SEA DANGERS

BY PHILIP MCFARLAND

A House Full of Women
Sojourners
Seasons of Fear
Sea Dangers

SEA DANGERS

THE
AFFAIR
OF THE
SOMERS

Philip McFarland

Schocken Books
New York

First published by Schocken Books 1985
10 9 8 7 6 5 4 3 2 1   85 86 87 88
Copyright © 1985 by Philip McFarland
All rights reserved

Library of Congress Cataloging in Publication Data
McFarland, Philip James.
   Sea dangers.
   1. Somers Mutiny, 1842. 2. Mackenzie, Alexander
Slidell, 1803–1848. 3. Somers (Ship)—History.
I. Title.
E182.M45   1985   973.5′092′2   85–1852

Design by Richard Oriolo
Manufactured in the United States of America
ISBN 0-8052-3990-1

For Joseph McFarland

QUESTION [*put by the captain to witnesses at the naval court of inquiry*]: From the time of the arrest of Mr. Spencer till the arrival of the *Somers* in port, did you observe that the officers exhibited any signs of unmanly fear, or of a desperate temper, or of anything unbecoming the character of an officer and gentleman?

ANSWER [*by Purser's Steward Wales, with much energy and decision*]: NO! SIR! I did not.
[*by Midshipman Rodgers*]: No, sir.
[*by Purser Heiskell*]: No, sir.
[*by Passed Assistant Surgeon Leecock*]: No, sir.
[*by Acting Master Perry*]: I did not, sir.
[*by First Lieutenant Gansevoort*]: I saw nothing of the kind. The conduct of the commander throughout the whole was of the most unexceptionable character, and I consider the country fortunate in having had such a commander, a man of so much decision, at such a time and under such circumstances of responsibility and danger as then existed. Too much praise cannot be awarded to all the officers.

CONTENTS

ILLUSTRATIONS

PERMISSIONS ACKNOWLEDGMENTS

Grateful acknowledgment is made for permission to reprint the illustrations listed from the following sources:

AMERICAN ANTIQUARIAN SOCIETY for Alexander Slidell Mackenzie; The decks of the *Somers;* The Greek lists. Courtesy, American Antiquarian Society.

BOSTON ATHENAEUM for the voyage of the *Somers*. Map from S. G. Goodrich's *A General Atlas of the World*. Courtesy of the Boston Athenaeum.

CHI PSI FRATERNITY for photograph of Passed Midshipman Philip Spencer.

LIBRARY OF CONGRESS for James Fenimore Cooper in the 1830s; John Canfield Spencer, lithograph by Charles Fenderich; Abel Parker Upshur, lithograph by Charles Fenderich; Charles Sumner, lithograph by H. W. Smith.

MASSACHUSETTS HISTORICAL SOCIETY for photograph from the 1840s of Richard Henry Dana, Jr.

JOHN MURRAY PUBLISHERS LIMITED for Washington Irving, Seville, 1828, painting by David Wilkie.

NATIONAL ARCHIVES AND RECORDS SERVICE for page written by Alexander Slidell Mackenzie, 0304-DMC-GCC.

THE NEW YORK PUBLIC LIBRARY for *New York from the Steeple of St. Paul's Church* (1849), aquatint by J. W. Hill; pencil sketch of James Gordon Bennett, courtesy of Print Collection, The New York Public Library, Astor, Lenox and Tilden Foundations. Also for photograph of Herman Melville (1885), courtesy of Gansevoort-Lansing Collection, Rare Books and Manuscripts Division, The New York Public Library, Astor, Lenox and Tilden Foundations.

THE TOLEDO MUSEUM OF ART for Oliver Hazard Perry, painting by Gilbert Stuart and Jane Stuart. Courtesy, The Toledo Museum of Art; gift of Florence Scott Libbey.

UNITED STATES NAVAL ACADEMY for Matthew Calbraith Perry, painting by William Sidney Mount; the *Somers*, lithograph by Nathaniel Currier and Napoleon Sarony; Spencer's service sword.

UNITED STATES DEPARTMENT OF THE INTERIOR, National Park Service, Longfellow National Historic Site for Henry Wadsworth Longfellow at age 28, sketch by Maria Rohl.

Grateful acknowledgment is made to the following for permission to quote from various manuscripts.

THE HOUGHTON LIBRARY, Harvard University for the use of excerpts from the Mackenzie and Sumner papers. By permission of the Houghton Library.

THE HUNTINGTON LIBRARY for permission to quote from Lieber (Francis) Collection. By permission of The Huntington Library, San Marino, California.

MASSACHUSETTS HISTORICAL SOCIETY for permission to quote from the Bancroft and Dana papers.

THE NEW YORK PUBLIC LIBRARY for quotations from the Duyckinck Family Papers, United States Navy Box. Courtesy, Rare Books and Manuscripts Division, The New York Public Library, Astor, Lenox and Tilden Foundations.

SEA DANGERS

PROLOGUE

AT ONE PERIOD OF HIS LIFE THE AFFABLE WASH-
ington Irving had for a particular friend Lieutenant Alexander Slidell,
United States Navy. Irving, friend of many, was in Madrid working on
a biography of Columbus; and in that capital during the early nineteenth
century—the date was 1827—Americans were few. Moreover, they came
and went. For instance, young Henry Wadsworth Longfellow, a year or
so out of Bowdoin and on an extended tour of Europe, passed through
Spain while his idol Irving was there. Lingering at the capital, the future
poet wrote home: "The society of the Americans here is very limited:
Mr. Everett and family, Mr. Smith his secretary, Mr. Rich the consul,
Washington Irving and his brother Peter, Lieutenant Slidell of the Navy,
and myself compose the whole." And Slidell, who had come into the
peninsula only the preceding fall, would be gone, like Longfellow, before
the summer ended.

The American naval officer, this Lieutenant Alexander Slidell, had
entered Spain from Roussillon in France, then proceeded south through
Catalonia to Valencia and westward to Castile—a journey over the Spanish countryside that had proved eventful. In fact, in the course of it the
twenty-three-year-old traveler had experienced one moment that he soon
was describing as "the unhappiest of my life": judgment uttered, to be
sure, while Alexander Slidell's life had much before it, though what he
had endured around that moment was dreadful in truth.

The incident had unfolded some distance from Tarragona, between Amposta and Vinaroz, on the road headed south. The coach in which the lieutenant was riding had set out at two in the morning. Not long after, he was huddled in a corner dozing, as were the other passengers, through predawn darkness, while the diligence, guided by its mule boy and a drowsy driver, lumbered along the deserted country road.

Suddenly Slidell had felt himself pitched forward.

The coach had abruptly halted. He rubbed his eyes and peered forth, toward shouts beyond the window. A lantern at the roof of the diligence revealed a road skirted by olive trees. Ahead the mules were clustered together, as if in apprehension, while nearer at hand, by the fore wheel, a *valenciano* in local dress was leveling a musket at the imperial overhead, yelling to the driver to surrender his purse: *la bolsa*. At the first sign of danger the wide-awake mule boy had "jumped from his seat to the roadside, intending to escape among the trees," but from those groves another armed bandit had emerged and led the child menacingly back and was making him lie in the road. Now, as Slidell among the helpless passengers watched from within, one robber ordered the frightened driver to descend from his perch and lie beside his fellow. That done, the thug lifted a stone from a nearby heap—"collected for the repair of the road"—and brought it down on the poor man's head. *No me quite usted la vida*—don't take my life! the driver screamed, and began to invoke saints and the Virgin to help him. "All in vain: the murderer redoubled his blows, until growing furious in the task, he laid his musket beside him and worked with both hands upon his victim." Cries for mercy turned into shrieks of terror out there in the darkness, then low inarticulate moans, "until a deep-drawn and agonized gasp for breath and an occasional convulsion" were all that signaled life remaining in the luckless driver, who had presumably recognized his assailants and so must be done away with.

"It fared even worse with Pepe"—the mule boy who had made a futile run for it. As the child lay facedown on the highway, a robber proceeded to pound his head in as well; from it came "low moans that died away in the dust beneath him." Then, while two of the band set about robbing the terrified passengers of their possessions, a third drew a knife and returned to the wretched boy as he lay rolling from side to side. Slidell in the carriage could not take his eyes from the lantern-lit outrage: the killer on his knees ripping aside the child's jacket, then thrusting his knife repeatedly into the defenseless body. "Though the windows at the front and sides were still closed, I could distinctly hear each stroke of the murderous knife as it entered its victim"—not the blunt sound of a weapon being resisted, but rather "a hissing noise, as if the household implement, made to part the bread of peace, performed unwillingly its task of treachery." This was the moment that seemed the unhappiest of all that the traveler had lived through so far, and "if any situation could be more worthy of pity than to die the dog's death of poor Pepe, it was to be compelled to witness his fate without the power to aid him."

Perhaps. Pepe did die in any case, miserably, at the end of two hours of suffering, after the robbers had fled and the bemused passengers had emerged and held the carriage lantern over that mangled form, silver buttons and proud silk sash hardly less disfigured by then than were the lad's piteous features. Slidell himself had helped lift the body into a passing cart, that and the body of the whimpering driver, who would die as well, a long week later, according to what the lieutenant was to learn from a Valencian wagoner whom he questioned about the matter subsequently, on his arrival in Madrid.

Alexander Slidell reached Madrid a couple of weeks afterward, in the late fall of 1826; he remained there until the following March. During his stay at the capital the young naval officer joined the little society of his countrymen that included Washington Irving, and soon he was helping that great author with researches on Columbus that were under way, lending his knowledge of technical details concerning shiphandling and navigation to solving problems connected with the discoverer's various voyages.

Incidentally, that Irving was a great author was undeniable. In those years the expatriate American's literary reputation stood at its height, so that this astonishingly eloquent citizen of a nation of red savages and tobacco spitters was everywhere regarded, both in Europe and in his homeland, as one of the three finest writers of English of the age. As for the other two, Byron, not long deceased, had been Irving's professed admirer, and Scott, very much alive, was his mentor and friend. So exalted an international standing—unprecedented for an American—rested upon the rollicking *Knickerbocker's History of New York*, first published as long ago as 1809, and on three more recent volumes that included most notably *The Sketch Book*. That work had appeared seven years before the present date, to wide and perhaps extravagant acclaim. Its genial descriptions of English scenes and its stories from the Catskills of Rip Van Winkle and Ichabod Crane had charmed not only readers of Irving's native language on both sides of the Atlantic, but also, in translation, readers in France and Germany, among which peoples the peregrinating American author had recently been living for extended periods. Now, however, he was in Spain—had entered it for the first time scarcely a year before, in February 1826—this bachelor of vast reputation, after more than a decade abroad past forty now, often homesick and worried that his powers were failing. He was nevertheless launched uncertainly on a project different from any he had ever attempted: serious history, the first full-length biography in English of the discoverer of America.

To accomplish his ends the conscientious Irving, alternately exhilarated and dismayed by the size of his task, was drawing on original sources, on old Spanish chronicles of ship stowages and lyings-to and sightings at sea. Lieutenant Slidell of the United States Navy found himself welcome as a timely visitor to assist the landsman in such exacting labors.

Slidell did help, but during his visit of some three months the new arrival also gave himself opportunities to see most of the sights that the Spanish capital offered: the Royal Palace, the crowded promenades along the Prado—ubiquitous friars, mustachioed soldiers flaunting their cockades, black-eyed, faultlessly shaped señoritas—the Puerta del Sol with its water-bearers and numberless beggars, the bullfights, the theater.

He also witnessed a hanging in the Plazuela de la Cebada, a spectacle "of deep and painful interest" that was scheduled to begin at ten one winter morning. Two robbers (not those whose cruelty he had earlier viewed through a carriage window) were to be executed as per announcement in the local newspaper. Once already, in southern France, just before entering Spain, Slidell had attended a similar scene, "and the feeling of oppression and abasement, of utter disgust, with which I came from it, was such as to make me form a tacit resolution never to be present at another." Thus, as he glanced over the *Diario* the morning of this latest execution, "the recollection of what I had seen and felt a few months before in Montpellier was still fresh in my memory; but when I turned to reflect that I was in a strange land, a land which I might never revisit, that a scene of such powerful excitement could not fail to elicit the unrestrained feelings of the multitude, and to bring the national character into strong relief, I made up my mind to be present on the occasion, and to overcome, or at least to stifle, my repugnance."

Accordingly, the visiting lieutenant arrived at the plazuela promptly, joining a crowd already assembled: ladies on balconies "saluting each other across the street or shaking their fans in recognition to those who passed below," in the thronged marketplace blind men singing ballads they carried for sale, clamorous boys quarreling for precedence as they clung to grates of windows for a better view, "sallow mechanics, tinkers, and cobblers with leathern aprons and dirty faces," gaily dressed Andalusians, thin-legged tailors, muleteers. Slidell arrived on time among the assemblage, but the doomed pair that all were waiting for were tardy that chilly morning. Ten o'clock came and went, and eleven was tolled from convent towers, and still no sign was given of their approach down the street that led from the prison. "I began at last to look with anxiety for the coming of the criminals," the lieutenant confesses. "But when I came to compare their condition with my own, I could not but reproach myself for my impatience. 'The remainder of their lives,' said I, 'is all condensed into the present hour, and that hour already on the wane! This remnant of existence may be infinitely valuable to them in seeking reconciliation with Heaven: and yet you, who perhaps have years in store, would rob them even of this to relieve yourself from a short interval of weariness and inactivity.' "

The reflection allowed him to wait more patiently, though now with a disgust not only toward the scene around him but toward the feelings that had entered his heart. Finally they did arrive, two prisoners attended by armed grenadiers and monks chanting the death dirge over the buzz of the multitude. One criminal, shrouded, "sat bolt upright on an ass, and his feet were bound tightly under the belly of the animal." His hands were bound, too, "and made to clasp a copper crucifix. But when it was pressed to his lips by the anxious and tremulous hands of the poor monk who walked beside him, he refused to kiss the image of the Saviour; nay, he even spit upon it. There was, in fact, more of the hardened villain about this malefactor than I had ever before seen"—catlike, sinewy fellow of fiendish countenance. By contrast, the other criminal, with a friar at his side, was singing hymns earnestly, from a paper that trembled in his fingers, through lips turned purple with terror. As if to save his life he chanted with vigor throughout the execution of his associate, while that unrepentant sinner was dragged to the oaken gallows, then up the ladder by the corpulent hangman, who having put the noose on him, hurled him from the high rung, the hangman himself riding aloft on the wretch's shoulders, even as others below "reached the legs of the victim and drew them down with all their might." By then the spectators in the plaza had grown solemn, murmuring prayers, crossing themselves as the first convict went plunging downward from the ladder, again moments later as the second followed, his hymns unavailing, the fat thighs of the hangman wrapped around his noosed neck as well.

Afterward, returned to earth, the hangman took from his hatband a half-smoked cigarillo and lit it complacently while the slowly revolving bodies above and behind him knocked against each other, even as the witnesses to the episode already were beginning variously to disperse, gathering together their brown cloaks or mounting their asses to ride about their business. "Surely," the lieutenant concludes of those two fatal punishments just inflicted, "there can be nothing in such a spectacle to promote morality, nothing to make us either better or happier—a spectacle which serves but to create despondency and to array man in enmity with his condition!"

For all that, he had observed the dismal occasion unflinchingly, noticing a wealth of detail that was set down with the "persevering and conscientious fidelity of a Flemish picture." So Washington Irving himself would adjudge in reviewing the book that the young officer was to fashion from this and other Spanish experiences.

Not that all the scenes in the traveler's book would be of such doleful matters as hangings and roadside murders. There was, for example, one frolicsome excursion of five or six days to Segovia and the Escorial, undertaken in mid-March, toward the end of Slidell's residence in Madrid. That outing the lieutenant made in company with a "countryman who had come to Spain in search of instruction. He was just from college, full of all the ardent feeling excited by classical pursuits, with health unbroken, hope that was a stranger to disappointment, curiosity which had never yet been fed to satiety." So agreeable a companion was, in fact, Longfellow himself, recently arrived in the Spanish capital. "We," writes Slidell, "had been thrown almost alone together in a strange and unknown land; our ages were not dissimilar"—the lieutenant three or four years older than his new friend, who was twenty—"and though our previous occupations"—sailor and scholar—"had been more so, we were nevertheless soon acquainted, first with each other, then with each other's views, and presently after we had agreed to be companions on the journey."

It took them, with their cloaks and knapsacks and in various unlikely conveyances, up into the mountains north of Madrid, where they were not long in discovering that their innkeeper at Segovia was "a regular rogue; the muleteer who brought us to La Granja was more than half a fool; and as for our posadero at the latter place, he was so thoroughgoing a sot that we found him as drunk as a loon at nine in the morning." The travelers had a fine time anyway, made no less so by the pretty girls at the various stopping places, one of whom—"hearty, well made, and active"—carefully scrutinized these strange beings from another world, turned their hats quizzically round in her hands, and stroked Longfellow's back, "saying, '¡Qué paño tan fino!' (What fine cloth!)." Nor were the two adventurers daunted even when they found themselves at dusk on the heights of a deserted mountain pass, mules unable to go forward, road uncleared, wind whipping up from the valley with such violence "that we could not check ourselves with so poor a foothold as was furnished by the snow, but had to scud before it down the opposite hill until sheltered from its fury. My long cloak gave me infinite trouble on this occasion," the lieutenant recollects, "for it fluttered about until I was afraid it would fly away with me." The situation was perilous; not until long after nightfall— eight or nine in the evening—did the wanderers hear the welcome bark of a dog in the darkness and stumble at last on the lights of an inn. Soon afterward they found themselves seated delightedly by a crackling fire, marveling in the warm parlor at the contrast to what they had just undergone: "dashing through the wet and snow, or roaming in a dark cold night over a wild waste, hungry, with wet feet, the prospect of being benighted, and the fear of footpads."

Slidell retold that adventure, along with others that befell him in Spain, in a manuscript that his friend Washington Irving would help him revise into a vivid book of travels through the peninsula. Irving did more.

He got his London publisher, the great John Murray—publisher of Scott and Byron and Jane Austen—to issue a handsome edition of the lieutenant's premier work. *A Year in Spain* it was called, by A Young American. Moreover, Irving himself reviewed the book, identifying the anonymous author by name and testifying to the accuracy of his account, in a long and favorable treatment that appeared in London in the influential *Quarterly Review* of February 1831. Slidell had by then obligingly collaborated on an appendix on the course of the discoverer's first voyage, to accompany Irving's monumental Life of Columbus; this much the older author might do for his young friend and their publisher, all the more willingly since the initial literary effort of a naval officer in his mid-twenties was so genuinely entertaining. "Throughout," pronounced no less a judge than the most famous American author alive, *A Year in Spain* "bears evidence of a youthful, kind, and happy spirit, and of fresh, unhackneyed feelings. There is a certain vein of humor and *bonhommie* running through it also, that gives it a peculiar zest; and not the least amusing circumstances about it are the whimsical shifts and expedients to which the narrowness of the lieutenant's purse now and then obliges him to resort in traveling, and which he records with delightful frankness and simplicity; the facility and good humor with which, from his rough nautical experience, he is enabled to put up with wind and weather and hard fare and hard lodging that would dismay and discomfit a landsman; and the true seafaring relish with which he enjoys every snug berth or savory meal, exulting over dishes that almost require the strong stomach of a midshipman or a Sancho Panza."

SLIDELL

SLIDELL'S FAMILY, LONG BEFORE THE LIEUTENANT
ever reached Spain, would have been acquainted with the family of
Washington Irving back home in New York. The fathers of both were
tradesmen—Slidell's a tallow chandler, Irving's father a sometime hardware merchant—and the town on the southwestern tip of Manhattan
when the expatriate author had lived there, before and during Alexander
Slidell's childhood, was still small enough to have allowed reputable
members of the community to be known to each other: Colgate with his
soap, Lorillard with his snuff and tobacco, Astor with his furs, Duncan
Phyfe with his chairs and tables, Irving with his hardware and wines and
sugar, Slidell with his candles.

To be sure, New York had been growing rapidly during those years
around the turn of the century. Washington Irving had been born at the
end of the American Revolution, in 1783, into a town that had numbered
scarcely twenty thousand people. When Alex Slidell was born in New
York twenty years later, on April 6, 1803, the town was thrice that size.
Visiting it about that time, ex-Senator Jonathan Mason of Massachusetts
set down in his diary what others would note again and again as the
century advanced: the progress of the city was "beyond all calculation—
seven hundred buildings erected the last twelve months; and Broadway"
—where the Slidells were living and the father conducting his trade—
"beyond all dispute is the best street for length, width, position, and

buildings in America." Even so, young Irving, when in his twenties, describing the place as he himself knew it in the spring of 1807, could speak in the pages of *Salmagundi* of a "queer, odd, topsy-turvy rantipole city," a town spread quaintly over hills and dales and through crooked streets and lanes and alleys. And elsewhere in that earliest of his popular works, the gentle ironist would evoke contemporary, small-town images of Courtlandt Street corner—a "famous place to see the belles go by"—of the mighty arch of Oswego Market and "the moss-crowned roof of the Bear Market," of the "tumultuous gutter" meandering down Pearl Street.

The cornerstone of the new City Hall—in use still, for the same purpose, in a metropolis now swollen to some seven million—was laid by Mayor Livingston the spring of Alex Slidell's birth, for a building not completed until eight years later, in 1811. During those years the child's father had been prospering. "A man of great intelligence and of a high moral and religious character," the elder Slidell was improving upon the trade of tallow chandler to become one of the wealthier and more respected merchants, bankers, and shipowners of the city, president now of the Tradesmen's Insurance Company and the Mechanics' Bank, as well as owner of a warehouse on South Street. The thriving businessman (and vestryman of Grace Church) was, moreover, a lover of books at his leisure, so that according to one recollection, he "passed his evenings in reading aloud to his family, a trait which his son continued" in his own manhood—specifically, the son Alexander, youngest of four boys in that comfortable household.

Others in the reading circle at 50 Broadway early in the century would have included the mother, Margery Mackenzie, a native of the Scottish Highlands, six sisters, and those three older brothers. The eldest—Alex's senior by ten years—was attending Columbia College, then a three-story edifice among shady sycamores at the end of Park Place west of what would become City Hall Park. He would graduate in 1810, and for a while thereafter would idle as a rich man's son about the city, dabble a bit at his father's trade, lose money at it, scandalize neighbors in his mid-twenties by seriously wounding the manager of the Park Theatre (one Stephen Price) in a duel, then flee town under a cloud to seek his fortune elsewhere. That was John Slidell, who was to establish himself in time as a politician of consequence: senator from Louisiana, the most powerful man in James Buchanan's administration, emissary for the Confederacy to the emperor of the French during the Civil War.

Another brother, Thomas, would graduate from Yale and, following John to Louisiana, would eventually become chief justice of that state. Impressive fraternal examples. For his part, the youngest son was to be denied whatever advantages Yale or Columbia College offered. Alex did attend a local academy briefly, but in later life his wife would hear him admit that "as a child he was no student and not at all precocious." By his own account, "what little education has fallen to me" was acquired "in much the same discursive and vagabond manner that a chicken gets his breakfast—a kernel of information in one corner and another in the next." For at the age of eleven Alexander Slidell ended his childhood, along with any opportunity for formal education, by leaving home to be initiated into the navy.

Doubtless before then he had witnessed pageants at the local theater celebrating exploits of American tars against Tripolitan pirates—a juvenile letter of Irving's describes just such a performance at the Park. And assuredly, like so many boys in seaport towns, this one was drawn to the docks and yards, as Irving had been himself: "when yet a child," Slidell later wrote, "I had loved to loiter about the wharfs of my native city, watching the arrival of ships from countries which I knew as yet only through my geography, or witnessing the casting-off of departing vessels, the last halloo . . ." But the strongest influence in deciding the course that the boy's life would follow was the War of 1812, especially the naval triumphs in that war—stirring victories over the hitherto invulnerable British by Hull and Decatur and Bainbridge and Macdonough and, above all, by Oliver Hazard Perry on Lake Erie.

Young Oliver Perry—twenty-seven when he met the enemy—was to his own era all that the youthful Lindbergh would seem to admirers early in the century that followed. All that and more: emblem of courage, resourcefulness, gallantry—as well as deliverer of his countrymen threatened by British domination in the Old Northwest. Perry's achievement was astonishing. In the wilderness at the lake shore he had directed the completion of a squadron of vessels, having lumber fashioned from the surrounding forest, causing guns, shot powder, sailcloth, and rigging to be carted in the rawness of late winter from Buffalo, from Pittsburgh, from as far away as New York, whence came blockmakers, blacksmiths, carpenters, "a distance of five hundred miles, through a half-settled country, destitute of good roads, and but partially intersected by water communication." The words quoted are Slidell's, those of a naval officer grown to maturity and marveling on his predecessor's accomplishment. Perry's own surviving letters to his superiors before the battle dwell on another obstacle to be overcome, as they repeatedly lament the lack of skilled hands, of trained seamen once the vessels have been launched. Finally, however, on the morning of September 10, 1813, the young captain in his flagship *Lawrence* did lead his fleet from Put-in-Bay onto the serene waters of the open lake to engage an enemy flotilla that from the beginning had controlled all access to the vast Michigan territory. Aboard the *Lawrence* shot was being collected in racks, pistols and cutlasses brought to quarters, preventer braces rove, matches lit, and the decks wet down and sanded "to prevent the explosion of scattering powder and create a secure foothold amid the approaching carnage." Just before noon the American line closed. Then, for more than two hours, the *Lawrence* fired upon and received the combined fire of the two heaviest enemy ships, the *Detroit* and the *Queen Charlotte*. By half-past two the destruction was all but complete. Though the British vessels had suffered gravely in the exchange, the *Lawrence* was utterly disabled, not a gun left aboard that could fire, not a mast or sail that could maneuver her, every brace and bowline shot away, most of the officers and crew wounded or dead.

What happened next seized and held the imagination of Perry's grateful countrymen when they learned of it, and made him their idol. For instead of surrendering, the American captain boarded a boat and had himself rowed to the *Niagara*, a vessel in his squadron that had so far escaped serious damage and now lay half a mile to windward. The British saw what was happening, saw the small boat with the commodore standing dauntlessly in the stern sheets making its perilous way from the battered flagship. Enemy fire was trained on the boat, so that during the fifteen-minute passage grape and shot fell all around it. Its oars were splintered. Spray drenched the exposed captain and his crew. But Perry made the passage safely, climbed aboard the *Niagara*, from Captain Elliott took command of the brig—"at the time perfectly fresh," the English commodore noted—and brought her into battle against the already damaged ships of the enemy. Earlier, soon after the small boat had set out on the crossing, the battered *Lawrence* had struck her colors, to the cheers of the exultant British; but before she could be taken, the *Niagara* was bearing down. "I determined to pass through the enemy's line," Perry reported in his official dispatch; "bore up, and passed ahead of their two ships and a brig, giving a raking fire to them from the starboard guns, and to a large schooner and sloop from the larboard side, at half pistol-shot distance."

The result was that within a quarter of an hour defeat for the Americans had been turned to victory. The British it was who struck; and before the day ended Perry would take their surrender on the bloody decks of his own disabled, recovered flagship. And there on the deck, scribbling amid the moans of the wounded, his officer's hat serving for a writing desk, the victorious captain (first in the history of the world to capture an entire British fleet) would pen his laconic report to General Harrison, commanding American land forces in the area:

> Dear Gen'l:—
> We have met the enemy and they are ours: two ships, two brigs, one schooner, and one sloop.
>
> Yours with great respect and esteem,
> O. H. Perry.

The Battle of Lake Erie proved to be the turning point of the war in the West. Before then the offensive campaign of the Americans had been at best unsuccessful, at worst disastrous. Now suddenly—with the enemy evacuating Detroit—they were left in control of the Upper Lakes, a control that they were able to maintain over that sprawling natural highway until the war's end, transporting their troops and supplies unhindered. Moreover, when the end approached, Perry's victory greatly strengthened the American bargaining position at Ghent, as earlier it had gloriously lifted the spirits of his countrymen, discouraged as they had been by news of humiliating defeats and surrenders on land during the opening part of the conflict.

Beyond any other battle of the time, all this had been won "by the courage and obstinacy of a single man." So Henry Adams concludes in his great history of the period; and that man—now a national hero, recipient of silver plate from Boston and Newport, a gold medal and a prize of five thousand dollars from the federal government, public dinners from the citizens of Philadelphia and Baltimore, applause and gratitude and numberless swords and torch processions and illuminations from the entire nation—that man Oliver Hazard Perry was the very officer who, in March 1815, a year and a half after his dazzling victory, among his other concerns took time to secure the warrant for an impressionable eleven-year-old, Alexander Slidell, as acting midshipman in the United States Navy.

Perrys and Slidells had become intimate by then. Oliver Perry's younger brother Matthew, twenty years old and himself a naval officer destined to achieve fame, had been spending the summer and fall attached to Decatur's squadron in New York. There he had fallen in love with Alex Slidell's seventeen-year-old sister Jane, and on Christmas Eve, 1814, had married her—making the hero's brother young Alex's brother-in-law. And early in the new year Alex himself, under the auspices of the victor of Lake Erie, assumed his midshipman's duties, attached to a brig fitting out for the captain's new flying squadron at Warren, Rhode Island, near the Perry home at Bristol, four miles away.

Years later Slidell would recall that first relocation of his life to strange surroundings: several times the boy had occasion at Warren "to see Captain Perry on his periodical visits to examine the brig" then under construction—the hero's person "of the loftiest stature and most graceful mould." And several times Alex was invited to take his place at the Perry hearth, "a lad not quite twelve, on a first absence from home, who sensibly felt and gratefully remembers the benevolent efforts of the old gentleman"—Perry's father, also a ship captain, from Revolutionary days—"to entertain him with anecdotes of past adventures in the profession upon which he was entering, and useful lessons for his guidance."

The midshipman was starting his career aboard the now fitted USS *Chippewa*, man-of-war brig, Captain Read, complement ninety officers and men, Alex's brother-in-law Matthew Calbraith Perry as first lieutenant, second-in-command. Early in July 1815 (Washington Irving, then thirty-two, having sailed from New York for Liverpool two months before, unaware that he was beginning an absence in Europe that would extend through nearly two decades), that summer of 1815 the vessel on which Midshipman Slidell was serving set sail from Boston to cross the Atlantic and treat with the Dey of Algiers along the Barbary coast. Slidell's first cruise lasted five months. At its conclusion, the twelve-year-old was home scarcely six weeks around Christmas before sailing again for the Mediterranean in early January, this time on board the *Java*, Captain Oliver Hazard Perry, out of Newport.

The life that the lad had entered upon could be harsh. With other midshipmen Alex was at school at sea one day, behind a canvas screen under the half deck on the larboard side of the *Java*. Surrounding waves were high. All at once a crewman was discovered to have fallen overboard from the bowsprit shrouds forward. "There was a scupper between the two guns where we sat, and the ship rolled to port as the man passed, bringing him within two or three feet of us and bearing his shrieks, which conveyed the inevitable impression of death-notes, to us with horrible distinctness." The seas were such that there was no chance of saving him, but "he could be seen from the mizzentop, whence his position was each instant reported . . . swimming steadily in the wake of the ship; and it was evident that he had advanced considerably, from his hat being some distance behind him." Ever afterward the image remained clear in Slidell's mind. "It has been the necessary fortune of the writer in the prosecution of his career," he noted a quarter of a century later, "to witness many similar scenes, but the memory of that first one has remained indelibly fixed, and those terrible shrieks, heard as he passed almost within an arm's length, seem still, when remembered, to vibrate painfully on the ear."

On the same cruise, when the *Java* was fourteen days out, men had been ordered aloft about noon to furl the topgallant sail. Suddenly the wind had freshened, and "the main-topmast parted above the cap and went over into the larboard waist, carrying the main-topsail-yard with it." The accident, caused by dry-rotted spars, led to the violent death of five of the crew: "one struck on the muzzle of a main-deck gun and was precipitated overboard, where he immediately sunk; another fell with his head on the keel of a boat turned bottom up on the booms and had his skull completely divided; three others lost their lives in modes equally horrible . . ."

A harsh life it often was—close quarters, exhausting watches, hot-blooded officers and mates, cruelties afloat, drunkenness and dueling ashore. But there was much of interest for a youngster to see: the bay of Tripoli with its minarets and mosques along the skyline, Mahón with its Spanish languor, massive Gibraltar, Naples and Vesuvius, Messina, Málaga. And much to learn: Matthew Perry—a surviving notebook reveals —had been teaching himself Spanish aboard the *Chippewa* on Alex's first cruise; the boy would take pains to learn the same language later. And much there was in navy life to admire, perhaps in time to emulate; on the *Java*'s homeward journey early in 1817, many of the crew had fallen ill of smallpox, giving scope, as the mature Slidell remembered, to Captain Oliver Perry's invariable benevolence toward the sick under his command. "He daily visited them, and inquired as to their condition and wants, and never failed to send from his own table whatever could be grateful to the convalescent."

In large part, Mediterranean service then was supporting Decatur's fleet, in the region to enforce an earlier treaty with the Barbary states— Tripoli, Tunis, Algiers, Morocco—their corsairs no longer able to prey on commerce with impunity, now that the hitherto preoccupied Americans and English were at peace. Having served in that duty and returned to Newport on the *Java*, Midshipman Slidell was next ordered to the brig *Enterprise*, to cruise the East Coast with President James Monroe aboard; on board as well was the President's aide, Oliver Perry. From the *Enterprise* the lad was attached to the *Macedonian* for an extended cruise on the other side of the world, along the west coast of South America—vivid interlude for an intent adolescent: "His letters written at sixteen and seventeen, when he was on board of the *Macedonian* in the Pacific, exhibit thus early his settled habits of study and his earnest sense of what was going on around him." Indeed, according to the same source, a correspondent of Slidell's widow after his death, "a series of letters from his early years, written from different parts of the world, which we have seen, are graphic, minute, and faithful."

He was growing into an appealing young man: amiable, studious, competent, if physically plain—of medium height, with high forehead and auburn hair—reserved in manner, temperate in habits, alert and curious about a world that he had already traveled widely in before he was twenty. We here sketch Slidell's career stage by stage in part because of the central role he is to play in a later, appalling episode of his professional life—partly so we can better understand his actions in that episode. But we sketch it also as representative of one career open to a young American gentleman thrown on his own resources, pursuing the profession most enticingly available to him in the first half of the nineteenth century. How such a one would spend his days—where he would go and what would concern him—is not without its own interest, aside from the later notoriety.

His duties about this time, in 1824, took the midshipman to West Indian waters, aboard the sloop *Terrier* in Commodore David Porter's squadron, charged with clearing the Caribbean of pirates. To merchants, travelers, and navy men of the period there seemed little enough of romance in piracy. The wanderer Irving, for instance, some years earlier off the Italian coast had passed one long, frightening day and sleepless night aboard the ship *Matilda* bullied by pirates, who had climbed aboard waving pistols and stilettos and rusty sabers as they bellowed out polyglot orders to shorten sail and surrender all valuables. For hours the thugs had swaggered about the decks and rifled the passengers' portmanteaus, before withdrawing to linger threateningly nearby in becalmed waters and swill down pipes of stolen brandy. That ordeal, hardly a rare one, had lasted from midmorning to the following sunrise—innocent travelers at the mercy of armed, unpredictable pirates on the unguarded sea.

In fact, so frequent were such occurrences then and later that "the present time," according to an article in *Niles' Weekly Register* in the fall of 1821, "seems to be entitled to the appellation of the *age of piracy*—caused chiefly by the spewing out of the late wars, and especially so of the contests between Spain and her late 'American colonies.' " Some of those vagabonds in sunlit waters, intercepting vessels engaged in a fruitful trade that peacetime had restored between the West Indies and the East Coast of the United States, were demobbed sailors from the Napoleonic conflict; but others were disaffected Americans, seizing the main chance under guise of lending support to Mexicans and Cubans and liberators farther south who had been asserting their independence from an enfeebled mother country across the ocean. Secretary of State John Quincy Adams as early as 1817 was referring to "the buccaneering and piratical spirit which has lately appeared among the South Americans, not of their own growth, but I am sorry to say, from the contamination of their intercourse with us. Their privateers have been for the most part fitted out and officered in our ports and manned from the sweepings of our streets." But wherever they came from, pirates of those days had an effect on commerce that was relentless and baleful.

By 1823, *Niles' Register*, published at Baltimore, could count over three thousand unlawful assaults against shipping of all nations that had occurred since the war with England had ended, eight years earlier. That averaged more than one outrage a day. In the same period, at least five hundred merchant vessels from the United States had been seized by pirates, to the value with cargo of twenty million dollars. Nor were the seizures managed gently. A typical encounter in the spring of 1822 involved the brig *Aurilla*, New York, from Baltimore bound for New Orleans. Two schooners, "well fitted with great guns and small arms, and manned by forty or fifty men each," overtook the vessel off Cay Sal. She was boarded, and the passengers and crew were beaten; one man was hung up to the yardarm, then dropped into the water "apparently lifeless." The brig was plundered, and the passengers robbed of "clothing, watches, breast-pins, etc." Then, having delighted in destroying what they were not pleased to take away, "the villains crowned their crimes by ravishing the women that were on board and committing the most brutal excesses on their bodies!" Facts, not breezy escapist romance. In this instance, the pirates did release the vessel to proceed on her course, though on other occasions passengers might be drowned and the ship taken, or the ship with all hands sent to the bottom to foil discovery or pursuit.

Young Alex Slidell, then in his early twenties, served aboard a fast schooner in tropic waters in 1824, attached to a squadron on the West India station bent upon removing the threat of piracy that would continue to distress sea lanes for more than a decade longer.

But while on that duty, the midshipman—he was promoted to lieutenant about this time—came down with yellow fever, prevalent in those parts. The disease was potentially fatal. In fact, five years earlier, the hero Oliver Perry, Slidell's model of a naval officer, had died of yellow fever near the mouth of the Orinoco, where he had ventured on a delicate mission at the request of the United States government—precisely a mission to protest extralegal interference with trade near Venezuelan waters.

Perry on the schooner *Nonsuch* had ascended the steamy Orinoco in mid-July 1819. "Confined on board a small vessel," he had recorded among his final words in a notebook: "rise in the morning after being exhausted by heat. The sun, as soon as it shows itself, striking almost through one: moschetoes, sandflies, and gnats covering you." No doubt one of those myriad mosquitoes had carried the fever that came on mortally during the three-hundred-mile journey downriver from Angostura, causing an agony of suffering: the hurried breathing, hiccoughs, vomiting, paroxysms as the young commodore lay on a mattress on the deck between berths in the stifling little cabin—all air excluded by coverings over the hatch to darken the space because light had become a torment. "Thus," Slidell would write later, after he himself had known yellow fever firsthand, "on his birthday, at the age of thirty-four years, died Oliver Hazard Perry, of a painful disease, surrounded by every discomfort, yet with a calmness and resignation honorable to his character and worthy of his renown."

The death of the hero had occurred at half-past three in the afternoon of Monday, August 23, 1819. Five years after that date Lieutenant Slidell had himself been stricken with the same disease in Caribbean waters, and—luckier this time than Perry—was returned from the West India station to New York to convalesce. When his health was sufficiently restored, he took advantage of a leave of absence from the navy of nearly two years' duration to travel in Europe, spending some months in France before finding himself in Roussillon, near the Spanish border, in the autumn of 1826.

This, then, was the young officer of twenty-three who ventured that fall over the Pyrenees to Barcelona and south in a diligence drawn by seven mules to Valencia, helplessly witnessing en route the brutal highway murders of a driver and a mule boy before one dawn. From Valencia he had continued westward to Madrid and the society of another New Yorker, Washington Irving. "My motives," Slidell wrote, "for going to a country which travelers ordinarily avoid were a wish to perfect myself in a language which is becoming so important in the hemisphere which it divides with our own"—that is, in South America—"and a strong desire to visit scenes so full of interest and attraction." And in time, as already noted, he would set down his impressions of those scenes in his first literary effort, one modestly scaled: "The author merely proposes to enable those who have not visited Spain, and have no expectation of doing so, to form an idea of the country and its inhabitants, without abandoning the comforts and security of the fireside." He would describe his travels, though in some ways hardly qualified for the task, as he admitted himself, burdened as he was with "the inexperience of youth and the disadvantages of an interrupted education."

Incidentally, as *A Year in Spain* confirms, Slidell's departure from the peninsula, like his entrance into it, had proven to be eventful. Irving had seen his young friend off from the capital April 11, 1827, and on the twenty-fourth had received a letter from him. "He has been robbed. I expected the event," so the older writer relayed to friends in Paris. "The robbery took place about thirty leagues from Madrid. Eight robbers, well mounted and armed to the teeth, attacked and drove off the guard, consisting of four men. They then took all the money, watches, etc., of the passengers, opened their trunks and helped themselves to whatever they fancied, and then, asking pardon of the passengers for the trouble they gave them, retired very slowly and tranquilly." Irving added one further, choice detail. "Honest Slidell," he explained to his friends, "had purchased a four-dollar silver watch to be robbed of, and had put his valuable watch in his trunk; but as in this instance the robbers were more curious in their researches, his holyday watch fell into their clutches, and his sham watch followed it."

Thus dispossessed, the lieutenant had made his way through Córdoba, Seville, Cádiz, and Ronda, on his way out of Spain by Gibraltar, from which fortress in early July he had written a letter back to his friend don Enrique Longfellow—that amiable former roommate, still at No. 17, calle Montera, Madrid. "I have at length determined to return home," Slidell explained, "and have taken passage in the ship *Atlantic* of Philadelphia, to sail at the end of a week. I tell you the name of the vessel so that if you should hear of her arriving safe or going to the bottom you may know that your friend Slidell is on board of her." The letter continues with abundant advice for Longfellow on his own projected journey south: what conveyances to try for, how much to pay, how long to linger in various places, which inns or houses to stay at, what to skip at the different stops. And it ends: "I am now about to leave the country and the quarter of the world which you at present inhabit, and I take this occasion to say that though our acquaintance has been a short one I shall ever be most happy to renew it, and that while I cherish your friendship I remain truly your friend, Alexander Slidell."

Artlessly expressed, the emotion was genuine; that friendship between sailor and poet would last through Slidell's lifetime. And he and Irving would also remain close. The lieutenant had been home in New York only a short while before receiving a letter from Madrid. "My dear Slidell," Irving wrote him cordially, "I enclose the charts you were so kind as to correct for me. . . ." As for the first landing place of Columbus in the New World, "I think," the older author observed with gratitude in a postscript, "you have settled the question satisfactorily." Indeed, when Irving's massive biography of the discoverer of America appeared to wide acclaim soon afterward, it contained an acknowledgment of his young friend's abundant help: "the author of this work is indebted for this examination of the route of Columbus"—through an appendix of twenty pages—"to an officer of the navy of the United States, whose name he regrets the not being at liberty to mention. He has been greatly benefited in various parts of this history by nautical information from the same intelligent source."

By then Slidell, returned home, had confessed in writing to Irving that he had himself felt "that irresistible impulse which prompts a man to perpetrate a book." To which confession the older veteran of literary campaigns responded from Madrid February 16, 1828: "It is some time since I received your letter imparting your project of a first expedition into the land of literature." Of course one familiar with the pitfalls of the terrain could not encourage a novice in such a venture, though good advice on that score is vain "to those who once come under the spell of its allurements; and I trust you are less likely than most to suffer from your indiscretion": typical specimen of Irving's ready grace and tact. "The plan of your proposed work," he went on, "is a good one, and from what I have been able to judge of the power of your pen, I think you will execute it in a creditable and very satisfactory manner." Moreover, Slidell's subject was interesting, information on Spain being scanty in English. "I shall be very impatient to see your work, and hope you will send me a copy," care of Horatio Sprague, Esq., at Gibraltar, in which direction Irving would soon be setting out on his own tour of Andalusia.

Thus encouraged, the lieutenant back home persevered. A year after leaving Spain his memories of that country remained vivid, as he demonstrated in June 1828 in a letter to Longfellow that made mention of the venta at Guadarrama, the kitchen fire, the backroom supper, the chocolate brought in the morning by that dark-eyed morisca, the mules and the mountain, the dread of robbers, the adventure of the snowbank . . .

Doubtless even then he was at work on his Spanish book in his family's Broadway home. "I have already told you that I am going to the country," Slidell continued in that same letter to his overseas friend, now at Paris, "but of the where and the how you as yet know nothing. Learn then that my brother and I set out tomorrow to walk to Niagara, or rather to undertake to do so." And, to anticipate, the outcome of so hardy an enterprise is told in a letter to the same correspondent the following winter: "Your friendly wishes that my journey to Niagara might be satisfactory were fully realized. My brother and I walked every step from our own door to Buffalo"—along towpaths of the recently completed Erie Canal?—"thence descending the thrice beautiful banks of the Niagara, until we came first within the roar of the cataract, then in sight of the ascending mists set in motion by the shock; nor pausing until we gradually discovered this wonder of wonders, and stood at length face to face against it upon the Table Rock."

No doubt Slidell had finished his *Year in Spain* before undertaking that ramble of some five hundred miles, but back home again during the fall he was feeling discouraged. "I am sorry," Irving wrote him from southern Spain in October 1828, "to find you have met with such difficulty in getting a publisher for your book of travels. Why do you not publish it at your own risk? I think there could scarcely be a likelihood of loss, and might be of gain. Books of travels are always acceptable . . ." And, acknowledging other news that awakened regret, "I am sorry to learn," he went on, "that your health is so affected by the sea that you are thinking of abandoning the profession. I had hoped to see you one day in a conspicuous rank in our Navy, and that it would be greatly benefited by the talent and information you would bring into the service." Should Slidell enter the diplomatic line? Irving thought such a life "barren for a man who has not political advancement in view." The poor pay exacted either heavy debts or humiliating economies. "I think some independent profession is always the pleasantest . . . but really I have such a regard for our navy that I feel a regret when I see any man of talent and worth abandoning it."

In the event, Slidell would stay in the navy after all. By the following February his letters reveal that for the last five or six months he has been expecting orders "to an expedition fitting out by our government to explore the Antarctic region, and also some imperfectly known portions of the Pacific Ocean. But fate, or rather the Upper House has ordered otherwise." This very day, February 15, 1829, he has learned that the appropriation bill has come to a dead halt in the Senate, meaning an indefinite postponement of the undertaking. And in fact it was not until almost a decade later, after absurd mismanagement and the successive refusal to command it by at least five naval officers including Matthew Perry, that the United States South Seas Surveying and Exploring Expedition—four small windjammers and a couple of pilot boats—at last got under way from Norfolk, with Lieutenant Charles Wilkes (arguably Melville's historical model for Ahab) leading the vessels on a formidable adventure of three and a half years' duration: polar nights, gales shrieking, hoarse cries of penguins in the piercing air, midday fog lifting to reveal colossal alabaster bergs, waves rising high as the ships' masts and flinging back clouds of spume and spray, ice weighting decks and rigging, crews numbingly aloft to reef stiff canvas on slippery spars under cawing seafowl . . .

Better for Slidell had he been along on that expedition, for the timing would have spared him a greater ordeal that was to dismay his friends, outrage his foes, and darken the latter days of his life. But by the time the little polar fleet finally sailed, the literary lieutenant had earned commands of his own.

For the present, as he wrote overseas to Longfellow this mid-February day in 1829, he planned to set out tomorrow for Washington, "where there are soon to be great doings: no less than a change of teams and drivers to the stage of state. Who knows but the General may after all make an excellent whip?" For thus far the cabinet appointments of President-elect Andrew Jackson—the people's choice—had (so Slidell thought) shown statesmanlike judiciousness. Like thousands of others the lieutenant meant to be on hand for Old Hickory's inaugural March 4; and when he got to Federal City he would find one of the most memorable scenes in all of American political life enacted, now when many of the Old Order like Judge Joseph Story were convinced that "the reign of King MOB" had arrived, and when the new President's noisy supporters appeared to confirm just that, as out of the West and South they descended on the capital to trod with their muddy boots through the rooms of the White House, downing ice cream and orange punch and standing in their clodhoppers on fine-cushioned chairs for the better view.

That summer Henry Longfellow returned from his extended sojourn in Europe to assume the position of professor of foreign languages at Bowdoin College, his alma mater. Down there in the Maine woods Slidell's *A Year in Spain* would be read and enjoyed. The book had finally been published by Hilliard Grey and Company of Boston; and according to the lieutenant's friend of Spanish days, who had received a copy when he and the author had managed a brief reunion in New York in September, it was "very much admired here. It makes me, however, very melancholy when I read it," Longfellow did admit, "for open where I will, I find something unknown to me before. I was as long in Spain as you were—enjoyed the same advantages whilst there—and now having before my eye a record of what you did, and the information you collected there, I feel rather sad that I should have effected so little, where you have effected so much." The young scholar was quarreling with himself every day, so he said, "for not having seen more bullfights—and sometimes fret myself into a fever for not having been hard-hearted enough to see the tragedies of the Plaza de Cebada": those hangings of two robbers that Slidell had witnessed in Madrid and described so vividly.

For his part, the lieutenant could fashion his own deft compliments. He was not long in assuring the discontented language teacher and future poet that "with a pen spirited, picturesque, and polished as yours, you would have done more than all my feeble and untutored efforts to draw attention to that most interesting country." As for any rewards that come from being a published author, "I do not find myself the happier for the qualification," he was insisting soon afterward; "I have had so much vexation, pecuniary and mechanical, that I feel no self-complacency on the subject." Indeed, Slidell had by then decided, after lengthy discussions with his friends, not to publish the remaining portions of his travels—a trip from Seville to Granada—and seemed in fact to be altogether content resuming his naval career aboard the frigate *Brandywine:* "I find myself delightfully situated on this ship, and hope to make an interesting cruise. We go to Mexico, Cuba, and as they say to Lisbon . . ."

That was early in 1830. During the course of that year Washington Irving would take the published edition of his young friend's travel book in hand and rework it for the English press, so that by March 1831, from London, where he had gone after leaving Spain, the world-famous author temporarily turned diplomat would forward to Lieutenant Slidell "the American copy of your work from which the London copy was printed. You will see," writes Irving, "I have made terrible cutting and slashing work with some parts of it, but it was necessary to do so . . ." Considering the English market, Slidell's friend at the American legation had had "to sacrifice some of your tirades against John Bull and some of your passages applicable merely to ourselves. Some of the historical parts also would have been trite in this country, so I threw them overboard." But benefits were to be gained from all that editing. "In checking over the corrected copy," Irving remarked, "you will notice a multitude of petty corrections which will be of service to you hereafter in point of style."

And *A Year in Spain*, as edited and republished under the prestigious imprint of the House of Murray, did prove successful with the often captious British. "Your work," Slidell was even then learning from his famous American friend on the spot, "has, upon the whole, had a triumphant launch, and has established a popular name for you in England, whether you choose to profit by it either as an author or a private individual. If you have any further manuscripts of any kind, Murray will be glad to treat for them, and I shall be happy to dispose of them for you." Handsome prospect! Nor was such heady encouragement uttered only to gratify an author's vanity. To other friends Irving was confirming that *A Year in Spain* "is quite the fashionable book of the day, and spoken of in the highest terms in the highest circles. If the Lieutenant were in London at present he would be quite a lion."

The lieutenant was serving a tour aboard ship, however; and while at sea this time, Slidell learned in the autumn of 1832 (soon after Irving, absent those previous seventeen years in Europe, had returned in triumph at last to his native city)—that autumn the lieutenant was informed that his father had succumbed to cholera, one of many victims of the summer's wide-ravaging epidemic in New York. Nearing the close of his life the old merchant—that "singularly urbane and scrupulously honest man"—had seen his fortune dwindle, and he had suffered the amputation of a leg, an operation that had for some time before his death made of his hobbling figure a distinctive sight along Broadway. Yet his end, despite those warnings of decline, arrived suddenly and unexpectedly. "I was in my Sunday school on the morning of 30th September about 10 o'clock," the Reverend Manton Eastburn wrote Slidell at sea, "when Captain Perry's oldest son came running to me with the intelligence that his grandfather was dying, and wished to see me. I went immediately" to a deathbed scene that reassured with its serenity: "he grasped my hand firmly, and though unable to utter anything, plainly showed that he felt all to be well. . . ."

The youthful messenger of that imminent demise—son of Jane Slidell and Matthew Calbraith Perry—would, by the way, enter the navy himself in adolescence, and later would serve as acting master aboard a sleek brig that Slidell would captain, on a cruise destined to awaken more public passion than would any other event focused around an individual in nineteenth-century America before the assassination of Lincoln. But the fateful voyage that would provide such news, as it shattered the complacency of Slidell's world, still lay a decade in the future.

Meanwhile, through the 1830s, the lieutenant continued alternately pursuing his two careers, as author and naval officer. By this time more than a third of his life had been spent on water: "for years together I have never slept out of a ship." Now on board the *Brandywine* on winter cruising in the Mediterranean, he found his eyes irritated—a chronic weakness—so that when the cruise ended in 1833, the invalid was granted another leave of absence, having in the interval at sea managed to write three long articles on naval subjects ("Ship," "Navy," "Navigation") for

The Encyclopaedia Americana, to be published in book form the year of his return home.

In the course of that same year, at ten on a beautiful autumn morning, "being the 1st of November, 1833," Slidell appeared—"punctual to the announcement of the newspapers" and with friends in company to see him off—on board the little steamboat *Hercules*, in attendance on the sailing ship *Hannibal* in New York Harbor, bound for London. But now he would sail merely as a passenger, on what was to be a rough crossing, for a visit of leisure to southern England to profit (as Irving had hinted he should) from his earlier literary success. Indeed, the lieutenant brought with him letters of introduction that Irving had written, to Lord Holland and others. And from this new experience would emerge his third book, *The American in England*, in 1835.

By his own admission this latest effort was joylessly put together, hampered as it was by the author's antipathy toward the English, by his discontent with the cheerless winter weather of his visit, and by an all but paralyzing self-consciousness arising from his expected larger readership, after the success of that earlier book of travels. Slidell's book on Spain had been composed, as he asserted, "with the same enthusiasm which attended the travels it described, and was truly . . . a labor of love." By contrast, this ill-natured account of London life in the early 1830s, though possessed of vivid detail, shows evidence throughout of the struggle it had taken to finish. The preface, dated October 1, 1835, from New York—on the lieutenant's wedding day—bluntly admits as much: "The result of this up-hill journey"—the two-volume work—"is before the reader, and, however distasteful it may prove to him, his feeling of aversion can scarce exceed that with which the author now takes leave of it."

Seldom can a book have recommended itself so tepidly. Nevertheless, *The American in England* does allow occasional sharp glimpses of the author-sailor-traveler, as when he is disclosed wandering London streets forlorn in his Spanish capa on a dreary, wet November Monday, debating whether to buy an umbrella: "In my professional pursuits the use of an umbrella was preposterous; and in the climate of my own country it rains so seldom that to a man of leisure, having no business avocations to call him inauspiciously into the open air, the umbrella is also a useless and disagreeable encumbrance." Those people of consequence to whom his letters of introduction would have made him known were out of town; left on his own, the solitary was grappling with a problem like that—that, and the boredom imposed by his weak eyes, which London smoke had all the more inflamed (no books or papers to help pass the time)—those problems, and the shock to his moral sense of English behavior in public: drunkenness and debauchery in the streets at Christmastime, loose manners at Drury Lane Theatre: "What with the kisses on the stage and the kisses off it, the evidence on all sides of unbridled licentiousness, the scene was such a one as in all my wanderings I had never beheld . . ."

Moreover, the weather continued wet and cold. His dismal visit was not yet two months old when the despondent Slidell gratefully seized an opportunity, New Year's Day, 1834, to escape England for a journey to the south of Europe. But "it may be proper," he concluded his account of that brief London residence, "to state that the writer returned to England some months subsequent to the period to which the foregoing pages refer, that he traveled, with far greater gratification than on his previous visit, extensively over the United Kingdom, keeping notes of whatever he saw . . ." And that on that second visit he was entirely cured of his eye malady through the ministrations of Mr. Alexander, "the celebrated London oculist."

Meanwhile, however, he would escape to Spain, charged with delivering to the American minister in Madrid dispatches that accredited that functionary to the regime empowered after the recent death of Ferdinand VII. "The service was then one of some difficulty, which, as an officer of the government, familiar, moreover, with the language and manners of the country to be traversed, I did not feel at liberty to decline." *A Year in Spain* had made its author officially unwelcome in the kingdom, the book having been confiscated by Ferdinand's government and a royal proclamation having been issued that the "joven anglo-americano teniente de la marina . . . llamado Ridell"—the young American naval lieutenant called Ridell—was to be escorted to the nearest frontier if ever he should attempt to reenter Spain. The work had offended the monarch with its mild disparagement of the royal family—although now, seven years later, Slidell found himself unmolested as he returned to Madrid; for the dissolute old king was dead, though little else appeared to have altered.

"The scene around me," the lieutenant observed, having gazed once more upon the crowded Prado, "was a familiar one; it seemed in all things unchanged by an absence of so many years. Here was the same collection of idle loungers, enveloped in their cloaks, which I had been wont to see." And there the vendors—watermen, orange sellers, egg and chestnut women with their nasally cries. "Accustomed as I was, at each return home after my professional cruises, to find the face of things changed, and my native city grown beyond my recollection, all was here so similar and so familiar that I was for a moment confounded, and half disposed to fancy that my absence was imaginary."

And unchanged, too, on this second Spanish visit, was Slidell's yielding to an impulse to attend a public execution: "It was sure to be a spectacle full of horror and painful excitement; still I determined to witness it. I felt sad and melancholy, and yet, by a strange perversion, I was willing to feel more so." Thus he was on hand this time at a garroting, the method of execution meticulously described: "A single upright post was planted in the ground, having attached to it an iron collar, large enough to receive the neck of the culprit, but capable of being suddenly tightened to much smaller dimensions by means of a screw which played against the back of the post and had a very open spiral thread." While Slidell watches, the prisoner is brought to the post and affixed there. "Quick as lightning the motion is given to the fatal lever; a momentary convulsion agitates his frame and horribly distorts his countenance, and the sinner is with God." At the instant, the crowd is muttering prayers; "ten thousand breasts are signed together with the cross of reconciliation." The bell of a neighboring church starts tolling, and a horseman darts off at a gallop to carry the news of this riddance to the Royal Palace . . .

Slidell's second visit to Spain lasted no more than two months, with stops at Pamplona, Salamanca, Valladolid, and Burgos. But it was long enough to provide him with material for yet another travel book, though an inferior one: *Spain Revisited*, which was published in 1836, after the lieutenant's return to America. And with three such works to his credit, he had found himself contemplating a fourth. Convinced as he was "that the popular manners of Ireland furnish a theme for amusing description," and that his present mode of writing "might be applied more advantageously in describing the sister kingdom" than in describing England in the dreariness of winter, Slidell had already promised readers of the earlier volume "to prepare for publication the account of his travels in that country." But the manuscript of his Irish journey he would be working on as late as the last month of his life, and at his death would leave unfinished what was not to be published after all.

The book on England did appear, however, late in 1835, and the following year appeared the second book on Spain, dedicated to Slidell's closest friend, Lieutenant George P. Upshur, United States Navy. The two young officers had served on shipboard for an extended period together, and on one notable excursion had traveled from Syracuse to Aetna during days of delight that provided "a temporary escape from the necessary, yet somewhat onerous thraldom of a well-regulated man-of-war." Though his brother was a celebrated jurist—judge of the Virginia general court—Upshur himself was as yet unknown to fame, merely one more all but anonymous naval officer. By now, of course, Slidell did know a number of illustrious people. Indeed, "the chief advantage of the slight reputation which has fallen to my share," he explains in his dedication, "has been its procuring me the favor and acquaintance of some distinguished individuals whose names might furnish a decoration to my pages which the world would, perhaps, more highly value. But I turn with far greater delight to the regard which, in the course of a long and

most familiar association, was conceded to me from personal considerations alone"—not from his having become an increasingly well-known
author—"and I feel a pleasure which I cannot easily describe in offering
this slight though heartfelt tribute" of *Spain Revisited* "to the truest and
most cherished of my professional friendships," to the friendship of this
same Lieutenant Upshur of the navy.

The dedication is dated from New York, January 1, 1836. Slidell had
returned home a year before to discover his native city further changed,
further aggrandized. Yet Bond Street marked the northern limit of the
town; fashionable residences clustered around the Battery, up Greenwich
Street, and along Broadway still. The year 1835 was the year of the great
fire that the pages of Philip Hone's diary describe so feelingly, the year
when the first issues of the *New York Herald*—James Gordon Bennett's
colorful penny paper for the multitudes—appeared for sale from his cellar office at 20 Wall Street. It was the year of the "Moon Hoax," and the
year that the Democrats nominated Martin Van Buren to succeed his
mentor Jackson in the presidency. And it was the year, on a personal
note, when Alexander Slidell, thirty-two, married, October 1, the
twenty-year-old daughter of the prominent New York lawyer and banker
Morris Robinson.

The marriage was altogether satisfying. After having experienced wed-
ded life with Kate almost a decade, the uxorious Slidell was able to describe their time together as "most truly one of increased and increasing
happiness, contentment, and enchantment." He had, he said, "no inade-
quate estimation of what a happy marriage is, for my own has been
eminently so." Three sons and two daughters would be born to the couple, two of the sons growing up to become naval officers, the third a
distinguished cavalry officer in the army (Grant said the most promising
young officer to come out of the Civil War). And now in the late 1830s
the lieutenant and his wife, not long married and about to start their
family, were planning a move from the city north to a home on the
Hudson near Tarrytown, in sight of the Tappan Zee.

Tarrytown was where Washington Irving lived. After ending his years
of wandering in Europe, that most adored of American writers had finally, in 1835, purchased an old farmhouse in rural haunts of his childhood, north of Manhattan some twenty-five miles, and settled down to
remake the place into Sunnyside, as it would come to be called. Slidell
had earlier expressed a longing for just such a domicile. When yet unmar-
ried, riding in the Dover coach toward London on his autumn visit two
years before, he had beheld a number of quaint ivy-covered villas with
paddocks stretching toward the road, ponies cropping the sward, flower
gardens with roses and dahlias behind neat iron railings. Any one of
those modest habitations, the lieutenant had fancied, if "placed in my
own country on any one of the thousand unnoticed and unimproved sites
of my native Hudson, would have bounded the circle of my unambitious

hopes." Like Irving, this inveterate wanderer had longed for a hearthside of his own. Now he would have that wish come true, at a small plain farmhouse on the Beekman acres, halfway between Ossining and Tarrytown. But Tarrytown would be the address his letters carried.

Assuredly the area was fashionable. Not only did Irving live down the road with his brother and nieces, but Matthew Calbraith Perry, married to Slidell's sister, would soon build a large home nearby for his wife and seven children. Another neighbor was Colonel James Watson Webb, "the Apollo of the press," colorful editor of one of New York City's leading newspapers. In such agreeable surroundings, then, did the Slidells come to establish their own domestic world, though no longer under that name. Rather, the family hereafter would go by the name of Mackenzie, the maiden name of Alexander Slidell's mother.

That lady's Scottish brother—Alex's maternal uncle, and a bachelor— had been unwilling to see the patronymic die out at his death; he would make a legacy available if his nephew would formally adopt *Mackenzie* as his own last name. The change was enacted by the New York state legislature in the late 1830s—the uncle's gift of money may have helped purchase the farmhouse near Tarrytown—and thereafter, though such long-standing correspondents as Longfellow required time to adjust their salutation, Alexander Slidell was and would remain for the rest of his life Alexander Slidell Mackenzie: Lieutenant, later Commander Mackenzie.

When the now Slidell Mackenzie took up residence at Tarrytown early in 1840, he had not long before returned from an eventful tour of duty, lasting two years, on board various vessels that had carried the navy husband from his wife eastward as far as St. Petersburg, southward as far as Montevideo. Aboard the *Independence* as first lieutenant (in the modern navy executive officer, next under the captain), he had sailed on an assignment to transport the American ambassador George Dallas to his duties in Russia. From the North Sea, Mackenzie had then sailed back across the Atlantic and south of the equator to the Brazil station. Rubber made cities on the South American coast desirable ports of call for merchantmen of the United States. But Brazil during those years was unstable: nativists fighting with Portuguese, federalists with centralists, radicals with conservatives, republicans with monarchists, inhabitants of the northern provinces with those farther south. As protectors of commerce, the American navy had a role to play down there. And there Slidell Mackenzie had been given a captaincy, of the USS *Dolphin*, aboard which schooner he would witness the siege of Bahia, and in that struggle would play his own small but creditable part.

Imperial troops were storming the gates; insurgents within the walls were setting the city on fire. "I got the *Dolphin* under way from her anchorage near the British and French cruisers," her captain later recalled, "and, crossing the fire of one of the batteries and an imperial cruiser that was attacking it, brought the *Dolphin* to anchor under the walls of the town opposite the residence of the American consul, received him on board with his family, and gave refuge to all who fled on board of her from the sanguinary onset of the assailants, from the conflagration and its drunken and desperate perpetrators." Again, at the end of one of several such chaotic civil conflicts, "when the constitutional government was overthrown and Ribera was about to enter Montevideo at the head of a horde of ferocious Indians, I gave refuge on board," writes Mackenzie, "to more than twenty individuals, including several high officers of state who were deeply compromised, abandoned to the females of their family exclusive use of my cabin, and conveyed them to a place of safety."

Deeds of a man of action, and a gallant one. "In like manner in the *Fairchild*"—on which the Spanish-speaking Mackenzie served as well about this time, in South American waters—"I withdrew from threatened death at Buenos Ayres several individuals compromised for political offences, and . . . I did this without forfeiting the favorable regard for myself and for my country of the authorities of Buenos Ayres, conciliated by the energetic measures which I had taken to resist the attempt of the French admiral to encroach on our neutral rights . . ." A man of action he had shown himself to be, forceful, diplomatic. But also a contemplative man. For returning from Brazilian duty, Mackenzie had no difficulty settling down with his family to the quiet joys of country living, tending his garden and pursuing his other career, as an author.

That love of rural existence was, as one contemporary noted, not unusual "with men who pass much of their lives upon the sea." Ocean air, or the air of the country. Slidell Mackenzie himself, earlier beset by London squalor, had written in the spirit of a Leatherstocking, floridly but with conviction, of "the tendency of a life passed amid crowds, confusion, the intimate and indiscriminate contact with the eager and mammon-seeking throng that congregate in cities, and all the manifold horrors that are to be found in smoke, dust, noise, omnibuses, and disgustful surroundings." The tendency of such surroundings was nothing less, he felt, than "to uproot the natural affections and to corrupt the heart." By contrast, this contemplative could assert his simple faith "that an existence gently gliding away amid the scenes of nature, and the calm and tranquil occupations of some rural abode, must oppositely and equally contribute to develop whatever is generous within us, and to give elevation and purity to the sentiments, and dignity to the character."

Such benefits—of dignity and generosity and pure, elevated feelings—were presumably being bestowed in those years from 1840 on, when the sailor at home was completing one literary task, casting about for others, and farming at his leisure. A neighbor recorded a visit that lets us see him at this time of life. One sunshiny Monday in 1841—the first of May it was—Washington Irving and two nieces paid a call on the Mackenzies, one of many such calls no doubt, though this one Irving described in some detail to yet a third niece, recently married and moved to Paris. "It was too early an hour for a regular visit," her uncle was writing Sarah Storrow two days later, "and I intended only to ask for Mackenzie, with whom I had some business. He was from home, however, and his excellent little wife received us with her accustomed warmth and frankness. We paid her a long visit, and to me it was a most interesting one, for I feel a strong and growing regard for this noble-hearted little creature and a deep sympathy in the fortunes of her worthy husband."

What about those fortunes was bestirring Irving's sympathy? Despite the naval career and six books published by then, Mackenzie was poor. "He has anxious moments, I fear, poor fellow, and looks forward with a dubious eye"—as well he might, as well he might—"but then he has a treasure at home better than all the world's wealth, and of which the world cannot deprive him." That treasure was a wife, of course, together with an infant child and a modest home. For modest the farmhouse was. "Mrs. Mackenzie told me," Irving relays to his niece, "she expected in the course of the spring to have her sister Fanny and her husband and several of her own family to pay her a visit of several days. Where the blessed little being is to put them all and how to accommodate them heaven only knows. One would think her mansion was as large as her heart. . . ."

The call that May morning had still been in progress when Mackenzie appeared. He "arrived from the landing, with his waggon filled with young trees, flowers, etc. I think he begins to look careworn," the caller notes, though compared to what lay in the officer's future, little enough had happened yet to cause him to look thus. Not Irving, however, or anybody else could know that. This spring day in 1841, the neighbor over from Sunnyside thought that Mackenzie "begins to look careworn, though he only wants a little money to make him one of the happiest of mortals. Indeed, when I saw him seated by his fireside, with his wife beside him and his bright-looking child on his knee, I would not have exchanged his lot for that of the richest man of my acquaintance. . . ."

That wagon full of trees and flowers: for some time the sailor ashore had been "laying out, digging and transplanting so assiduously in a new garden . . . that I have neglected many things that I ought to have done." So Mackenzie a while before had written his old friend Longfellow, by then at Harvard and nationally known. To the successful poet he had turned a year earlier for literary aid and counsel. In February 1840, the lieutenant had asked Longfellow to look over proofs "of my little book" on John Paul Jones, a naval life prepared at the editor Jared Spark's request as one in his series of biographies of eminent Americans. "I would beg you to make the freest possible use of your pen, which can not be otherwise than very improving in its effects." And more: "When you have time to write to me pray tell me whether you have thought anything further of the story you were suggesting to me as offering good materials for a novel. I think if I could once get underweigh with a naval subject I might be able to go on."

Longfellow had responded in May, expecting to read .the Paul Jones proofs with the greatest pleasure; "I am very glad to have it in my power to serve you in any way, and will make any suspicious-looking sentence show his passport." But another matter had called for a judgment: "In regard to the Piña de los Enamorados"—Slidell Mackenzie's effort at a different literary form—"I shall advise you not to publish it. The sack of Martos is very finely done, and the midnight scene in the count's palace very striking. But as a whole I do not think it would raise your reputation as an author. When you enter the realm of fiction, I want you to march in with a more lofty step." Nor was that all. Yet another matter Mackenzie had solicited his friend's help on, a question of research down Maine. Longfellow had dealt with that too, dutifully forwarding details in the life of the Baron of Castine, seventeenth-century French army officer who, after the Treaty of Breda, had come to America, fought in Canada, acquired a plantation at Penobscot, traded in fish and furs, and married an Indian. Could he be made into a hero of romance? "To tell the truth," Longfellow confessed, "my heart rather misgives me about this subject. I do not want you to fall into Cooper's trail—or *wake*, I *should* say. People would cry out *imitation!* which heaven forfend. Your good genius will guide you to some good theme ere long . . ."

In fact, just such a theme was soon at hand. Within weeks Mackenzie was being urgently petitioned—by the late naval hero's grown son—to write a life of Oliver Hazard Perry, victor of Lake Erie. And that subject, and the book the lieutenant would make of it, would bring him into vigorous public conflict with the very writer whom Longfellow feared he might be charged with imitating. Lieutenant Mackenzie was about to be "menaced with the high displeasure" of James Fenimore Cooper.

Fenimore Cooper and Slidell Mackenzie were acquaintances. In a letter from Philadelphia dated January 29, 1837, the creator of Leatherstocking and Long Tom Coffin had written his wife, at home in upper New York State: "Tell Paul"—their son, not yet in his teens—"I shall give him the Cyclopedia of Geography, if I find he has made good use of his time and Sue makes a good report of him." Sue was a daughter, staying with her mother at Cooperstown. The novelist added a cheering afterthought: "Slidell, who is here, promises me a cure for Sue's eyes."

Doubtless the cure was Mr. Alexander's, that of the London oculist. The lieutenant was offering to share so beneficial a treatment with the illustrious Mr. Cooper early in 1837. Relations between the two were cordial then. Within three years, however, all cordiality had vanished.

The illustrious Mr. Cooper. To say that this prodigious storyteller was illustrious requires qualification. On the continent of Europe he assuredly was—the only American writer, in fact, whose reputation rivaled that of the beloved Irving. But at home Washington Irving was much the more popular of the two. Indeed, for many of his countrymen Cooper by this time was less an illustrious writer than a notorious one, though it had not always been so.

He had been born—twelfth of thirteen children—in 1789, six years after Irving, and had spent his childhood in a fine home in the wilderness beyond the Catskills, in Otsego County, as the pampered son of a judge and prosperous landowner—friend of Washington and Jay and Hamilton, founder of the town on Lake Otsego that bears the family name. At thirteen Cooper was enrolled in Yale, where in his junior year he was expelled for playing some prank more or less serious—a gunpowder explosion at the keyhole of a college room? a donkey placed in a professor's chair? Out of Yale for whatever delinquency (family legend is inexact), the spirited boy was at his father's insistence sent to sea as a common sailor, aboard the merchantman *Stirling*, bound for Europe. Cooper was seventeen at the time—October 1806, with the Napoleonic wars in progress.

The voyage offered its share of adventures: near collisions, storms in the foggy Channel, press-gangs boarding, a felucca in pursuit off Portugal, James among others of the crew managing liberty to wander the streets of London, having "a rum time of it in his sailor rig." That standard apprenticeship completed—before the mast as an ordinary seaman —the young man returned home with his newly acquired knowledge of shiphandling and, on the first day of January 1808, was commissioned a midshipman in the navy.

Cooper served in the navy three years, aboard vessels in New York Harbor and on the Lower Lakes; later he would claim to have been "the first officer who ever carried the button on to those waters," a United States naval uniform seen in those wilderness outposts for the first time five years before Lieutenant Perry on the same waters was to win his great victory.

But unlike Oliver Perry, Cooper played no part in the War of 1812—a fact that at least one of his numerous enemies would have occasion to remind his countrymen of later. One day in 1809, his father the judge, an active Federalist, had been emerging from a meeting in Albany, descending the statehouse steps, when a political opponent struck him from behind, a blow that led to his death soon after. The son was accordingly obliged to assume larger familial responsibilities. But now financially independent, young Cooper was not long in becoming engaged, some months after his father's death, to the eighteen-year-old Susan DeLancey, and on New Year's Day, 1811—exactly three years from the date of his commission—was married. That spring, at his bride's urging, he resigned from the navy.

His married life, like Slidell's, was to prove exceptionally happy. "Few men," he could write Horatio Greenough twenty-seven years later, "know more, or have known more of domestic felicity than myself, or can better speak on the subject of the value of a good wife." (His sculptor friend had raised the subject by forwarding news of his own recent marriage.) "Our family circle," Cooper confided, "is our world, and has long been so, and every day I prize it more, and become more fondly attached to all its members."

Besides their happy marriages, their naval interests, and their literary propensities, he and Alexander Slidell had, curiously, one other matter in common. As already noted, the lieutenant late in the 1830s successfully petitioned the New York legislature to change his name to Mackenzie. A decade earlier, in 1826, James Cooper petitioned the same body toward the same end, and for the same reason: to change his name in order to perpetuate the name of his mother's family, about to expire without male descendants. Accordingly he would be known from then on as James Fenimore-Cooper, though the hyphen between maternal and paternal names was dropped within a year or two.

By that time, by the late 1820s, Cooper had become internationally famous as an author, a profession happened upon almost by chance. Since his marriage he had been living the life of a well-to-do gentleman farmer, at Otsego and in Westchester County (not far from Tarrytown), speculating, interesting himself in agricultural pursuits and in the state militia. But in 1820, on a dare from his wife, the thirty-one-year-old squire had tried his hand at writing a novel. The first attempt he destroyed. A second attempt, on an English subject, was published to mild praise. But the third, set in Westchester County during the Revolution and published late in 1821, was a resounding success; three editions of *The Spy* were rapidly exhausted.

Thereafter, like the contemporary British novelist Scott, with whom he was often compared, Cooper proved to be amazingly prolific and his works extraordinarily popular. *The Pioneers* appeared in 1823, *The Pilot* in 1824, *Lionel Lincoln* in 1825, *The Last of the Mohicans* in 1826. And honors accrued. The suddenly successful novelist was granted membership in the American Philosophical Society in 1823. The following August he received an honorary degree from Columbia College. In May 1826, the corporation of the city of New York awarded him a silver medal "as a testimony of their high respect for you, as a citizen of the U. States, who, by his writings has added to the glory of the Republic." And through piratings and translations, this other New Yorker's reputation was, like Irving's, extended overseas, where Balzac was only one among many to extol his achievement.

But along with triumphs, those same years brought misfortunes. Cooper's house burned in 1823. His young son Fenimore died soon after. And through a series of forced sales of his late father's land—sales necessarily completed at ruinous losses—his inheritance was swept away in the early 1820s, so that profits from his novels were more than consumed by debts from other sources, debts in some instances incurred by relatives but for which he felt bound to assume responsibility. Like Scott again, Cooper must go on writing to pay off indebtedness. But in the case of the American, the debts were paid by 1826; and in June of that year, he set sail with his family for an extended residence in Europe.

In comparable self-exile Irving passed seventeen years, from 1815 to 1832. Cooper's residence abroad—mostly in France—lasted no longer than seven. But patriots in the young republic were displeased by the absence of both those writers from their native land. Both felt called upon to demonstrate loyalty during their protracted stays in Europe, Irving through the choice, as he conceived it, of so solid an American subject as his life of Columbus. For his part Cooper in Paris, at the suggestion of his friend Lafayette, willingly undertook to defend his countrymen from the numerous slanders and misinterpretations published by churlish Europeans who had traveled to the New World and returned laden with letters and journals unflattering to their hosts. *Notions of the Americans* (1828) is just such a defense, but its composition started the novelist thinking analytically about his homeland, and about contemporary social and political matters in general.

Cooper was, as Irving put it, "a very 'castle of a man' "—over six feet tall, over two hundred pounds, a man of forceful opinions, outspoken, eloquent, utterly undaunted by controversy, and with an Olympian moral sense. He had, for example, little use for Irving himself, not on personal grounds but purely on moral ones. Back in the early 1820s, near the start of his own literary career, Cooper had undertaken to review the latest production of the expatriate Irving's, published simultaneously in America and England. *Bracebridge Hall* had been generally hailed as a worthy successor to the astonishingly popular *Sketch Book;* but Cooper didn't like it, seeing in its warm evocations of manor life and customs a servile flattery of the mother country. "While he proudly, and no doubt sincerely, declares his increasing attachment to republican principles," that stern moralist back home wrote of his fellow New Yorker, "he eulogizes the aristocracy of Great Britain." Such apparent hypocrisy seemed at the very least offensive. Nor would Cooper ever revise his low estimate of Irving's moral worth that so fawning a performance appeared to substantiate.

Friends of both authors were dismayed, all the more so because Irving in speaking of Cooper was always the soul of generosity. When, for example, *The Pathfinder* appeared years later, Irving was "all enthusiasm about this book. He spent an hour with me yesterday," Fitz-Greene Halleck bore witness, "pointing out its fine passages and talking of the absurdity of denying that Cooper is a man of genius of the first order." Bryant insisted that Irving was in actuality one of Cooper's "warmest friends and admirers," and Charles Fenno Hoffman reported that his good friend Irving, who had spoken with him long and sympathetically on the subject of the novelist's "writings, quarrels with the newspapers, etc.," expressed the conviction that "there is hardly any American prose that will live except Cooper's."

Such praise from Irving, relayed by friends, was without effect. "My opinion," Cooper pronounced flatly, "has been independent of what that gentleman might have said of me, or my writings, or character. It has been solely formed on what are admitted to be his acts, and what I think of *them*." That Irving could toady to the English, for instance. That he could publish in a periodical so consistently anti-American as *The London Quarterly*. That he could even stoop to reviewing his own productions anonymously (though Irving did that only once, reluctantly, of *The Conquest of Granada*, at his publisher's urging, and not to praise the work but to clarify its rather confusing narrative method). "I never understood that Irving was severe on me, either as a man or an author," Cooper continued in this letter to a well-intentioned admirer of both. "If I had, pride might cause me to suppress what I think of him . . ." But, he insisted, "a published eulogy of myself from Irving's pen could not change my opinion of his career. . . . I have never had any quarrel with Mr. Irving, and give him full credit as a writer. Still, I believe him to be below the ordinary level in moral qualities, instead of being above them, as he is cried up to be."

It was a singular judgment of Irving's nature, by no means generally shared—a judgment that held a fellow human being to a very high standard of conduct indeed. But Cooper was sincere and even disinterested in uttering such judgments. And he was consistent.

Returning home after his seven years' absence, in 1833, the novelist had been dismayed to discover a country different from what he had left: less free, less tolerant, more vulgar—or so it appeared to one who by then had lived observantly in several European nations. Nor was he long in publishing his revised opinion of his native land. (Irving, for his part, on his return had expressed his own decided reservations, but only privately, in letters to relatives and intimate friends in Europe.) In various works, but especially in the novel *Home As Found*, Cooper conveyed a sense of the new America he had come upon, where mediocrity seemed in the ascendant, where manners no longer signified, where wealth more than breeding set the tone, where the very towns and dwellings in that age of rapid growth had become as tawdry as the lives led in them were coarse. Moreover, republican simplicity and independence had given way, he thought, to pretension and the tyranny of the mob; examples of just such tyranny informed the plot of this new work, in which a well-bred, cosmopolitan gentleman from upper New York state asserts his legitimate hereditary rights of property against grasping and boorish neighbors.

Home As Found contained not the first of Cooper's strictures on the values of his countrymen, but it provoked the most vehement reactions up to that time. Colonel James Watson Webb, Slidell Mackenzie's neighbor at Tarrytown, reviewed the novel in the influential paper he owned and edited, *The Morning Courier and New York Enquirer*, in the issue for November 22, 1838. The review begins: "We may in truth say that we have never read an American book with the same feelings of regret, pity, contempt, and anger, as the last work of Mr. Cooper." Webb, who in his youth had worked at a store near Cooperstown before running off to join the army, did not scruple in the course of his review to draw upon personal recollections: "We . . . know him"—the author— "as a base-minded caitiff, who has traduced his country for filthy lucre and from low-born *spleen*." More specifically, "the leading purposes of the author," wrote the clairvoyant Webb, "were, *first*, to create a market for his works in England, in imitation of other hireling writers; *secondly*, to give vent to his spleen against his countrymen for not hailing his return as they did that of Washington Irving; and *thirdly*, to produce the impression abroad that he is the descendant of a long line of noble ancestors, and, in point of antiquity, of family not only far above his countrymen, but the equal of the noblest blood in England."

Yet on that last point readers of the *Courier and Enquirer* were to be undeceived. Cooper's father—that friend of Washington's who had acquired those hundred thousand acres of New York State—was in fact, so Webb went on to explain, "a highly respectable WHEELWRIGHT of *New Jersey*, who has frequently been heard to declare that he was proud of his occupation and only regretted that while he labored at it, he was unable to manufacture as good waggons as his brothers in the trade." And as for Cooper's mother, Webb's readers were later to learn that she was "the daughter of a notorious huckster woman, who for a quarter of a century was known in the Philadelphia Market as the very best *pedlar of green vegetables* in that best of markets."

So much for a proud man's claim to family. "The Courier & Enquirer of this morning," Fenimore Cooper was writing in cold fury that same day to William Cullen Bryant's *Evening Post*, "in a pretended review of *Home As Found*, contains a series of libellous falsehoods of a personal nature." Some of the allegations leveled against him in the "review" the author would answer on the spot: for instance, that a motive for writing his novel had been to increase his market in England; in fact, *Home As Found* was sold to his English publisher for less than the earlier Cooper romances of broader appeal. "The editor of the Courier & Enquirer," the novelist concluded, "writes as if we were well acquainted. This I deny. He is my junior, and I knew him slightly when a boy, and slightly when a young man. I do not think I have spoken to him on five different occasions in fifteen years.

"As the libels of the article will be made the subject of a legal investigation, I shall say no more."

And on that note he ended his letter. A criminal suit followed, only one of a number of suits—criminal and civil—that Cooper instituted for libel against various newspapers in the late 1830s, in a self-declared effort to tame them and teach them manners. The editors of eight different papers he sued in all, including some of the most powerful: Webb and Thurlow Weed and Park Benjamin and William Leete Stone and Horace Greeley. He took them all on—entered into the necessary correspondence, went through the ordeal of preparing his briefs, traveled over the state to the various courts of venue, on occasion brilliantly argued the cases himself. And he won. After five years of such exhausting, time-consuming endeavors, he could truthfully write, in 1843: "I have beaten every man I have sued who has not retracted his libels." And looking back at that litigious interval in Cooper's life, Bryant, poet and himself an editor, summarized what his friend had achieved. "He put a hook into the nose of this huge monster"—the hoglike daily press—"wallowing in his inky pool and bespattering the passers-by; he dragged him to the land and made him tractable."

At the time, the chastened newspapers—all that institutional strength whipped into line by a single individual—had responded by tacitly agreeing to ignore Cooper's writings altogether. They might no longer slander him, but they would take no further notice of works from his pen. And despite his preoccupations with libel trials, the author had been continuing to publish: novels, essays, accounts of travels. Behind him, among other achievements, lay *The Prairie* (1827), *The Red Rover* (1828), *The Water-Witch* (1830), *The Bravo* (1831), *A Letter to His Countrymen* (1834), book-length descriptions, totaling ten volumes, of England, France, Switzerland, and Italy (1836–38), and *The American Democrat* (1838). *Homeward Bound* and *Home As Found* had appeared that same year, 1838. Soon would emerge two of his greatest imaginative efforts: *The Pathfinder* (1840) and *The Deerslayer* (1841)—both generally decried or ignored by the American press of the time.

But for a decade and longer Cooper had been contemplating yet another enterprise, and an enormous one: a work of history, in the truest sense patriotic, something he would take far more seriously than he did those costumed chases through forests or on the high seas that embellish his romances. This, in fact, would be his magnum opus.

He had spoken publicly, as long ago as 1826, of the debt he owed the solemn Muse of History for having so often invaded her domains for plunder for his frivolous fictions. Now he would pay that overdue debt. To his English publisher Richard Bentley he had written at the end of 1837 that the new and long-contemplated work—a weighty History of the United States Navy—"will be ready to be sent in March. I think this book will not disappoint you, as, if I know myself, impartiality will form its great feature. Some of the combats, too, will have the interest of a fiction, though strictly true." But the March that Cooper mentioned came and went, and that next year ended, and still he was laboring over the quantities of material that his research had uncovered. In late January 1839, he was writing a friend, "As respects the History, I can only say I have never worked half as hard in my life"—this from one who knew what work was. He had, for example, come upon new information about the Revolution that had led him to rewrite more than half of the first volume. He was corresponding with such as John Quincy Adams, inquiring whether that aged statesman could recall the fate of certain Revolutionary naval vessels. He was traveling in December, arduously, by steamboat, stagecoach, and railroad, to use the library of the American Philosophical Society in Philadelphia, and later to visit Washington for further research. He was soliciting his many friends in the navy for help.

But the results of all that digging would be worth the effort. These were hard times, in the aftermath of the Panic of 1837. Cooper, who had earlier in his life suffered through financial loss and indebtedness, was acutely aware that his novels earned less than they once had done, still less because of the attitude the American press had taken toward him. But the History of the Navy would rectify all that. It would be something different—an indispensable work, accurate, impartial, a work that would sell and sell, year after year, to the benefit of Cooper's family, including those four daughters and that son Paul whom he loved.

"The History, first and last," he wrote his wife in the fall of 1839, after a gratifying visit to his publisher in Philadelphia, "will make me from $10,000 to $15,000—with the third volume quite the latter I think." And a month later, more good news from the same source: "When abridged, it will be worth $500 a year to me for the next twenty-eight years; and of course for my life—" His publishers, he reported, "value it, as a selling book, very high . . . The Naval History, in short, is the best hit I have made . . ."

Yet a few of its early readers were disturbed by one portion of that vast work—specifically, by those fifteen pages (out of eight hundred and seventy-five) in which the author had dealt with Oliver Perry's victory over the English in the War of 1812. Slidell Mackenzie—sailor and writer himself—had been one who was made unhappy by what he had read. He had proceeded to develop his opinion for *The North American Review*, in an anonymous, thirty-five-page notice of Cooper's achievement that was published that same October of 1839. Mackenzie's review was, to be sure, for the most part favorable (of a work of "liberality, talent and ingenuity"; "a valuable addition to the history of the country"), but the reviewer did take the historian strongly to task for what he called an "unfair account of the Battle of Lake Erie."

The issue between Cooper and his opponents in this instance concerned the posthumous reputation of Captain Oliver Perry, and the conduct during that battle of Perry's second-in-command, an officer named Jesse Duncan Elliott, who in the late 1830s was still loquaciously alive. Those many years earlier, when the engagement had been fought on a golden fall afternoon in 1813, what had happened aboard Elliott's brig *Niagara*, that undamaged American vessel to which Captain Perry had been rowed under fire, after his own brig, the *Lawrence*, had been battered into submission? For two hours and longer the *Lawrence* had gallantly exchanged fire with the enemy, at fearful loss of life, and all that while the captain of the *Niagara* had held his vessel out of range to windward. Why?

"I'll tell you," Elliott responded, many years after Perry's early death at the mouth of the Orinoco. "Where two fleets are about to engage in battle, a knowledge of naval tactics and evolutions must be resorted to. The line once formed, no captain has a right to change, without authority, or a signal from the commanding vessel." To be sure, late in the battle "the crisis had arrived, in my opinion, when, at the risk of losing my own head, I changed the order of battle." On his own authority he had left his assigned station and sailed into a position from which Perry, climbing aboard soon after from his small boat, could turn the struggle around by bringing the *Niagara* victoriously down upon the enemy.

Others would maintain that a ship closing with her assigned enemy vessel in the confusion of battle could never be out of station, no matter what friendly vessel she had been ordered to guide on before the battle began. Some even whispered that Elliott had stood out of range until presuming Perry dead—who could have survived the battering the *Lawrence* had taken?—then begun his maneuver to close and win all the glory. In any case, with the battle ended and in the immediate aftermath of his triumph, in a report to the secretary of the navy dated September 13, 1813, Captain Perry himself had awarded praise to all his officers and men, including his second-in-command: "Of Captain Elliott, already so well known to the government, it would be almost superfluous to speak. In this action he evinced his characteristic bravery and judgment, and since the close of the action has given me the most able and essential assistance."

Later, however, the victor would come to regret having written those words, those and even stronger words: "I am indignant," he had been led at the time to express himself directly to Elliott, "that any report should be in circulation prejudicial to your character as respects the action of the 10th instant. It affords me pleasure that I have it in my power to assure you that the conduct of yourself, officers, and crew was such as to merit my warmest approbation. . . ." But if such testimonials were false—as Perry later averred—why had he protected Elliott's reputation thus, at a time when others were already hinting that that officer's conduct during the battle had been either cowardly or treasonous?

"On the evening of the action," Perry would finally explain, "I was elated with our success . . . At such a moment there was not a person in the world whose feelings I would have hurt." Moreover, he had been reluctant to let the enemy know that the second-in-command had failed in his duty. Better to screen a coward, so the commodore professed to have concluded, than to reveal that one was in the American fleet.

Accordingly, Elliott possessed in writing testimony from his superior confirming his courage; but rumors of his treachery persisted, to the extent that four or five years later he was demanding that a naval court of inquiry review his conduct on that fateful day. And later still, having learned that Perry in conversation was no longer defending his subordinate's valor, Elliott instituted correspondence with his former commodore that led to a demand for a duel. "It is humiliating," the superior officer responded to that invitation, "to be under the necessity of replying to any letter written by a person who so little knows what becomes a gentleman." To that point had their relationship deteriorated: Elliott's was "a pitiful letter, which none but a base and vulgar mind could have dictated." Did its writer now need to be reminded of an earlier meeting, immediately after the battle, when Perry had discovered Elliott "sick, or pretending to be sick in bed, in consequence of distress of mind, declaring that you had missed the fairest opportunity of distinguishing yourself that ever man had, and lamenting so piteously the loss of your reputation?"

But such a reminder on this later occasion Elliott was prompt to dismiss as "a masterly production of epistolary blackguardism." An interview in the field was demanded. Perry, however, declined to meet his opponent unless the latter was first cleared of charges of cowardice to be presented at a court-martial, which was to convene because of new evidence that the commodore planned to submit to the Navy Department. "Should you be able to exculpate yourself from these charges, you will then have a right to assume the tone of a gentleman." Only then could arrangements for a duel move forward.

Yet when President Monroe learned of what had been going on, he proved averse to a public airing of so ugly a dispute between two naval officers, two heroes. For the time being, in that era of good feeling, the President shelved Perry's request for a court-martial; and before any further action could be taken, the victor of Lake Erie had sailed south on a mission of state, to negotiate with the liberator Simon Bolivar for the control of piracy off the South American coast. From that mission he had not returned, perishing in misery in a darkened, stifling cabin aboard a schooner thousands of miles from home.

That was in 1819. Time passed. Some fifteen years later Perry's former adversary Jesse Elliott had advanced in his career to a position where he was serving as commandant of the Boston navy yard. Old Ironsides was berthed there—the frigate *Constitution* of thrilling memory, recently saved from destruction after the Harvard medical student Oliver Wendell Holmes had published a poem of protest in the newspapers:

> Ay, tear her tattered ensign down:
> Long has it waved on high . . .

Old Ironsides had been saved by public sentiment that a poem had awakened, and there at its berth in Charlestown it rode—as it rides still—a reminder of past naval glories. Commandant Elliott, a Jackson man, was moved in his ardor to have a wood carving of the then President of the United States affixed below the bowsprit as a figurehead. Jackson's enemies, of whom commercial Boston was full, were incensed at such a partisan display. The local Whig papers wailed their indignation day after day—image of a scarcely lettered frontier pol desecrating the bow of a national treasure—and on a stormy July night in 1834, one Whig supporter shouldered his anger and under cover of darkness managed to reach the frigate, scale her sides, and saw Jackson's head right off.

Daylight uncovered the outrage—the President beheaded—producing counterscreams of fury from Jackson's followers, from the navy, from Captain Elliott—screams that grew even louder after it was learned that the severed head had reappeared at a dinner gathering of prominent Whigs, where it had been "LAID UPON THE TABLE, AND BACCHANALIAN ORGIES WERE HELD OVER IT!!!"

So Elliott's name was back in the news (he shrouded the damaged figurehead until a new carving could be made to replace it), and his enemies were resurrecting those charges of cowardice from two decades before, republishing during this same summer of 1834 the long-dead Perry's side of that earlier controversy. The opposing camp responded promptly with a version authorized by Elliott of what had happened aboard the *Niagara* on that distant afternoon. During the coming years Elliott himself repeated his account to whoever would gather to hear him.

The versions could hardly have been more dissimilar. According to what Perry had told one of his officers the night of the battle, he had reached the deck of the *Niagara* soon after two o'clock to find her captain at the gangway. Elliott had "inquired how the day was going"—surely an inane question under the circumstances. "Captain Perry replied, badly: that he had lost almost all of his men, and that his ship was a wreck." Then he in turn had demanded to know why the gunboats of the squadron were so far astern, where their firepower was useless. "Captain Elliott offered to go and bring them up; and, Captain Perry consenting, he sprung into the boat and went off on that duty"—leaving his superior aboard the *Niagara* to close with the enemy, in what would prove to be a victorious maneuver, completed within a quarter of an hour.

Elliott's own version was this. He had met Captain Perry at the gangway and asked him "what was the result on board his brig. He answered, 'CUT ALL TO PIECES,—THE VICTORY'S LOST,—EVERYTHING'S GONE: I'VE BEEN SACRIFICED BY THE DAMNED GUNBOATS.' To which I replied, 'NO, SIR, VICTORY IS YET ON OUR SIDE. I HAVE A MOST JUDICIOUS POSITION . . . YOU TEND MY BATTERY, AND I WILL BRING UP THE GUNBOATS.' 'Do so,' said he, 'FOR HEAVEN'S SAKE'—I immediately passed over the side into his boat," and fearlessly rowing between the *Lawrence* and the enemy "hailed each gunboat as I passed, ordering it to make sail."

There was more. When he returned to the *Niagara* after the victory, Elliott "was met at the gangway," so he claimed, "by Capt. Perry, who asked me if I was wounded. I answered him, 'No.' He then observed to me that 'he thought it was impossible I could have pulled down the line without being killed.' He further remarked, 'I OWE THIS VICTORY TO YOUR GALLANTRY!' "

The truth of the matter will never be settled, though historians almost without exception—from Bancroft to Lossing to Adams to Mahan to Clark to Roosevelt to Morison—have supported Perry's version. Admiral Morison, for one, notes that "Elliott was a very odd fish, even for a naval officer," his career studded with quarrels, challenges, duels, and courts-martial. Indeed, at the very time that Cooper and Mackenzie were entering upon their own public dispute, five or six years after the beheading incident at Charlestown, Jesse Elliott was again under investigation by a naval court of inquiry, instructed to examine into thirteen charges of misconduct amassed during the captain's command of the Mediterranean squadron in the mid-1830s. On the basis of those charges, preferred by his subordinates, the court of inquiry recommended that Captain Elliott be tried by a court-martial. He was, in 1840, and was convicted on several counts, a conviction that led to his forced retirement from active service during this same period when Fenimore Cooper's recently published History of the Navy was being judged by its early reviewers.

While preparing that history, Cooper had received a letter from one who at the time was a friend, Commodore Matthew Perry, the dead hero's brother and Mackenzie's brother-in-law. Perry wrote to say that someone aware of Cooper's current project feared that "the machinations and falsehoods of others had diverted your mind," though Perry himself was confident that "you are too intimately acquainted with naval matters to be deceived" about Lake Erie. Papers relating to the quarrel between Oliver Perry and Jesse Elliott would make all things clear; those were being forwarded.

When they arrived Cooper studied them, and studied the battle diligently. From that study he concluded that the controversy surrounding the subject was "not in a fit state to be transferred to the pages of history." Thus he determined to ignore the matter entirely, choosing to follow the official version that Oliver Perry himself had set down in the jubilant aftermath of victory.

That account, of course, had made heroes of everybody; on the basis of it Elliott as well as Perry had been awarded a gold medal by vote of a grateful Congress in 1813. Never mind that Perry later renounced his own original version. "I was not," Cooper explained, "recording the quarrels of the Navy, but its deeds." And again: "As respects the Battle of Lake Erie, my aim was to avoid anything that could admit of dispute, or disgrace the service. . . . More contradictory testimony was never given. Now, I could not insert the testimony of one side and omit the testimony of the other. Had I given both, besides laying a very pitiful exhibition of contradictions before the world, I should have taken up a large portion of the work with statements that are not sufficiently substantiated, and which in their nature are unfit for history." The sober annals of history are no place, the author sincerely believed, for gossip and slander. "What had a historian to do with petty quarrels of those engaged?"

Cooper's motives are clear and principled. Nor was his account of Perry's behavior anything but laudatory. Nor was Elliott given any prominence at all in the account of the battle. But the Perry faction was nevertheless incensed by the course the historian had chosen to follow. He had failed to excoriate Elliott's conduct. Matthew Perry's hero brother, dead these twenty years, could not defend himself, whereas the glib coward Elliott was alive and by this time claiming most of the credit for the victory. In their rage the Perrys struck back.

"The following work," Alexander Slidell Mackenzie was soon explaining in the opening sentence of the preface to his own most recent literary effort—a biography of the man who had provided him with his midshipman's warrant, the officer whom he adulated and under whom he had served—"was undertaken at the request of Doctor Grant Champlin Perry, the eldest son of Commodore Perry, who, perceiving in the Naval History of Mr. J. F. Cooper an attempt to diminish that admiration with which the people of the United States have been accustomed to regard the memory of Perry, with a view of raising the standing of his second-in-command in the battle of Lake Erie, was desirous that a full account should be published of his father's life and services." The request that Slidell Mackenzie render such an account had been willingly assented to; his biography of Oliver Hazard Perry appeared accordingly, early in 1841.

But the Perry faction attacked Cooper's book from other positions as well. Mackenzie himself, as noted, had preliminarily made his objections to the work known in that lengthy examination of it in *The North American Review*. Tristram Burges, a former representative to the federal legislature from Perry's home state of Rhode Island, had some years earlier delivered a lecture on the Battle of Lake Erie; that panegyric to Perry was now enlarged, with diagrams and appendices, and published as an authoritative account of the battle, to refute Cooper's version. And the president of Columbia College, William Alexander Duer, had come forth, in June 1839, with his own extended review of Cooper in the pages of the *Commercial Advertiser*. This Duer was a member of a notable New York family, uncle by marriage of Slidell Mackenzie, brother of the John Duer to whom Mackenzie had dedicated his book on England. "But with all our experience of the waywardness, inconsistency, and love of paradox which had distinguished the author of *Home As Found*," President Duer was lashing out with scarcely professional disinterestedness near the start of his review of the Naval History, "we could hardly persuade ourselves that he"—Cooper, that is—"had become so utterly regardless of justice and propriety as a man, so callous to the preceptions of good taste as a writer, so insensible to his obligations and responsibility as a historian, and so reckless of his character as a public candidate for literary distinction and immortal fame, as to forego and disregard the opportunity of retrieving, in some degree, the reputation and standing which he must have been conscious of having lost. We were certainly not prepared to find that the infatuation of vanity or the madness of passion could lead him to pervert such an opportunity to the low and paltry purpose of bolstering up the character of a political partisan, an official sycophant, and to degrade the name and object of history, in a work claiming by its title to be national in its design, by salving the wounded reputation of an individual [Captain Elliott] who, from the time of the transaction referred to by his apologist, has been regarded as one doing at best but doubtful credit to his profession, and who owes his continuance in the service, after the events of that day" on Lake Erie, "solely to the forbearance and magnanimity of his superior, which he subsequently requited with ingratitude and perfidy."

Columbia's distinguished president fulminated thus at length, through four issues of the newspaper, his vituperation trained exclusively on Cooper's fifteen-page account of events on the lake, with not a word aimed at the other eight hundred and sixty pages of the book he was professing to review. But Duer's attack, and Burges's, and Mackenzie's were all taking effect. Cooper would successfully sue the publisher of the Duer review, on the grounds that it was not a review at all, but simply mendacious character assassination. The verdict, however, was arrived at long after the damage was done. Meanwhile, the consequences to his magnum opus, as Cooper himself noted, had been "irreparable. No work ever sold better or faster than the naval history, until the lies about the Battle of Lake Erie were published, and from that moment the sale dragged. I am a loser of several thousands . . . The labor of years is lost to me." So embittered had he grown that he came to feel "were the manuscript of what has been printed now lying before me *unpublished*, I certainly should throw it into the fire as an act of prudence to myself, and of justice to my children." Looking back, he felt that the Naval History, which he had labored so hard to make accurate and impartial, "was much belied, and the lies injured both book and author, in a way that no subsequent reparations ever can or will repair. When masses do wrong, it is never by halves; and the evil is irremediable."

One final irony—a final twist of the knife in the wound. John Canfield Spencer, superintendent of the New York common schools, rejected Cooper's abridgment of his Naval History for inclusion in the New York district school libraries. "He declined putting the Naval History into the District School Library," wrote Cooper in amazement to a friend, "on the ground that the *book was controversial on the subject of the Battle of Lake Erie, and he had uniformly declined admitting any controversial works.*" But "it is the *want* of controversy in the History that has made the clamor about it—my abstaining from accusing Elliott, etc. But the d——d scoundrel" —i.e., Spencer—"had actually put Mackenzie's Life of Perry, which is *all* controversy, which avows itself to be controversy in its preface"—had put that volume in the library several months before he wrote the letter rejecting Cooper's work!

The novelist couldn't get over it. The one decision of Superintendent Spencer's meant profits to be earned from Mackenzie's propaganda, put together over a season or two, whereas the superintendent's other decision condemned the impartial and definitive Naval History, which had been labored over for years, to official neglect in its author's own state. Writing another friend a month later, after that same John C. Spencer had moved on to become a member of President John Tyler's cabinet, Cooper found himself still brooding on the matter: "What do you think of the new Secretary at War? He was our Superintendent of Common Schools, and a publisher applied to him to recommend the abridged Naval History. His answer was, he could not, as it was controversial as relates to the Battle of Lake Erie, and he uniformly rejected all controversy. When he wrote this, the scamp had recommended Mackenzie's Life of Perry six months before, a book that avows itself to be contro-

versy in its Preface! He is a precious fellow"—is John Canfield Spencer—
"as they will find out at Washington."

Meanwhile, though the naval historian, treated thus unfairly, might
bide his time, he did not mean to let his attackers go unanswered. Jesse
Elliott could lecture to those who would listen about "that paltry collection of trash and falsehood, Mackenzie's Life of Perry," about "that
wretched farrago of errors and nonsense, the Life of Perry, by A. S.
Mackenzie," which "has been admitted into the libraries of the public
schools of New York." Cooper's response to his critics would be more
measured, more deliberate, and more effective. First, he would sue William Leete Stone, publisher of Duer's so-called review of the Naval History. And that suit, like all his others, the novelist won; the court confirmed in time "that Stone has libelled me . . . 2. That the History is
true, 3. That it was written in a spirit of impartiality, 4. That the review
is *untrue*, 5. That the review is not written in the spirit of impartiality. . . ."

Next, with the case against Stone finally settled by the spring of 1842,
he felt ready to take a further step, by publishing a pamphlet to answer
"all the charges against the Naval History connected with the Battle of
Lake Erie"—specifically those charges leveled separately by Messrs.
Duer, Burges, and Mackenzie. Such a pamphlet was finally about to
appear, as Cooper announced in the columns of the *New York Evening
Post*, June 28. "I feel little doubt that these answers will effectually dispose of the matter, as it would be affectation in me to say I have not the
utmost confidence in the entire justice of my own side of the question."

But by then—by late June 1842—Slidell Mackenzie was out of the
country. He was back on active service, on a shakedown cruise, as captain, with officers and crew on the high seas, sailing from Puerto Rico
homeward toward New York Harbor aboard a trim new naval vessel. In
the event, publication of Cooper's pamphlet would be postponed because
of occurrences about to take place aboard that vessel, the USS brig-of-
war *Somers*.

THE *SOMERS*

SLIDELL MACKENZIE HAD TAKEN COMMAND OF THE
Somers that spring.

Despite a pinched purse, this officer and author and father must have experienced his present days as fulfilling ones in a varied life. A son had been born to him in the summer of 1840; another would be born two years later. In 1841 the author had seen two books appear: biographies both, of John Paul Jones and Oliver Hazard Perry. And in the same year the naval officer had been promoted to commander. With the promotion he had resumed active service, aboard the steam sloop *Missouri*. But now in the spring of 1842 Mackenzie was being provided with a new command, and a choice one: command of a special sailing vessel dedicated to carrying out an assignment in temperate latitudes dear to the heart of the influential commandant of the New York navy yard, the captain's brother-in-law, Matthew Perry.

The vessel was a little beauty: just built, just rigged and outfitted there in the yard in Brooklyn, her brass agleam, her gear all snug and sound. She was small—103 feet overall, 266 tons—but trim and shaped for speed. Her decks were flush; and onto the racily canted mainmast, which rose 130 feet above those decks, could be crowded five separate tiers of canvas. The foremast, sloping in the same streamline, rose some 90 feet into the sky, and the bowsprit, with the jib boom and flying jib, thrust swordlike forward nearly 50 feet overall beyond the bow. This on a brig that measured at the beam no more than half that, no more than 25 feet. A beauty of a ship, pierced for 14 thirty-two-pounders (though only 10 were aboard), square-rigged, low bulwarks, lovely slim lines: the fastest sailing vessel in the service.

The *Somers* was designed to carry a complement of some ninety officers and crew. The majority of those were at present apprentices. Most of them the captain had personally selected, from among personnel aboard the receiving ship *North Carolina* there in the navy yard. And a remarkably young complement it was. The *Somers* was crowded when it sailed on its second cruise in September: one hundred and twenty aboard, instead of the projected ninety. And of those hundred and twenty, only about one-quarter were past their teens. Three-fourths of the men aboard were nineteen and younger. Two of the twelve officers were only sixteen years old; forty-five of the crew were between thirteen and sixteen years of age: all those children blundering about the decks in the early days of the voyage.

But that was the point of the mission that had been planned. After her shakedown cruise in early summer to Puerto Rico and back, the *Somers* was berthed at Brooklyn through August 1842, preparing for a crossing of the Atlantic to the coast of Africa in order to continue the training and schooling of apprentices in a manner more systematic than had been the custom since the service had been established. The Naval Academy had not yet been founded. Aspiring midshipmen would still for the most part learn the ropes as young Cooper had done thirty some years before, as Slidell and all the others had done—simply by going to sea, before or abaft the mast, picking up from old salts whatever they could. Precisely that was what Commandant Perry of the navy yard at Brooklyn, and his friend and protégé Slidell Mackenzie, had both been eager to change.

Matthew Perry was a man of vision. Early in his naval career he had been involved in the settlement of Liberia, indeed had selected the very spot, at Cape Mesurado on the West African coast, where the capital Monrovia was established. Currently, during this present tour of duty ashore, he had been interesting himself in the uses of steam aboard warships, with such diligence and effectiveness that he would be remembered by later generations as the Father of the Steam Navy. A few years into the future he would distinguish himself above all but one or two other naval officers of the time by his services in the Mexican War. And later still, in 1853, he would cross the Pacific and lead the squadron that negotiated a treaty to open the Empire of Japan to Western trade.

In addition, Perry throughout his career applied himself to raising the quality of men in the naval service. It was he who had agitated for the apprentice system in the first place, and had seen it installed in the navy in 1837, five years before the present date. Crews benefited thereby; but as for young officers, they were still instructed—when instructed at all—

in lax shore schools, ineffectually administered, only voluntarily and sparsely attended, at various East Coast ports for midshipmen awaiting assignment on board. To improve the caliber of those professionals Perry had organized the United States Naval Lyceum and sponsored *The Naval Magazine*, which were aimed at disseminating nautical knowledge. (Both Cooper and Mackenzie had written for the latter.) But the commandant was intent upon establishing schools at sea, for apprentices and officers as well, under captains of merit, on cruises designed explicitly for naval training. The *Somers*, sailing again in mid-September, was to be the first of such training-school ships afloat.

There was a need for such vessels. All kinds of boys in the 1840s went to sea. Until halfway through the nineteenth century the sea would retain its hold on the imagination of America's young: the sea more than the land. The population of the republic remained for the most part concentrated along the Eastern Seaboard, with ties—cultural and commercial—maintained over ocean lanes to Europe. Thus seaward was where restive thoughts turned; the sea was where lives might most easily begin again, where fortunes might be made and glory gained.

In fact, through the first half of the century the ocean remained our true frontier; it held out the very promises that after 1850 would be extended by the Far West. But by then, by midcentury, the Mexican War would have been fought—a triumph for the army, as the War of 1812 had earlier been a triumph for the navy. That later conflict, which ended in 1848, thus not only exalted the cavalry officer at the expense of the naval lieutenant (one of Mackenzie's own sons became a cavalry officer, in the Civil War and afterward against the Plains Indians, with conspicuous success). The later conflict also delivered California with other vast lands north of the Rio Grande into American hands. Moreover, by midcentury gold had been discovered in California. And as the century moved beyond its midpoint, the centers of population were all the while continuing to creep westward, away from the Atlantic Coast and into the interior, so that the commercial nation of the earlier half of the century— all those prospering New York merchants—was dissolved at last into the industrial nation of the latter half. By that time, instead of shipping aboard at New Bedford for adventure, wealth, glory, a new start at sea— as their fathers had done—boys and young men would light out for the territories, would go west with their dreams.

But for many in 1842, as the *Somers* was preparing to sail, that dreaming westward lay in the future. For now most young men looked eastward still. Tocqueville had written, in 1835, that Americans would "one day become the foremost maritime power of the globe," because "they are born to rule the seas, as the Romans were to conquer the world." And indeed it seemed that way. The Polar Exploring Expedition would soon set sail, in 1838, charged specifically with finding additional Pacific trading posts and sealing grounds, though even now America's merchant vessels were everywhere, exchanging furs and ginseng for tea at Canton, pursuing the sea otter off the Northwest coast, chasing seals off the coast of South America and whales in the Pacific. They were gathering hides from California and sandalwood from Hawaii and rubber from Brazil, trading in the Mediterranean, at Madagascar, at Zanzibar, transporting to the most distant outposts American rum, American ice, American firearms, American blankets and nails.

Accordingly, the navy, protector of such commerce, sailed on long cruises as well: to the West India station, the Brazil station, the Africa station, the Mediterranean station, the Pacific station. And the naval service still held first place in youthful imaginations: navy blue, gold braid, anchor buttons and epaulets, those heroes and the victories: Paul Jones, Decatur, Perry, the *Bonhomme Richard* against the *Serapis*, the *Intrepid* at Tripoli, Old Ironsides, the *Lawrence* on Lake Erie.

A proud tradition for a young republic, at a time when traditions were few. But since 1815—that is, through a quarter of a century and longer— the nation had been at peace, with few calls to exercise its military. To be sure, through all those years the navy continued to have its champions. Irving as early as 1814 had written a series of lives of naval heroes for a Philadelphia magazine, and here in the early 1840s—at this very time— Fenimore Cooper, sea novelist and naval historian, was writing another such series, for *Graham's*, also published in Philadelphia: lives of William Bainbridge and Edward Preble and John Templer Shubrick and the others, just as Slidell Mackenzie had produced his own such lives, and at book length too, of Perry and Paul Jones, with one on Decatur to come.

Many continued to hold the American navy in high regard throughout the period, though in actuality long years of peace had made the service stagnant. Promotion was very slow. Pay was poor. The higher ranks were overfilled. Desertions emptied the ratings of sailors eager to escape military rigor for the more relaxed, more modernized, and better paying service of the merchant marine. This, then, was the situation—of a military arm atrophying in an era of peace—that had urged Commandant Matthew Perry's various reforms in the 1830s to benefit naval personnel.

Chief among the reforms was the improvement of the quality of training for officers and men. Put them to sea under a captain of demonstrated intelligence, knowledge, and ability; Perry's own brother-in-law Slidell Mackenzie was such a man. Give the captain a capable and compatible second-in-command. In this case, on board the *Somers* would sail as first lieutenant Guert Gansevoort, with nineteen years' experience in the navy, and from a fine old family in upper New York state. Guert's father, incidentally, was a brother of Maria Gansevoort, mother of Herman Melville. Indeed, it had been this same Guert Gansevoort, in the years preceding his signing aboard the *Somers*, whose example during leaves spent in Albany had helped to encourage young Melville, his first cousin, to go to sea.

An experienced and respected officer was Gansevoort, and the others in the *Somers*'s wardroom were in their own ways comparably fit for duty. Two of them were Matthew Perry's sons. Another young officer was the brother of John Slidell's Creole wife, wife of the captain's brother, who years earlier had left New York for Louisiana and was now enjoying success down there as an attorney and aspiring politician. One other midshipman aboard the *Somers* was a son of the heroic Commodore John Rodgers, whose brother had married a sister of Matthew Perry.

A close bunch; and with such a wardroom and a handpicked crew, could the cruise of the fall be any less successful than the shakedown cruise in early summer had been? There was, however, another young officer—an acting midshipman—newly assigned to the brig. His name was Philip Spencer, son of that John Canfield Spencer who had awakened Cooper's ire as superintendent of the New York district schools. Spencer's father was at Washington now, as President Tyler's secretary of war. The son reported aboard the *Somers* in late August 1842.

"When young Spencer first reported himself to me for duty on board my vessel," Commander Mackenzie later recalled, "I gave him my hand and welcomed him on board."

The scion of such a father, and such a grandfather, would have appeared to add further distinction to an already distinguished wardroom. The grandfather, still alive at the time, was Ambrose Spencer, former mayor of Albany, chief justice of the Supreme Court of New York State, brother-in-law of DeWitt Clinton, and for two decades at the start of the century the most powerful figure in New York politics. His son, Philip's father, was notable in his own right: erstwhile member of the federal legislature, speaker of the New York Assembly, secretary of state of New York, and now an influential officer in the cabinet of the President of the United States.

Having returned the salute of the son of such a man, Commander Mackenzie had cordially extended his hand, welcoming Philip Spencer aboard the *Somers*.

"I heard not long after," the captain had occasion to explain in a later account, "that he"—this new addition to the wardroom—"had been involved in difficulty when on the Brazil station, and that he had been dismissed for drunkenness. Upon hearing that I earnestly desired his removal from my vessel—principally on account of the young men I had with me." Given the ship's mission and the age of the crew, it seemed of particular importance that the officers aboard display exemplary conduct. Moreover, several in the wardroom had been, so Mackenzie noted, "entrusted to my special care"; a delinquent among them in close quarters on shipboard could cause trouble. "I had heard," wrote the captain, "that Spencer had expressed a willingness to be transferred." After two additional midshipmen had reported aboard for duty, crowding the steerage still further and to excess, there seemed reason to hope that Philip and his captain might both get their wish. "I desired Lieutenant Gansevoort to state to Mr. Spencer that if he would apply to Commodore Perry to detach him from the *Somers* I would second his application."

The application was accordingly made and seconded, but the commandant of the navy yard declined to accept it. The son of the secretary of war would be aboard when the overcrowded *Somers* sailed in mid-September.

He was a problem all right—had been for some while. At present Philip Spencer was eighteen years old. He had been born in Canandaigua in 1824, soon after his father had completed his third term in the New York legislature, and not long before that public servant distinguished himself by revising in their entirety the tangled statutes of New York State. The achievement (managed with the help of Attorney Benjamin Butler and the John Duer whom Slidell Mackenzie admired) was only one of several vast undertakings that the industrious John Canfield Spencer would complete to his credit during an active lifetime. Such a father, ceaselessly occupied, unstinting in the demands he placed on himself and others, by nature stern—"the apparent austerity and haughtiness of his manner detracted something from his popularity," as an early biographer carefully put it—such a man may not have been easy to live with. But Philip's two brothers and a sister apparently had not so hard a time growing up in the Spencer family, for the three of them reached respectable maturity without leaving records of unusual strain behind.

Not so with Philip. Assuredly he had found his father a trial; at least from early adolescence, the stress between father and son was unremitting. How could the elder understand the younger? Whatever problems confronted young Philip, John Canfield Spencer had had in his own youth to confront—and had done so more than adequately. Hadn't the elder's father, for example, been awesomely successful and famously severe in his own right? "His manner"—that of Chief Justice Ambrose Spencer—"while on the bench was grave, dignified, austere, stern and decided . . . He permitted no familiar approach, no importunity from counsel. Lawyers who addressed him used the most respectful language, while he in turn observed a high-toned courtesy toward the bar." That, of course, was the manner of many a judge and father then. Yet reared amid sternness, the son of one such had thrived through youth, graduating from college with high honors after "close and thorough application to his studies"—he who later would be required to watch his own son Philip remain a freshman three years running, before being dismissed for continually neglecting college exercises.

Such cases are not uncommon. Like his father and grandfather, this youngest Spencer was bright enough. One who knew Philip during his idle college days around 1840 remembered him as "a talented young man, very quick to learn . . . The ease with which he mastered the Greek and Latin was remarkable. Frequently he would be applied to for assistance by other members of the class, some, in fact, whose standing was higher than his." Not an uncommon case, but wondrously aggravating to a parent, then as now—this spectacle of a gifted son doggedly wasting his opportunities. Doubtless there was less understanding then of such behavior. What was wrong with the boy? Don't tell me how hard it is to be my son. His brothers are my sons too, and I was my father's son.

The days and long nights of exasperation that Secretary Spencer had lived through by the early 1840s may be imagined.

This John Canfield Spencer—Philip's father, Ambrose's son—who had risen to become the present secretary of war, had "fierce and quick-rolling" eyes in a face that naturally bore "an unpleasant character of sternness." He was tall, clean-shaven, thin—and notoriously hot-tempered. John Quincy Adams referred to his proud spirit, with the implication in context of testiness, of a nature hard to deal with. Erastus Root one day in 1820 had been chatting with Spencer on the steps of the capitol at Albany. "Everybody is afraid of you," Root told him friend to friend. "They think you are sour, proud, and crusty." Get rid, he urged, of that "confounded haughtiness." To which Spencer had replied resignedly, "Nature never made a Chesterfield of me." No surviving reference to the man casts doubt upon the accuracy of that self-assessment.

Yet despite his manner, Spencer had been able to conduct his affairs in a way that had earned him regard as one of the most capable lawyers of the day. His mind was logical and abstract; "he was not easily excited by the delicate and exquisite beauties of poesy," according to that early biographer already quoted—him of the gift for saying blunt truths mellifluously. Not an imaginative mind, but a brilliantly logical one. And the man who possessed it had presence: in any assemblage he joined, Spencer attracted attention even when silent.

He had been born in Hudson, New York, in 1788, the eldest son of Ambrose Spencer by that notable personage's first wife, Laura Canfield, daughter of John Canfield, under whom Ambrose had studied law. (Ambrose's own father, a Connecticut ironmonger and ardent Whig in Revolutionary times, had been named Philip—hence the names of those descendants whose lives were intertwining with Slidell Mackenzie's in 1842.) John's childhood had made him aware of distinction: his father's associates included Burr, the Clintons, Hamilton, King, the Livingstons. And with that awareness the boy had entered first Williams College, then Union, from which he had graduated with high honors in 1806, even as his father had been an honor graduate at Harvard a quarter of a century earlier. After college John had returned to his father's law office—this dutiful and responsible behavior occurring at precisely that point in his life, age eighteen, that would correspond to his own son Philip's age when signing aboard the *Somers*, although in that later case Philip would have by then failed even to advance beyond the freshman class at either of two colleges, and would already have come close to dismissal from the naval service.

When I was your age. By the time I was eighteen. Doubtless the idling son was informed of the career of his industrious sire; he would have learned among other things that John Canfield Spencer's professional rise had been rapid. Out of college by his late teens, the elder Spencer had studied law in his father's office. Soon he was serving as the private secretary of the governor of the state, and in 1809 he gained admittance to the New York bar. From the beginning he would thrive in law: diligent, perspicacious, ambitious, stable, and—the trait would separate him further from his son—"free from personal vices."

Stability was reflected in the young lawyer's marriage that same year, 1809. John's wife was estimable—"of rare accomplishments"—one Elizabeth Scott Smith of New York City. And if the couple later had problems between them in that more reticent age, they succeeded in keeping them behind doors. Nothing survives to suggest that the marriage between Spencer and his wife was any less fulfilling than those notably happy marriages between Cooper and the former Miss DeLancey, between Mackenzie and his Kate, between Matthew Perry and his devoted Jane Slidell.

Not long after their marriage Spencer moved with his bride to western New York, settling in the frontier village of Canandaigua, where the husband would make his way on his own. At the time, sixteen years before the opening of the Erie Canal, a journey that far west was "long and weary"; the couple had taken with them in their wagon a few personal belongings, some lawbooks, and fifteen dollars. They rented a house in the village and partook of a memorable first dinner in it: "It was eaten off from a common kitchen table," Spencer later recalled. "I was seated on a cheap old-fashioned chair, and Mrs. Spencer occupied a common wooden stool. But everything on the table, though simple, was nicely cooked, and we enjoyed our meal with a relish rarely equaled at the more sumptuous repasts of our prosperous days." They meant to be frugal; they meant to be self-reliant. Accordingly, within six months the energetic attorney had succeeded to the point where he could purchase the house they were renting, the home where he and his wife would continue to live for the next quarter century—that same house in which were born all their children, the youngest one, Philip, when John Canfield Spencer was in his mid-thirties.

That was in 1824. Already by then the father of the newborn had served the public as master in chancery, as brigade judge advocate in the War of 1812, as tax assessor, as postmaster of his village, as attorney general and district attorney for the five Western counties of the state, as elected member of the federal legislature (at twenty-eight, one of the youngest members of the House), and as speaker of the New York Assembly, in which body he sat for three terms, from 1820 through 1822.

As an orator before those various bodies, Spencer expressed himself characteristically with "keen sarcasm," with "terse, severe diction . . . in which no redundant word or fanciful expression was permitted." In addition to public speaking, he had done some writing when younger, including one pamphlet in his early twenties, as war clouds were gathering, that had been noticed abroad. It had been entitled *The Probable Results of a War with England;* and "who does not see the fatal truths contained in Mr. Spencer's article on the results of this war?" one sympathetic British reviewer had remarked approvingly. A second of Spencer's pamphlets had been published abroad as well, this on *The Pretensions of England as to the Right of Searching American Vessels on the High Seas.*

Clearly he was a man alive to his times, as writer, as speaker. But above all Spencer was a worker, indefatigably. Years later John Tyler, by then a former President, recalled serving in Congress with the young New Yorker—"a man of extraordinary capacity in the dispatch of business and of the most untiring industry." Having noted "his habits of unceasing labor," Tyler paid tribute to Spencer's "information upon all subjects," information that was both "extensive and practical." Indeed, those habits and the possession of that information kept the lawyer busy through most of a lifetime. It is noted, for example, that "Mr. Spencer participated in all the contests of the session of 1825 (the 48th Senate)," and "between his senatorial duties and professional ones"—his private practice—"was never subjected to more severe and ardent labor than at this period," immediately following the birth of his youngest son.

Two years after that domestic event Spencer was engaged in the horrendous job of revising the statutes of the state of New York, a labor performed so efficiently that it has not had to be undertaken on the same scale since. And in 1829, when young Phil was five years old, his distinguished father was appointed special attorney to prosecute offenders in the Morgan case.

The Morgan case has been all but forgotten now, but in the late 1820s it dominated the news in the Northeast and nationally, not for weeks or months but for several years, leading to the formation of a political party that would provide the basis for what was to become the Whigs—those same Whigs who by the end of the following decade had gained strength enough to elect their candidate President. Thus the fate of the otherwise obscure William Morgan—or more precisely, the mystery concerning his fate—was to have far-reaching consequences; and near the center of the controversy surrounding that case was John Canfield Spencer.

Briefly what had happened was this. Morgan, a bricklayer from Virginia aged about fifty, had moved into western New York state and settled with his twenty-three-year-old wife in the frontier village of Batavia. There he had joined the local Masonic lodge. The Masons were (and are) a society claiming descent from medieval artisans who built the great cathedrals of Europe—those superb workers in stone who had passed secrets of their craft from generation to generation down through the decades and centuries that were required to complete such structures as those at Chartres and Cologne and Salisbury. Indeed, some Masons trace the antiquity of the order back to the building of Solomon's temple, though in fact modern Masonry has been shown to have been organized, in England, as late as the seventeenth century.

Its purposes by the time William Morgan came to know of it were primarily social and fraternal. From England the order had spread to Europe and across the Atlantic, to thrive in the New World of colonial days, where it offered variety, color, and companionship to the often bleak lives being led in American towns and villages all but destitute of social amusements. General Washington was a Mason. So was President John Adams. So was Jefferson. So were many other male citizens, among both the exalted and the humble, in the young republic.

Among that latter number was this same William Morgan. But the bricklayer was in debt; and in need of money, he had determined to publish a book that would expose the secrets of Masonry. What goes on behind the frosted blue windows of the various lodges? What is the meaning of all those ceremonies, all those arcane signs, those squares and coffins and stars and eyes and columns and suns and crescent moons that initiates guard so jealously? What oaths do they take? What private loyalties do they swear to uphold?

Morgan had written and made plans to publish a book that would tell. But before *Illustrations of Masonry by One of the Fraternity* could appear, his printer's office had been set on fire and the author himself thrown in jail, in the county seat of Canandaigua, on a trumped-up charge of default on a two-dollar debt. Next, mysterious benefactors had appeared at the jail and paid the debt. But even as they were leading Morgan out of the jailhouse, the unfortunate man was seen abruptly being forced against his will—he was crying out in "a most distressing manner, at the same time struggling with all his strength"—into a carriage, which in turn was sighted subsequently at various junctures making its way westward, toward Buffalo. But after the early morning of September 13, 1826—and a last glimpse of the carriage at Hanford's Landing—Morgan was never seen or heard from again.

His young wife, left with two children, was in despair. In time—a year later, in fact—a body was discovered washed ashore at Lake Ontario. It had long fingernails, a scar over one eye, a toe chopped off: physical characteristics said to be Morgan's own. Accordingly, the corpse was brought to Batavia and buried before the bricklayer's outraged and newly aroused fellow citizenry (though later it had to be dug up again and carted to Canada, having been identified as the body of one Timothy Munro). Reports, meanwhile, of Morgan's whereabouts continued to circulate. He had been bribed by Masons to leave his native land forever, then taken to Canada on penalty of death should he return. He was supposed to have been sighted in Vermont, in New Brunswick, working in the fisheries, in Boston "selling his *Illustrations of Masonry* . . . and reaping a harvest from the speculation." One report placed Morgan as far away as Smyrna, dressed like a Turk, notwithstanding which "he had been discovered by an acquaintance" and had "kindly sent messages to his anxious friends in this country."

But the most persistent version of his fate had him taken in his abductors' carriage to a federal fort in Buffalo, where for a time he was incarcerated in a dungeon, before being rowed out onto Lake Ontario and drowned. Indeed, twenty years later a Henry Valence confessed to having been aboard the very boat on the lake, with two oarsmen and with Morgan in the bow. "The night was pitch dark; we could scarcely see a yard before us." They had rowed a certain distance from shore. "Then in a whisper, I bade the unhappy man to stand up; and after a momentary hesitation he complied with my order. He stood close to the head of the boat," his back to the others. Weights had been bound to the victim. As the oarsmen lifted the weights and kept the boat steady, Valence moved toward the luckless bricklayer "and gave him a strong push with both my hands, which were placed on the middle of his back. He fell forward, carrying the weights with him, and the waters closed above the mass." After the splash, and a silent pause that lasted a moment or two, Valence's companions (or so he later confessed) had resumed their places without a word and rowed the boat through the blackness back to shore.

All that because an American citizen had threatened to reveal the secrets of a fraternal order of foreign origin, "an institution which made concealment of the most atrocious crimes one of the most solemn obligations," as it came to be believed. For a Mason's first loyalty was not to his country, but to the select fraternity of which he was a member. I do promise and swear that I will aid and assist a companion royal arch Mason wherever I shall see him engaged in some difficulty, so far as to extricate him from the same, whether he be right or wrong. I swear to advance my brother's best interests by always supporting his military fame and political preferment in opposition to another—whether he be right or wrong. And for determining to make public such secret oaths,

Morgan had had his prerogatives as a citizen set at naught: the poor man removed from the bosom of his family, betrayed under the guise of friendship, forcibly abducted in the nighttime and confined in a citadel of the United States, in a dungeon "over which floated that flag which is the nation's pledge of protection to every one of its citizens." Doubtless even now he was dead.

To protest such an enormity, meetings were being held in various villages across western New York. Rewards were offered, and the governor himself had issued a proclamation enjoining all officers to do their duty to apprehend offenders. President John Quincy Adams at Washington was soon being made aware of "a universal excitement and popular fermentation in that vicinity, which has extended throughout New York, and has at length brought a mass of obloquy upon the institution of Masonry itself." Indeed, the issue was operating on voters of the forthcoming presidential election more powerfully, Adams noted, "than all other electioneering topics put together." And all the while Morgan's murderers remained at large, unidentified, aided no doubt by the sinister network of the Masonic fraternity, with its members in places high and low, on the bench, at the bar, able to interfere at will with justice.

A special prosecutor must be named with authority and funds sufficient to enable him to apprehend the murderers. To that position in January 1829, Governor Van Buren appointed John C. Spencer. Spencer proceeded promptly to conduct investigations, summon witnesses, bring forth indictments, and conduct trials, despite what were seen as obstructions placed in his path by members of his committee known to be Masons, despite death threats ("*Sir*—As you are seeking for the blood of those who never injured you, remember that your own blood will run quite as easily and red as theirs . . ."), and despite two attempts on his life. On a country road late one evening Spencer was fired at, the bullet whistling past his head; and on another occasion, again at night, an assailant armed with a cane sword lunged at him in the street, failing to inflict a wound only because he clumsily stumbled as he sprang. Such efforts, the record assures us, caused Spencer "not the least uneasiness." He had brought two cases against suspects in the Morgan murder—the *People* v. *Mather* and the *People* v. *Jewett*—and though the prosecution was unable to convict in either case, his committee was continuing to gather evidence when allotted funds ran out. Seeking an additional two thousand dollars to press forward with the investigation, the special attorney was astonished and chagrined to have his request denied, whereupon he immediately tendered his resignation to Acting Governor Enos T. Throop, May 3, 1830, in a long, blistering letter in which he charged, moreover, that the contents of his confidential correspondence to the executive had been divulged so as to reach counsel for the accused. "Public duty," Spencer wrote, "does not require me to forfeit my own self-respect and the esteem of others by continuing in a situation where I should be exposed to treatment like that already received, and where I am practically disavowed and disowned by my employers."

But the episode had far-reaching consequences. Though the murderers of Morgan were never identified for certain—nor indeed was it established beyond doubt that Morgan had been murdered at all—Spencer himself became a leading figure in that odd new political party, the Anti-Masons, that included William Seward, Thurlow Weed, Thaddeus Stevens, and thousands of others throughout New York, Pennsylvania, and New England. For the most part the leaders of the movement were bright young men (Spencer in his early forties was among the oldest) disaffected with Jackson's policies and unwilling to align themselves with the moribund National Republicans who formed the party of Jackson's predecessor John Quincy Adams. The new political grouping would meet to nominate its own candidate for President in 1832, and it would succeed in electing various candidates to positions in state governments in the Northeast and Midwest. But before long the Anti-Masons were absorbed into the Whig party, its leaders becoming Whig leaders, its program attached to the rickety Whig platform, adherents of which would in time triumph nationally, in the federal election of 1840.

Spencer meanwhile, through this recent experience, had acquired an even stronger aversion to the absurd mummeries that the likes of Masonry seemed to perpetuate: secret initiatory rites, fantastic titles so offensive to a democrat—Most Excellent General Grand High Priest, Worshipful Grand Generalissimo, Most Worshipful Grand Master—the oaths, those oaths sworn to, to keep secrets of the order "under no less penalty than to have my throat cut across, from ear to ear, my tongue torn out by the roots, and my body buried in the rough sands of the sea, a cable tow's length from the shore at low water mark . . ." Revolting to a sober, logical, God-fearing mind: those unlawful oaths, those "ridiculous ceremonies . . . the dangerous obligations and the blasphemous mockeries of order." Masonic frivolities profaned religion. "Drinking, singing, and carousing," as Spencer, a lay officer in the Episcopal Church, concluded in disgust in 1832, "form a regular part of the business at every meeting of a lodge or chapter. How many victims of intemperance may trace their ruin to this single cause?" Guarded from intrusion within their lodges, shut away from the eyes of the world, "separated from their homes and families, enveloped in the darkness of night . . . the bacchanals," wrote Spencer, "have every inducement to excess, no motive for restraint." Such murky socializing appalled his unromantic, analytic mind; his disciplined temperament was outraged by such irresponsible, such potentially sinister self-indulgence.

*   *   *

How would this concerned citizen feel, then, about his youngest son's obsession during those adolescent years through which Philip was living in the late 1830s? The boy's obsession was with piracy: with the free, wild life—covert, lawless—oaths, black flags, low, black schooners, death's heads, planks from the quarter rail projecting over the waves, ships scuttled, lovely, tearful female passengers cringing at one's mercy, treasure to bury in tropic coves or squander.

The subversive young: for Phil Spencer was by no means alone in his obsession. Many an adolescent mind in America before midcentury fed its fantasies on the abundant cheap fiction that recounted desperate piratical adventures. Fenimore Cooper's *Red Rover* had started it all back in 1828, but within a decade that entertaining historical romance had been imitated in the work of scores of less gifted writers, the genre rapidly degenerating into worthless scribbling for the amusement of the scarcely literate, comic-book stuff, paper-covered, double-columned precursors of the dime novel with such titles as *Ramon: The Rover of Cuba, The Haunted Brig, The Pirate of the South Pacific, The Farewell at Sea*. Careers of Blackbeard, Captain Kidd, Jean Lafitte, and other historical figures may have provided some tenuous factual basis for those fantasies, but the fictional world that resulted was not to be found on any map: a world of hairbreadth escape from shipwreck, of females in flight disguised as sailors or cabin boys, of incredible reunions after years of separation, of the miraculous on the high seas mingling with the diabolical. For always at the center of that world stood the pirate captain, Byronic, his face absorbed in "stern and darksome thought," his manner suggesting "passion uncontrolled and unrestrained," his speech disclosing "an acquaintance with the courteous rules of the world somewhat above the sphere in which he was acting." Scowling outcast from society: "Ah, bitter, relentless fate! I can never know the joys of domestic bliss. No sweet prattler will ever call me father. No fond, confiding woman will ever lean upon my bosom or honor me with the title of her protector." Against all mankind, against the whole world, the pirate waged his war: "How many hearts have been rendered desolate by this blood-stained hand!"

The skewed eyes of young Spencer had taken in sentiments like those. "Avaunt! ye images of murdered men! Silence! vain echoes of mingled groans and curses, long since hushed. Disturb me not! I do but fulfill my destiny." His fantasies thrived on such stories, as his counterparts later in the century would find compensation for their inadequacies in tales of Western outlaws: Jesse James, Billy the Kid. "I have sought . . . to forget myself—the past—everything, in a life of action and adventure," asserts Ramon, the Cuban rover, whose fictional solutions to life's problems were recounted by an anonymous hand in the 1830s. And a far more skilled hand, Melville's own, about this time—only a little later—described the lure of the sea that Spencer's choice of reading was responding to: "I am sick of these terra firma toils and cares, sick of the dust and reek of towns . . . [sick of] the dull tramp of these plodders, plodding their dull way from their cradles to their graves. Let me snuff thee up, sea-breeze! and whinny in thy spray . . ."

Not that young Spencer seemed destined to go to sea, except in imagination. He had been given, as he told an acquaintance later, "religious example and culture enough during his early years," though apparently it had all been "a mere matter of memory without any potency to shape, control, and exalt his maturer life." In any case he had been sent to school to learn what culture he could, first at Canandaigua Academy, then, beginning in 1838, at Geneva College, Geneva, New York. That was the college (present-day Hobart) where Fenimore Cooper's only son Paul—the same age as Spencer—was enrolled, but Paul and Phil had not a lot in common. The novelist's son would graduate valedictorian of his class; the politician's would not graduate at all. Even so, Paul Fenimore Cooper years later recalled that other member of the little community (twenty in the freshman class, down to seven in the senior) with marked kindness and generosity: "His manner was remarkably good, quiet, courteous, and self-possessed. His voice was very low and pleasant. My recollection is that he had a decided cast in his eyes and that otherwise he would have been thought good-looking, if not handsome." Spencer at college had seemed to Cooper "to live very much by himself and to mingle little with the other students. If he had any intimates, I do not know who they were . . . His class standing for scholarship and attendance was very low, but it was generally thought that he had ability enough had he chosen to exert it in the direction of his studies."

Those who work among the young will recognize the boy. When exerted, Phil Spencer's acknowledged abilities were aimed in directions other than studies. The Whig party, his father's party, had won the presidential election of 1840, and students joined tens of thousands across the country in celebrating the victory of the log-cabin candidate: Tippecanoe and Tyler too. Old Tippecanoe was that same General William Henry Harrison to whom, a quarter of a century earlier, had been addressed Captain Perry's brief announcement of victory at Lake Erie: "We have met the enemy and they are ours." Now, after a riotous campaign—the first such complete with slogans, banners, parades, bonfires—the aged veteran of the War of 1812 had been elected President on the Whig ticket, and his followers let the party drink flow. Hard cider was the down-to-earth beverage that the new President was said to favor. Consequently, the Geneva College records took note, according to one who examined them some years later, that "on November 23, 1840, Philip Spencer was a participant in the cider disturbance so called, but does not appear to have been regarded as a leading spirit": campus drunkenness involving fifteen or twenty young partisan roisterers. Earlier, in February of that same year, "Philip Spencer for negligence and going to Canandaigua without permission was formally sent to Greene to remain for a time under the care of Rev. I. V. Van Iryen." Those are the only two disciplinary matters of record concerning Spencer at Geneva, though it was remembered later that, at one commencement, to the end of an academic procession the boy had clownishly attached himself "wearing a lofty conical hat elaborately decorated with a streamer showing the legend, 'Patriarch of the Freshman Class!' The president and faculty were walking at the head quite unaware of this characteristic demonstration in their rear."

Assuredly an elder of his class by then: he had entered Geneva as a freshman in 1838; in April 1841, when his father withdrew him, he was a freshman still. "Philip Spencer, at the request of his father, received a dismission from the college. The request was made in consequence of his continued neglect of college exercises and this neglect stated in the letter of dismission; but inasmuch as a change of association might prove favorable, it was also stated that the faculty of this college would make no objection on account of his deficient standing here to his immediate reception at any other college."

He would, in fact, be promptly received at Union, where his father had distinguished himself some thirty-five years earlier. But before leaving Geneva for Schenectady it had been young Spencer's whim, according to one later report, to present a book to the students' library: *The Pirate's Own Book*, which a couple of years later "still remains there with his name in it." Perhaps that same book was the source of some of the "murderous stories and tales of blood" he was said to have related to the children of a professor "in whose family he was domesticated" during a part of his Geneva years. But how much truth was there in such recollections, how much was later embellishment? Was it true, as later asserted of Spencer, "that on stepping into the stagecoach to leave Geneva, the last words he said to a friend who took leave of him were, that he would next be heard of as a pirate"?

Maybe so. He couldn't in any case have known many moments of fulfillment in that New York village during those college years, reading his blood-and-thunder novels, moodily playing the violin in his unprepossessing room with the cabalistic signs burned into the woodwork. The walleye that Cooper remembered: the boy might have passed for good-looking without that: tall, slender, well-spoken, hair dark and abundant, a nose only a bit too generously scaled. But the eyes. The first thing one noticed about him were those dark eyes diverging. A less rare affliction then than now, but an affliction nevertheless. While at Geneva he had submitted to a painful attempt at correcting the condition, gamely refusing "to be bound or held during the operation." The results were disappointing; still the two eyes diverged. "The operation, as usual, left a fixed, staring look that was occasionally very marked." He couldn't have found much to relish in that and all those other failures: physical, academic, social, familial. A fellow student had found Spencer one afternoon "in bed, greatly depressed, yet feeling indignant and bitter toward his father on account of his severe reproof, which latter, Philip told me, was that unless he turned over a new leaf and did better in the future than he had in the past, he would disown him. Brooding over this, he had planned to leave college, go West, change his name, turn land pirate, freebooter or buccaneer on the Mississippi River . . ."

But he wouldn't go west, wouldn't even leave college yet. Union had accepted him that same spring of 1841, and for a few weeks the boy was enrolled there in Schenectady. Fraternities enlivened campus life. "Phil Spencer, who did not like the kind of men who composed the other secret societies then in college, conferred with us," an acquaintance at Union later remembered, "about forming a new society, to be composed of kindred spirits. We readily agreed to the proposition." Thus was founded Chi Psi, which would grow to be national in scope. Thereafter this founding son of the scourge of Masonry "gave most of his time to the business of organization, devised the signs, grips, and passwords, and made arrangements for the badge of Chi Psi to be worn by the members. . . . He always took great delight in the initiations, grips, signs and passwords, and studied how to make them more mysterious and impressive"—that recollection from a Chi Psi who remembered Spencer affectionately, as "noble-hearted and generous to a fault."

Or was it that, right or wrong, one spoke well of a brother?

Helping organize a social fraternity was about all the young man got done during his brief stay at Union. He had come there in May 1841. By summer he was out of college for good. By the fall, through his father's influence, he had been appointed a midshipman. In late November of that same year Philip Spencer reported for duty aboard the receiving ship *North Carolina* at the navy yard in Brooklyn.

A certain Passed Midshipman Craney, nine years a navy man, had the quarterdeck as Spencer arrived aboard in the company of his uncle. "Captain Spencer of the navy, brother of the Secretary of War, came on board, bringing with him his nephew Philip Spencer, who had just received a midshipman's warrant." The captain introduced his nephew to the officer of the deck, asking that Craney assist the novice in learning the ropes and establishing himself in the service. "Mr. Craney was pleased with the opportunity of befriending the son of the Secretary of War and nephew of an officer of high rank, and thought it might be an advantage to himself if the young man turned out well."

Philip Spencer was accordingly made welcome to the use of Craney's stateroom, and was urged to borrow Craney's books whenever he wanted to.

The two young men—the veteran in his twenties, the recruit in his teens—got to talking. Craney learned that his newly acquired protégé had left Union College some months before and "returned to his friends, where he remained some time," presumably at Albany, to which his father had moved from Canandaigua three or four years earlier. But "being of a wandering turn of mind, and fond of anything bordering on the dangerous and marvelous," Philip had during the summer (so he told Craney) run away from home, making his way to New York, and from there by schooner to Nantucket.

Hiding his identity, the boy had meant to sign aboard a whaler, undertaking those lowliest and filthiest of duties in the merchant service. Craney when told of it expressed surprise, that Spencer "should ever think of adopting that hazardous life, sought only by those whom friends and fortune had discarded . . ." But Philip, recounting his summertime escapade, merely "smiled at my astonishment at his deserting his happy, luxurious and delightful home." And why a whaler? "His reply was that he 'should like to harpoon a whale and see the blood spilt,' that he 'was not afraid of danger and liked an adventurous life.' "

The Nantucket ship was still being fitted out when Philip had gone aboard. Much work had to be done making her ready to receive her casks, so that "he was compelled," as he was telling Craney some time later, "with many others to work from morning till late at night in getting them and her stores on board, being allowed only thirty minutes for their meals, which were of the coarsest kind, and only five hours rest at night in a miserable forecastle in close communion with the dregs of New-York streets."

That might have satisfied any curiosity to see the world: that servile, squalid, exhausting labor. But had Philip been telling the truth? "In confirmation of his assertions, he showed me his hands, and they, from their horny, hardened appearance, corroborated his statement of what he had undergone at Nantucket. Having disposed of his wardrobe and replaced them by the coarse and homely garb of the whaler, he was ready, as was also the ship, in two days to sail for their cruising grounds in the South Seas."

By then, however, diligent inquiry had discovered the boy's whereabouts. Steps were being taken to get him off the vessel. That same month of October, John C. Spencer had assumed his duties as Tyler's secretary of war; "his father's position," newly occupied, "as one of the cabinet at Washington procured for him a midshipman's appointment, which was sent with all dispatch to Nantucket, with a description of his person, etc., to the care of the owner of the ship. This and a letter from his father was placed in his hands." By no means had Philip welcomed so timely a rescue from the drudgeries of the forthcoming voyage. Still, through "the earnest persuasions of the owner and captain, after learning who he was, he was induced by them to give a volunteer $30 to take his place in the ship."

From Nantucket, the young man had then returned to New York. This was late in the fall. His uncle the navy captain had fitted him out as a midshipman and brought him aboard the receiving ship and placed him under young Craney's care. What else could be done with him? Send him out west to some army post—out there under the big sky, awaiting the rare arrival of a riverboat, there at the stockade with Indians and fur traders and prairie dogs and not much else—and he'd be off to the hills inside a week. No, get him to sea, where discipline was strict and desertions not easy. Get him into the navy—though it was precisely this misuse of the service, as dumping ground for the fractious and incorrigible, that Commodore Perry's current reforms were aimed at correcting.

In any case, Spencer was aboard the receiving ship at Brooklyn, awaiting assignment to whatever vessel might need his services for a forthcoming cruise. His time idling aboard "was passed," so Craney later asserted, "as is much of the time of some other young men in like circumstances, in occasional, and, I am sorry to say, frequent dissipation, principally at night, but not unfrequently in the face of day."

Craney by now had come to regret the offer of his cabin; the new midshipman had taken to storing his liquor bottles there. Of one incident the older officer had opportunity during the spring of 1843 to tell Richard Henry Dana, Jr., who set it down in his journal. Thus: "One night Craney was in his berth asleep when he was waked up by a noise and saw Spencer in his stateroom trying to draw a bottle from under some place where it seems he had hidden it. Craney ordered him out of the room. Spencer, who appeared to be a little intoxicated, said he would go when he chose. Craney ordered him out again, and then Spencer raised his arm and struck him a severe blow as he lay in his berth. Craney sprang out of his berth and pushed Spencer from the room. Spencer resisted, and the noise brought the officers down. Spencer was ordered below."

The morning following that scuffle, according to Craney's account, he was sent for by the first lieutenant. Do you mean to report Mr. Spencer? Of course; it was his duty to do so. What more serious offense could occur aboard ship than striking a superior officer? "The lieutenant then told him that he would advise him as a friend to do no more about the matter. That it would do him no good at the Department; that Spencer's friends were powerful, and he had better let it drop." Craney thought about that, and in time convinced himself that the incident might just in fact have alarmed the youth into better behavior. He determined to take the lieutenant's advice and press the matter no further.

Among Craney's possessions was a superior sextant, the uses of which he had offered to explain to the midshipmen at their daily school in the steerage. The instructor of navigation was delighted. "One day"—the date happened to be Thursday, February 10, 1842—"the professor asked Craney to go down and explain the sextant to the young gentlemen, and having no duty on hand he did so. While there, in the presence of the professor, explaining the instrument to the midshipmen, he received a violent blow upon the side of the face, which pushed him backwards in his chair and threw him and the chair over on the floor." Spencer it was who had struck the blow, moving among the clustered midshipmen to a position behind Craney in order to do so. At the same time he had "wrenched off Craney's epaulet, tearing off the button, and ripping down his coat." Craney had leaped from the deck and lunged at his assailant, but was grabbed by others and held back, while Spencer was being dragged from the room.

This latest offense, committed publicly and soon known by the entire ship's company, could not be ignored. Craney would report it through the chain of command to the Navy Department in Washington. But officers at the yard saw his report and moved again to intervene. "Either Captain Spencer or the commander of the ship, Commodore Perry, sent for the professor and several of the midshipmen present, and learned from them that Mr. Craney's report was rather understated than otherwise." Nevertheless, Commodore Perry himself, so Craney told R. H. Dana over a year later, had called the aggrieved officer in and "tried to persuade him not to report Spencer, telling him that he would do himself no good by it . . ."

This time, however, Craney was adamant. "The Commodore then told him it would be of no use, as Spencer had been ordered to join the *John Adams* at Boston, and offered him back his charges, which he had not sent to the Department." What had happened seemed obvious. In Dana's words: "Captain Spencer, finding Craney determined to report his nephew, had written to the lad's father and procured orders for him to join another vessel and prevailed upon Commodore Perry to retain the charges until Spencer should be sent away."

Craney was furious. He proceeded to communicate directly with the secretary of the navy, who responded by "slighting the whole matter and treating Craney, as he thought, in a very insolent and contemptuous manner." The upshot was that Passed Midshipman William Craney soon tendered his resignation from the service and saw it accepted. After more than a decade taken from the prime of his life, and ill-suited to do much else, he found himself "thrown out upon the world."

At least that was the disgruntled Craney's version; and Dana, to whom he was later applying for a position in Boston, found it credible: a story told in a "precise, methodical, and calm manner," the teller himself im-

pressive in his "calmness, self-respect, and candor." Yet Dana was ignorant of one fact that has a bearing on judging Craney's credibility. This
same officer had earlier, in his late teens while attached to a ship at
Veracruz, been dismissed from the navy for intoxication, absence without leave, disorderly conduct, misrepresentation, and disrespect to his
superior officer. In fact, he had been reinstated and assigned to the *North
Carolina* only weeks before Spencer had reported aboard. One notes
among those charges misrepresentation. For certain, Craney in Boston in
the spring of 1843 was misrepresenting himself to Dana as a lieutenant;
he was a passed midshipman—and as such would not have been wearing
an epaulet to be torn from the shoulder. He was misrepresenting his
years in the navy at the time of his resignation as totaling "twelve or
fourteen"; the actual total was just under ten. And he was suggesting that
his resignation had followed by some weeks the sextant incident with
Spencer; in fact, his resignation is dated the very day of that incident,
February 10, 1842, and refers to Craney's having been at the time suspended and confined to the ship for four weeks.

Does his suspension, for whatever unnamed reason, account for why
the young man had been free that day in February to explain the workings of his sextant in the steerage? In any case Craney may not have been
entirely blameless in the affair. Certainly not if we accept as true the
contents of a letter dated February 11, 1842, from Acting Midshipman
Philip Spencer to Commodore Matthew Perry aboard the *North Carolina*:

> You have informed me that Passed Midshipman Craney has made
> an official report of the transaction which occurred between us on
> Thursday the 10th inst. I would respectfully represent that the ag-
> gravation which induced the assault was of such a character that my
> feelings were highly excited, and laboring under the imputation of
> being a liar, I was led to an act of insubordination and breach of
> discipline which reflection has taught me was highly improper. May
> I respectfully request that this letter may accompany the report of
> Commander Moorhead and Midshipman Craney to the Hon. Secre-
> tary of the Navy.

Young Spencer, who came by his temper honestly, had been extricat-
ed from this current scrape through transfer to the *John Adams*. By the
spring that frigate, with Philip aboard, had sailed from Boston south of
the line to Brazilian waters. So the young man had got under way at last,
and had journeyed some five thousand miles from home.

But this was not a life he was learning to care for. Another officer who
met him in Rio judged the acting midshipman to be "of that irresolute
and arbitrary temperament which frets and rebels under the restraints
and limitations society imposes for its own conservation." That same
acquaintance had occasion to address the matter forthrightly. "Spencer,"

he said, "it seems to me that you are a mutinous"—but did he say that really? or only later think he had?—"a mutinous, insubordinate sort of a fellow, constantly kicking against discipline, always in hot water. What in the devil's name induced you to enter the service?"

Spencer had answered that he hardly knew. "The fact is, I wasn't a model boy by any means—pretty bad, lawless, if you like that better; and my father, perhaps to get rid of me—perhaps to reform me—put me in the navy. I am disposed to think it has done me harm."

"And you do not like it, then?" asked his fellow officer.

"Like it! Like it!" exclaimed Spencer. "Hell, no; I hate it!"

What had led this other, a Midshipman Rogers, to form his impression of Spencer's unruly nature is not far to seek. His first sight of Philip had occurred not long before, on a sultry midday in Rio, when sounds of a fracas in the street had brought Rogers to the window of his pied-à-terre at Pharoux's Hotel. Below in full view an American officer and a brawny Brazilian were about to come to blows, fists clenched menacingly amid an outpouring of "English and Portuguese expletives by no means decent or peaceful." The dispute, which had arisen over a boat fare, was made unequal partly because the officer was drunk, partly because the boatman was about to be reinforced by compatriots hurrying along the mole in his direction. Rogers had run down to the street and paid off the boatman "and led the unsteady middy into the hotel. That was my introduction to Philip Spencer."

We learn from the same source, from this Robert C. Rogers reminiscing as an old man in 1890, that Spencer while in Rio that half century earlier, through drunkenness and generally churlish behavior, had soon become "the most unpopular of the junior officers of the squadron." His squadron mates shunned him, with regrettable consequences. "That punishment by Coventry affected him so far," wrote Rogers, "as to lead him to an indulgence of his love of liquor as often as he had an opportunity. When he went on shore he rarely sought persons of his own class, was indifferent to places of note." Instead, according to this recollection of a man in his late sixties, young Spencer had "wandered into places where gathered the odds and ends of society, in and out of *cabarets borgnes*, the reeky bagnios of the Rue Sabôa, and with people who would not have paused to cut his throat, except that there was no need of it, for his maudlin and promiscuous hospitality impoverished him quicker than a sheath-knife could have done."

One occasion in May the aged Rogers recalled with particular clarity. On the mole, "that crowded point of embarcation," Spencer in full daylight, in abusive befuddlement, had been incoherently berating an English officer against whom he held some grudge or other, threatening to shoot the man on sight. "He was in uniform, and he was too obstreperous to escape observation. He was seen by the late Admiral Wyman, who sent him to his own ship, and the facts were duly reported. Commodore

Morris was the very last person in the navy to condone so gross an in-decorum. The *Potomac* was on the eve of her departure for home, and Spencer was ordered to her in disgrace."

The old man's memory had served him well. In the national archives reposes corroborating correspondence, including a letter from then Mid-shipman R. Harris Wyman, aboard the *Delaware*, to Philip Spencer, aboard the *John Adams*, dated Rio, May 29, 1842, replying to a query by the latter about the report made to Commodore Morris: "I would have you to understand that I did it considering it my duty . . .—of anything further I am not to be the judge." And the official copy of another letter survives, dated four days earlier, May 25, from Philip Spencer to Com-modore Charles Morris, commanding the United States naval station, coast of Brazil: "I have taken the liberty," wrote Spencer, "of addressing you for the purpose of giving you an exact account of my conduct on the 21st inst. . . . On the morning of the 21st, I had been on shore in the market boat; when there I had drank considerably. When I came off I also drank with several persons, and when I went on shore for the day, by permission of the first lieutenant, I was overcome by the liquors I had drank." The young officer's defense, after conceding the disgracefulness of his conduct, was built on the fact that others had behaved as disgrace-fully, and yet had been given "a chance of retrieving themselves." Spen-cer, now under arrest, ventured a further reason for leniency: "my previ-ous good conduct. This is my first offense, and I know my last."

But if only by punishing him could law and discipline be satisfied, would the commodore receive instead the young man's resignation from the navy, thus saving his name "from that disgrace that would accrue to it by sentence of a court-martial"? For Spencer was remembering, some-what tardily, that "my father's station is such that my disgrace would be widely spread and he would deeply feel it." The appeal for mercy con-cluded with an acknowledgment that "perhaps I am asking too much; but if it could be that the offence could be overlooked, I would solemnly pledge myself that the offence should never be repeated."

In the event, Commodore Morris refused to accept Spencer's resigna-tion, on the grounds that he lacked authority to do so. On May 30 he ordered the officer to report to the U.S. frigate *Potomac* two days hence, "to return to the U. States in that ship, there to receive the decision of the Secretary of the Navy."

Thus abruptly, by the end of July, after a fifty-day run, Midshipman Spencer was back in America, at Boston, where he wrote his brother John:

> You will be surprised to hear that I have returned to the U. States. But it is so. I had a difficulty while at Rio de Janeiro and the Commodore ordered me from the *John Adams* to the *Potomac* which

was about to return home. So here I am. While I was at Brazil I visited but two places: Rio de Janeiro and San Salvadore. I staid more than a month in Rio but was only a few days at Bahia (San Salvadore). I was so short a time in the country that I had not time to collect curiosities but employd myself in visiting the country and eating fruit, the most delicious in the world.

I shall probably be in Albany in a few days as soon as I can get detachd from the ship. But shall not stop more than a day as I shall apply for sea service immediately—I should be extremely obliged to you if you could conveniently lend me forty or fifty dollars as I am at this time in great want of money. I assure you it shall be punctually paid on the first of October.

Remember me to all friends and believe me Your Affectionate Brother.

I shall expect a line from you immediately.

The letter is dated from the *Potomac*, Boston navy yard, July 31, 1842. Within a week of writing it Acting Midshipman Spencer had been informed of the decision in his case. The secretary of the navy—incidentally, Abel P. Upshur, Virginia judge, and brother of the Lieutenant Upshur to whom, as his best friend, Slidell Mackenzie had earlier dedicated his *Spain Revisited*—the honorable secretary had "perused with pain the correspondence transmitted to me by Comdr. Morris." From the perusal he had been mortified to learn "that one more young officer of the Navy, and one brought up as you must have been, has been guilty of the degrading and disqualifying vice of drunkenness." However, all was not yet lost. "Your frank and manly acknowledgment of your offence," wrote Secretary Upshur, "your penitence for it, the fact of its being the first known to your Commander, and his interposition in your behalf have upon the whole induced me to overlook the transgression reported to me, and to put you upon trial by your future conduct. If that is such as the country has a right to expect from one who wears her uniform, what has passed will be forgotten. But if otherwise, it will be remembered against you."

Spencer's resignation from the service was accordingly declined. His appointment was returned to him, and he could look forward to receiving orders promptly.

Those came August 13: "Report to Capt. M.C. Perry for duty on board the U.S. brig *Somers*."

The *Somers* would be sailing soon, shrinking her world to a population of a hundred and twenty males, most of them young, crowded within two decks that measured at the maximum scarcely more than a hundred feet by twenty-five. But for now, in late August and early September, the brig at the navy yard in the East River was the center of much activity connected with the shore, drawing and stowing away supplies and provisions to see her over the breadth of an Atlantic crossing. Visitors were coming and going, and laborers from the navy yard getting the ship ready—carpenters, caulkers, blacksmiths, coopers, armorers— doing another day's work aboard before returning ashore for the evening.

Some of the workmen and visitors lived in still vernal Brooklyn; others got home by means of the frequent ferries that plied between Brooklyn and New York on the opposite side of the river. Much survives to help us picture that setting—New York in 1842—but nothing perhaps both as brief and as vivid as the impressions set down by Charles Dickens after a visit some few months earlier to this East Coast seaport now grown to 300,000 people.

Just turned thirty and already beloved on two continents for *Pickwick* and *Oliver Twist* and *Nicholas Nickleby* and *The Old Curiosity Shop*, young Dickens during this first triumphal visit to America had on one occasion taken a seat at an upstairs window in the Carlton House in New York City and from there looked down on Broadway. At the time that "great promenade and thoroughfare" extended north from the Battery Gardens three miles or so before terminating in a country road at Union Square. The hour was noon on a strikingly unseasonable day like midsummer, though actually only in late February or early March. The window was wide open, the sun hot on the visitor's face. Opposite, "red bricks of the houses might be yet in the dry, hot kilns," so warm did they seem. Below was glimmering the pavement of the roadway, polished by the tread of many feet. Omnibuses passed, their roofs looking as though water poured on them would hiss and smoke: "No stint of omnibuses here! Half-a-dozen have gone by within as many minutes. Plenty of hackney cabs and coaches too; gigs, phaetons, large-wheeled tilburies, and private carriages." And the crowds down there among the traffic: coachmen white and black and variously behatted, precocious urchins bellowing out names of the fifty-some city newspapers for sale, posturing gentlemen— "Byrons of the desk and counter"—and the colorful ladies. "We have seen more colors in these ten minutes than we should have seen elsewhere in as many days. What various parasols! what rainbow silks and satins!"

Abandoning his window perch Dickens had descended to the street, then made his way through the throngs eastward along a narrow thoroughfare, "baking and blistering in the sun," that was Wall Street. He paused at the river's edge, with Brooklyn and the Long Island hills beyond: pausing "here by the waterside, where the bowsprits of ships stretch across the footway and almost thrust themselves into the windows," like rafters overhead. Much else he noted in his walk that day: great blocks of ice being carried into bars and glittering shops, watermelons and pineapples profusely displayed, spacious houses with open doors revealing a plenitude of plants within, at one window a child peeping out at a dog below. Leafy squares he saw, and cellar oyster bars, and a horse-drawn trolley taking passengers to the Bowery, where in that cheaper section of town "the lively whirl of carriages is exchanged for the deep rumble of carts and wagons." Everywhere the vagrant dogs, the indifferent hogs rooting in gutters and nudging beneath green area railings. Everywhere signs of all sorts, "in shape like river buoys or small balloons, hoisted by cords to poles," some with candles inside to light their messages at nighttime.

On a particular evening Dickens leaves the gaslit thoroughfares and, accompanied by two stalwart policemen, plunges into the unspeakable squalor of the Five Points, where the poorest of the city's poor endure and somehow survive, beside muddy lanes and alleys, in ramshackle tenements at the top of dilapidated wooden stairs. All is filth and decay and loathsomeness. Every other house seems to be a low tavern, inside one of which ("as seamen frequent these haunts") the English visitor discovers pictures in abundance, "of partings between sailors and their lady-loves, portraits of William of the ballad and his Black-Eyed Susan, of Will Watch the Bold Smuggler, of Paul Jones the Pirate, and the like: on which the painted eyes of Queen Victoria, and of Washington to boot, rest in as strange companionship as on most of the scenes that are enacted in their wondering presence. . . ."

So passed one of Dickens's evenings in New York. Another, February 10, 1842, began at seven with the assembling of two hundred and thirty gentlemen, invited to a memorable dinner to commemorate this visit of the already beloved English novelist. The dinner had transpired at that same, elegant Carlton House, at the corner of Leonard Street and Broadway, some fifteen blocks north (thus far had the center of fashion moved) of the City Hotel, scene a decade earlier of the only other public dinner of comparable renown, that in which fellow citizens had welcomed the return of Washington Irving after an absence abroad of seventeen years. Indeed, of all the Americans to whom young Dickens was introduced, none was he more eager to meet and none delighted him more than did Washington Irving, whose works he professed to know by heart. Irving it was who had been chosen by the dinner committee to give the toast of welcome to the conquering Englishman. Irving and Dickens: Boz and Geoffrey Crayon. And the two vastly popular writers from opposite sides of the sea had got on famously, to the delight of everyone, here and later in the spring in Washington, where both were guests at the White House, and later still when they had used two straws to share a mammoth julep in Baltimore.

Irving, in his late fifties now, was stirring from Sunnyside, those few miles up the Hudson, in order to assume, as he said, an entirely unexpected position of responsibility bestowed on him by his government. He was setting out that spring to return to Spain, this time as American ambassador, and thus would be out of the country by May, would remain at his diplomatic post overseas through the next four years, far removed from the crisis that was shaping around his Tarrytown neighbor Alexander Slidell Mackenzie. Much had changed since those two had been in Spain together fifteen years before. Now Irving, author of numerous books on Spanish subjects and at ease with the Spanish language and culture, would be arriving in Europe in an official capacity, appointed ambassador at the recommendation of Daniel Webster, secretary of state. The appointment was to prove the most popular of all the acts of the then President John Tyler, during a markedly unpopular administration that lasted one month short of four years, from 1841 to 1845.

His Accidency, Tyler was called, first Vice-President to succeed to the White House through the death of his predecessor. Would the system for transferring power even work? Tippecanoe and Tyler too: Old Tippecanoe, General William Henry Harrison, had delivered his prolix inaugural address bareheaded and coatless on a raw March midday in 1841; it had consumed the better part of two hours. The effort may have cost the old man dearly. Within three weeks he had come down with pneumonia. He died April 4, 1841, in his sixty-ninth year, on the thirty-first day of his presidency.

Harrison had been a Whig, the first elected to the White House. To simplify: insofar as they had a program Whigs represented the commercial and industrial East and their allies in the Midwest; Harrison was from Ohio. In fact, however, like the Anti-Masons, they were more of an antiparty: Jackson's policies as carried on by Martin Van Buren were what Whigs abhorred. But to balance their ticket in 1840 they had needed an anti-Jackson Southerner for Harrison's running mate—and got one in John Tyler of Virginia. But Tyler had been a Democrat, albeit an anti-Jackson Democrat. And when he moved into the White House after General Harrison's untimely death, the new chief executive was not long in urging a program—free trade, states' rights, an aggressive stance toward Mexico, opposition to a national bank and to internal improvements—agreeable to the South but little short of treasonous to Northern Whigs. New York's Philip Hone voiced the outrage of many an upright Harrison supporter as he became aware in succeeding months of "the faithless and wayward conduct of Mr. Accidental President Tyler . . . It was a dark day for the country when the brief but glorious reign of Gen. Harrison was brought to an end, and Virginia abstractions and fine-spun theories came in." Whig newspapers grew roundly critical of Tyler's Southern bias. Whig politicians appointed by Harrison, led now by Henry Clay, indignantly resigned from Tyler's cabinet. Of the principal officers, only Webster as secretary of state stayed on, and even he for less than the duration of the President's term.

Long enough, however, to sponsor the nominee for ambassador to Spain. "Washington Irving is now the most astonished man in the city of New York," Webster was quoted as saying of the appointment in February 1842. For Irving, although pressed financially, had by no means sought or expected the pecuniary relief of any governmental favors—indeed, had earlier declined to pursue political opportunities urged upon him.

Or so people insisted at the time: the diffident author, retired to Sunnyside with a house full of relatives, had taken no steps to secure this high and attractive honor. Fenimore Cooper, however, didn't believe that. In his hearing, a Mrs. Willing "had let out the secret of Irving's appointment," so Cooper in New York was explaining in mid-March to his wife back home. It seems that Irving "wrote to Webster to remember him *if anything good offered*. So that instead of not asking for the office, he asked for any that was going. There has been more humbug practised concerning this man than concerning any other now living."

What survives leaves Mrs. Willing's gossip unconfirmed. Perhaps Secretary Webster wrote the celebrated author at Sunnyside offering his services; perhaps the author's answer had been equivocal. Irving in any case would be off to Spain, while Cooper would remain through the year busy here at home with his own various projects, at Philadelphia, at New York, and at Cooperstown.

During this same spring of 1842, for instance, in the United States courtroom in New York City, the naval historian, through a speech that lasted eight hours, brilliantly and successfully argued his case concerning Lake Erie before expert referees and against formidable legal opposition that represented William Leete Stone and the *Commercial Advertiser*. Commander Mackenzie had appeared in court as a defense witness, though it did no good. Stone, like others before him, was forced to retract and pay damages.

But matters besides the Duer libels in Stone's paper occupied Fenimore Cooper that year. His pamphlet defending his Naval History against the attacks of Messrs. Duer, Burges, and Mackenzie was ready for publication by midsummer. He was at work on his novel *The Wing-and-Wing;* and for Rufus Griswold of *Graham's Magazine* he was researching and writing the life of the naval hero Richard Somers, first in a series of such sketches that would be published in the months ahead.

July 11, from Cooperstown: "Somers is ready. I shall send the manuscript this week . . . You will see I want the Christian name of Somers's sister. She lives nearly opposite to Dr. Harris, in, I believe, South Eighth, and is a Mrs. Keen. The directory will give you her address . . ." The sketch, which would come to fifty pages when republished in book form, describes the accomplishments of a young officer of promise who in a gesture of grand futility had sacrificed his life by blowing up the fire ketch *Intrepid* while guiding her down on the enemy's anchored fleet in the inner harbor of Tripoli the night of September 4, 1804. Or had shore fire blown her up for him? No one knew for sure, but Somers was a hero anyway. At the conclusion of the sketch Cooper observes that his name had been perpetuated on one of the gunboats in the Battle of Lake Erie: "Perry had a schooner which was thus designated under his orders on the memorable 10th September, 1813; and a beautiful little brig"—the same that Slidell Mackenzie was currently in command of—"has lately been put into the water on the seaboard, which is called the *Somers*. In short, his name has passed into a watchword in the American Navy . . ."

Cooper's sketch appeared in *Graham's* October 1842, even as the new brig named for the hero was making her way eastward across the Atlantic. For the rest, besides his novel, and his magazine articles, and his court suit against Stone, and his pamphlet, and his reviews (from Cooperstown June 19, the author revealed that he was planning to "review Mr. Burgess in the Boston *Notion*, a paper of wide circulation, in a few days. Capt. Mackenzie will follow, and rely on it, *he will be demolished*")—besides all that, Cooper was managing suits through the year against Thurlow Weed, editor of *The Albany Evening Journal*. With victory in that succession of suits gained at last, on December 14, the litigant had won them all. Thereafter newspapers would proceed cautiously when they wrote of him, now that even the powerful Weed had been cowed: "On a review of the matter and a better knowledge of the facts, I feel it to be my duty to withdraw the injurious imputations . . . on the character of Mr. Cooper. It is my wish that this retraction should be as broad as the charges . . ."

Besides Stone and Weed, Cooper's other major adversary in the newspaper wars, Colonel James Watson Webb of Tarrytown, had been forced by the courts to issue his own retraction a year earlier, after a trial that had been settled in November 1841. Now, in the summer of 1842, on June 25, the scrappy colonel had got himself into a duel with Congressman Tom Marshall near Wilmington, Delaware. Three days later Cooper was writing his wife that "Webb's duel makes a good deal of fun. They say the wound looks serious from the condition of his body, but I fancy it will not come to much." And it didn't. Marshall had emerged unscathed; Webb had taken a ball in the calf that put him on crutches awhile. But later in the year, in October, he was charged with breaking a New York statute against dueling. Indicted, Colonel Webb was sent to pass a couple of weeks in comfortable lodgings in the jury room of the Tombs, there receiving daily visits from friends and supporters as at a levee. Clerics and others to the number of fourteen thousand petitioned the governor for mercy, after a sentence had been handed down of two years at hard labor; on November 28, Seward pardoned the unrepentant offender. That set Webb free to resume attacks he had been engaged in for months against John Canfield Spencer, secretary of war.

Near the end of the year, for instance, on December 10, 1842—with the *Somers* three months at sea—Webb's paper, the *Courier and Enquirer*, made reference to "the pliant Mr. Spencer . . . the veriest political trimmer and the most unprincipled politician in the country . . . Here in New York he was an *abolitionist* when he thought that band of fanatics might give him power and influence; and no sooner does he get a place at Washington than he openly sells himself to the head and front of the *slavery* party," that is, to the Virginian Tyler.

For as Cooper had earlier offended by criticizing America in *Home As Found* and elsewhere, so Spencer had offended by seeming to abandon the true party. Of course the busy public servant did not see it that way. Harrison's appointees had resigned from Tyler's cabinet during the early fall of 1841—had even read the President out of the Whig party, September 13, 1841. His Accidency accordingly had been forced to look about for replacements. One the new President thought of was John C. Spencer; for Spencer and Tyler had worked on committees together when both had been young representatives to the federal legislature back in 1819.

Since that time Spencer's activities had been confined to his home state, where he had sat in the assembly, had served as special prosecutor in the Morgan affair, had returned to serve two more terms in the assembly, had edited (1838) the English-language edition of Tocqueville's great essay on American life, and had lately been serving as secretary of state—and ex officio superintendent of schools—under the Whig governor Seward. That office Spencer was holding when President Tyler summoned him to Washington in October 1841.

This New York Whig of impeccable credentials agreed to come and assume the burdens of national office; and as Tyler remembered it later, "the great multitude of cases which had accumulated in the War Department, many of which involved large sums of money, melted away before his sleepless industry," even as Whigs back home went on berating the secretary for his apostasy. Colonel Webb, for one, was still ranting a full year and longer after the secretary of war had undertaken his duties: "In all that regards honor and honesty," bemoaned the duelist that December of 1842, "John Tyler and John C. Spencer are well-matched; and the admitted talents of the latter will give respectability and éclat to the ignorance and treason of the former."

By December the *Somers* had long been gone from New York, had sailed, with the secretary's youngest son aboard, three months earlier, September 13, 1842—coincidentally, a year to the day after the Whigs had formally expelled President Tyler from their party, sixteen years to the day after the bricklayer William Morgan had been last seen in a carriage traveling westward toward Buffalo, twenty-nine years to the day after the victorious Oliver Perry had ill-advisedly penned his official report that praised all hands including Captain Elliott, six years to the day before the *Somers*'s present captain, Alexander Slidell Mackenzie, would end his stay on earth.

September 13, 1842. One scans the pages of New York newspapers to dispel the obscuring mists of time. In early September those pages are full of the court-martial of Captain Charles Wilkes on board the *North Carolina*. Over the summer the leader of the Polar Exploring Expedition has returned from three years and more of arduous sailing in Antarctica and throughout the Pacific, in the course of that great voyage having surveyed 280 islands, having constructed 180 charts (with enough accuracy that some will be used as late as World War II), and having gathered descriptions and specimens of countless unfamiliar birds, animals, insects, shells, fish, and fossil remains. But instead of praise on their return, the explorers are met generally with indifference. Wilkes specifically meets with something worse. Ahab come home and charged by subordinates with various offenses, he is being tried aboard ship in the New York navy yard as September opens.

Slidell Mackenzie, who years before had hoped to be part of just such an expedition, must have followed the proceedings aboard the *North Carolina* attentively. Wilkes sums up his defense by reading "fifty-six closely printed pages" to the court September 6. On the seventh the verdict is handed down. Not guilty of two charges, guilty of the third: illegally punishing men of his squadron. The court orders that Lieutenant Wilkes be publicly reprimanded. Accordingly, Commandant Matthew C. Perry administers an official censure, subsequently read in Wilkes's absence to naval crews in the area. To that punishment Secretary Upshur in Washington will add his own written rebuke.

September days pass, events of those days recorded among the announcements, complaints, reports, and advertisements of the numerous city newspapers: for Parr's Life Pills, for Portuguese Female Pills, for artificial teeth on the principle of atmospheric pressure, for stoves and buttons and gymnastic exercises. The condition of the East River ferry boats is deplored: doors that won't shut, broken windows, drafts, cushionless seats. News comes from a distance: "The anniversary of the Battle of Lake Erie was celebrated at Providence Saturday with an unusually large and spirited military display." "Reporting this date the death of Mrs. Tyler, who expired at the White House on Saturday evening, after a protracted illness." Trinity Church is abuilding, for the third time on the same site. The Croton reservoir, just completed, is bringing fresh water to town from thirty miles away; an eel three feet long "that had traveled all the way from the Croton Dam" is found in a water cock in the city. On record from the early days of this month are instances of brawls, thefts, abandoned babies, quarreling congregations, rapes, murders, Wall Street swindles. Pickpockets are caught, gangs singled out by name: the Alms House Rowdies, the Dock Rats. The Conover Boat Club's Pic Nic Party of the eighth is noted, at Weehawken, on a spot "the most romantic in all this fairy region, commanding a view of your city, of the harbor, the bay, islands and neighboring villages . . ."

Monday the twelfth is hot. This day will uncover a couple of drownings, a body found in an alleyway, a death in prison, a death of a sawyer when lumber falls on him at a yard on the corner of Clinton and Water streets.

The thirteenth dawns. About daylight two watchmen at Gold Street and Maiden Lane catch a certain Thomas Butler with twenty pounds of stolen opium. Between eight and nine rain pours down; then the sun comes out. A final brief shower just before noon is followed by brilliant sunlight for the rest of the day. Chartered steamboats—the *Saratoga*, the *Indiana*, the *Boston*, the *Gazelle*, the *Napoleon*, the *Convoy*—have left at about nine to take some fifteen hundred citizens up the Hudson twenty miles to Hastings to witness a prizefight between lightweights Cris Lilly and Tom McCoy, upon the result of which have been staked several thousand dollars.

And perhaps even as that fight is in progress, the *Somers* at Wallabout Bay is hoisting her launch in, roving her stunsail gear, passing the messenger, storing the gangway below. On shore, relatives of officers and crew cheer and call farewell and wave, while the vessel stands out into the stream, drops down the bay. Mackenzie himself has described the scene that the motion discloses, as it appeared only a few years earlier: "the smoke, from the city and the countless steamers that were everywhere urging their busy way and disturbing the calm waters with their bustling passage, rose in perpendicular threads toward the sky." Crewmen aboard are casting last glances at the receding skyline: "its encircling forest of masts; at the Battery, with its trees and promenades, the spires . . ."

Pilot disembarked, the captain issues his orders: yards trimmed, studding sails set. Everything is secured: cables unbent and payed below, fenders hauled in, ropes coiled clear for running. Shouts come from the deck, from the yardarms, as the brig drops her lee rail and stands out toward sea.

Not for a while will the *Somers*'s wardroom or crew be amused again onshore. None will partake of the genial clatter of Bowery taverns tonight. None will attend *Secrets Worth Knowing* at the Park, *The Butcher of*

Ghent at the Chatham, *Petty Sins and Pretty Sinners* at the Olympic. All will miss the season's last exhibition of fireworks, that grand gala this evening at Castle Garden.

Wednesday the *Somers* is gone. Awakening New Yorkers learn the outcome of yesterday's prizefight. Cris Lilly has won it, and the purse of $200. But his opponent is dead. The fight ended when McCoy fell to the ground mortally hurt. Round by round the *Herald* reports the harrowing event, one hundred and twenty rounds: jeers and taunts of the crowd, the beating, Tom's eyes swollen shut, his flesh cut loose in strips, blood spurting, lips huge, choking on blood, game but unable to find his way, to see the other through round after merciless round: "Brutal murder. We refer to our report in another column for the details of a cold-blooded murder, committed yesterday at Hastings in this state under the name of a prize fight . . ."

No mention, incidentally, is made of the *Somers*'s departure. Not in the *Herald*. Not in the *Courier and Enquirer*. But in Greeley's *Tribune*, all but lost on page 2, buried in the middle of the third column among much else of interest, is a brief notice of a voyage under way:

☞ The following is a list of the officers attached to the U.S. brig *Somers*, sailed September 13th, bound for a cruise on the coast of Africa: Alexander S. Mackenzie, Esq., Commander; Guert Gansevoort, Lieutenant; M. C. Perry, Acting Master; H. M. Heiskell, Purser; Richard W. Leecock, Passed Assistant Surgeon; Henry Rodgers, Egbert Thompson, Charles W. Hayes, Midshipmen; Adrian Deslonde, Philip Spencer, John H. Tillotson, Acting Midshipmen; Oliver H. Perry, Commander's Clerk; J. W. Wales, Purser's Steward.

WASHINGTON IRVING, SEVILLE, 1828.
Drawing by David Wilkie. In Madrid the preceding year, Irving had
gratefully made use of his friend Alexander Slidell's nautical skills in
writing his biography of Columbus.

HENRY WADSWORTH LONGFELLOW AT AGE TWENTY-EIGHT.
The lifelong friendship between Longfellow and Slidell had begun in
Spain in 1827, when the future poet was twenty.

OLIVER HAZARD PERRY.
The portrait, by Gilbert Stuart, was done in 1818, five years after
Slidell's mentor had triumphed at the Battle of Lake Erie.

JAMES FENIMORE COOPER IN THE 1830s.
The celebrated novelist had returned home from an extended stay in
Europe and was beginning to awaken the ire of certain of his
countrymen. For now, however, Slidell remained a friend.

MATTHEW CALBRAITH PERRY IN 1834.
Slidell's brother-in-law had recently begun a decade of shore duty at the
New York naval yard in Brooklyn.

NEW YORK IN THE 1840s.

The view is from the steeple of St. Paul's, showing the business district south from Vesey Street. Broadway runs diagonally upward toward the right, with Trinity steeple in the right background. Brooklyn is on the horizon to the left.

PASSED MIDSHIPMAN PHILIP SPENCER.
The accuracy of the likeness was attested to by those who had known
the young man, fellow members of Chi Psi fraternity, which Spencer
had helped to found.

ALEXANDER SLIDELL MACKENZIE.
The sketch was made at the court of inquiry called in late 1842 to
investigate the commander's conduct as captain of the *Somers*.

VOYAGE

THIS WOULD BE HARDLY A CRUISE AT ALL. THE FEW old salts aboard knew what cruises were: gales around Cape Horn and the ship on her beam ends, lamp in the forecastle burning blue with the fetid air, seas hitting the bows down there like sledgehammers a plank's thickness away, bulkheads leaking, scurvy among the seamen with legs bloated and breath rank and gums so swollen that the mouth wouldn't open. Cruises lasted three years and more. But this: a greenhorn crew of boys with hayseed in their ears, off for a few weeks of autumn sailing in horse latitudes, wafted by trade winds and not even crossing the line.

The brig was bearing dispatches for the sloop-of-war *Vandalia*, Commander Ramsay, on the Africa station, that favorite training and cruising ground for the navy. Sailors might prefer the Mediterranean, but there was work to be done in warmer waters. When Charles Dickens had set off for America early this same year, he had traveled aboard the steamer *Britannia*, which brought news from England of the appointment of Lord Alexander Ashburton as a special envoy. To conduct delicate negotiations with that English diplomat, Secretary of State Webster had remained at his post while other cabinet officers were forsaking their President in Washington. The Webster-Ashburton Treaty that resulted from his and the nobleman's diplomacy not only averted war by settling a long-standing boundary dispute between Maine and its neighbor to the north. The treaty also provided that England and the United States would cooperate henceforth in suppressing the illicit slave trade. Accordingly, the *Somers* might do her bit now, patroling waters off the West African coast, her crew on the alert to give chase to any strange vessels sighted. That would allow the saplings, those recruits aboard, to get practice handling sails, and meanwhile they could look forward on the easting to regular exercises with the broadswords, and to target practice with muskets and pistols on the spar deck, popping away at floating barrels or whatnot. They would learn, too, to take and give orders, as routines of this new seaborne world grew into second nature.

But first get their sea legs on. Homesick, confused, they staggered about the decks and scrambled aloft in response to scarcely understood commands, feeling the initial waves of nausea hardly off soundings, as the little brig hit ground swells and started her rolls, land and home now dropped below the horizon, far astern. With all that cannon weight topside, the rolls were heavy. And the apprentices, "those *children* entrusted to the care of the officers," as First Lieutenant Gansevoort expressed it later, "for whose safety we were responsible,—to God, to their country, and to their *parents*, to many of whom, before we sailed, I had pledged myself to extend parental care and advice"—many of those apprentices and boys, fifty aboard sixteen years of age or under and "some very small," would have been clinging to the weather bulwarks that second day out, when the *Somers* hit her first gale, and all the beef kids and bread barges and pots and pans were tumbling about the berth deck below them at midday's ill-attended meal. Uplifted young faces would have been white as foam.

Sick or well, new crew members had little trouble finding their way about. Lay forward; aft was officers' country. The brig was small in any case, tiny by the lights of our twentieth-century navy. To repeat: she measured one hundred and five feet from knightheads to taffrail, in usable space roughly the length of a basketball court, which reaches ninety-four. The *Somers*'s maximum breadth was a fraction over twenty-five feet; the width of the singles court in tennis is twenty-seven. Two decks she had in all, the spar or gundeck above, the berth deck below, with a hold for storage, packed full. The spar deck, minuscule to begin with, was cluttered with those ten great guns and carriages protruding six feet inboard either side, with the wheel and binnacles and pump and, between the two masts, the booms, taking up forty-five feet of deck space fore and aft—spare spars in case a mast should break, with the brig's launch and cutters stored on top of them. Ship's standing order: no idling on the booms. There were other orders: no going below for coffee from the galley (only Cromwell got to do that). No tobacco for the youngsters; no grog aboard for the crew—no tot of whiskey twice a day as on some naval vessels. Captain Mackenzie had made that clear to each sailor signing on.

And midshipmen will keep their journals up to date and turn them in each Sunday.

Such orders were deemed necessary to govern this compact, over-crowded autocracy of a hundred and twenty souls (ninety had been the designated complement)—one hundred twenty human beings crammed together on a floating basketball court, pared to the width at the widest of a singles game of tennis, and that space cluttered abovedecks with braces and buntlines and spars, with capstan and hen coops forward and arms chests port and starboard astern.

As for the berth deck below, where the crew slung their hammocks, that twilit space, over the bilge water that stank in rough weather, was cramped as well: "all small vessels," according to a navy-yard official of the time, "sail from New York so full that stores and provisions are stored on the berth deck." They kept a spare anchor down there, for instance, and no doubt the gangway and coils of rigging and additional sails and ship's stores that wouldn't fit into the hold: flour and vinegar and dried peas and such like. The headroom was four feet, ten inches between beams; only the smallest of the crew could straighten up below decks. The space itself was fifty feet long, seventeen wide. Filling the forward end, abaft a storeroom, was the galley. As roaches and rats in-fested every vessel of the time, the *Somers* doubtless carried her share of them; and among those vermin, in that perpetually dim abode, nightly slept some hundred men and boys, a foot and a half allowed as the ham-mock width, no spreaders—no shoes or sticks to spread them out—the lowest hammock in a tier of three swinging no higher than a foot above the deck. Moving among them meant groping and ducking, progress made audible by the curses of the disturbed: the off watch that had griped and farted and joked its way to sleep during the close, short night before morning.

Ship's bell sounding: eight slow tolls. All the starboard watch, ahoy! On deck there, below! Wide awake there, sleepers! Pipe's rough voice at the hatchway above: chief boatswain's mate, silver whistle at his mouth. Samuel Cromwell was his name, a bearded giant, biggest man aboard. From Virginia, an ugly scar partly hidden by his hairline, but his violent temper nakedly on display. Look sharp when Cromwell calls you. Uproar below decks to relieve the watch, jostlings up the narrow ladder to come topside.

When you arrive, it's to a salt breeze, and brilliance of early morning, sunlight on the vast blue empty sea. Nearer at hand the decks are freshly holystoned snow-white, rigging neatly flemished, caulklines black, black the carronades, the masts varnished, brightwork gleaming. Tar smells. And sounds: shrouds awhistle, ceaseless creak of the yards, slap of belly-ing canvas, captain's pig grunting, fowls cackling, human voices borne aloft.

This day the sun rose clear. The wind was auspicious; all seemed bright and cheerful. Ship's routine continues, including that daily holy-stoning of the decks at dawn—sand and ponderous stones on the decks, laboriously, then wet them down and squilgee them: shipshape and Bristol fashion. Pipe hammocks up, bags down. Then breakfast at eight. Morning muster at nine.

Midshipmen touch their caps, report to First Lieutenant Gansevoort in his blue coat with the gold anchor buttons. Clutching his bright speaking trumpet, the lieutenant goes to summon the captain. Report: All present and accounted for, sir. Captain, hugging the sword at his thigh, emerges to inspect the crew and battery. Hands stand at attention, all neatly attired, all those children.

Very good, sir. Beat retreat.

Later the short, broken shuffle of the drum: general quarters. Three minutes to get to battle stations. All hands scrambling up the hatchway to man guns or scurry aloft. Powder monkeys pitching shot hand to hand from the magazine below the wardroom. Gun crews at the tackles thrusting cannon outboard, handspikes under them, quoins in place.

Report: All on station.

Very good, sir. Beat retreat.

Eight bells and the forenoon watch. Lunch at midday. Supper at four: broken biscuit, boiled beef: scouse, burgoo, soft-Tommy. Twice a week butter and cheese served out. Scoff away, lads. No snacks between meals, no snacks at any time. Setting sails, reefing. Exercising the great guns in the afternoon, loaders standing by. Gun captain trains his thirty-two, sees it well loaded, grape and canister rammed home. Prick the cartridge, take the sight. Matchman, apply your wand.

Fire!

Gunner's mate solemnly firing away, ears humming in the din of it, smoke stinging the eyes and nostrils before drifting through the portholes leeward.

Orders all day long, shouted from aft. Boatswain's pipe: All hands on deck to tack ship! Out reefs, my hearties! Haul braces! Pull, you black-guard! You don't pull an ounce! Lend your pound of beef to it! Fore and aft, set the topgallant sails! Stand by to give her the main-topmast stun-sail!

Afternoon. Master-at-arms exercising the men with the musket and broadsword. Chores: scraping hatch combings, tarring, oiling, greasing, scrubbing, polishing brightwork about the great guns . . .

Evening muster: six o'clock. All hands present and accounted for, sir. Then the leisure of the second dog watch. Men taking sailor's pleasure, assembled at the scuttlebutt or mending clothes between the guns, lounging against the bitts, against the topmast shrouds. Horseplay: sparring together, singlestick in the lee waist. A fiddle scrapes for dancers on the forecastle. And talk among men idling in groups about the deck at dusk: old hands sharing details of their past careers, instances of their luck in gambling, how they squandered a windfall fortune, their generosity ashore to porters, to poor relations, their conquests, the hearts they've broken.

Sunset. Moonlight. Maybe some song from aloft: "Poor Tom Bowline," "List, Ye Landsmen," "The Roaring Brandywine."

> When we return from distant seas,
> We'll take our children on our knees,
> And kiss the lass, and drink a glass . . .

A little after sunset hammocks are piped down.

Darkness. Evening watch, middle watch through the night. Phosphorescence on the sea, rhythmic slap of waves on the bow, astern the helmsman's face lit dimly by the binnacle lamp, gurgle of wake, staccato creak of the yards aloft, hollow, intermittent hum of voices.

Then sunrise. From the giddy heights of the masthead the first gray streaks visible beyond the forecastle along the horizon, dim light on the distant water, the first brilliant spot of red appearing, the molten globe itself lifting astonishingly into the sky.

Another day.

September 16, three days out, three sailors are given six colts by the boatswain's mate. A colt was a kind of whip, a three-strand rope frayed at the end and of the thickness of a little finger, doubtless thick enough to hurt like hell. Six strokes are administered by the giant Cromwell across the backs of Edward Anderson, of Peter Hanson, of James Travis. Their offense: skulking, evading work. Travis, who is thirteen years old, is described elsewhere as of "good character." He will receive a total of thirty-nine lashes before being detached from the *Somers*. The first six lashes are given him this day.

On the day following, the seventeenth: Charles Van Velsor, twelve colts—the maximum allowable—for "striking Bradshaw." Richard Gilmore, twelve colts, for skulking.

Five days later, on the twenty-second, nine seamen are punished, one for skulking (twelve colts), seven for disobedience of orders (variously six, eight, and nine colts), and one, Josiah Smith, by "order of Captain," nine colts, for a reason not specified. On the following day Dennis Manning, described as "smart and active," receives twelve colts for disobedience of orders; Manning is fourteen.

The log entries of punishments continue: six colts to the "dull and stupid" John Finneday for skulking. Colt lashes for theft, for dropping a knife from aloft, for sleeping on watch, for impertinent answers to the master-at-arms, for being dirty at muster, for fighting, for pushing a man against the head rail, for washing clothes without permission, for using profane language (twelve colts), for throwing tobacco on deck (twelve colts), for spilling tea on deck (six colts).

Forty-three separate floggings were administered aboard the *Somers* between her departure from New York and her arrival at Funchal in the Madeiras three weeks later. What is to be made of that? The captain alone could authorize punishment. Was he a monster? We make allowances for differences in pedagogical theory, remembering those dreary schools and cruelly conscientious schoolmasters in the fictions and fact of Victorian England. American schools would have derived theory from those models: spare the rod and spoil the child. And this school afloat was a naval school. No doubt Captain Mackenzie, that amiable friend of Irving, of Longfellow, saw himself as doing no more or less than his duty. Ashore he was repeatedly described, and on the best authority, as humane and mild-mannered. The excellent Dr. Francis Lieber recorded that Slidell Mackenzie was "one of the simplest, unfashionablest, kindest, plainest men I know." The perspicacious Charles Sumner found Mackenzie to be "a modest and unassuming man." The estimable Cornelius Felton, professor of Greek at Harvard, remarked on Mackenzie's "calmness, self-possession, gentleness and refinement of manner." The astute Richard Henry Dana, Jr., who had sailed before the mast himself a few years earlier, concluded after meeting Mackenzie that his "appearance and manners are very prepossessing. He is quiet, unassuming, free from all military display in manner, self-possessed, and with every mark of a humane, conscientious man."

Conscientious no doubt he was. Mackenzie's idol was Oliver Hazard Perry, adored by his crews; and Perry had run a tight ship. "Captain Perry was a strict and exacting commander," Mackenzie himself reminds us in his life of that officer, "enforcing rigid discipline in his ship." But Perry was humane as well, regularly visiting the sick and sending them food from his table. Similarly, Captain Mackenzie, who had served under the hero, was, in the words of one aboard the *Somers*, "very humane. I have frequently seen him send dishes from his own table to the sick. I have known him give fruit from his own private stores to the crew." To be sure, the numbers in sick bay so far would not have laid a heavy tax on the captain's provisions. The health of the men, generally good to start with, was improving on this first leg of the voyage; according to the ship's surgeon, "most of the cases were slight and trivial complaints, occasioned by bruises, etc., from a number of the boys not having been at sea before."

But the commander's humanity was manifested in another way. The burly Cromwell, chief boatswain's mate and in his mid-thirties, was charged with carrying out sentences of those brought to the mast for punishment. Older hands were punished with the cat-o'-nine-tails, younger ones with the colt. But Cromwell would whip the younger apprentices as hard as the older seamen, "would strike with all his might," Purser's Steward Wales remembered, "as though it was pleasing to him to whip them. He whipped them hard, the same as though they were men instead of boys. I have frequently heard Commander Mackenzie censure him for whipping them so hard, and he has often ordered him to stop."

But Cromwell seemed a brute, not at all tamed by his having got married shortly before sailing. Indeed, that same Wales had been shocked, two or three days out at sea, to hear the boatswain's mate below in the berth deck speak of his new wife "in a very light manner, for a man who has just been married at least"—something to the effect that he cared not a whit for her chastity while he was gone. This crudeness from one not without advantages; Cromwell had had some education. But he had a fearful temper, and scorned the saplings on board, those raw hands just from the bush, green as cabbages, who didn't know a girtline from a backstay. "He would often," according to the first lieutenant, "go into the most violent fits of rage from some small matter . . . at times used most outrageous and blasphemous language toward the boys." Van Norden overheard the boatswain's mate say of the youngsters—on a vessel that size much could be overheard—that "he would like to get them on the cathead and shove them overboard." And on one occasion the ship's carpenter had had to intervene to prevent what might have ended in murder. An inept apprentice and ship's barber named Sears, eighteen years old, had inadvertently stirred the ever-smoldering ire of the boatswain's mate, having allowed a stick to roll from the forepeak across the deck against his feet. Cromwell had grabbed the stick and hurled it at Sears's skull. That missed, whereupon the boatswain's mate picked up another in his great fists and threatened to drive it through the boy's heart, even if doing so meant that "he swung on the mainyard the next minute." Sears had crumbled to his knees, expecting his death blow, when Carpenter's Mate Dickerson, with nineteen years in the service, intervened, calling down from the hatchway above. Though Cromwell stayed his hand, he was not pleased with such meddlesomeness. "Your time's damn short," he snarled up at Dickerson, according to what the carpenter himself remembered.

As for the midshipmen, they would hardly make matters easier for the crew. As a class, those middies, or reefers, were notorious throughout the navy—"terrible little boys," cocking their hats, strutting about the decks self-importantly, slapping their dirk hilts and stroking the stubble on their chins, sputtering out their oaths like the full-fledged officers they aspired to become: You fellow, I'll get you licked before long! I'll get you a tight dozen! You, Scotty, and be damned to you. I'll teach you to be grinning over a rope that way!

But that was the manner of navy life since time immemorial: me with this sailor's frock on, them swobs and reefers with the anchor button—and nothing for it till the cruise was done. First Sunday of every month (in this case it would have been October 2, twenty days out and three days before arriving at Funchal) officers and crew assembled, as throughout the navy they assembled, at capstan or coat of the mainmast, to hear read aloud the articles of war:

"Article 13: If any person in the Navy shall make or attempt to make any mutinous assembly, he shall on conviction thereof by a court-martial suffer death; and if any person aforesaid shall utter any seditious and mutinous words, or shall conceive or connive at any mutinous or seditious practices, or shall treat with contempt his superior, being in the execution of his office, or, being witness to any mutiny or sedition, shall not do his utmost to suppress it, he shall be punished at the discretion of a court-martial."

Sabbath muster at ten in the morning, four bells of the forenoon watch, all hands scrubbed with their prayer books and at attention, bare-headed. The voice of the captain's clerk is lifted above the breeze of the open sea:

"Article 24: Any officer, seaman, marine, or other person who shall disobey the orders of his superior, or begin, excite, cause, or join in any mutiny or sedition in the ship to which he belongs, or in any ship or vessel in the service of the United States, on any pretence whatsoever, shall suffer death or such other punishment as a court-martial shall direct; and further, any person in any ship or vessel belonging to the service aforesaid who shall utter any words of sedition and mutiny or endeavor to make any mutinous assembly on any pretence whatsoever shall suffer such punishment as a court-martial shall inflict."

Those two and the various other articles of war were read in their entirety. Then under that shadeless sun came the sermon, which in the absence of a chaplain was delivered by Captain Mackenzie himself, standing on the trunk house—with its two skylights over officers' country—of a height a couple of feet above the deck and extending aft abaft the mainmast as one more encumbrance of those crowded spaces. A fitting sermon it would have been from the exalted and literate captain, author of *A Year in Spain* and *The Life of Commodore Oliver Hazard Perry*, both of which were among a select group of books, along with Bowditch's *Navigator* and four or five others, required by order of the secretary of the navy to be aboard every vessel in the service.

Midshipman Rodgers, who had served with Mackenzie before, was aware of the brig's good fortune in having such a captain. Most of the wardroom were, although Acting Midshipman Spencer seemed not to be. In fact, Rodgers had heard Spencer say "that if the commander should have another *S* to his initials, it would spell his character"—pre-

sumably by reversion to Alexander Slidell, if young Spencer's witticism
is to be played out. "On another occasion, shortly after leaving New
York," so Rodgers later recalled, "I was in conversation with some of the
midshipmen in regard to the vessel and character of our commander. To
some observation of mine"—clearly laudatory—"Mr. Spencer remarked
that he did not know that he was that kind of a man. He thought he was
a damned old granny."

Ill-feeling between the commander and this midshipman with the outboard eye had been prompt in forming. Indeed, it was hinted that even
before the *Somers* sailed, Captain Mackenzie had warned the rest of the
wardroom, most of them closely allied to him, to give the newcomer a
wide berth; his nephew, Matthew Perry, Jr., acting master, had "a slight
recollection of something being said" along those lines. Did their collective demeanor toward Spencer lead him to seek friends elsewhere? If
Craney aboard the *North Carolina* and the squadron officers at Rio are to
be believed, the boy had no knack for making appropriate friends. In any
case, once the *Somers* had got fairly out to sea, Captain Mackenzie himself
was not long in observing that this son of a distinguished father "was in
the habit of associating but little with the other officers, but that he was
continually intimate with the crew. He was often in the habit of joking
with them and smiling whenever he met them, with a smile never known
but on such occasions . . ."

Midshipman Rodgers had noticed the same behavior, disapprovingly:
Spencer chatting at his ease with the men "when he was on duty during
his watch—laughing and talking with them in a more familiar manner
than became an officer or gentleman." The midshipman seemed to be
courting the crew's favor in other ways. Purser's Steward Wales saw
Spencer "several times throw money upon the deck—a shilling or so—
and tell the boys to scramble for it." And he would give tobacco to the
youngsters against naval regulations. With ship's ledgers and daybooks to
tabulate, Wales was in a position to know that Spencer's purchases of
tobacco exceeded those of anyone else aboard. If Granny Mackenzie—
that "damned old humbug," as Spencer was overheard calling the captain
on another occasion—wouldn't let the boys have tobacco, why then, "*he*
could accommodate them."

The young man had one trick that was particularly aggravating. Later
the commander was to describe it in a context of almost palpable annoyance. "He was in the habit of amusing the crew by making music with
his jaw. He had the faculty of throwing his jaw out of joint, and by the
contact of the bones playing with accuracy and elegance a variety of
airs." But picture it: this son of one of six cabinet officers in the government at Washington, here on the little deck under that wide sky, grimy
tars gathered round and grinning in wonderment at a walleyed officer in
the uniform of the United States Navy, jaw awry, making freak music

like some street clown with cap extended for coppers on Ludgate Hill!

He got brandy, too, and gave it to the men. Though discouraging indulgence, the captain had not presumed to legislate what the wardroom could or could not drink. But for the men the orders were clear: none of their blue ruin aboard this ship, no liquor whatever. Yet Charlie Stewart, captain of the forecastle, got a glass of grog off Mr. Spencer for scrubbing a pair of pantaloons for him, and for lending the midshipman his mattress when Spencer lost his overboard. Landlubberly trick in any case: losing your mattress overboard.

Of course such attentions and favors from an officer in that ungentle world made him a favorite forward. Manuel Howard, the mulatto steerage steward, was rubbing the midshipman's head one day. Mr. Spencer "asked me if I would go with him—he did not say where. I told him I would, and he said I should have nothing to do but rub his head, and brush his clothes, and clean his boots, and he would give me good wages." That wooing of naval personnel from their present employer was doubtless common then, though much of it mere idle talk. Enlistments, technically for two or three years, actually lasted no longer than the length of the cruise, at the end of which seamen were paid off, many vowing never again to set foot on a deck. (A couple of nights of roistering in taverns ashore brought the bulk of them penniless back with their ditty bags to the receiving ship.) And indeed, this same head-rubbing Howard was soon being tempted by Midshipman Rodgers, who asked him "if I would go on his farm as overseer, and Mr. Spencer overheard it, and asked him"—Rodgers—"I think, if he wanted me, and he"—Spencer—"said, 'oh, damn you now, you're going with Mr. Rodgers, not with me.' " The tone of that exchange is left for us to supply: surprised? mock-petulant? genuinely annoyed?

The oft-punished Billinger Scott, aged fifteen, was Mr. Spencer's hammock boy. Spencer asked "how I would like to sail with him; I told him I would like it very well." Scott, second-class apprentice, was encouraged to believe he would be rated seaman if he sailed under that different command.

Yet of all the crew, Mr. Spencer's most intimate associate was Old Bunting, the quartermaster, Elisha Small, a Maine native and aptly named, for at thirty years of age he was the most diminutive man aboard. As quartermaster, Small with his lead-weighted signal book would have been in charge of hoisting communication flags, and would have had navigational responsibilities as well, under the sailing master. This Small and Mr. Spencer had grown close even before the *Somers* left port. In New York, on the eve of departure, on the evening of the very day that the wayward midshipman had solemnly pledged his word to Commandant Perry to reform, he was lending fifteen dollars to Small, a shaky sort who had already forfeited a good position in the merchant service through drunkenness; Seaman Charlie Rodgers had seen the rhino pass hands.

Their fondness for drink no doubt encouraged that anomalous friendship between the well-born Spencer and the humble though not illiterate petty officer. They could chat together in Spanish, another bond. And Small, who had served in West Africa as agent for a Salem shipowner, was full of lore about slaving. He even claimed to have sailed on a guineaman once, bearing contraband slaves westward to the New World. Obsessed with piracy, young Spencer must have found colorful the yarns that Small, veteran of a slaver, could spin.

The *Somers* had been steering against opposing winds that drove her north of her course. Thus she would touch at Madeira first, before proceeding to carry out orders that directed her to Tenerife and Porto Praya. Shortly before reaching Funchal—it would have been on the third or fourth of October—the brig sighted a sail, doubtless the first in days of cruising on an empty sea. Captain Mackenzie ordered course altered to speak the vessel. Small was standing by to bend on signal flags, hoist and receive signals. Those not on watch lounged along the bulwarks, enjoying this break in an already monotonous routine.

Signals were exchanged; the other proved to be a vessel from home.

Acting Midshipman John Tillotson, sixteen years old and new to the service, found himself alongside Acting Midshipman Spencer observing the maneuvers. He and Spencer got to talking, and the latter made one remark that lodged firmly enough in Tillotson's mind that he was able to recover it weeks later. "When we were bearing down on the brig *America* before our arrival at Madeira," according to what Tillotson remembered, Spencer "said he should like to have the launch full of armed men and take possession of her."

There had been more bad feeling between Carpenter's Mate Dickerson and Chief Boatswain's Mate Cromwell. Lieutenant Gansevoort had had the carpenter make him a couple of singlesticks. Dickerson had gone to store them in the boatswain's locker, telling Cromwell as he did so that "they belonged to the First Lieutenant." Cromwell was unimpressed. "He said he did not care a damn, they should not stay there. On my leaving the storeroom," Dickerson recalled, Cromwell had repeated his earlier threat: *"Your time's damn short."* But the singlesticks had stayed where the carpenter put them.

"Another time he"—Cromwell—"had a rule which was broke, and he said that one of the carpenters had broken it. I told him they had not, it had got broken in the chest, and as I was going up the ladder he said, 'God damn you, I'll fix you.'"

*   *   *

But then suddenly a change came over the mammoth boatswain's mate. More than one person would comment on it. Purser's Steward Wales, for instance, ever since leaving New York had been listening to Cromwell bawling day after day at the apprentices and boys, cursing them, behaving "very tyrannical" toward them, though otherwise "having no conversation with them, and keeping aloof from them altogether." Now, however, "just previous to our arrival at Madeira, I noted a sudden change in his manner toward the boys: he then 'made free' with them, and let them talk and play with him and pull him about."

The transformation must have delighted the hitherto cowed and anxious youngsters—a delight that the sight of land must have heightened, after three full weeks and a day at sea.

Land ho! Dead ahead! Land ho!

It rose first dim as a cloud on the horizon—see, just there?—then gradually grew sharper, turning green at last, most brilliantly green and miraculously stable in the midst of all that wavy blue world. Through succeeding hours the little brig edged nearer. Lines down from the heights of the peaks became ravines, and along the coast were high precipices, and behind them ridges and gorges, and little bays at sea level before tended land, little houses, roadways.

Spirits were rising aboard. On deck Cromwell was good-humored with the youngsters, no longer the fearsome giant. And in fact, despite floggings, despite the boatswain's terrible temper throughout most of that first leg of the voyage, despite the bewildering newness of it all for many, the officers would later concur with Wales that discipline and morale aboard "between New York and Madeira . . . was very good indeed." Before Madeira, as the first lieutenant corroborated, the crew's "conduct was very good."

On October 5, 1842, the *Somers* dropped anchor in Funchal, chief port of the island.

By then the ship had sailed some thirty-eight hundred miles.

Madeira, known to the Romans, rediscovered by the Portuguese in 1418, lies out at sea some four hundred miles west of the African coast on a line with Morocco. The island, which is now and was then a Portuguese possession, measures about thirty-five miles in length, thirteen miles in width at its widest point; its highest peak rises to six thousand feet. In the nineteenth century, as until recently, it continued to be a convenient stopping place on trans-Atlantic voyages, and it remains a favorite retirement spot for English and other northern Europeans, blessed as it is with a year-round average temperature of sixty-five degrees. Its principal product is wine.

A crate of Madeira, "wine of a rare value," was, in fact, soon being brought off from the island and loaded "with much care" aboard the

Somers at its anchorage. The wine was a present from I. H. Burden, Esq., United States vice-consul at Funchal, to Commodore J. B. Nicholson, that jolly-tar lifelong friend of Washington Irving under whom Captain Mackenzie had served earlier on the Brazil station. No doubt so valuable and tempting a commodity would be stored in officers' country, perhaps in the captain's own tiny stateroom, which was entered through a hatchway in the after end of the trunk house. In any case, many of the crew would have observed the crate being carefully loaded aboard—not that there was much time for gawking. Look lively there! The *Somers* would linger at anchor only long enough to replenish supplies—the purser had returned ashore in the market boat already—and to take on fresh water. The *Vandalia*, for the captain of which Mackenzie was bearing dispatches, might even now be at Tenerife, in the Canaries. The commander accordingly meant to get under way promptly.

His first lieutenant, Guert Gansevoort, in the midst of those preparations for departure, was on deck with Mr. Spencer, Boatswain's Mate Cromwell, and Purser's Steward Wales. "There was a good deal of work to be done—getting in water, provisions, etc." So he later remembered. "Cromwell was grumbling about the amount of duty required. I heard him say that 'it was damned hard usage': he said that to the crew. He did not appear to drive on the duty and assist in carrying out my orders as he had done before. He would repeat my orders and then stand on the forecastle without making any attempt to see them executed: he would do nothing more than repeat what I said to him."

Which sounds like skulking, though no one took the cat to Cromwell. Now the launch had brought the last of the water casks alongside. Fruit and other foodstuffs were aboard. The order was passed to get under way.

All hands up anchor, ahoy!

But the boatswain's mate remained out of sorts. "At Madeira, when we were getting under weigh," according to Wales, "Cromwell spoke against Commander Mackenzie. Captain Mackenzie asked why some rigging had not been attended to. Cromwell was stationed forward and Captain Mackenzie went aft. Cromwell then said he 'did not care a damn about the rigging: Captain Mackenzie was desirous of getting too much work out of the crew; that there was no necessity of getting under weigh that night at all,' at the same time wishing the 'commander and the brig farther in hell than they were out.' This he said loud enough to be heard by all forward. Several of the officers were forward at the time, but in the hurry of getting under weigh, paid no attention to it. . . ."

The sails were filling. The *Somers* set her course south-southeast, toward bluer, ever warmer seas. Soon she had run the island out of sight. Over the horizon, three hundred miles ahead of the bow of the little brig, lay the Canaries.

*   *   *

But aboard ship the mood seemed to have changed. After leaving Madeira, Lieutenant Gansevoort noted that "the crew were very slack, and I had frequently to drive them to their work. They would frequently disobey small orders, such as putting clothes away, etc. . . . Before, if I told them to put away an article of clothing they would do it readily; after that they paid no attention to it."

Which of us who have worked with adolescents could doubt that such a change might come about? What parent could doubt it? The opportunities for sojering, for shirking duty aboard, were many. Send a boy below for something, and he could take his own time finding it. It might require twice as long as usual to scrape clean a belaying pin. You could pull feebly. You might stop pulling altogether as soon as the officer went aft. All the more likely because of the altered manner of the chief boatswain's mate. Cromwell appeared to be attending absently to duties himself now. Once, according to the first lieutenant, the mate "was sitting near the forecastle. I called to him three or four times, to order him to pipe the bags down. He got up very lazily with a pipe in his mouth. His manner was disrespectful, and he merely ordered the bags piped down, letting his own bag remain on deck." This from someone whom Gansevoort had judged invaluable early in the voyage. Indeed, "such instances were continually occurring—all of which it is impossible for me to recollect. A change of manner on board ship is very easily observed . . ."

As another example, Master-at-Arms Garty took note that thefts aboard increased after Madeira; only one such case had occurred during the first leg of the voyage. Incidentally, the sergeant, lone marine aboard, on this second leg was seated one day on the combings of the main hatch when he was joined by Mr. Spencer. They started talking, first about Carty's Marine Corps standing—would he lose his sergeant's rating if he went ashore?—then about the brig. Both agreed that the *Somers* was a fine vessel.

Spencer said: I could take her with six men.

To which the master-at-arms replied: You couldn't with three times six.

He could though, the acting midshipman insisted, "provided he knew where everything lay as well as I did, and the keys of the arm chest." Those the marine kept himself. Spencer "went on to describe"—injudiciously, one might suppose—"how he would take her. First he would secure the captain and officers, then take possession of the arms, turn up the crew, and he made no doubt as soon as they saw his men in arms they would give in to him. I told him then," Carty recalled, "that after the crew had been turned up they could rush on him, and before there might be six killed we could throw him and his six overboard, and he must think us a poor crew to think he could take it with six men. Oh no, or something like it, he muttered out as he went away. That ended that conversation."

One of many such to help while away slow hours at sea—and doubtless no stranger than many another.

On Saturday, the eighth of October, two or three days out of Madeira, the *Somers* raised the Canaries. In due course she came to anchor in the harbor of Santa Cruz.

As at Madeira, the stay at these Spanish islands was brief. Yet one watch did get ashore, into that picturesque, lassitudinous world among Mediterranean foliage, beaches brilliant in sunlight, one green peak before them rising twelve thousand feet into the sky. Liberty, after mighty piping at the forward hatchway: D'ye hear there, all you starboard watch: get ready to go ashore! After the scrubbing on deck, the scrounging together of a proper uniform: frock, trowsers, neckerchief, flat tar hat. The muster; the men impatiently boarding the cutters alongside, to be rowed ashore by mates of the luckless larboard watch. Charges called out, jokes, clowning at the shoreline.

And from that excursion one man was, inevitably, late returning. McKinley was his name, Daniel McKinley, who had already been punished for drawing a knife on Ford before the ship had ever set sail from home. Commander Mackenzie ashore had ordered him back to the ship, and he had dallied instead. Sunday, day of ten o'clock muster and the captain's sermon, McKinley was being punished for the infraction, receiving twelve cats across the bare back "for breaking liberty." The flogging was severe, at the legal limit—welts turning purple, blood spurting as the nine knotted strands slashed again and again across writhing flesh. On the same day James Mitchell got nine cats for "cutting a rope," and Dennis Manning got nine colts for fighting, and James Travis got nine colts for "using bad language," and three others were colted for disobedience of orders—in all, seven punished that day, as three had been punished two days before, and nine men had been punished at the gratings the day before that.

The log of the *Somers* records as much. Again we wonder: how interpret such a record by the lights of the time? Aboard ship the purser, Horace Heiskell, was present throughout the voyage "as a gentleman unacquainted with the naval service, and fresh from private life": accountant, bookkeeper. When asked later if he had ever seen "any treatment of the crew not in perfect accordance with your sense of justice, and humane and kind as the proprieties of life required," that gentleman responded, "I never did." Was he lying? Had he been inattentive? Or was punishment of the sort meted out on this vessel no more than was expected, judged by all hands to be reasonable and necessary?

The *Vandalia* had departed Tenerife before the *Somers* arrived. Captain Mackenzie would continue the pursuit, across twelve hundred miles that separated these Canaries from the Cape Verde Islands to the southwest, and from that Portuguese archipelago onward if need be another twelve hundred miles to Monrovia, capital of the newly founded commonwealth of Liberia, on the coast of Africa.

The weather during the current passage turned from balmy to hot. In succeeding nights and days parching winds off the African coast brought men from close quarters below to linger on deck for what breath of air they could get, seeking the shade of the guns, and some to sleep up there off watch. The sun at midday made sticky the tar in deck seams; the deck was kept sprinkled with water. And in that heat the crew's dispositions grew ever more sour.

Spencer continued, apparently, to brood on his one idea. He spoke to Midshipman Thompson, veteran of the Polar Expedition, who at twenty-one had four years in the service. Did not Thompson think the *Somers* could be easily taken? Spencer "said a person could go in the cabin and murder the captain without detection. He also asked me about pirates rendezvousing in the islands in the Pacific, and whether a vessel could not go in there and refit. I think Howard heard this conversation," below decks in the steerage, where Howard was steward.

Lately Midshipman Spencer and Boatswain's Mate Cromwell had become close friends. Crewman Charlie Rogers recalled that the two had not appeared to be intimate until after the brig reached Madeira (though early in the voyage Spencer had given Cromwell, as he had Small, fifteen dollars, which the master-at-arms was charged with looking after). Now, though, Mr. Spencer and Cromwell seemed always together, "more so than I ever saw an officer with any of the crew before." Conferring, whispering on the forecastle, turning their backs on others. Jonas Humbert, sixteen, was topside after an early morning rain somewhere between Madeira and Mesurado. On this particular morning the apprentice had noticed Mr. Spencer lurching like a drunk man; he was approaching to where Cromwell was seated on the forehatch. Humbert overheard the midshipman asking the chief boatswain's mate if he wanted something to drink. Mr. Spencer went aft again and beckoned. Cromwell rose and walked to the mainmast, hard by the hatchway at the forward end of the trunk house, through which Mr. Spencer was descending into the steerage. A moment later the midshipman had put his head back up above the hatch and was looking around to make sure the officer of the deck was aft. Then Mr. Spencer handed Cromwell a cup. The boatswain's mate drank and returned forward, with the midshipman following. Soon after, Humbert was piped below to breakfast, but by then he was sure of what he had seen. Though it had rained earlier that morning, the weather was calm now. Yet Mr. Spencer, with sea legs in place, had been staggering like somebody drunk.

Twelve days after departing the Canaries, the *Somers* came to off Praia, in the Cape Verde Islands. The date was Friday, October 21, 1842.

Nine crewmen were punished at the gratings that day: two for fighting, four for disobedience of orders, and one each for using improper language, for striking a boy, for stealing. There is no evidence that liberty was granted; but this would have been toward the end of the rainy season, when the climate of those islands, after insufferable summer heat, had turned even more noxious to white men.

The Mediterranean world had been left behind by then, so that from aboard the anchored vessel what could be seen of those rugged, volcanic outposts was African: black slaves at their labors along the waterfront, muddy streets wending through the dismal settlement, goats, steamy lushness of surrounding vegetation. Again the *Somers* lingered only long enough to replenish her hold. Soon she was once more under way, the islands diminishing astern as she steered a course east by southeast toward the African mainland.

Nearly three weeks were consumed in covering the distance. Another first Sunday of the month fell within that passage, this one November 6, when once again the crew stood to muster, as was the naval custom, to hear the reading of the articles of war.

However, despite such admonitions as that document broadcast, some of the men and boys continued shirking their duties, or performed them grudgingly; others aboard would later confirm that fact. Even so, and oddly enough, punishments recorded after Madeira seem comparable to those logged before. As was true early in the voyage, so now some were colted for disrespect and disobedience of orders. But the numbers of men and boys punished did not swell dramatically after the first leg of the cruise. And the reasons for punishment continued to be various, log entries casting their flickering light on routines and expectations aboard an American naval vessel a hundred and forty years ago: twelve colts on the back of Joseph Weaver for sleeping below during the watch, twelve colts across Thomas Bywater's back for his wasting fresh water, twelve colts on the back of Henry Miller for not having a white hat, twelve colts on the back of Peter Fenton for being dirty and slovenly.

On the new course, in those torrid latitudes, the ship's progress was slowed. Day followed day without relief, smooth water scarcely bubbling at the bow, wake scarcely rippling astern. And the sun beat down. Meanwhile Midshipman Spencer, new chum of the boatswain's mate, continued his long-standing friendship with Elisha Small. That former petty officer had recently been disrated, reduced to seaman, for his "care-

lessness of duty" as quartermaster, and for "disobedience of orders." Had
he got drunk, as before on the Salem merchant's vessel? Now, in any
case, he was merely sailmaker and captain of the maintop, though his
attachment to Mr. Spencer seemed unaffected by the change. They were
together constantly, still finding much to gab about.

Spencer chatted with other crewmen too. Charlie Rogers, Small's
successor as quartermaster, the midshipman approached "one calm night
on the passage from Cape de Verde Islands to the coast of Africa." Somewhere over the horizon lay the infamous slave coast. Had Rogers ever
been on a slaver? He had not. Mr. Spencer proceeded to express a wish
that he might have a launch and ten such men as he would pick from
among the crew; then he could make his fortune. While the two talked,
another brig was in sight, bearing down on the *Somers*. You would take
that brig? Rogers wondered aloud. I would. But, the quartermaster ventured, it would be hard to find ten men. Not at all; and Mr. Spencer
proceeded to name Willson, Cavanaugh, McKinley, Green . . .

Such easy converse with crewmen—while with his fellow officers
Spencer's dealings continued tentative. He seems to have got along with
Wales, from whose store he would draw the cigars that he distributed
liberally among wardroom stewards and petty officers. But with Mr.
Thompson, for instance, he would soon blunder into a fight: "a scuffle,"
as Thompson described it. In the steerage Spencer "struck at me, I ward-
ed off the blow, slapped him with my hand, then threw him down. The
first lieutenant came in and ordered me to desist." Even though smaller
than his opponent, Mr. Thompson had got the better of the exchange: "I
pitched into him before he knew it."

Mr. Gansevoort parted them and saw that the two made up, with no
hard feelings. But Spencer would continue to seek to please the crew
more than his fellow officers. He asked his hammock boy, Billinger
Scott, if he wanted some tobacco. "I told him it was against the commander's orders. He said, 'if I got hauled up for it, he would stand
between me and the commander.' I took the tobacco."

And on another evening the boy "heard Mr. Spencer ask Small how
they got slaves. Small said they went up the rivers in Africa; they would
anchor off in the brig they went up in, and take the long boat and go
ashore. . . ."

On the horizon off the port bow, out of the colorless tropical haze, was
emerging a shadow that became in time a mottled bulk, underscored by
a long pale line where sea foamed with eternal patience against a continent. Gradually the bulk took on definition, color. In the foreground a
rocky promontory rose out of the haze to a height nearly three hundred
feet above sea level. Slowly the cape was revealed to be covered with
dense underbrush and massive forest trees—tall palms, the globular man-

go. At its summit stood a tiny fort and lighthouse; and behind, over the lower ridge, coming into view as the ship rounded the headland, spread the village of Monrovia.

You could see the stores and warehouses at waterside now, the red, rutted streets higher up, one-story buildings where the thousand inhabitants who composed the settlement worked and lived. Farther along, a stream opened a hole into the dark interior, though in fact that little Mesurado River extended no greater distance inland than eighteen miles or so, as though nature itself were unable to penetrate far through so tangled, so formidable a mass of vegetation.

And Africa loomed awesomely in view: deep unbroken forest, with hill rising beyond hill as far as the eye could see. Over those hills, within that forest, roamed elephants and leopards; forest trees held monkeys, slithering boa constrictors; down to the riverbanks waddled crocodiles, hippopotami. And back there in that huge continent were anthills twelve feet high, scorpions, giant centipedes.

November 10, 1842. The *Somers* comes to anchor in the cove near the base of Cape Mesurado, at the edge of a world of wonders.

Young Matthew Perry had picked this site twenty years earlier, as an alternative to an unhealthful location on Sherbro Island farther north. But the well-intentioned venture that had initiated the colony had from the start been unlucky. Founded in 1817, the American Colonization Society had within three years, in February 1820, embarked the first group of eighty-eight free black emigrants from New York to return them to Africa, though it would require another two years before the group found permanent asylum, here at this cape of the then Lieutenant Perry's choosing. The brief history of the settlement had so far been a troubled one. Natives in the area, resenting the presence of interlopers, tried to drive them off. For their part, the freed blacks from America did battle against local slave traders. Liberia, as the colony was named in 1824, sought to expand its borders through purchase, but encountered resistance doing so. Meanwhile, American vessels began to deposit at Monrovia slaves captured at sea—one more community burden—while France and England set about protesting the claims to sovereignty of what seemed to them no more than a commercial experiment by an American philanthropic society. Nevertheless, by 1838, and despite manifold hardships, Liberia had become a commonwealth. It remained feebly viable four years later, as Perry's brother-in-law was bringing his little vessel, with two of the founder's sons aboard, from across an ocean to within range of the spot, kedging her beyond the sandbar close offshore.

The *Vandalia*, as common report here affirmed, had sailed from Cape Palmas October 5 for home. Informed of the fact, Captain Mackenzie determined to break off pursuit. He would get under way and point the bow of the *Somers* westward, delaying at Monrovia no longer than a day or two to resupply and give his crew liberty.

Accordingly, after allowing some fishing off the forecastle, he had cutters made ready the following day to row the men ashore. Midshipman Spencer was serving as officer of one of the boats, with Purser's Steward Wales aboard. "I believe," said Wales later, "Mr. Rodgers was also in the boat, though I am not sure. The commander had told Spencer before he got into the boat that he was not in uniform. He was just going into the boat as this was said. He muttered some reply, but I could not hear what it was. After we had got some twenty or thirty yards from the brig, the captain hailed us"—one imagines that proper form back on deck at the railing, speaking trumpet to his lips, calling across the water to the little cutter filled with eager men and boys, bobbing toward shore—"the captain hailed us and asked if we had the American ensign in the boat."

What's he say? What's he yelling about?

"Spencer replied that he had not got it, and added (not, however, so the captain could hear) that he'd 'be God damned if he was going back after it either, for the damned old humbug. Go to hell.' He continued cursing all the way to shore—though I cannot call to mind," said Wales, "the particular expressions that he used. I think McKinley was in the boat, and Golding also—though I am not sure. This was the second cutter. This was all that took place at that time. Spencer's remarks seemed to please the crew."

Those cheeky seamen got their liberty anyway. Henry Waltham, the mulatto wardroom steward, went ashore and in the course of his stay was handed letters to take back to New York and deliver to emigrants' friends in America. McKinley onshore got the purser to buy him a knife, a bone-handled African knife about six inches long and sharp on both sides. Others no doubt wandered over the weed-infested streets of the settlement to feel firm earth, while gaping at locals in their cast-off finery and wondering at the rediscovered strangeness of shore life: all those oxen and swine, those exotic fruits—tamarinds and soursops and papaws and guavas. And assuredly many steered for the nearest grog shop to slake their sailor's thirst.

As for young Spencer, that officer of the cutter had, according to ship's clerk Oliver Perry, used his time ashore to go see an Italian slave dealer: "I heard Mr. Spencer say that he had derived a deal of information from him. . . ."

All hands up anchor! Man the bars! Heave round!

Crew at the capstan. Cable rises slowly through the hawse hole. The anchor is short apeak.

Lay aloft to loose the sails!

Some are already in the rigging, topmen on both masts closely watching each other's movements.

Lay out!

Men scramble to positions along the yards.

All ready aloft?

Ready on the foremast. Ready on the mainmast.

Stand by. Let fall!

The heavy sails burst from their gaskets, sail being made as the anchor is calted and fished, yards are trimmed to the wind, and the brig begins to gather headway.

Fifty-five hundred miles of ocean by way of St. Thomas lie between the little vessel and New York Harbor, but never mind: we're homeward bound! Homeward bound! as astern the green line of the African coast diminishes and gradually loses color in the haze.

By slanting northwest the *Somers* leaving Africa followed the sea road that slave runners had traveled for three centuries and longer, from barracoons on that sultry coast, from those beaches into the sands of which terrified slaves had futilely dug their fingers to keep from being thrown aboard the big canoes, aboard the dread ships standing off and waiting to carry them to those same Caribbean islands from which none ever returned. Toward those islands far over the horizon the *Somers*'s bow was pointing, even as, from this same coast, bows of other ships still pointed with their illicit cargo of human souls to smuggle to the New World these thirty some years after the slave trade had been outlawed. November 11, 1842: dispatches for the *Vandalia* having been left with Dr. I. S. Day, United States agent, the naval brig-of-war under Captain Mackenzie's command leaves Cape Mesurado. Soon she will catch the trades to run before them in an autumnal passage that old salts continue to insist contains simply the very best sailing in all the world: easy days, night after easy moonlit night gliding westward in pleasant latitudes before a favoring breeze.

To be sure, the weather was warm on this, the fifth leg of the voyage. The ship's log shows midnight readings hovering around eighty degrees through the thirtieth of November. Thus, much of the off watch would be scattered now about the spar deck topside with the day's work done. Around dusk in the evening all that was needed was to take in and make sail as the rare occasion required. But for the most part the men could lounge through the second dog watch jawing together; it was, so one of them reported of this stretch of the voyage, "a very usual thing for the officers to talk with the crew after dinner about affairs at home." Others of the wardroom and steerage besides Mr. Spencer would be conversing with the men now—Mr. Deslonde, for instance, and Mr. Tillotson, with Browning, the boatswain's mate: typical talk for such a time. When exactly would they reach New York? What was the first thing they'd do when they got there?

A few evenings after leaving Cape Mesurado, Mr. Spencer on the forecastle was showing crewman William Neville how to take an altitude of the moon. In the course of the demonstration the young officer brought up the question he had asked others: would Neville sail with him when he got command of his own vessel? But such a question was growing odder as time passed, because nothing on the cruise so far suggested that the acting midshipman's future in the navy was bright. What kind of vessel did so feckless an apprentice officer imagine himself commanding?

About the twentieth of November, a week and more from Africa, Master-at-Arms Garty was sitting on the combings of the forecastle during an idle hour. On hand were a number of the crew, including Cromwell. Mr. Spencer was there too. The talk was about one thing and another, until somebody introduced the subject of the army. Garty, as he remembered, "asked Mr. Spencer if it would not be better for him to go in the Army than the Navy. He told me that his father"—that cabinet officer—"told him he would get him a lieutenant's commission in the Dragoons; that he thought he wouldn't like it, and he thought he was not going to be long in the Navy. He said he was going to have a vessel of his own shortly."

But how? From where? It would take money to get a vessel, as Spencer had himself acknowledged a few days earlier in another leisurely conversation, this time with Purser Heiskell by the forward hatch. That conversation had got onto the adolescent obsession with piracy. If I had my own band, said Spencer, and a vessel, I'd cruise the Spanish Main, never chase a ship if another was in sight, never attack if uncertain, never carry spare sails or spars on deck. Strip her down for speed; and when I grew tired of the life, I'd quit it by simply deserting the crew some night onshore.

Pirates haunted the boy's imagination still, out there with the broad seas all around him. A few days after the conversation with the purser, he was showing Midshipman Hayes a drawing he had made of a brig with a pirate's flag. "This was in the steerage. It had a black flag, with a skull and bones." Was it the *Somers* that Spencer had sketched? No, it was a hermaphrodite brig, rigged differently, but the outlaw flag flew defiantly from the masthead. And the young man had made a remark that stuck with Hayes; "he said I would have occasion to remember the name of Spencer someday."

So was that schoolboy sketch like sketches many a boy would later make of warplanes, of racing cars? And the vows of future fame: were they no more than the talk of dreamy, discontented youth in every age?

Not all was idleness and yarn spinning on shipboard. According to later report, the mood of the crew continued sulky even homeward bound; but work got done, although on at least one occasion Spencer, in charge of a work party, was negligent in attending to the task. So Commander Mackenzie adjudged. The captain called the young man aft and dressed him down. A few minutes later the junior officer returned forward in a rage. Wales was nearby. "Whatever is the matter?" the purser's steward asked, while the working party gaped and Spencer went on storming. "The commander said I did not pay attention to my duty," he was quoted by Wales as replying, "and requested me in the future to do better." But do captains request midshipmen to do better in the future? What had Mackenzie really said? "God damn him!" Spencer added, in diction that sounds more convincing. "I'd like to catch him on that roundhouse some night and plunge him overboard. God damn me if I don't do it, too."

Time at sea was not altering the low opinion skipper and acting midshipman had formed of each other. In the course of this leg of the voyage Mr. Spencer on one occasion asked Neville, apprentice whom Captain Mackenzie had rated an ordinary seaman—a promotion for the length of the cruise—did he not think the damned son of a bitch of a captain "was very hard in flogging the boys"? But no, answered Neville loyally; the captain only did his duty. Incidentally, punishments at the gratings homeward bound were continuing at the usual pace, for the usual reasons: disobedience, insolence, filthiness, fighting, skulking. Specifically, during this interval after leaving Mesurado one crew member received eight colts "for not cleaning of his battle axe"; another, nine colts "for not having his hammock lashing blacked." Spencer's question seems not unreasonable to us who consider that bleak record a century and a half later: sixteen men routinely flogged in two weeks' time.

Other signs showed discontent aboard, though perhaps no more than might have been expected two months and longer into such a voyage— and so many spirited men and boys crammed together. Third-class apprentice Peter Tyson, eighteen and on his first cruise, one early morning before daylight was lying aft between the fourth and fifth guns to the leeward side. His shipmates Willson and McKinley wandered near, as he later asserted. Willson, who had no hat on, was carrying a battle-ax and a sharpening stone. Better be careful, McKinley was saying, to which Willson had answered menacingly, "He need not fear, for he knowed him, knowed he had been in too many scrapes, and that he did not fear anything, but went right straight ahead."

Seated on the gun tackle they had begun to talk about slavers at St. Thomas. This Willson, a large, stout fellow, ship's butcher and sailmaker's mate, was of a type met with on many a naval vessel. Earlier the boy Weaver had done something for which Willson had struck him in the face. Weaver had reported the offense to the officer of the deck, Acting Master Perry. The captain, informed of it in turn, had ordered Willson flogged. Later the offender was heard muttering that he would take Weaver's life, and he would pay back the captain and the master too. Now to McKinley he had grumbled where the drowsy Tyson could overhear: "*He* knows well enough that I did not come on board this vessel willingly." No, as soon as they got to St. Thomas, Willson meant to desert, would join a slaver.

Others more consequential than the ship's butcher had got into rows lately. The hot-tempered Midshipman Spencer had had that fistfight with Midshipman Egbert Thompson in the steerage; and Acting Midshipman John Tillotson, sixteen years old, later recollected "Mr. Spencer striking me because I did not relieve him quick enough, and I struck him back." That kind of behavior from a statesman's son, a young officer reared with every advantage—that kind of behavior even as Spencer's manner toward the captain was becoming downright obsequious, so much so of late as to suggest a mocking irony.

The same could be said of Cromwell. In these recent days, so Midshipman Rodgers noted, the giant boatswain's mate "had become more obsequious when addressing an officer, while at the same time there was a sneer upon his countenance." And on at least one occasion Cromwell's contempt erupted for anybody on hand to hear. It was the twenty-third or -fourth of November. A strange sail had hove in sight, bearing down. The first lieutenant was ordering the master-at-arms and the gunner's mate to load all weapons: twenty-three flintlock muskets, twenty-eight flintlock pistols loaded, though not primed, all but six or seven muskets, which would not fit into the arms chest if pointed aft, as loaded muskets had to be. And still the pursuing vessel came on.

The captain now beat to quarters and had the brig cleared for action. Much scurrying about, assuming postures of readiness aboard: carronades run out and gun crews at their stations, shot passed up, skipper on the roundhouse peering . . .

Until the ship in pursuit had been identified as a British cruiser, misled by the sleek lines of this rakish little brig—black and sinister as she must have looked—and giving chase to what had appeared to be a slaver. The misunderstanding was soon cleared up, and aboard the *Somers* the crew resumed its normal duties—though not before Cromwell had pronounced scornfully, and loudly enough to be heard by others of the men, that "there was a damned sight of humbug about this vessel; he had been aboard vessels where shot was fired and there was not so much humbugging. . . ."

Over the ocean's blue surface a speck is moving slowly westward, the long V of its wake astern, tension aboard and time passing. Westward, homeward bound, perhaps no more than eight days from St. Thomas now. Reprovision there, then northward to be home by Christmas, to solid American earth, space to move in, city streets, Bowery taverns, farms of the surrounding countryside. And time was passing. Aboard, young Spencer leaned over candlelit charts in the wardroom, or told fortunes out of palms in the steerage, or sat on the forecastle "having marks pricked in his arms and breast"—tattoos on that fair, favored skin.

And time passed. It had gone three bells one evening. Two persons stood under the booms by the galley pipe. Dickerson the carpenter's mate was watching them: Mr. Spencer and Chief Boatswain's Mate Cromwell. "They never altered their position till I went aft, which was in about fifteen minutes." And aft, the captain was seen coming on deck. He leaned on the roundhouse through another quarter hour, seeming to muse out there in the empty darkness, taking the familiar salt-laden air aboard this benighted ship of his before moving forward to the gangway to give the order to haul in the weather fore braces . . .

Spencer had the midwatch the night of the twenty-fourth. In the course of that watch the lee main topgallant brace parted, causing the yard to swing forward. And the acting midshipman on watch never noticed. Rodgers was aft as officer of the deck. "I went on the forecastle," that more attentive youth later reported, "to discover whether it had parted or let go by mistake, and passed Mr. Spencer standing on the lee hen-coop conversing in an apparently familiar manner with John Brunt the lookout. I called the boy to hand in the running part of the brace that was towing overboard, when Mr. Spencer appeared to see me for the first time. He immediately got down and went to his station on the weather side of the forecastle. He afterwards asked me why I had braced the yard sharp up with the weather brace. I relate this as an instance of his familiarity to his inferiors and of his inattention to duty."

And that same fellow meant soon to have a vessel of his own? On the following evening—Friday it was, November 25, 1842—during the second dog, Spencer off watch was huddled once more in conversation, this time with Purser's Steward Wales. The day had been (the logbook tells us) fair and mild. Supper was over, beef kids cleared away, darkness fallen swiftly as it does in tropic latitudes. The moon shone bright. The trades were in the rigging, flutter of sail aloft. Moonshine along the tarred shrouds and backstays, black shadows of sails and spars sliding across the blanched deck with the ship's motion. Sounds of the sea swishing at the vessel's bow, darkness surrounding. And Mr. Spencer had summoned the purser's steward from the bitts forward, where Wales had been lounging, to climb aboard the booms with him, on those spars piled midships. There, against ship's orders, the two were huddled out of sight, on the starboard side forward over the forehatch. And there, around eight in the evening, young Phil Spencer had opened a fateful conversation with this chosen confidant by asking him three questions:

Do you fear death? Do you fear a dead man? Are you afraid to kill a man?

MUTINY

WHEN HE WAS BROUGHT THE REPORT, COMMANDER
Mackenzie at first dismissed it out of hand: "it seemed to me so monstrous, so improbable, that I could not forbear treating it with ridicule."
What Lieutenant Gansevoort was telling the captain had been passed on
by Purser Heiskell, who had heard it not long before direct from the
purser's steward himself. In the wardroom during quarters that morning
Mr. Wales had seated himself by his superior "as if to converse on their
joint duty." But it was not of their duty that the young man had spoken;
it was, instead, of his alarming conversation the previous night on the
booms with Midshipman Spencer.

Spencer's dark words had been tormenting Wales ever since. In fact,
he had tried last night until late to share what he had been told with
others, though without success, and thus had been required to go to his
hammock to lie among snorers of the berth deck, waiting sleeplessly for
morning. That had given him time enough to review the horrific implications of all that Spencer had confided to him.

Do you fear death? the voice had probed at his shoulder. Do you fear
a dead man? Are you afraid to kill a man?

The questions had startled Wales. Was the midshipman serious? Spencer had waited intently for an answer.

"I replied that I was not particularly anxious to die quite yet, that I had no cause to fear a dead person, and that did a man sufficiently abuse or insult me, I thought I could muster sufficient courage to kill him if necessary."

Good, very good. "I don't doubt your courage at all," the other had responded. "I know it. But"—and his voice had been, so Wales recalled, "very serious, very much in earnest"—"can you keep a secret? And will you keep one?"

If so, take the oath.

Unseen on the booms the purser's steward had taken an oath at Spencer's bidding, "administered by word of mouth, no Bible being used."

Never make known to any person the conversation about to take place between us. So help you God. Swear.

I swear.

And with that, this son of a worthy father had unfolded his plan. About twenty of the brig's company were leagued with him, so he told Wales. Names are all here, done up in my neckerchief, stations, all in a secret writing. Feel.

Wales had felt the neckerchief. A "rumpling" sound "showed that there was a paper in the back part of it."

On Spencer's person a plan of what would happen one night soon, when he had the midwatch. By arrangement "some of the men would get into a fight on the forecastle." The acting midshipman himself would intervene, lead the sham brawlers to the mast, summon Midshipman Rodgers from aft as officer of the deck to settle the matter. But as Rodgers was approaching the gangway, the men would abruptly seize him and hurl him overboard, all in a muffled instant.

"They would then have the vessel in their own possession."

At any moment, so Spencer had said, he could lay his hands on the keys to the arms chests. He would open the chests, distribute arms to his men, station them at the hatches. Swiftly, "with the least noise possible," the midshipman would move next to the after cabin and murder Commander Mackenzie, "then proceed with some of his men to the wardroom, and then murder the wardroom and steerage officers."

Eight of them in the depths of night as they slept. "He stated that the officers had no arms in the wardroom with the exception of the first lieutenant, and all the arms that he had there was an old cutlass, which he should secure before the affray commenced."

Figures advancing fast, darkly purposeful in the small hours. Bare feet hurrying back topside. Now slew the two after guns around to rake the spar deck. Call the crew up. Puzzled, scarcely awake, they would emerge one by one through narrow companionways to find armed men on station at the hatches. Select from those coming up "such as would suit his purposes"; throw the others overboard. Splashes, sea silvered briefly,

froth slipping aft into wake, screams diminishing aft, consumed in darkness. "(The words 'suit his purposes' were the very ones he used.)"

But such a scheme was preposterous. Or was it? Next morning the
captain was being informed of what the purser's steward had learned.
"Although I received the first communication with incredulity," Commander Mackenzie wrote later, "yet when I reflected upon the earnest-
ness and solemn manner in which the disclosure was made, and the
strong impression of the reality and imminence of the danger made upon
the mind of Mr. Wales himself, my doubts vanished . . ."

It had not been easy getting word to the captain, though speed had
seemed imperative. That very night of Spencer's revelation the acting
midshipman was to stand the midwatch—like the midwatch of calami-
tous enactments planned for some night soon. He had said as much to
Small. Seaman Small had been passing near last night, and Spencer had
called to him. "He came and stood by the railing, but did not get up on
the booms." Those two had talked together in Spanish, which Wales
could not understand. But he could see Small's face, saw the look of
surprise. Spencer had reassured his crony in English. Oh, you need have
no fear of Mr. Wales. "I have sounded him pretty well and find he is one
of us." The sailmaker had looked pleased—"I saw Small's face very plainly"—and said he was glad to hear it. The two would talk later tonight, on
Spencer's midwatch, but Small was to " 'see that foretopman' meantime.
(He did not name him.)"

After the seaman had left, talk between Spencer and Wales had
resumed. Having taken possession of the ship, the mutineers would make
the "small fry"—those useless thirteen- and fourteen-year-olds who ate
up biscuit—walk the plank, and would heave overboard spare spars and
launches that only lumbered up the decks. Strip her down. Race west to
Cape San Antonio or the Isle of Pines, there "take on board *one who was
familiar with their intended business, and who was ready and willing to join
them.*" Then commence cruising for prizes: "whenever they took a vessel,
after taking from her that which would be of use to them, they were to
murder all on board and scuttle the vessel, so as to leave no traces of her."
Dead men tell no tales was the motto. And "should there be any females on
board . . . they would have them removed to the brig for the use of the
officers and men—using them as long as they saw fit, and then making
way with them . . ."

What did the purser's steward, promised the rank of third officer,
think of the plan? "I thought it prudent to dissemble . . . told him that I
was favorably disposed toward it." But by then they had been on the
booms an hour or more. His duties called Wales. "Spencer remarked that
we would have another interview on the morrow, when he would show
me the plan he had drawn up. He followed me to the gangway saying

that if I lisped a syllable of what he had communicated to me I should be murdered; that if he did not do it himself those connected with him would; that go where I might my life would not be worth a straw."

But you could count on the purser's steward: "No, I would not make any mention of it."

By that time it was about nine at night. Spencer had gone below to turn in. Wales went aft, "as far aft as the cabin, intending to communicate the intelligence to Commander Mackenzie, but I observed that Small was watching me closely." Turn back; down through the steerage to the wardroom. "But there I was again put off"; for Spencer, whose hammock hung in the steerage over the wardroom door, raised his head and demanded to know "what the devil I was about, cruising around there." Wales had pretended to be heading for the purser's storeroom beyond, did so and then returned above deck. "About one hour after, I went again to the steerage and found Spencer still awake." Beyond him now the lights were out, for "the ward-room gentlemen had retired."

So the steward must sleep with his fears until morning. In fact, Wales "did not go to sleep, though I tried. In the morning, as soon as I could get in, before breakfast (about 7 o'clock I should think), I communicated the matter to Purser Heiskell," seated beside him in the wardroom—"in a low voice," as his superior remembered—"and then went on deck and told the first lieutenant that the purser wished to see him immediately . . ."

Lieutenant Gansevoort recalled that meeting with Wales at the fore-hatch as having occurred at about ten o'clock; but in any case the second-in-command had gone directly below, Wales following to open the door of the purser's storeroom, which nearly closed the entrance into the wardroom and thus allowed the two gentlemen to talk unobserved. The purser "asked me," as Gansevoort remembered, "if I was aware that a plot existed on board to take the vessel out of the hands of her officers and murder them all?" He had been aware of nothing of the kind. However, as the lieutenant listened to what Mr. Heiskell proceeded to tell him (Spencer could be seen beyond the door in the steerage, so that the purser worried lest he might be attending), Gansevoort grew alarmed, enough so that he did not linger to hear all that Mr. Heiskell had to say, but went straight topside and aft to the captain's cabin to make a report.

For would not this discovery explain the otherwise inexplicable behavior of the crew since leaving Funchal?

Commander Mackenzie in that tiny space at the ship's stern (it measured two feet wide at its entrance aft, and was eight feet long, eight feet at its forward bulkhead, with ladder and lockers to reduce the room further)—there in his cabin the captain received the news, as Lieutenant Gansevoort remembered, "with great coolness." Indeed, Mackenzie himself explained later: "I was under the impression that Mr. Spencer had been reading some piratical stories and had amused himself with Mr. Wales."

Even so, as he went on to note, "this was joking on an improper theme."

Should the first lieutenant question Wales?

No, the captain thought not. Keep a lookout on Mr. Spencer; watch him today without seeming to do so. Commander Mackenzie was, of course, duty-bound to be on his guard, "lest there should be a shadow of reality in this project." So keep close watch on Mr. Spencer, and on the rest of the crew as well.

What Lieutenant Gansevoort learned from his day's scrutiny was not reassuring. Part of that morning Spencer passed "rather sullenly in one corner of the steerage, as was his custom, engaged in examining a small piece of paper and writing on it with his pencil, and occasionally finding relaxation in working with a penknife at the tail of a devil-fish, one of the joints of which he had formed into a sliding ring for his cravat." But what had the man been writing? And where did he disappear to at dinnertime, when the lieutenant suddenly became aware that he was missing from the deck? "This was about 2 o'clock." Up there in the foretop: wasn't that Spencer? Gansevoort climbed the rigging to see what the midshipman was about.

He was "sitting on the lee side of the top, with his chin resting on his breast—apparently in deep thought. He did not observe me till I had got into the top and was standing erect. He raised his head, and as soon as he discovered me got up and evinced some confusion. He asked me some questions about the rigging, and about the foremast head, which I answered in my usual manner."

But did Mr. Spencer mean to dine today? Dinner was ready in the steerage.

No, he didn't care about it just then.

So, leaving the other aloft, the lieutenant returned to the deck; and an hour later, back on deck with the crew slinging clean hammocks, he observed that the midshipman was still up there. Apprentice Benjamin Green had joined him—with India ink was pricking love devices in Spencer's arm. "I hailed the top," Gansevoort was to report, "and ordered Green to come out. Mr. Spencer put his head over the top-rail, and from his manner I thought he wished Green to remain"—to finish the tattoo?—"though he asked no question. I repeated the order, and then ordered Spencer to send Green and other men that might be in the top on deck. Green came down immediately but no others. Spencer remained in the top."

The first lieutenant next ordered Green to sling his hammock. "He answered that he had done so already. I was engaged in mustering the men for the purpose of having the hammocks stowed. When I got abreast of the Jacob's ladder on the starboard side forward, I observed Mr. Spencer sitting on the ladder. I turned my eye towards him—"

And a chilling, protracted exchange took place, in perfect silence. Glancing toward Spencer, the first lieutenant had "immediately caught his eye, which he kept staring upon me"—that crooked eye—"for more than a minute, *with the most infernal expression I have ever seen upon a human face. It satisfied me at once of the man's guilt.*"

No doubt about it from that time forward; as far as Mr. Gansevoort was concerned, the mind behind those glaring, divergent eyes in the refined face of the statesman's son could coolly resolve on committing murder.

Hammocks stowed, the first lieutenant went aft at once to report to the commander.

Captain Mackenzie heard him out. Mr. Gansevoort was recommending that something be done: Spencer should be secured. But the captain "did not wish to do anything hastily." By evening quarters he would decide what it was best to do, meanwhile maintaining a sharp lookout.

In the course of that afternoon the commander was made aware of additional troubling information, either by Mr. Gansevoort himself or by others of the ship's company. For one thing, young Spencer, it was learned, "had been endeavoring for some days to ascertain the rate of the chronometer by applying to Midshipman Rodgers, to whom it was unknown and who referred him to the master. He had been seen in secret and nightly conferences with boatswain's mate S. Cromwell and seaman Elisha Small. I also heard that he had given money to several of the crew . . ." Wales had been told (what was not true) that the box brought aboard with such care at Funchal, ostensibly containing rare wine, contained in fact money; according to Spencer, "the commander had a large amount of money on board. This, he said, with what the purser had, would make a pretty little sum to commence with." And there was that other disturbing business with Rodgers, who would have the midwatch when the mutiny was to be set in motion. Spencer "had quite recently examined the hand of Midshipman Rodgers, told his fortune, and predicted for him a speedy and violent death." That, and the young man's drinking. And the drawing he had made of a pirate brig. And a report that he had been heard to declare, "that it would give him real pleasure to roll me"—the captain—"overboard from the roundtop." And—yet more —one singular occasion in the wardroom a few days earlier, with Purser Heiskell lounging on the first lieutenant's bunk, Surgeon Leecock at the table. Spencer had come in. The doctor had been examining charts of the coast of Africa and the West Indies. Did Mr. Leecock know where the Isle of Pines was? Spencer was curious. "I told him it was somewhere on the coast of Cuba, and I believe I asked him at the time if he knew anybody there, and remarked that I had heard it was a great piratical resort. Mr. Spencer made no further observation that I know of, but continued for some time looking over the chart . . ." So the surgeon remembered; so the purser confirmed.

But why Wales? Why attempt to seduce from his duty that particular member of the ship's company? On reflection, the answer seemed obvious. Not only was the purser's steward currently acting as master-at-arms (the "sheriff" aboard, and in charge of the berth deck, where the crew slept) during a bout of sickness that had laid Sergeant Garty low. Wales might also be presumed to bear a grudge against his captain, since the two had fallen out during the *Somers*'s shakedown cruise to Puerto Rico last June. Everyone aboard knew that: some unspecified dissatisfaction on Commander Mackenzie's part with the way the steward had been performing his duties, grave enough to have led to a threat of dismissal on their return to New York—though the threat had not been carried out, and Wales had shipped again, on this second cruise. But as a malcontent? No doubt Spencer presumed so.

So what steps should the captain take now, to deal with this matter that Wales had reported? Mackenzie recalled what he had heard of Spencer's "scandalous conduct" in the Brazilian squadron, what he himself had heard and observed since the young man's coming aboard. Jaw music. Coins on deck. "These various recollections, added to what had been revealed to me, determined me to make sure at once of his person, though I had before meditated allowing Mr. Wales to have another interview with him that evening, for the purpose of ascertaining more of his plans . . ."

But evening was almost upon them. As the time of muster approached —it was just before the drumbeat to quarters—the captain conferred again with his first lieutenant: "he asked me," Gansevoort recalled, "what I would do if I were in his situation as commander of the vessel. I told him that I would bring that young man aft (alluding to Mr. Spencer) and iron him and keep him on the quarter deck. He told me that that was the course which he intended to pursue; and that he was very glad to find that I agreed with him. . . ."

Evening quarters aboard the brig-of-war *Somers* in mid-Atlantic, Saturday, November 26, 1842. Captain's Clerk O. H. Perry relays the captain's orders. Mr. Hayes to remain at his station on the forecastle. All other officers lay aft. Any crew stationed abaft of midships lay forward to the mainmast. The sailing master, third in command, is ordered to take the wheel.

Crew at their stations. Officers and warrant officers assemble on the quarterdeck. The captain approaches Acting Midshipman Philip Spencer.

"I learn, Mr. Spencer, that you aspire to the command of the *Somers*?"

"Oh, no, sir."

The boy's answer was deferential, his expression (as the captain noted) "gently smiling," his manner "unmoved."

"Did you not tell Mr. Wales, sir, that you had a project to kill the commander, the officers, and a considerable portion of the crew of this vessel and convert her into a pirate?"

"I may have told him so, sir, but it was in joke."

"You admit then that you told him so?"

"Yes, sir; but in joke."

"This, sir," said Captain Mackenzie, "is joking on a forbidden subject. This joke may cost you your life. Be pleased to remove your neck handkerchief."

Take Mr. Spencer home a prisoner, see him tried. Any officer who shall begin, excite, cause, or join in any mutiny in the ship to which he belongs shall suffer death or such punishment . . .

The midshipman had removed his neckerchief as ordered, was handing it to the first lieutenant. Gansevoort opened it.

Nothing inside.

What, asked the captain, have you done with the paper you told Mr. Wales of?

"It is a paper containing my day's work"—navigational calculations—"and I have destroyed it."

"It is a singular place to keep a day's work in."

"It is a convenient one," Spencer replied blandly, still deferential.

"You must have been aware," said the captain, "that you could only have compassed your designs by passing over my dead body, and after that, the bodies of all the officers. You had given yourself, sir, a great deal to do. It will be necessary for me to confine you, sir."

Commander Mackenzie turned to Mr. Gansevoort. "Arrest Mr. Spencer," he said, "and put him in double irons."

At the command the first lieutenant stepped forward and relieved the acting midshipman of his sword. Spencer was then ordered "to come out from among the officers. He did so." With Wales as master-at-arms gone to fetch irons below, the young man under arrest obligingly began rolling up his sleeves. Did he have other weapons on him? Spencer answered the first lieutenant that "he had not, but perhaps I had better overhaul him, as he supposed I would not believe anything he said." He was searched. Nothing was found but scraps of paper and part of an old pipe.

Fetters having been produced, the prisoner was next ordered to sit on the sternpost. Double irons were fixed to his ankles, handcuffs clamped around his wrists—a humiliation "to which he appeared willing to submit." There was, according to Wales, no conversation. Unable to walk now, the encumbered officer was led to the larboard arms chest and seated beside it on a campstool.

There, for want of a better, was to be his place of incarceration, on deck in full view. Where else? Not in the suffocating hold. Not on the berth deck or in the tiny steerage or wardroom or captain's cabin. Where else could he be placed aboard? Lieutenant Gansevoort was being ordered to "watch over his security," see that the prisoner had "every comfort which his safekeeping would admit of." But should he attempt to communicate in any way with others of the crew, by word or by sign, he was to be put instantly to death.

Spencer, too, was informed of those orders. His very life henceforth depended on silence.

Now, so the captain noted, "Mr. Spencer being confined, the officers were remanded to their quarters, the crew and battery inspected, the ordinary reports made to the first lieutenant, and by him to me, and the retreat beaten."

But not before Small had been questioned, summoned from forward and asked what he knew of the affair. The sailmaker admitted to talking with Spencer, but denied knowing anything about a mutiny. He was allowed to return to his station. And forward the crew after quarters were gathering in threes and fours, studying the singular sight of an officer in irons at the stern. Was it for fighting with Midshipman Thompson in the steerage? Willson, McKinley, others huddled together. Was he in irons for fighting with another reefer?

Now hear this: all hands stay clear of the quarterdeck except on duty! All hands stay well forward!

Midshipman Hayes at his station on the bow had meanwhile been noticing one man in particular. During Spencer's arrest Boatswain's Mate Cromwell had "assumed the utmost indifference as to what was going on"—leaning against the bitts, hat over his eyes—"and gave me the impression that he knew what Mr. Spencer was confined for, while the rest of the crew were looking aft and appeared desirous of knowing what was going on. Cromwell was on the forecastle at the time, and remained there until I ordered him below to move the iron chest."

That chest containing the fetters, which usually sat in the space where the crew slept, was now to be lugged into the wardroom. Other changes would occur to promote the ship's safety. Hereafter, no clubbing on the berth deck. Handcuffs and double irons were to be examined every half hour by lifting the prisoner's wrists and ankles. Officers of the watch would go armed with cutlasses and pistols, would make frequent rounds topside and below "to see that the crew were in their hammocks, and that there were no suspicious collections of individuals about the decks."

And the prisoner's locker would be overhauled.

Down the forward hatch of the trunk house to the steerage space, midshipmen's quarters: eight feet by fourteen, part taken up by the pump housing and a table. Five warrant officers were supposed to sleep there, though seven were aboard, with the result that "the two oldest and most useful"—Mr. Rodgers and Mr. Thompson—had had no locker to put their clothes in, and had slept "on the steerage deck, the camp stools, the booms in the tops, or in the quarter-boats" throughout the cruise.

In the steerage, over the after door that led to the wardroom, was where Spencer's hammock had been slung, where last evening he had lain and caught Wales "cruising about." This evening the acting midshipman would not swing that triced-up hammock there, or on any other evening before the voyage ended. He would nap through nights as best he could in irons on deck, on the gathering dew of the arms chest till they could get him home to trial.

Here was his locker. On captain's orders Lieutenant Gansevoort opened it.

Letters inside, from the young man's father, one from a certain Eliza. Letters from his mother. And a shaving case with a looking glass. Mr. Gansevoort was examining the case as Mr. Rodgers and other officers watched—saw him pull out the drawer, remove a piece of paper of the sort used to wrap around razors. The instrument itself was missing, but inside the paper the searchers came upon Spencer's list.

Two sheets, creased and soiled, one torn from a geometry book. Columns—unmistakably a list of some sort, and in Spencer's hand, though the script was unreadable. Was it Greek? Did anybody know Greek?

Mr. Rodgers did, and would oblige by undertaking a translation. But soon the midshipman was discovering that he need do no more than transliterate words: ςμιθ to Smith, Αρμ χέοι to Arm ches*l*, or arms chest, ςμαλλ to Small.

The two papers transliterated were found to contain on one sheet station assignments, on the other, three groups of names, one under "Certain," another under "Doubtful," a third "To be kept, nolens volens." Obviously names of accomplices: four (including the names of Wales and Spencer himself) who could be counted on for certain, eighteen men to be kept whether willing or not (including θε Δοχιερ, The Doctor), and ten who were "doubtful," though of those last, four had crosses by their names, indicating (so the list spelled out) who "uill probablu be induked to Goin, bephore the progek*l* is karried in*l*o ekeku*l*ion. The remaindor oph the Dou*l*phul will probablu Goin uen the thing is done; iph no*l*, theu mus*l* be phorced." And a closing thought: "Iph anu no*l* marked doun, wish *l*o Goin aph*l*er i*l* is done, ue uill pich ou*l* the bes*l* and dispose oph the res*l*." Or as it read in the original:

Ιφ αυυ υοι μαρχεδ δουυ, υις῾ιο τοιυ αφιερ
ιι ις δουε, υε υιλλ πιχ ουι θε βεςι αυδ
διςποςε οφ θε ρεςι.

Throughout, as Rodgers noted, Roman S was used for Greek Σ, Roman italic *l* for Greek *τ*. But otherwise the message was transparent enough, and the ship's good fortune seemed God-given: among these were the very men—Spencer's "chickens," as Captain's Clerk Perry promptly dubbed them—to keep close watch over till the cruise was done.

These and one other, whose name oddly enough did not appear on Spencer's lists. But the carpenter's mate and the gunner's mate both thought him the most dangerous of all, and were not long in telling Mr. Gansevoort so. "The next day in the morning I had a conversation with some of the men whom I suppose to be true," so the first lieutenant remembered, "though I am not positive that it was not the evening of Spencer's arrest." Dickerson, the carpenter, said "that big fellow forward is more dangerous than the rest; he ought to be confined." The chief boatswain's mate. Cromwell. "I am positive that Dickerson and King, in that and all other conversations I had with them up to Cromwell's arrest" —for he would be arrested—"impressed me with the belief that it was necessary to have him confined; and after that they appeared relieved. They said they believed him to be dangerous and desired that he might be ironed."

He would be, whether the Greek lists named him or not. There was, for instance, that earlier business with the singlesticks the carpenter had made for Mr. Gansevoort and gone to store in the boatswain's locker. Words had passed. Ascending the ladder Dickerson had registered Cromwell's surly threat: *"I'll pay you for this before long."* For storing sticks in the locker? Your time's damn short. The carpenter brought that exchange to the first lieutenant's attention now. And Mr. Gansevoort himself was remembering instances of Cromwell's insubordination—one night in particular, when the lacings had jammed in the stays while the headsails were being hauled down. "God damn the jib and stay," the chief boatswain's mate had cried out for all to hear, "and the damned fool that invented it." For that remark the first lieutenant had reproved him severely, for Cromwell had known the captain himself had devised that particular fitting, "as I," Mr. Gansevoort, "had told him of it before. When I reproved him for this and other offences, his manner was sullen. . . ."

Sullen, and often disrespectful, and on occasion menacing. King, the gunner, Dickerson, "I think Browning, and Anderson, captain of the forecastle . . . all thought Cromwell the *most dangerous man concerned in the plot*. I had several conversations with them every day"—doubtless including this day immediately after Mr. Spencer's arrest, with the sun finally up on a Sunday, November 27, over the empty sea, the anxious ship, the arms chest at the stern portside whereon a prisoner in officer's uniform sat complacently with a first night in double irons behind him.

Commotion on deck. Four bells of the morning watch: crew mustering for inspection. Commander Mackenzie takes his station aft, "with the intention of particularly observing Cromwell and Small," Mr. Spencer's closest cronies. For Small was already implicated; and someone—he or Cromwell?—had tried to communicate with the prisoner during the night. In what way, for what purpose the record leaves hazy. In any case, this morning the captain meant to look those two men over narrowly, where they were mustering as usual in the third division on the afterpart of the quarterdeck.

"The persons of both," he was to discover, "were faultlessly clean; they were determined that their appearance in this respect should provoke no reproof. Cromwell"—facing starboard—"stood up to his full stature, his muscles braced, his battle-axe grasped resolutely, his cheek pale, but his eye fixed, as if indifferently, on the other side. He had a determined and dangerous air." And Small? "Small made a very different figure. His appearance was ghastly, he shifted his weight from side to side, and his battle-axe passed from one hand to the other; his eye wandered irresolutely, but never toward mine. I attributed his conduct to fear. . . ."

And rightly so. For fear was what the doctor concluded had brought that same Elisha Small to sick bay these last two mornings. Friday night had been when the sailmaker had learned from Mr. Spencer on the booms that their plan was being shared with Wales, huddled in moonlight at the acting midshipman's side. Later that same night Wales was approaching the captain's cabin—had veered off only after noticing Small's stare upon him. Already Spencer's crony must have felt alarmed. The purser's steward thought so; at least by next morning, in the difficult process of getting what he had learned passed on to others, Wales had found himself being "watched as closely as possible by Small, Cromwell, Wilson, McKinley, and Spencer, and therefore kept out of the way of the officers as much as possible. These men I frequently noticed clubbing together, and I believe they knew I was playing them false."

If so, that may have been what had sent Small to sick bay that morning, which was Saturday. He had complained to Surgeon Leecock of nausea and vomiting. The doctor had put him on the list and given him medicine. And again the following morning—this morning, Sunday—Small was back, with the same complaint. "From his appearance, tone of voice, and the quivering of his hand when I felt his pulse," Leecock would later recall, "I perceived he was laboring under manifest fear and anxiety." But by this time Mr. Spencer had been arrested on Wales's evidence that implicated Small; the surgeon, who knew that, was canny. He checked with other crew members. Had anyone on the berth deck seen Small throw up? "Nobody having seen him do so, and believing he was feigning sickness, I refused," said the doctor later, "to keep him on the list longer and discharged him."

Here, then, was Seaman Small, this same morning at Sunday inspection, shifting his weight, his eyes, his battle-ax, making an irresolute and "ghastly" appearance before Commander Mackenzie. Such a demeanor led the captain to reach his own conclusions about the little sailmaker demoted from quartermaster: "I have since been led to believe that the business upon which he had entered was repugnant to his nature, though the love of money and of rum had been too strong for his fidelity. . . ."

Beat retreat from quarters. Church was being rigged—jury-rigged altar, shot boxes put out for seats. Commander Mackenzie later recalled something unusual about the crew's behavior: they "mustered up with their prayer books and took their seats without waiting for all hands to be called, and considerably before five bells, or half past ten, the usual time of divine service." Were they expecting to hear some explanation of the spectacle on the arms chest? Mr. Gansevoort came to report that all was ready, and to ask if he should call all hands to muster. No, replied the captain, intent on following routine in these extraordinary circumstances. "I told him to wait for the accustomed hour."

It came. The men were called, and the captain emerged and mounted the trunk house to conduct the service. Nothing was said about events of the previous evening. "The crew were unusually attentive," Commander Mackenzie remembered of that occasion, "and the responses more than commonly audible. The muster succeeded, and I examined very carefully the countenances of the crew, without discovering anything that gave me distrust." These were, after all, men he himself had chosen from the receiving ship, for (in his words) "their physical appearance and their indications of health, activity, intelligence and spirit." All might yet be well, even with Spencer's accomplices lurking among them.

How many days until home? Three weeks yet? Ship's position just after midnight that had opened this Sunday was Lat. 13°24'16" N, Long. 41°24'45" W, making good progress, though still some twelve hundred miles east of Barbados.

Then, during the afternoon, between three and four, the wind slackened.

Intent on maintaining speed, Captain Mackenzie instructed the officer of the deck to increase sail. Mr. Hayes gave the order: set skysails and royal studdingsails. Fifteen-year-old Ward Gagely, "one of the best and most skillful of our apprentices," hurried aloft to the topmost part of the ship, a hundred and more feet up, to set the sails, while hands on deck lined up to haul.

The sails were the slightest of the ship's outfit, the topmost sails on spars scarcely thicker than broom handles. "In going large," the captain later explained, "I had always been very particular to have no strain on the light braces leading forward, as the tendency of such a strain was to carry away the light yards and masts." And yet in setting these sails, with the brig proceeding at seven knots and more, what did Small think he was doing there at the forefife rail, suddenly jerking the weather main-royal brace, hauling on the very line that should have stayed slack? And Gagely was still aloft, high on the main-royal yard.

Mr. Gansevoort, Mr. Rodgers, and Acting Master Perry were in the wardroom when the top of the mast went. They could hear the crack, the commotion on deck, the scampering of feet, Mr. Hayes's urgent voice: "Belay! Belay!" and the captain, leaping from the roundhouse, urgently repeating the order: "Belay there! Belay!"

Looking through the skylight and up the hatch, officers below beheld the main-topgallant mast dangling. Topsail, gallant staysail, head-gaff topsail, and rigging all were flapping loose aloft, the mast buckled at the upper part of the sheave hole of the topgallant yard rope. And Gagely? "I scarcely dared to look on the booms or in the larboard gangway, where he should have fallen," the captain himself recalled of that instant. "For a minute I was in intense agony"—his mind visited perhaps with that long-ago day on the *Java* when, before the horrified gaze of a novice twelve-year-old—as Alex Slidell was then—a rotted mast had snapped and tumbled five seamen to their deaths below on guns and boats and overboard. But this time the alert Gagely had caught hold of the royal-shroud when the topmast went, had fallen on the belly of the topgallant sail and somehow climbed his way back to the topgallant yard. Indeed, the captain could see through the sail the shadow of the boy rising rapidly toward the yard, which remained at the masthead. A moment later, and Gagely was sliding deftly to the deck by the yard rope, unharmed.

At the time Commander Mackenzie felt no suspicion "that the carrying away of this mast was the work of treachery." But it would be just such an occasion, as he did promptly realize—"the loss of a boy overboard, or an accident to a spar, creating confusion and interrupting the regularity of duty—which was like to be taken advantage of by the conspirators, were they still bent on the prosecution of their enterprise." Accordingly, he moved at once to restore order. The first lieutenant was directed to take the deck. The wreck was sent down from aloft, and all hands kept busy unreeving and coiling down the rigging, bending sails afresh to the yards, scraping and slushing the spare topgallant mast, cutting the fid hole.

But as this necessary work was going forward, the commander was astonished to discover "all those who were most conspicuously named in the programme of Mr. Spencer, no matter in what part of the vessel they might be stationed, mustered at the maintop masthead": Small and Will-son (Υιλλςον) among others, including Cromwell, animated perhaps, as Mackenzie noted dryly, "by some new-born zeal in the service of their country"—or had they collected aloft out of earshot "for the purpose of conspiring"? To the captain, the coincidence of those very men together on the canted mast high over the quarterdeck "confirmed the existence of a dangerous conspiracy, suspended, yet perhaps not abandoned." All the more likely because of Mr. Spencer's behavior at the arms chest during the disruption, his gaze traveling perpetually to the masthead, his eye casting thither "many of those strange and stealthy glances which I had heretofore noticed."

It took the rest of the afternoon to clear the wreck and prepare the replacement rigging. Supper was piped before the new mast could be sent up. After supper, quarters having been dispensed with as night closed in, the same assembly of suspicious crewmen could be seen at their singular muster in the now dusky maintop. It grew dark. Hands worked as fast as they could to fid the new topgallant mast, cross the light yards, set the sail.

But while the work was going forward, the ship's observant captain must have had a lot on his mind. Last night in the closeness of his cabin he would have studied Spencer's remarkable list with care, would have put a face to each name in the lamplight, so that today he had known very well which ones were implicated. As well as he knew what piracy was, this New York merchant's son who in his own young manhood, in Commodore Porter's squadron, had chased pirates bedeviling commerce near these very waters. And his travels since then had taught him what ruffians were, too, and thieves, and murderers. This morning the muster —those youngsters lined up, among them the ghastly Small and the dangerous, stolid chief boatswain's mate. And later the mast snapping, Gagely scrambling along the far side of the sail up there, and afterward the conspirators aloft together doing little to help. The wreck cleared; supper; and after supper the same ones reassembled until darkness had hidden them.

Under the circumstances it seemed "scarcely safe to leave Cromwell at large during the night: the night was the season of danger." With the mate still aloft, Commander Mackenzie was consulting his first lieutenant. Both agreed that Cromwell should be confined. Mr. Gansevoort would hail the top and order him down. But the captain said no, wait till he came down of his own accord, then bring him aft.

Meanwhile, they would be ready for him and the others when they did descend.

During that interval Acting Master Perry recalled being in the wardroom when the lieutenant came to him with a pistol and cutlass and told him to take station on the starboard gangway: "he was going to confine Cromwell," who was on the cap of the mast at work. Midshipman Rodgers remembered that Mr. Gansevoort "armed each of the officers with pistols and a cutlass and stationed me at the gangway, with orders to watch that rigging strictly, as he expected they would come down that way. They however came down the weather rigging," Cromwell's voice audible in the top descending. And no sooner had the foot of the boatswain's mate touched the Jacob's ladder than Mr. Ganesvoort was aiming his cocked Colt pistol at the bewhiskered giant; "and when he got on deck I told him the captain wished to see him."

If Cromwell was surprised at that reception—"all the officers . . . armed . . . stationed about the mast on different parts of the deck ready for action"—he was doubtless even more taken aback when the lieutenant's firearm went off, the report reverberating loudly over the astonished faces on board and out to the surrounding nighttime vacancies. Fortunately the lieutenant had lowered the weapon, so that the accidental discharge propelled the bullet harmlessly into the deck. But the accident was enough to encourage prompt compliance in the boatswain's mate, now being marched aft to the dimly lit quarterdeck to learn what his captain wanted.

At the quarterdeck Cromwell was ordered to sit down on the trunk. Had he not tried to communicate with Mr. Spencer last night?

"It was not me, sir; it was Small."

Nevertheless, the commander (so Mr. Gansevoort recalled) told the boatswain's mate "that there were many suspicions about him, and that he considered it necessary to confine him. He was told by the commander that he would be confined in the same way with Mr. Spencer, and taken home, where he would be tried by the laws of his country and acquitted if he was innocent. If guilty he would be punished."

Cromwell made no objection, other than to reiterate his innocence of wrongdoing: "Yes, sir; but I don't know anything about this. I assure you that I don't know anything about it."

And in fact soon afterward Mr. Spencer himself was sending urgently to speak with the first lieutenant. On his larboard perch the midshipman would have been near enough to see if not hear what had been going on, see Cromwell being led in irons athwartships and seated beside the starboard arms chest. Had he been arrested because of their earlier intimacy? "Cromwell is innocent," said Spencer. "That is the truth, Mr. Gansevoort."

But a court back home would determine the truth. Meanwhile, Elisha Small had been arrested as well, having been "pointed out by an associate"—Cromwell, just a few minutes ago—"to increased suspicion." With the chief boatswain's mate secured, the captain had again been conferring with his first lieutenant. Was it not best to confine the sailmaker as well? "I told him I thought it was, and he then told me to order him aft. Nearly the same conversation then passed as with Cromwell. The commander told him he would be confined as the others were, brought home and tried. Small did not deny having had conversation with Spencer. The captain said to him, 'Spencer has talked with you about the plot,' in which Small acquiesced and said Yes sir. He did not deny it and made no objection to being confined."

So they had ironed the demoted quartermaster and placed him on the starboard deck aft of the No. 5 gun, not far from where Cromwell sat. The mood aboard was tense. All the officers, having been issued pistols and cartouches and cutlasses to arrest the boatswain's mate, would henceforth wear those bulky arms night and day.

Work resumed. The new mast was being pointed, was about to be swayed from the deck. Mr. Gansevoort and the captain were standing on the larboard side of the quarterdeck, at the after end of the trunk. "We were in conversation," the lieutenant remembered. "It was dark at this time. I heard an unusual noise—"

But what was it? A crowd, a mob of seamen abruptly rushing aft, all of a sudden, down both gangways!—"a rushing on deck, and saw a body of men in each gangway rushing aft toward the quarterdeck."

"God," screamed the lieutenant, "I believe they are coming."

Seize the two officers at the roundhouse! Kill them! Overboard with them! Free Mr. Spencer! Take possession of the vessel!

Mr. Gansevoort drew his Colt pistol and cocked it. The commander's pistols were below. As Mackenzie ducked through the darkness to his cabin for arms, "I jumped on the trunk and ran forward to meet them. As I was going along I sung out to them not to come aft. I told them I would blow the first man's brains out who would put his foot on the quarterdeck. I held my pistol pointed at the tallest man I saw in the starboard gangway . . ."

That would be Willson; and as Gansevoort pointed the barrel of the weapon at him, another voice was heard bellowing from forward, Mr. Rodgers's, desperately, even as the lieutenant felt the trigger nestled at his forefinger:

"It is me, sir; I am sending the men aft"!

One voice alone from that crowd had called out, even as the captain was reemerging armed with his brace of pistols, ready abaft Mr. Gansevoort by the after gun. O but they must make no such unusual movements aboard. Not now, not at this time, not with the ship in this condition. The lieutenant hesitated, then returned the Colt to its holster. "They knew the state of the vessel, and might get their brains blown out."

Thus in the darkness, after that nerve-wracking interruption, hands would haul the new rigging into place, while three prisoners chained on the quarterdeck watched the proceedings.

Night was the season of danger. With darkness upon them again, Midshipman Rodgers noticed—and others confirmed it—that the behavior of many of the men had grown worse. "The change was very marked. The elder part of the crew would collect together in knots about the vessel, and were slow to obey the orders of the officers. Their looks were sullen. If an officer approached one of these knots, they would sometimes remain together and their tone of voice would become louder." What they were saying, according to Apprentice William Neville, concerned the arrests: "The greater part of the crew seemed dissatisfied, and gathered about the decks talking about Spencer, Cromwell, and Small. They said they thought it was not right to put them in irons." George Warner, another apprentice, went so far as to speak directly to Sergeant Garty, up out of his sickbed to resume his duties as master-at-arms, though he hardly felt able to. This same evening he heard from Warner that "there was great work going on. I said there was no more than I thought was necessary. He made a remark that the officer of the deck was armed with three pistols and the officer of the forecastle with one. He said what would *we* do if they made a rush on them in the midwatch. I told him," so Garty remembered, "I thought thirteen or fourteen of them would drop if they did. That was all the conversation I had with him, but it excited my suspicion. . . ."

Understandably so. Throughout the ship suspicion and fear were rampant. "I feared a rescue would be made very much," Gunner's Mate Henry King admitted, "and was afraid to turn into my hammock at night. The men were about the deck and we did not know who to trust." After the confinement of those three on the quarterdeck, "we could not get much rest," he said; "we did not get our usual rest. I was afraid to go to sleep I had such a dread on my mind."

Thus passed a second long night, bells sounding every half hour, ship creaking eerily, the watch changed at midnight, again with fuss at four. Below in the berth deck those in outboard hammocks lay listening to the sweep and gurgle of seas just beyond the bulkhead, inches away. Any sudden noise alarmed, hearts standing still.

Then during the morning watch, sometime after four, activity on deck: a sail sighted on the larboard bow, standing southwest. The *Somers* on her course (N 65° W) would make no effort to overhaul her: another little world out there, orderly innocence afloat, sound sleepers aboard as her sails were diminishing, were lost to view.

After sunrise Monday morning, November 28. Swabbing the decks, scouring them. Was this when Mr. Spencer requested pen and paper? One morning he did, of the first lieutenant: "He wished to keep an account of the occurrences which took place." Mr. Gansevoort would ask the captain—though "of course it was not allowed." The lieutenant's impression, "and I think I communicated it to the commander," was "that he would probably make use of it to communicate with the crew." No, "it was at once refused. This conversation, I think, sprung up some morning when he was taken out of his irons to wash himself, which was done every morning; he was asked if he wanted anything . . ."

So far two nights, one day ironed on the arms chest, the son of the secretary of war. Home lay three weeks ahead, and another day commencing.

On this morning that began a new week, "two crimes of considerable magnitude appeared on the master-at-arm's report of prisoners." Captain Mackenzie in his cabin was studying the report. "Charles Lambert, apprentice, had been guilty of theft, in stealing sinnit for a hat from Ward M. Gagely [sennit is cordage formed by pleating strands of rope], and Henry Waltham, the wardroom steward, had stolen brandy from the wardroom mess and given it to Mr. Spencer. These," says the captain in words that sound excessive, though doubtless they reflect the mood aboard—"these were vile offences. The present was not a time to bring the discipline of the vessel to a stand, and the prisoners were both punished to the extent of the law."

Thus in the logbook:

> 28—Chas. Lambert, app., 12 cats stealing.
> Henry Waltham, seaman, 12 cats stealing.

That would have been around nine, at morning quarters. The name of Waltham, the mulatto, had appeared on the Greek paper: Υαλλάμ, "to be kept nolens volens." But like others' since the imprisonments, his manner had grown increasingly surly; he had been heard "mumbling out threats and grumbling about the decks and cursing and swearing," more volens than nolens now. For their present offenses he and Lambert would each get a dozen, and accounts from other sources (young Herman Melville for one, observant crewman aboard a U.S. man-of-war the following summer) let us experience what the logbook records so sparely: gratings rigged, offenders stripped, a shipmate binding Lambert's hands and feet as Waltham waits his turn, boatswain (Browning? or Gunner's Mate Collins? promoted now with Cromwell in irons) holding the green bag. When ordered, he removes the cat from inside, combs its tails with his fingers. The captain stands by to give the signal to commence. Crewmen look on, some whispering, most silent, some "carrying suppressed indignation in their eyes." Officers are grouped to starboard, the surgeon close by.

At Captain Mackenzie's signal the boatswain's mate steps forward, sweeps the cat around his neck, with full force brings the nine tails down across Lambert's surging back: "a cutting, wiry sound." With every blow the man twists and twists from side to side in his bonds, "pouring out torrents of involuntary blasphemies." And the back is bloodied, grows black like burned flesh.

. . . Ten. Eleven. Twelve.

After the twelfth stroke of those nine lashes has cut through his skin, the offender is finally released and thrown his shirt to go back among his shipmates. Blood stains the deck and gratings and bulwarks.

Waltham is next.

But last night while in irons after the discovery of his crime, the mulatto steward had told the wardroom cot boy, McKinley, where three bottles of wine had been hidden—crime on crime—"his object being, no doubt, to furnish the means of excitement to the conspirators, to induce them to rise, release Waltham, and get possession of the vessel." McKinley was down on the Greek list as certain, his mutiny station assigned at the arms chest. Yet this morning this same McKinley had reported Waltham to the master-at-arms—"an extraordinary denunciation under the circumstances, probably occasioned by his desire to relieve himself from suspicion." In any case, the mulatto would get a dozen today for stealing brandy from the wardroom mess, would spend the day and another night in irons, then across his disfigured back would get twelve more tomorrow.

Cat!

Captain's finger lifted. The signal.

One. Two. Three. Four. Five. Six. Seven. Eight. Nine. Ten. Eleven. Twelve.

Cut him down!

For now the punishment was over; and with the steward being led away doubled in pain, this seemed to Commander Mackenzie "a fit opportunity to endeavor to make some impression on the crew." From the elevation of the trunk house he addressed them as they stood mustered before him, prisoners within earshot. "The character of his speech," the first lieutenant recalled, "was that of kindness and mildness, and for the purpose of bringing their minds back to the proper situation, if they had been influenced by Mr. Spencer. He pictured to them their homes and friends, and endeavored to show them that even if they did succeed in this plot, they would be much worse off than they were at that time. Many of them probably would be thrown overboard, and they had everything to lose and nothing to gain. That was the amount of it."

Tenses make clear he was describing a mutiny that persisted in his mind as a possibility. Commander Mackenzie remembered sketching for the men Mr. Spencer's general scheme to seize the brig, make the small boys walk the plank, sail to the Isle of Pines. But in the course of his speech he had taken care not to awaken "any suspicions that I was in the possession of the names of those who were implicated. I was willing, in fact, that the worst of them should repent and hide themselves among the well-disposed portion of the crew." He did remind his listeners that the prisoners' plans would have doomed the majority of them. And "I endeavored to divert the minds of the slightly disaffected from the picture of successful vice which Mr. Spencer had presented to them." Most of the crew—"unlike crews in general"—had kin ashore who made life dear to them. The commander "expressed the hope that within three weeks we should be again among our friends. I thanked God that we had friends to follow us with solicitude and affection: for to have friends, and not to be unworthy of them, was the best guarantee that could be given for truth and fidelity."

To those words of their captain the men responded in various ways. Some, he said, seemed filled with horror at the revelation of what they had escaped from. Others felt terror "at dangers awaiting them from their connexion with the conspiracy. The thoughts of returning to that home and those friends from whom it had been intended to have cut them off forever caused many of them to weep." In short, the response would seem to have been all that he could have hoped for: "I now considered the crew tranquilized and the vessel safe."

She would proceed to St. Thomas, in the Danish West Indies. Perhaps the *Vandalia* or some other American naval ship would be in port at Charlotte Amalie to take into more commodious spaces prisoners causing such strain on this little brig. But St. Thomas lay more than a week away. And had Captain Mackenzie's reading ever by chance encompassed the story of Jörgen Iversen, first governor of those Danish West Indies toward which his helmsmen were steering? Iversen, who had served at St. Thomas in the 1640s, had been returning to that Caribbean island from Copenhagen in 1683 when a crew rose in mutiny and threw him overboard, after having first shot the ship's captain and decapitated seven or eight aboard. Those mutineers had been bent on piracy too, though with little knowledge of navigation they had not got far before going aground in the North Sea. For their pains they were hanged outside the gates of Copenhagen—cold comfort, of course, for the luckless governor at the sea's bottom.

But wasn't a lesson to be learned from that, and from many another such nautical episode? Aboard the *Somers*, among these later malcontents, the only three who knew anything of navigation were now in irons. Still, their presence on deck was increasingly troublesome. Purser Heiskell for one remarked the crowded gangways and forecastle, so crowded that merely moving about the ship had become a chore. It had not been so earlier: "I requested the officer to have the passage kept clear." But that was hard to do, and all those boys and slow-moving men sullenly in the way.

And it was proving hard to keep signals from passing between prisoners and crew. Spencer was seen to laugh, to knock his feet together and wave a hand. Mr. Rodgers had "observed McKee standing forward, looking very intently on Mr. Spencer, apparently endeavoring to catch his eye, but seeing me he commenced skylarking with one of the boys near." Well, something might be done about that. During this same Monday afternoon Commander Mackenzie ordered the three prisoners to be faced aft: let them study the stern the rest of the way home. "I also directed that no tobacco should be furnished them after the supply they had on their persons when confined should be exhausted." Mr. Spencer would have his officer's mess, the others their regular governmental rations. Indeed, "everything should be supplied to them that was necessary to their health and comfort." But tell them, Mr. Gansevoort, that tobacco is a stimulant. Tell them the captain wishes them "to tranquilize their minds and remain free from excitement"—this though all three upon learning of their new deprivation "earnestly begged to be allowed tobacco."

No, they must tranquilize their minds. And was it not sometime during this same Monday afternoon, the twenty-eighth, that the captain first entertained a different fate for the prisoners from the one he had pronounced to them at their separate arrests? Would he be able to take them home after all? Later he wrote a letter to explain what had changed his mind—for change it he did, now or within the coming hours. "First: I was influenced by my deep conviction of the reality of the plot disclosed by Mr. Spencer to Mr. Wales." Under that conviction he had already "determined to adopt no measure but after mature deliberation," yet "to shrink from none that the preservation of the lives of those entrusted to my care, the honor of my country, and my sense of duty should demand." There was, after all, a murderous plot aboard, one in which, "by the declaration of Mr. Spencer, at least twenty of the crew were concerned, and which in my own opinion the majority of the crew were willing to be accomplices."

These men the captain had come to know in the course of eleven weeks of sailing with them. He knew that some aboard were capable of "committing any atrocity." He referred in his explanatory letter to "the depraved character of the crew," and to "the fact that many of them, although men in strength and size, were still boys in age, and consequently would be little likely to resist temptation, and more easily allured by the pleasures held out to them as accompanying the life of a pirate." Red Rover, Blackbeard: free to go where you want, get rich, have thrilling adventures—those ladies in their smooth dresses cowering on doomed decks, bright fear-filled eyes, bosoms heaving, their fine voices quavering, begging for mercy . . .

He explained that he was influenced to change his mind "by the insubordination of the crew . . . very much increased after the arrest of the prisoners: their gloomy and angry looks; their secret conferences, broken off when an officer approached; their increased reluctance in the performance of their duty; the actual disobedience of some; the attempts of several to communicate with the prisoners." All that influenced him— that and "the confident and even insolent air of the prisoners themselves, though confined for a crime which rendered them liable should they be taken home to the punishment of death, clearly showing that they expected and had prepared a rescue."

Even in irons Spencer was insolent. Did the boy understand so little the plight he was in? For eleven weeks his captain had tolerated that young man's behavior, his ridiculing of "efforts to have the duty performed with skill, dispatch, and uniformity," his representing to the crew that necessary punishment aboard "instead of justice was persecution," his casting of odium upon his captain "and the excellent and hitherto most popular first lieutenant." By contrast, Alexander Slidell Mackenzie (who had begun his own career aboard a ship the size of the *Somers*), at Spencer's young age—or only slightly older, at nineteen—was already captain of a merchant vessel, on leave from the navy to gain experience in seamanship and command. Slidell by that age had sailed with Oliver Perry in the Mediterranean, dutifully sailed along the East Coast with President Monroe aboard, had sailed on the *Macedonian* in the Pacific station, had diligently studied French and Spanish and dancing and swordsmanship in free hours at sea, had written those informative letters to share far places with loved ones back home . . .

The commander was recalling the broken mast on Sunday, with Spencer's "strange and stealthy glances" to the masthead. Had that not been planned as a prologue to rescue, with Small yanking on the weather brace to topple poor Gagely overboard? A boldness among the conspirators had informed the act, meant (so the captain may now have felt certain) to create "dismay and confusion on board, an act committed moreover in fair weather and broad day, too surely evincing what they were capable of in tempestuous weather and in darkness." And there would be tempestuous weather: not till mid-December could the *Somers* hope to reach New York, sailing day and night from the Caribbean northward through ever more wintry seas.

Secondly, he wrote: "Secondly: by the uncertainty under which we labored as to the extent of the mutiny"—that, too, had influenced Mackenzie to alter his plans. For what could he do to get at the truth: examine the whole crew? Say that all protested their ignorance of any plot. "Could we have believed and trusted them? Would the uncertainty have been removed or diminished?" On the contrary, a profession of universal ignorance might, so the captain reasoned, have "justified our suspicions of universal guilt." Or say the examination had uncovered some others among the crew guilty: "our difficulties would have been still greater. To confine and guard them was impossible. To leave them at large, with a knowledge that their guilt was known, and that—if they arrived in safety—death might be their doom, was to render them desperate, and an outbreak inevitable."

That particular awareness seems crucial. Others aboard had sensed it: desperation among undetected mutineers growing with every passing hour that brought the vessel closer to settlements ashore. Meanwhile, even the prisoners under guard posed a threat to those same conspirators not yet identified, who would have felt increasing urgency to rescue them, as Acting Master Perry put it, "from thinking that they"—the ones at large—"would be discovered to the officers through those already confined."

In his letter the captain specified still other reasons why he was led to abandon his original plan of carrying Mr. Spencer, Cromwell, and Small to New York for trial. He noted that the officers were exhausted, and growing more so with their watch load necessarily augmented. "From loss of rest and continual exertion we were daily losing strength, whilst that of the mutineers, from increasing numbers, was daily becoming greater." Then too, at any time, day or night, more likely so as the season advanced, a storm might come up, "calling the attention of the officers and petty officers from the prisoners and mutineers still at large to the necessary duties of taking care of the vessel." At such a tumultuous time a few resolute men might easily seize control of the brig and release the prisoners, so the captain reasoned. Moreover, the very size of the vessel posed yet one more argument, a critical one; for she was too small for her officers "to confine more prisoners, and prevent those already confined from communicating with each other, and with those of the crew at large."

That last consideration was on the minds of others, on Mr. Gansevoort's mind, for instance, this very Monday afternoon, the twenty-eighth. He was asking the opinion of Acting Master Perry, third in command. "I told him," Perry later confirmed, "that I did not think we could take charge of more prisoners with safety to the vessel . . ." Mr. Leecock agreed, and Mr. Rodgers, and Mr. Hayes.

Yet more prisoners would have to be confined. That seemed obvious in part from what was happening on board this same day. For one thing, Mr. Spencer had got his hands on one of the battle-axes mounted on the bulwarks outboard of the arms chest. Ironed as he was, he had been hefting it and glaring at Wales, who was taking his turn as prisoners' guard. Wales had reported the infraction; Spencer had released the weapon at the first lieutenant's approach. ("I told him," said Mr. Gansevoort, "he must obey the orders strictly; that his life depended on it." The lieutenant would do his duty whatever: "I would put him to death with my own hands.") But had the prisoner been trying to arm himself expecting rescue? Was that the reason? Mr. Perry, for one, presumed so, in part because Spencer's manner, now as throughout his confinement so far, "appeared to be perfectly easy." Why else would one in his circumstances be easy?

The battle-axes were removed and locked in the arms chest. This same afternoon Mr. Gansevoort came upon the gunner and the carpenter's mate, King and Dickerson, talking together—two whom he knew he could trust. Dickerson thought Knevals and Golderman and Sullivan and Willson and Hamilton and Gurabrantz and Waltham—Waltham especially—were concerned in the plot. They were the ones "who gathered about the decks." And what did he think of those fellows aft, their backs to the crew now? "The damned fool is on the larboard," the carpenter confided to Mr. Gansevoort, "and the damned scoundrel is on the starboard arm chest." The judgment was lodged in the lieutenant's mind: Mr. Spencer the fool, Cromwell the scoundrel—"the most dangerous man on board the ship." But though a fool and a scoundrel and one other had been confined, the crew seemed not at all cowed. On the contrary, they continued "disorderly." They were, according to Wales, "surly; they went to work, when orders were given, with evident dissatisfaction."

More of them would have to be taken prisoner. That seemed unavoidable. Ahead, the sun sank low in the sky. Signs were pointing to this as the night for attempting rescue. Accordingly, the captain ordered that the strength of the deck patrols be increased. Officers would stand four hours on, four off, four on again, watch and watch. As for the crew, any topside and not actually working the vessel must henceforth lie prone on deck through the hours of darkness.

Nerves aboard were thus stretched taut through another long night. In making their rounds now, patrols stepped over prostrate forms. The prisoners huddled aft, their eyes astern toward the spreading wake, chains rattling with each shift of position. And suppose a squall should come up? Not unlikely in these latitudes at this time of year. Imagine the black emptiness, black water all around, on deck shadowy forms of officers ordering sail taken in, and it would be "hard to tell who were engaged in it or not, and it would be easy in a dark night for a parcel of men where the officers were running about the deck, for each man to pick out his mark, stick his knife in him, and after killing all the officers but the commander, it was easy to take command of the vessel . . ."

That was the waking nightmare of many, as Boatswain's Mate Browning articulated it, a nightmare to be brought close and made a sudden reality at any moment through the long hours tonight, or if not, then tomorrow night, or if not, the night after that. Time was with the mutineers, coolly awaiting their opportunity.

First faint gleams astern. Sunrise. This Tuesday morning, November

29, dawned "pleasant" as days before, with "moderate breezes." Wales was guarding the prisoners while decks were being holystoned. "I observed signs," he recalled, "passing between Spencer, Wilson, and McKinley. They put their hands to their chins, and Cromwell, who was lying on the arm chest, rose up. I told him my orders were to shoot him down, and I should do so if he did not lie still. He lay down. I then went back with my pistol cocked to the launch, where Wilson was poking about, and found that he had a number of the holystones out"—those heavy hunks of sandstone for scouring—"and that he was taking out a handspike. I told him that if I saw him making any farther signs I would blow his brains out. He said nothing, did not put the handspike back but went to draw some water. I put the handspike back myself."

But shouldn't such potentially lethal implements be under lock and key? Wales would suggest that to the first lieutenant.

This was the morning, incidentally, this the day when young Mr. Spencer broke down. By now he had been some sixty hours chained at the stern. Lieutenant Gansevoort, come to question him before quarters, found the prisoner hunched under a sheltering grego, or great cloak. He couldn't talk now. Captain Mackenzie would later refer to the "day after Mr. Spencer's tobacco was stopped," when "his spirits gave way entirely. He remained the whole day with his face buried in the grego, and when it was for a moment raised, it was bathed in tears. He was touched," so the captain presumed, "by the gentle and untiring attentions of Lieutenant Gansevoort," whose grego it was. Spencer "told him that he was in no state at that time to speak of anything—when he felt more composed he would tell him all—he would answer any questions that the commander might desire to put to him."

That day they left the midshipman alone. Some ship's business to finish after quarters: all hands to witness punishment. Henry Waltham was led forth, irons removed, arms and legs bound to the gratings. His bare back would have swollen by then to look like a dark, lined pillow. The cat was brought out—was the disconsolate Spencer watching? was Cromwell, facing aft? Small?—and twelve hard strokes of nine lashes each were sliced across the already cut and puffy flesh. That for offering McKinley three bottles of wardroom wine. Let him down; and afterward the captain addressed the crew again, though not with yesterday's success. Commander Mackenzie was "urging them to conform to the discipline of the vessel: the orders were all known, and of easy observance. I mentioned that every punishment inflicted must be known to the secretary of the navy, and that the less punishment there was, the more creditable it would be to the commander and the crew. But the whole crew was far from being tranquilized. The most seriously implicated began once more to collect in knots . . ."

Willson, there by the mainmast. With McKinley, McKee, the tattoo artist Green: the ones who had taken it upon themselves to bring the prisoners their victuals. During the course of this day Gunner's Mate King was talking with the first lieutenant. *"Has Wilson drawn two or three knives from the store-room lately?"* Mr. Gansevoort was not aware of it. "I heard," King said, "that he had several knives in his sail-bag, and I think it would be a good plan to overhaul it." Most of the morning the bag had been sitting at the after part of the gun nearest Mr. Spencer—"and a knife hid away in the rigging," which King thought Willson *"intended to put into the hands of Mr. Spencer."* The first lieutenant accordingly overhauled the sail bag. He found inside it an African dirk—souvenir of Monrovia—"very sharp, and having the appearance of having been lately sharpened." That was locked into the arms chest for safekeeping. The gunner's mate had thought, moreover, that there was a collection of arms in the storeroom, so Mr. Gansevoort searched about in there too, "but found none." Nevertheless, and to Wales's relief, he collected "all the monkey-tails, holystones, marling-spikes, and such things as might be used against us. They were locked up in the store-room and otherwise secured. I did not know then," the first lieutenant adds, "that any other of the crew were implicated; but I think it was King who told me that he thought all the older boys were . . ."

Willson, at any rate, had been acting oddly. This same evening Sergeant Garty observed the sailmaker's mate "quite restless in his hammock, raising up his head and looking round the decks; and I had a suspicion of him in consequence, so that every time the watch was called I turned out myself, having my sword under the blanket and my hand on the hilt of it"; for all that harrowing night the marine was tensely expecting a rush on the steerage.

On deck meanwhile, at the end of yet another wearing day and with darkness back upon them, Acting Master Perry was discovering that the boom tackle had been carried away. The ship was rolling "very heavy at the time; the boom kept sweeping across the deck. I took in the slack of the weather sheet myself, without thinking of the prisoners at the time, and gave the order, 'Some of you lay aft.'" Immediately fifteen or more came rushing down the gangway—many more than were needed to haul in a spanker sheet. "Some of you lay aft" had been the order—three or four to lend a hand. Yet the mob would not leave the quarterdeck until the captain himself emerged from his cabin. "They then went forward; that is all."

But enough to give pause. And, that same evening, had the commander below been pondering a recommendation from his first lieutenant? Much else, at any rate, had been crowding upon Mackenzie's mind. "I considered the imminent peril which hung over the lives of the officers and crew. I thought of the seas traversed in every direction by merchantmen, unarmed and defenseless. I thought of what was due to the interests of commerce, to the safety of the lives of thousands upon the deep, to the sanctity of the American flag entrusted to my care, and to my own honor. All these considerations impressed me with the absolute necessity of adopting some further means of security for the vessel which had been given to my charge."

Had he come to a decision down there in his tiny cabin? Had he already written the letter he would deliver to his officers in the morning? The captain later admitted that this evening "I felt more anxious than I had yet done." He would remain on deck throughout the night; and before that long night with its "risks and uncertainty" had finally ended, he would resolve "that another such should not be passed."

Midnight.

The watch was called, and "McKinley, Green, and others seriously implicated missed their muster. That they should have been asleep at all that night," so the captain concluded, "was not likely. That they should have missed their muster on that particular occasion, having never done so before otherwise than intentionally, was impossible. Those who missed their muster had all some lame excuse. There was probably," their commander felt, "an agreement to meet around the officer of the deck and commit some act of violence."

But McKinley, for instance, was claiming his mate McKee hadn't wakened him. McKee was pleading that, made to lie prone on deck, he had fallen asleep. As for Green—all those names prominent on the Greek paper—Green the captain heard "give as an excuse for missing his muster that he was on deck but could not get aft for want of room. I immediately went forward, rejected his excuse with some exclamation of impatience" —the commander's edginess evident—"and ordered him to take the lookout forward for four hours, directing the midshipman on the forecastle to watch him closely." But when those four hours had passed, and the watch was again being changed, to the captain's dismay "others of the implicated also missed their muster. I could not contemplate this growth of disaffection without serious uneasiness. Where was this thing to end?"

He had had time meanwhile, on that moonlit deck in mid-Atlantic as the *Somers* was running her westing down, to brood further on her situation. Trustworthy petty officers, working directly with the crew, felt "that the vessel was yet far from safe—that there were still many at liberty who ought to be confined . . ." Moreover, "individuals not before supposed to be very deeply implicated were now found in close association with those who were." The captain reports, without further specifying, that this bright night "seditious words were heard through the vessel, and an insolent and menacing air assumed by many . . . Several times during the night there were symptoms of an intention to strike some blow. . . ." This when the moon shone bright. What of moonless nights?

What of storms? And as he brooded on the starboard quarterdeck, did it not steadily press upon the commander that the issue involved more than his own safety or the eventual ragged triumph of lawfulness at whatever bloody cost? Rather, he must act to keep that cost minimal, must act to shield the ship utterly from peril and remove from risk every trusting life aboard.

Morning came finally, benignly—last day of November, pleasant (says the logbook), with breezes now "brisk" after the miracle of sunrise. The *Somers*'s crew yet again reenacted ship's dawn routine: scouring, swabbing the decks.

With daylight restored to them, the first lieutenant was going to interview Mr. Spencer "for the purpose of his proving more clearly his guilt." Guard and prisoner would look at the Greek paper together; "I took him the paper that he might translate it, so I could understand it. My object was to obtain from him an acknowledgment of his guilt."

Today the disgraced midshipman seemed in somewhat better spirits. About that list of his there was a problem, however. Four names he had set down as certain: McKinley, Wales, E. Andrews, and his own. Yet no Andrews was aboard the vessel. "I asked him," the lieutenant recalled, "if that name did not stand for Cromwell. He said no, that it meant Small— that was his real name. I said, 'Ah! how is that, when you have Small's name twice on the list?' "—as stationed in the captain's cabin for mutiny, and in the steerage. "Mr. Spencer appeared to be surprised, and said 'Ah! I did not know I had written it that way.' "

He said more, some of it highly incriminating: that he had formed mutinous plots, for instance, on other vessels he had served aboard, "both in the *John Adams* and in the *Potomac*. He said he knew that it would get him into difficulty—that he had tried to break himself of it— but it was impossible: *it was a mania with him*. I think he wished me to mention it to the commander."

The lieutenant would do so. But two bells were about to sound: nine o'clock muster. By that time Willson the sailmaker's mate had approached the commander to make a confession of his own. Captain Mackenzie does not specify what it was, but it was "lame and absurd," and followed by a "request that he should not be ironed." Yet what of the dirk in the sail bag—"of no use for any honest purpose," in the captain's opinion, "fit only to kill"? And the way the man had been hovering glumly around the mainmast; his recent suspicious behavior both topside and below. Willson must have sensed—"having failed in his attempt to get up an outbreak in the night"—that his confinement was near and confessed to avoid it. "I immediately told him," Mackenzie reports, "that if he would make a real confession, he should not be molested, and that it was only an insult to offer me such a lame story as that which had been already repeated to me by Lieutenant Gansevoort. Nothing more could be got from him," however, "and at quarters he was ironed."

Thus additional firm steps were being taken on board. Willson was ironed, and so was McKinley, on the Greek list "down among the certain, and beyond a doubt correctly." So was Green ironed, his "demeanor during the past night" having caused the captain this morning to send for him, interrogate him, and order him seized as well. So was Alexander McKee put in irons, he who on the mutiny list would have taken the wheel, "and who was entirely in the confidence of Cromwell . . . These individuals were made to sit down as they were taken; and when they were ironed," says the captain, "I walked deliberately round the battery, followed by the first lieutenant, and we made together a very careful inspection of the crew. Those who (though known to be very guilty) were considered to be the least dangerous, were called out and interrogated. Care was taken not to awaken the suspicions of such as from courage or energy were really formidable . . ."

The most formidable in any case had already been arrested, during this very muster. Prisoners now numbered seven, "filling up the quarterdeck and rendering it very difficult to keep them from communicating with each other," while at the same time "interfering essentially with the management of the vessel." Green had been put aft of No. 4 gun portside, Willson aft of No. 5. McKee and McKinley had been put on the starboard side of the quarterdeck. But where was this thing to end? And hadn't the officers already agreed that no further prisoners could be taken safely? The first lieutenant was standing over the sailmaker nevertheless, aft of the No. 5 starboard gun. "Small, you see we have taken more prisoners. . . . Do you know of any others that are at large from whom we may apprehend danger?"

But that was hard for Small to say.

Well then, was not Cromwell engaged with Mr. Spencer in this plot?

Protestations of innocence by the boatswain's mate, seconded "eloquently" by Spencer himself, must have been on Mr. Gansevoort's mind. "That's a hard thing for me to say, sir"—although Small would reveal that he had seen Mr. Spencer give Cromwell money, "more money than *he'd* like to give him or lend him, either.

"I said to him—'That's not the thing: I want a plain answer to a plain question. Is not Cromwell deeply engaged with Mr. Spencer in this plot of Spencer's to take the vessel out of the hands of the officers?' "

And Small had at length replied, "If anybody aboard of the brig is, *he* is, sir."

Ah. I thought so, said Mr. Gansevoort. And it would have been soon after Small's gratifying corroboration that the first lieutenant, there on the gangway with muster ended, was handed a letter by his captain, from the captain and addressed to all the officers aboard except for the acting midshipmen. The letter solicited the collective counsel of the wardroom and steerage—though in truth, as Commander Mackenzie would assert at the earliest opportunity in writing to the secretary of the navy, "I had before made up my own mind on the subject, and determined if necessary to do without counsel what I knew to be necessary to my duty to the flag and vessel . . ."

What had led Alexander Slidell Mackenzie to his solemn resolve? All those reasons previously set down—and one final reason. Finally, there had seemed only one sure way (as he put it in rather cumbersome prose) to "relieve the minds of the rest of the mutineers from apprehension occasioned by the consciousness that the ringleaders possessed secrets that might be fatal to many whose guilty participation in the plot might otherwise remain uncertain." That one way would also deprive the crew "of the power of navigating the vessel, as none of the survivors would be capable of taking charge of her" thereafter. That way "was the only effectual method of bringing them back"—all those muttering, scowling reprobates—"to their allegiance and preserving the vessel committed to my charge." The ship's company aboard the *Somers* would not pass another such night as those last few, for her captain had determined to execute Spencer, Cromwell, and Small.

"Gentlemen," he had written under the date November 30, 1842:

> The time has arrived when I am desirous of availing myself of your counsel in the responsible position in which, as commander of this vessel, I find myself placed. You are aware of the circumstances which have resulted in the confinement of Midshipman Philip Spencer, Boatswain's Mate Samuel Cromwell, and Seaman E. Small, as prisoners, and I purposely abstain from entering into any details of them, necessarily ignorant of the exact extent of disaffection among a crew which has so long and so systematically and assiduously been tampered with by *an officer*. Knowing that suspicions of the gravest nature attach to persons still at large [these, he subsequently explained, were Willson and the three others, not yet arrested when the letter was written], and whom the difficulty of taking care of the prisoners we already have makes me more reluctant than I should otherwise be to apprehend, I have determined to address myself to you, and to ask your united counsel as to the best course to be now pursued, and I call upon you to take into deliberate and dispassionate consideration the present condition of the vessel and the contingencies of every nature that the future may embrace throughout the remainder of our cruise, and enlighten me with your opinion as to the best course to be pursued.
>
> I am, very respectfully, gentlemen, your most obedient

Alex Slidell Mackenzie,
Commander.

To Lieutenant Guert Gansevoort, Passed-Assistant Surgeon R. W.
Leecock, Purser H. M. Heiskell, Acting-Master M. C. Perry, Midshipman Henry Rodgers, Midshipman Egbert Thompson, Midshipman Chas. W. Hayes.

Those officers proceeded at once to assemble in the wardroom. Eight
by ten feet were the dimensions of that space under the trunk house.
Around the little table (four feet by three), seven grown men packed
themselves to listen, throughout a long, hot day, first to the captain's
letter read aloud, then to testimony from thirteen witnesses. Mr. Wales
testified, and twelve of the crew in turn. Purser Heiskell acted as secretary, keeping penciled notes. All day it went on. Sergeant Garty, master-
at-arms, "believes Small and Cromwell were determined on taking this
brig . . . Thinks the vessel would be safer if Cromwell, Spencer, and
Small were put to death." And why, the officers questioned Apprentice
Warner, had he told Green that "the damned son of a bitch (meaning
Cromwell) ought to be hung? Because," that crewman answered, "I
thought him guilty," and moreover, "I told Green I thought Mr. Spencer
as great a villain as any of them." Boatswain's Mate Browning was of the
opinion, "to tell you God Almighty's truth . . . that some of the cooks
around the galley—I think they are the main backers. Viz. Waltham,
Constin, Howard, Gallia. I have my suspicions also about some of the
boys . . ." Andrew Anderson, brought down for his turn before the officers, allowed that the vessel might be safe at present, but what about
later, off the North American coast in winter? For then ten would be
needed to do the work of two now—"and the boys will be of no use to us.
I don't know," he went on, "about the *niggers* at the galley. I don't like
them." Dickerson thought "the following persons still at large are concerned in it. Viz. Knevals, Golderman, Sullivan, Hamilton, Van Velsor,
Whitmore, Gurabantz, Godfrey (partly concerned in it), and Waltham.
He more so than ever within two or three days . . ."
During which the wardroom steward would have been nursing those
two hundred and sixteen stripes cut into his bare back, the back of him to
whom Mr. Spencer had earlier in the cruise given a frock coat and "bundle after bundle" of segars. The crew's testimony took time: Van Velsor
himself, and Collins and Stewart and Gedney and King and Tyson and
Charlie Rogers were yet to be heard from. The day wore on. On deck the
captain was standing watch, aided only by the three acting midshipmen:
Mr. Deslonde, seventeen, Mr. Tillotson, sixteen, and Mr. Perry, seventeen, doing men's duty though still only boys ("it would have been hard,
at their early age, to call upon them to say whether three of their fellow-

creatures should live or die"). But Commander Mackenzie, keeping the crew occupied squaring ratlines and scraping the masts, was eager that the business below be ended before another nightfall; he was "exceedingly anxious to know the result of the investigation." Late in the afternoon he sent down for a report on the council's progress. No, they were not yet finished, even though the officers had "passed the whole day in this occupation without interruption and without food." Now at six, with darkness at hand, the captain was reluctantly ordering them to break off deliberations; the vessel's safety required that they resume their watches: "He considered the vessel in danger and wished to show a force about the decks."

Thus not until the following morning, after an additional hour or so of testimony, could the results of the investigation be made available to Captain Mackenzie, by means of correspondence delivered through his first lieutenant:

> U.S. Brig *Somers*
> Dec. 1, 1842

> Sir: In answer to your letter of yesterday, requesting our counsel as to the best course to be pursued with the prisoners, Acting-Midshipman Philip Spencer, Boatswain's Mate Samuel Cromwell, and Seaman Elisha Small, we would state that the evidence which has come to our knowledge is of such a nature as, after as dispassionate and deliberate a consideration of the case as the exigencies of the time would admit, we have come to a cool, decided, and unanimous opinion that they have been guilty of a full and determined intention to commit a mutiny on board of this vessel of a most atrocious nature; and that the revelation of circumstances having made it necessary to confine others with them, the uncertainty as to what extent they are leagued with others still at large, the impossibility of guarding against the contingencies which "a day or an hour may bring forth," we are convinced that it would be impossible to carry them to the United States, and that the safety of the public property, the lives of ourselves, and of those committed to our charge, require that (giving them sufficient time to prepare) they should be put to death in a manner best calculated as an example to make a beneficial impression upon the disaffected. This opinion we give, bearing in mind our duty to our God, our country, and to the service.

> We are, sir, very respectfully, your obedient servants,
> > Guert Gansevoort, Lieutenant
> > R. W. Leecock, Pas'd Ass. Surg'n
> > H. M. Heiskell, Purser
> > M. C. Perry, Act'g Master

Henry Rodgers, Midshipman
Egbert Thompson, Midshipman
Chas. W. Hayes, Midshipman

From Lieutenant Gansevoort the captain had received the council's recommendation first verbally, then in writing at ten-thirty that same morning. He forthwith proceeded to take all steps necessary to put the recommendation immediately into effect. Forty fathoms of 2¾-inch rope were ordered to be got from stores for whips, or hauling line. Forty fathoms of signal halyard stuff were expended for downhauls, and three 7-inch sail blocks brought up on deck. The crew was set to work fitting the blocks and stretching the rope. Where? On the forecastle, along the gangways? The prisoners, in any case, seem in their postures facing aft to have been unaware of what was happening. Commander Mackenzie had gone below to his cabin, Purser Heiskell following to read him the minutes of the council proceedings. When the captain reappeared, he was in full-dress uniform: blues, gold braid and buttons, epaulets, eagle-hilt sword, cocked hat. McKinley, catching sight of such splendor from his position confined on deck, thought that another vessel must be bearing down, and a visit between ships about to occur. It was nearly noon. The petty officers of the *Somers* were being mustered on the quarterdeck, the first lieutenant arming those seven, each with cutlass, pistol, and cartridge box. That done, the captain addressed them:

"My lads, you are to look to me, to obey my orders, and to see my orders obeyed. Go forward."

At noon the mainsail was hauled up, and two whips rose on the main yardarm starboard, one whip on the yardarm port. The ensign and pennant were bent on, ready for hoisting. Now—proceeding (in his words) "to execute the most painful duty that has ever devolved on an American commander"—Alexander Slidell Mackenzie approached Philip Spencer where that young man was seated on a campstool facing aft, head down on the forward part of the arms chest portside.

He had been sitting at the arms chest a hundred and fourteen hours. High noon, the blue sky, a few high clouds, the blue sea. Captain Mackenzie, in full uniform, speaks. The prisoner lifts his head—those eyes askew with their staring look. A minute's puzzlement. The captain speaks, and gradually his full meaning comes clear:

When you were about to take my life, sir, and dishonor me as an officer in the execution of my rightful duty—without cause of offence to you, on speculation—it was your intention to remove me suddenly from the world in the darkness of night, in my sleep, without a moment to utter one murmur of affection to my wife and children, one prayer for their welfare. Your life, sir, is now forfeited to your country; and the necessities of the case, growing out of your corruption of the crew, compel me to take it. I will not, however, imitate your intended example, as to the manner of claiming the sacrifice. If there yet remains to you one feeling true to nature, it shall be gratified. If you have any word to send to your parents, it shall be recorded and faithfully delivered. Ten minutes shall be granted you for this purpose.

He ended.

Spencer's response to that disclosure was dramatic. The captain reports that the boy was entirely overcome: "He sank, with tears, upon his knees and said he was not fit to die. I repeated to him his own catechism" —Are you afraid of death? Do you fear a dead man? Would you dare to kill a person?—"and begged him," says the captain, "to let the officer set, to the men he had corrupted and seduced, the example of dying with decorum."

So timely a sentiment "immediately restored him to entire self-possession." With that the prisoner began to pray; and the captain, having ordered Midshipman Thompson to notify him when ten minutes had elapsed, made his way across deck to inform Cromwell of the fate that was rushing upon him.

On the starboard arms chest the boatswain's mate had been reading *The Penny Magazine*. At the captain's pronouncement, the magazine fell from those manacled hands, and Cromwell, struggling in his irons, rolled heavily from the chest with a cry. "God of the universe," he screamed, "look down upon my poor wife. I am innocent." He was on his knees, "completely unmanned." But the captain had left him, was moving resolutely forward, was standing now before Elisha Small where that prisoner sat on deck aft of the No. 5 gun.

This one Mackenzie admits to have regarded as the poltroon of the three, yet Small surprised him by accepting the news of his doom with composure. The commander was asking solicitously whether the sailmaker had any preparations to make, any message to send home. The little man answered no; "I have nobody to care for me but my poor old mother, and I would rather that she should not know how I have died."

Nearby, a crewman noticed that "when the captain went away, Small looked at me and smiled. I thought by that he thought he was not to be hung." And meanwhile Spencer, not far off, had signaled that he had something important to say. Mackenzie was crossing the deck to attend.

"What is that?"

The midshipman spoke: "As these are the last words I have to say, I trust they will be believed. Cromwell is innocent."

The assertion, made in full solemnity, "staggered" the commander, by his own admission. Evidence against the boatswain's mate had seemed conclusive; yet Spencer's statement caused the captain to hesitate, at least long enough to consult with Lieutenant Gansevoort. No, "there was not a shadow of doubt." But the lieutenant would speak with the petty officers. He did, and Cromwell soon "was condemned by acclamation" of those seven: "He was the one man of whom they had real apprehensions."

So why would the midshipman have been trying to save him? Maybe "in fulfillment of some mutual oath"? Maybe in hopes that, released from confinement, the boatswain's mate might yet manage to seize the vessel? "I returned to Mr. Spencer. I explained to him how Cromwell had made use of him. I told him that remarks had been made about the two not very flattering to him . . ." What remarks? Spencer "expressed great anxiety to hear what was said," so the captain enlightened him about what Carpenter's Mate Dickerson had told the first lieutenant, that the fool was to port, the scoundrel to starboard. Someone else aboard had volunteered that Cromwell after the mutiny would have allowed the midshipman to live only if he—that statesman's son—could have made himself useful, maybe as Cromwell's secretary. "I do not think," added the captain suavely in relaying that latter opinion, "this would have suited your temper."

At those confidences Spencer looked grim—looked "demoniacal," in fact: "he said no more of the innocence of Cromwell." But he did speak at length with Captain Mackenzie of other matters. They talked together an hour or longer, out of earshot of everyone else aboard. From a distance Lieutenant Gansevoort observed them in conversation: "Mr. Spencer had a Bible in his hand, and the commander was seated near him with a paper upon which he appeared to be writing." A campstool had been brought up from the captain's cabin, and paper, and ink. Midshipman Thompson had long since reported the passage of ten minutes; still the prisoner and his confessor talked on at the forward end of the arms chest, with only Mackenzie's version to tell us what they said.

Even so—even as reconstructed by the captain some weeks later—the exchange is remarkable, the more so for the light it casts on Slidell Mackenzie. He began this way: had Spencer no message to send his friends? "None that they would wish to receive." Come, no words of consolation in so great an affliction? "Tell them," said the young man under urging, "I die wishing them every blessing and happiness. I deserve death for this and many other crimes—there are few crimes that I have not committed. . . . I have wronged many persons, but chiefly my parents . . . this will kill my poor mother."

That last struck the captain with the force of revelation. "I was not before aware that he had a mother"—but what can he mean? We all have mothers. Moreover, a correspondent from Washington would later remind Thurlow Weed that Mackenzie had been at the capital some months before he took command of the *Somers*—had there, as captain of a steam frigate, entertained on board Mrs. Upshur and Mrs. Spencer, wives of the secretaries of the navy and war: "is it not strange that he should say in his dispatch that he did not know that Spencer *had* a mother living until Spencer mentioned to him that it would kill his mother, meaning his conduct—?"

Strange, indeed. Yet so affected was the captain by the boy's disclosure that he needed time to collect himself there at the stern before proceeding. He recovered his poise. Wouldn't it have been "still more dreadful" if the young officer had succeeded in his mutiny, still worse for his mother than what was about to happen? He put it to the prisoner. Spencer was expressing his fears that the scandal would injure his father. "I told him it was almost"—almost?—"too late to think of that—that had he succeeded in his wishes, it would have injured his father much more—that had it been possible to have taken him home, as I intended to do, it was not in nature that his father should not have interfered to save him—that for those who have friends or money in America there was no punishment for the worst of crimes—."

And is not that strange, as well, that gratuitous admission of mixed motives for the hanging? "Perhaps," writes Mackenzie in a footnote to the passage, "this was an extreme and erroneous opinion, which I do not attempt to justify. I am only faithfully recording what passed on the occasion." And he insisted (resuming the account of his words to Spencer), that "this"—this awareness of crimes of the rich and influential going unpunished back home—"had nothing to do with my determination, which had been forced upon me in spite of every effort which I had made to avert it"; though such being the case with criminals on American soil, "I on this account the less regretted the dilemma in which I was placed . . ."

That he told Spencer too. The sanctimony of the interview makes for painful reading. "The best and only service he could do his father was to die. . . . It was, if possible, more criminal to seduce another to commit crime than to commit crime one's self. He admitted the justice of this view. . . . I placed before him their opinion," the unanimous opinion of his brother officers, set down in writing. "He stated that it was just, that he deserved death." And in what manner would he die? "I explained it to him. He objected to it and asked to be shot. I told him that I could not make any distinction between him and those whom he had corrupted. He admitted that this also was just."

"But," asked Spencer, "have you not formed an exaggerated estimate of the extent of this conspiracy?"

"I told him 'No,' that his systematic efforts to corrupt the crew and prepare them for the indulgence of every evil passion since the day before our departure from New York had been but too successful. I knew that the conspiracy was still extensive—I did not know how extensive. I recapitulated to him the arts which he had used."

And the boy's mania for mutiny, indulged aboard every vessel he had served on: " 'Do you not think,' I asked, 'that this is a mania which should be discouraged in the navy?' "

Spencer did, "most certainly." Then later: "But are you not going too far," the boy implored, "are you not fast? Does the law entirely justify you?"

"I replied that he had not consulted me in making his arrangements—that his opinion could not be an unprejudiced one . . . He objected to the shortness of the time for preparation, and asked for an hour. No answer was made to this request, but he was not hurried, and more than the hour he asked for was allowed to elapse. He requested that his face might be covered. This was readily granted, and he was asked what it should be covered with. He did not care. A handkerchief was sought for in his locker, none but a black one found, and this brought for the purpose."

Frocks would be taken from the bags of the other two prisoners to cover their heads; that way none aboard would witness the facial distortions at execution, "horribly," that Slidell had seen and recorded at a public garroting in Spain eight years before. Spencer was asking to have his irons removed. "This could not be granted." He asked for a prayer book. That he was given, as were his accomplices. "I am a believer," he told the captain. "Do you think that repentance at this late hour can be accepted?" And Commander Mackenzie was ready with a little sermon, about the penitent thief "pardoned by our Savior upon the cross"—though he felt aggravated at not being able to put his finger on the biblical text. Spencer had begun reading the Bible now, was kneeling in his irons, was reading the prayer book. Mackenzie consoled him. "GOD, who was all-merciful as well as all-wise, could not only understand the difficulties of his situation, but extend to him such a measure of mercy as the necessities might require."

"I beg your forgiveness," the midshipman was saying, "for what I have meditated against you."

"I gave him my hand and assured him of my sincere forgiveness. I asked him if I had ever done anything to him to make him seek my life, or whether the hatred he had conceived for me, and of which I had only recently become aware, was fostered for the purpose of giving himself some plea of justification. He said, 'It was only a fancy—perhaps there might have been something in your manner which offended me.' "

The manner of that granny, so proud of his command—as the midshipman had expressed it to others. Through the preceding the captain had been taking notes. Now young Spencer read them over, pausing at one hastily written sentence: "He excused himself by saying that he had entertained the same idea in the *John Adams* and *Potomac*."

Might that be corrected? "I did not offer it as an excuse; I only stated it as a fact."

The correction would be made.

There passed an interlude when the captain vacated his campstool. Spencer had been seated in irons on a stool alongside. Now he sat alone, head bowed over his shackled hands. Others later would recall the sight . . .

And now came the moment for leading the prisoners beneath the main yardarm. Watch stations had been assigned earlier; petty officers were to conduct the three according to rank, the two most senior aboard to accompany Mr. Spencer over the sixteen feet or so that separated his place of confinement from his place of execution. The order was passed to do so. The prisoners were helped up. All three in double irons hobbled forward.

"At the break of the quarterdeck," Mackenzie tells us, "is a narrow passage between the trunk and pump well. Mr. Spencer and Cromwell met exactly on either side." The captain ordered the boatswain's mate to halt so that the midshipman might pass to the starboard side of the vessel. But Spencer was asking to speak with Wales, and while he waited and the purser's steward was sent for, Cromwell lurched onto the portside, "almost touching Mr. Spencer. Not one word was now said by Mr. Spencer of the innocence of Cromwell; no appeal was made by Cromwell to Mr. Spencer to attest his innocence."

Surely that silence was significant: Cromwell and Spencer confronting each other a final time with all pretense abandoned.

Now Spencer and Wales were face-to-face. Having received the summons to this spot, what might the latter have dreaded? Ah, but the midshipman was extending his manacled hands: "Mr. Wales, I earnestly hope you will forgive me for tampering with your fidelity." The prisoner's manner was calm, but Wales was so moved that he burst into tears. "I do forgive you from the bottom of my heart, and I hope that God may forgive you also." Wales was "weeping and causing others to weep," as the fettered youth lumbered on, reaching the starboard gangway.

There, under the rigged yardarm, "he placed himself in front of Small, extended his hand, and said, 'Small, forgive me for leading you into this trouble.'"

But the little sailmaker was not of Wales's mind, or in Wales's circumstances. He drew back. No, by God. I can't forgive you! "Mr. Spencer, how can you ask me that when you have brought me to this?" And he remained firm even after the midshipman repeated his plea: "Small—I can not die without your forgiveness."

At that the captain intervened. "I went to Small," says Mackenzie, "and urged him to be more generous—that this was no time for resentment." And at once the seaman relented. He did what his captain told him to—"since you request it, sir"—and held out his hand "to take the still-extended hand of Mr. Spencer, and said with frankness and emotion, 'I do forgive you, Mr. Spencer. May God Almighty forgive you also.'"

Having spoken thus to the youth who had led him this far, the sail-maker turned to Mr. Gansevoort and sought that officer's forgiveness, asking to bid him good-bye. "He told me," the lieutenant recalled, "that he was guilty and deserved his punishment. I think the commander said to him, 'Small, what have *I* done to you that you won't bid me goodbye?' Small replied, 'I did not know that you would bid a poor *bugger* like me goodbye, sir.'"

But of course Commander Mackenzie would. Small was, after all, "the one of the three who was most entitled to compassion. I took his hand and expressed my complete forgiveness in the strongest terms that I was able. I asked him," wrote the captain later, "what I had ever said or done to him to make him seek my life, conscious of no injustice or provocation of any sort. I felt that it was yet necessary to my comfort to receive the assurance from his own lips. If any wrong had been done him—if any word of harshness, in the impatience or excitement of duty, had escaped me, I was ready myself to ask also for forgiveness. I had hardly asked the question before he exclaimed, 'What have you done to me, Captain Mac-kenzie? what have you done to me, sir?—nothing, but treat me like a man.'"

Such a tribute led the commander to further self-justification. He was very sorry he had to take this course. "I told him . . . that I had high responsibilities to fulfill—that there were duties that I owed to the government which had entrusted me with this vessel—to the officers placed under my command—to those boys whom it was intended either to put to death or reserve for a fate more deplorable. There was yet a higher duty to the flag of my country."

That reminder touched Small in turn. "You are right, sir," he said—and others heard him say it. "You are doing your duty, and I honor you for it. God bless that flag and prosper it!"

The first lieutenant noticed that Small's words affected the commander "very much"; and we can believe it, aware of Mackenzie's lifelong regard for the flag of the fledgling nation—how once as a lieutenant in his mid-twenties just arrived in Spain, the then Alex Slidell had stood deeply moved along the coast near Barcelona, overlooking an American vessel on the blue Mediterranean as she displayed "in the bright sunshine the stars and stripes of that banner which has never been branded with dishonor nor sullied by strong-handed injustice." The republic was younger then; people could talk that way and mean it. Lieutenant Slidell as he then was had brushed a tear from his cheek, "rather in exultation than in sorrow" before so gallant a sight. And here, sixteen years later, Commander Sli-dell Mackenzie had felt his eyes dampen anew. Indeed, Wales remembers tears streaming down his face. "Now, brother topmates," Small was turning to call out to those who held the whip, "give me a quick and easy death." His guards lifted the little man onto the hammocks forward of the gangway, face inboard. The noose was bent on. Mr. Spencer, we are told, "was similarly placed, abaft the gangway, and Cromwell also on the other side."

That bear of a man, noosed like the others, waited on the hammock cloths. Mr. Deslonde passed close by. The boatswain's mate called to him, entreating him "to tell the officers to overlook this." But Mr. Deslonde walked on, ignoring the entreaty. Lieutenant Gansevoort approached to say good-bye. Cromwell "seized my hand, grasping it very violently. He said that he was innocent, and hoped that we'd find it out before six months." And indeed, he was saying that at the very last. "Cromwell's last words," Mackenzie records, "were, 'Tell my wife I die an innocent man; tell Lieut. Morris I die an innocent man.' But," the captain adds, "it had been the game of this man to appear innocent, to urge Mr. Spencer on, to furnish him with professional ideas, to bring about a catastrophe of which Mr. Spencer was to take all the risk, and from which he, Cromwell, was to derive all the benefit."

Now with death moments away, the doomed midshipman was summoning the first lieutenant to his side. "You may have heard," Spencer said to his superior, "that I am a coward, and *you* may think that I'm not a brave man. You can judge for yourself whether I die like a coward or a brave man."

His head and the heads of the other two prisoners were covered: jumpers, black neckerchief. For more than an hour the crew had been standing at their stations, afterguard and idlers of both watches on the starboard quarterdeck at Mr. Spencer's whip, forecastle men and foretopmen on portside at Cromwell's ("to whose corruption they had been chiefly exposed"), maintopmen of both watches starboard at Small's, as former captain of the maintop. "The officers were stationed about the decks according to the watchbill I," the commander, "had made out the night before; and the petty officers were similarly distributed, with orders to cut down whoever should let go the whip with even one hand, or fail to haul on it when ordered." The crew was to hold on, and "when they got forward, to stand still and hold the rope till ordered to belay."

From No. 4 starboard gun the apron was removed. Mr. Spencer through his face covering was asking the captain what the signal would be.

"I told him that being desirous to hoist the colors at the moment of execution, at once to give solemnity to the act and to indicate that by it the colors of the *Somers* were fixed to the masthead, I had intended to beat the call as for hoisting the colors, then roll off, and at the third roll fire a gun. He asked to be allowed himself to give the word to fire the gun. I acceded to the request, and the drum and fife were dismissed."

Was the gun under him? It was the next one over. Would there be a delay? Mr. Spencer "begged that no interval might elapse between giving the word and firing the gun." The captain looked into that: were they firing with the lock and wafer? No, with a tube and priming, and a match for backup. Commander Mackenzie passed the word to keep live coals coming aft from the galley, and thus could assure Mr. Spencer that the firing would on the instant follow the order to fire.

Yet more minutes passed. (Belongings of the doomed midshipman would need to be returned to his family: pair of woolen drawers, two and a half pairs of cotton socks, blue cloth jacket and pants, cotton drawers, towel, two sheets, pair of suspenders, comb, pencil, wooden spoon, an elephant's tooth . . .) Small was requesting permission to address the crew. "Mr. Spencer, having leave to give the word, was asked if he would consent to the delay. He assented; and Small's face being uncovered, he spoke as follows—'Shipmates and topmates, take warning by my example. I never was a pirate. I never killed a man—' "

The captain, alarmed, looked at his first lieutenant. "Is that right?"— meaning (as Gansevoort presumed) "ought he be suffered to go on?" But Small was continuing:

"It's for saying that I would do it that I am about to depart this life. See what a word will do. It was going in a guineaman that brought me to this. Beware of a guineaman." Beware of serving on slave ships. He turned then and spoke to his fellow sufferer on the starboard side. "I am now ready to die, Mr. Spencer. Are you?"

But still the young man hesitated. The captain had climbed on the trunk house, "in a situation from which my eye could take in everything." Boatswain's Mate Browning was one of those holding the noosed prisoner from whom the word must come, through the black cloth gathered about the throat, white rope rising behind him. Seconds passed. The prisoner mumbled something muffled to Browning. The boatswain's mate stepped to the trunk, saluted the captain. "Mr. Spencer says he can not give the word. He wishes the commander to give the word himself."

On the instant Captain Mackenzie cried, *Fire!*

The cannon thundered. The first lieutenant threw up his arm and sang out, *Whip!* As officers watched with pistols cocked, the crew moved smartly beyond blue smoke along the length of both gangways forward, hauling lines that lifted three hooded bodies aloft toward the yardarm, dark clinking forms rising—Cromwell's out over the water—in arcs that grew shorter as ropes ran fast through the sail blocks. Ship's ensign and pennant were streaming at the gaff. And up there under the furled mainsail three bodies swung, turning, steadying, finally swaying together with the ship's idle roll.

"Surely," Mackenzie himself had written of a similar sight in Madrid fifteen years before, "there can be nothing in such a spectacle to promote morality, nothing to make us either better or happier—a spectacle which serves but to create despondency and to array man in enmity with his condition. . . ."

Lines were being belayed on deck. After that was done, the crew filed on order aft to hear their captain, at this later time, point them a different moral.

He stood on the trunk house, his officers and men gathered attentively around him, under the hooded bodies that swayed some twenty feet overhead.

"I called their attention first to the fate of the unfortunate young man whose ill-regulated ambition, directed to the most infamous end, had been the exciting cause of the tragedy they had just witnessed. I spoke of his honored parents, of his distinguished father, whose talents and character had raised him to one of the highest stations in the land, to be one of the six appointed counselors of the representation of our national sovereignty. I spoke of the distinguished social position to which this young man had been born, of the advantages of every sort that attended the outset of his career, and of the professional honors to which a long, steady, and faithful perseverance in the course of duty might ultimately have raised him. After a few months' service at sea, most wretchedly employed so far as the acquisition of professional knowledge was concerned, he had aspired to supplant me in command, which I had only reached after nearly thirty years of faithful servitude, and for what object I had already explained to them.

"I told them that their future fortunes were within their own control. They had advantages of every sort, and in an eminent degree, for the attainment of professional knowledge. The situations of warrant officers and of masters in the navy were open to them. They might rise to command in the merchant service—to respectability, competence, and to fortune. But they must advance regularly and step by step. Every step, to be sure, must be guided by truth, honor, and fidelity.

"I called their attention to Cromwell's case. He must have received an excellent education. His handwriting was even elegant. But he had also fallen, through brutish sensuality and the greedy thirst for gold. The first fifteen dollars given to him by Mr. Spencer had bought him; and the hope of plunder held out to him by Mr. Spencer—who, to completely win him, had converted a box of old wine into treasure—had secured the purchase.

"There was an anecdote told by Collins in his mess which, with Cromwell's commentary, had reached my ears. I caused Collins to stand up on the pump well and relate it to the boys. Collins had been in an Indiaman on board of which the supercargo, a Mr. Thorndyke, had brought a keg of doubloons. Collins stowed it in the run, and was alone entrusted with the secret of its being on board. He said not a word about it until it went ashore. Cromwell, on hearing this, laughed at Collins, and said had the case been his he would have run away with the keg. The story, and what had passed before their eyes, contained all the moral that it was necessary to enforce.

"I told the boys, in conclusion, that they had only to choose between the morality of Cromwell and that of Collins—Cromwell at the yardarm and Collins piping with his call.

"Small had also been born for better things. He had enjoyed the benefits of education, was a navigator, had been an officer in a merchantman. But he could not resist the brandy which had been proffered to him, nor the prospect of dishonorable gain. He had, however, at least died invoking blessings on the flag of his country."

Anything else? The captain consulted with his first lieutenant on the trunk to larboard. How would it do to cheer the flag? Mr. Gansevoort thought it would do very well—would allow officers to assess the crew's loyalty. So Captain Mackenzie called for the cheers. "I gave the order, 'Stand by to give three hearty cheers for the flag of our country.'"

And the lads did. And "never were three heartier cheers given. In that electric moment, I do not doubt that the patriotism of even the worst of the conspirators for an instant broke forth. I felt that I once more was completely commander of the vessel that was entrusted to me, equal to do with her whatever the honor of my country might require."

For his part, Mr. Gansevoort thought the cheers had "appeared to relieve the minds of the officers and men from the gloom that hung about us." And what feelings were uppermost in the heart of the first lieutenant at that moment? "I felt like an officer who had done his duty to his God and his country." And were the four surviving prisoners cheering too? Doubtless—having only after the execution of the others learned that they were fated to live, at least for now, to be returned to the United States for trial. In his irons McKinley (the captain would judge McKinley to be "the individual who, if the mutiny had been successful, would have made way with all his competitors and risen to the command")—on being told of Commander Mackenzie's leniency, that formidable conspirator McKinley broke down and cried.

The watch was set. The crew was piped to dinner. Going below decks, some of the younger boys glanced up at the mainyard where the three bodies swung and as they did so "indulged in laughter and derision." The commander on the way to his cabin was pained by the sight of such behavior.

Ever a captain by the book, he was troubled about one detail. "I still earnestly desired that Mr. Spencer should be buried as officers usually are, in a coffin. I ordered one to be forthwith made from a portion of the berth deck." But no part of the ship would have to be dismantled, for

Mr. Gansevoort was prepared to relinquish for the purpose a couple of wardroom mess chests. These the carpenter was set to work converting into a substantial receptacle.

Dinner was meanwhile eaten below while the corpses swung in their nooses overhead, under a sky that had darkened. When the men came back topside, the dead had hung at the yardarm about an hour. Now the bodies were lowered to the deck, their irons and handcuffs and face coverings removed. Messmates prepared for burial Spencer's body—skin scarcely healed from the fresh tattoos. Those among the crew who had been in Cromwell's and Small's divisions were assigned to their corpses, farther forward on the quarterdeck. Under gathering clouds the work proceeded: cleaning the bodies, dressing them, combing their hair.

Later in the afternoon the first lieutenant came to the captain in his cabin and invited him to inspect the results, "to see that these duties had been duly performed." The captain found Mr. Spencer "laid out on the starboard armchest, dressed in complete uniform except the sword, which he had forfeited the right to wear. Further forward, the two seamen were also laid out with neatness. I noticed with pain that the taste of one of the sailors had led him to bind the hands of Cromwell with a riband having on it, in gold letters, the name of the chivalrous Somers who had died a self-devoted victim in the cause of his country. But that particular badge had been dishonored by the treason of its wearer, and it was suffered to remain."

Except for that, all was as it should be. Yet even as the captain was concluding his inspection, the skies that had grown black erupted, a tropic squall that forced all hands to break off—rain pouring onto the canted decks—and scurry to reduce sail and hastily toss tarpaulins over the corpses.

It blew past at dusk.

With the storm ended, Small and Cromwell were placed in their hammocks, shot to weight them at their feet. The sailmaker sewed the hammocks shut, taking the last stitch, as by immemorial custom, through the nose. Mr. Spencer's body was put in its weighted and perforated coffin, and the three corpses were lined up on deck along the lee side according to rank, the officer's farthest aft.

Darkness had fallen before all hands could be called to bury the dead. It was about seven in the evening. All the lanterns aboard were lit and distributed among the crew, holding their prayer books and taking their stations on the booms, in the gangways, in the lee quarter boat.

The ensign was lowered to half-mast.

By candlelight the captain read the service, "the responses audibly and devoutly made by the officers and crew . . ."

Points of light flicker on a vast emptiness. Murmur of voices in unison. At an order hammock sails are lifted to consign three bodies to the deep, lumps that splash into the black water, foam slipping aft as the captain's voice rises in that prayer "so appropriate to our situation, appointed to be read in our ships-of-war":

> Preserve us from the dangers of the sea and from the violence of enemies . . . that we may return in safety to enjoy the blessings of the land with the fruits of our labor, and with a thankful remembrance of thy mercies, to praise and glorify thy holy name, through Jesus Christ our Lord.

Those aboard later agreed that discipline, deteriorating on the vessel up to the execution, thereafter (weighted bodies drifting downward, downward) was entirely restored. Wales "noticed a change instantly after that. Those who had been the most surly immediately turned about." From then on (downward back there through three thousand black fathoms), the first lieutenant found for his part that "orders were obeyed with more alacrity, and there was less sullenness than there had been before in the manner of some of the men." Nevertheless, the passage home was a trial. Gunner's Mate King, for one, "never unbuckled my arms from me, and slept with them from the time they were given me until our arrival in New York."

That would not be for another two weeks. The execution had occurred Thursday, December 1, some 525 miles west of St. Thomas, at Lat. 17°34′28″ N, Long. 57°57′45″ W. Three mornings later, Sunday the fourth, the vessel running northwest by west three quarters west, her crew was mustered for divine services at five bells, "after the laws for the government of the navy had been read, according to our invariable custom in the *Somers* on the first Sunday of the month." Commander Mackenzie took the occasion to address the men and boys once more, drawing "from the past history and example of the criminals whose execution they had so recently beheld all the useful lessons that they afforded, to win back to the paths of duty and virtue the youthful crew which they had been so instrumental in leading astray." He who had conceived the mutiny was shown again to have turned aside from the example of his honored parents, trampling on all the "wise counsels and solemn warnings" lavished upon him. And Small: "in the Bible of poor Small I had found a letter to him from his aged mother, filled with affectionate endearment and pious counsel. She expressed the joy with which she had learned from him that he was so happy on board the *Somers* (at the time Mr. Spencer had not joined her)—that no grog was served on board of her. Within the folds of this sacred volume he had preserved a copy of verses taken from *The Sailor's Magazine*, enforcing the value of the Bible to seamen. I read these verses to the crew." And the captain urged them to cherish their own

Bibles, which could medicine to every ailment of the mind. Moreover, he "endeavored to call to their recollection the terror with which the three malefactors had found themselves suddenly called to enter the presence of an offended God. No one who had witnessed that scene could for a moment believe even in the existence of such a feeling as *honest* atheism—a disbelief in the existence of a God." The captain presented the recent tragedies aboard in ways that allowed his young listeners to draw two useful lessons: "a lesson of filial piety, and a piety toward God. With these two principles for their guide they could never go astray." And he ended this way:

"I told them that they had shown that they could give cheers for their country. They should now give cheers for their God, for they would do this when they sang praises to his name (the colors were now hoisted) . . ." Thus over those blue seas came forth from the little vessel sounds of all aboard singing the hundredth psalm, their leader contrasting so inspiriting a spectacle with what by this time would have been transpiring on board had the *Somers* fallen into pirate hands.

And now, at last, might the captain retire below for rest. During the crisis of these recent days he had been topside eighteen or nineteen hours out of every twenty-four. But in the aftermath of the execution it was noted that "he was not so much on deck, as he was indisposed." What thoughts were visiting that fevered mind in the solitude of the cramped cabin, the *Somers* holding her course westward toward Sombrero?

Some thirteen hours after his Sunday sermon, fifteen minutes past midnight civil time on December 5, Slidell Mackenzie brought the brig-of-war into port, before the red-tiled roofs of Charlotte Amalie, St. Thomas, Danish West Indies. Regard "for the health and comfort" of his crew required that the captain "stop to obtain a supply of bread, water, and refreshments." But he would not delay there. The following morning he was rowed ashore to supervise the dispatching of provisions, in a hurry to clear the islands before nightfall.

Once ashore, however, Mackenzie thought to write a letter to Secretary of the Navy Upshur, brother of his closest professional friend. Accordingly, in great haste "and with a wretched pen" the captain set down his first account of what had happened aboard the *Somers* in recent days, in case "the overpowering violence of the elements, collision with another vessel in the night, or other accident of this order" should "cause us nevermore to be heard of." But "if you never again hear of the *Somers*," he wrote the secretary, "be assured, sir, that she has not been captured from her commander and her officers . . ."

Before dark the vessel got under way once more and set her course northward. The last leg of the voyage was completed in nine days. With that behind him, off New York Harbor and a pilot aboard to take his ship in, the captain again wrote his superior, lamenting that he had been unable as yet to find time to prepare "a detailed statement of my cruise and of some extraordinary events which have attended it." But since St. Thomas, the weather had been "so boisterous throughout the passage" that the vessel's care had left him no time for such an endeavor. "During the last three days I have not had my clothes off, nor have I slept continually for an entire hour for the last fifteen days."

Be that as may, the *Somers* had finally reached home port. Having been at anchor no more than a hundred and seven out of some twenty-three hundred nearly continuous hours at sea, those aboard the brig-of-war on this wintry night of December 14, 1842, had heard the rattle of her cables through the hawse holes a final time, the battered vessel stopped at last near the navy yard across from sleepless Manhattan. A quarter of a year had passed since her bright September departure from these same waters, these waters onto which even now was being lowered a small boat to row young Oliver Perry, captain's clerk, stealthily, darkly to shore, hastening him on his way to Washington.

TRIAL

PHILIP HONE WAS A PROMINENT CITIZEN OF THE
New York from which the *Somers* had sailed in September, the New
York to which she had now returned after three months and a day at sea.
Sixty-two years old in this December of 1842, Hone had made a fortune
in his youth as merchant and auctioneer, had served briefly as mayor of
the city, had in early middle age retired from business, and had thence-
forth passed his generally comfortable days supporting the Whig party,
socializing with important personages of the time—Webster, the Astors,
the Schermerhorns, and the like—and keeping a full and observant diary
through nearly a quarter of a century.

In no other document do the two decades before midcentury as one
person lived them in Manhattan emerge so distinctly. During the preceding May, for example, the diarist had noted Fenimore Cooper's suit in
this city of "poor Stone, editor of the *Commercial*, who is really one of the
most decent of the city editors," but who had published the defamatory
attack on the naval historian by William Alexander Duer, president of
Columbia College. "The plaintiff," wrote Hone of Cooper, "tries his own
cause and displays forensic abilities equal to those he possesses as a novelist. What a pity it is that so good a head should be joined to so bad a
heart! He will not let people like him." Again, in June, Hone records
details of the duel "fought on Saturday morning at sunrise near Marcus
Hook in the state of Delaware by James Watson Webb, editor of the

Courier and Enquirer, and Thomas H. Marshall, member of Congress." In July he describes a visit on the twelfth with his wife and son to the just completed Croton reservoir, at Murray Hill, "about two miles above my house. . . . A wide flagged walk surrounds the whole which will form a delightful promenade for the millions who will visit it in all future time for centuries after the present generation shall have passed away"—that prodigious reservoir situated at Fifth Avenue and Forty-second Street, on the site of the present New York Public Library. In mid-September, the day after the *Somers* had slipped her moorings at Wallabout Bay, Hone is complaining about "the amusement of prize-fighting, the disgrace of which was formerly confined to England," but which has now become "one of the fashionable abominations of our loafer-ridden city." The complaint arises from the Lilly and McCoy fight in Westchester the afternoon before, during the hundred and twentieth round of which Tom McCoy, blinded and choking on blood, had fallen dead in the ring. A cross-eyed, cadaverous blackguard from Scotland, James Gordon Bennett, had been in the habit of publishing in his regrettably popular penny-press *Herald* "the horrid details" of such encounters—as he did that morning of this one—"with all their disgusting technicalities and vulgar slang . . . to gratify the vitiated palates of its readers, whilst the orderly citizens have wept for the shame which they could not prevent." Lilly, indeed, would escape unpunished, making his way aboard the *George Washington* to England, where, according to the disgusted diarist in a later entry, "he will be all the fashion in that refined country, whose sensitive tourists faint at the recollection of the tobacco-chewing and spitting Yankees . . ."

Meanwhile, New Yorkers among those Yankees had been exulting during October (with the *Somers* bearing eastward toward Madeira) over the abundance of fresh water now available from the far-off Croton River, after years of coping with the brackishness of local wells. "It is astonishing how popular the introduction of water is among all classes of our citizens," Hone writes on the twelfth, "and how cheerfully they acquiesce in the enormous expense which will burden them and their posterity with taxes to the latest generation. Water! Water! is the universal note which is sounded through every part of the city . . ." Two days later, Friday, October 14, the ex-mayor participates in the official Croton Water Celebration, which starts from the Battery at ten that morning, with Hone, Governor Seward, and other dignitaries distributed among "about a dozen barouches" that are accompanied by a military escort up Broadway circuitously to the jetting new fountain in City Hall Park. The procession winding its way through the streets on the sunlit occasion is five miles long; it includes butchers on horseback, regiments of troops, fifty-two companies of firemen from as far away as Philadelphia, temperance societies, mechanic associations, civic and scientific institutions—

and "nothing struck me with more pleasure and surprise than the perfect order and propriety which prevailed among the immense masses of male and female spectators on the route of the procession; not a drunken person was to be seen. The moral as well as the physical influence of water pervaded everything."

Mid-November would witness the appalling climax of the Colt murder case. (The *Somers* near the middle of that month lay briefly at Monrovia, on the twelfth had weighed anchor to steer a course westward for St. Thomas and home.) Back there, in the Tombs—New York's dismal prison behind City Hall—was languishing John C. Colt, of a respectable family (his brother invented the firearm), as he had been languishing throughout the year, convicted in January of the murder of a job printer named Samuel Adams. The previous September, officers of a cargo vessel at the New York docks had on a tip opened a crate about to be shipped to New Orleans; inside was a human body. It proved to be Adams's. Subsequent investigations had pointed to Colt as the suspect in what was a particularly gory murder, for Adams had been struck over the head five crushing times with an ax, his body then dumped into the three-and-a-half-foot box and his legs stood on till the limbs broke to fit; the corpse was then salted, and the box nailed down for shipment. As for Mr. Colt, a debtor of Adams's, he had been acting strangely of late in any case, and at the trial one witness testified to having peeped through a keyhole and seen the gentleman at an appropriate hour wiping a puddle of blood from his office floor. The jury had brought in a verdict of willful murder; but Colt had continued protesting his innocence of the charge, while influential friends were petitioning for his pardon amid excitement that lasted through spring, summer, and fall. By mid-November, with execution scheduled for the eighteenth and Colt now confessing but claiming self-defense (against an unarmed man), Governor Seward had made it clear that he would not pardon the prisoner, who had meanwhile been issuing widely read and affecting letters from his jail cell. "His friends are moving heaven and earth to save him," another New York diarist noted on the fifteenth, this one the twenty-two-year-old George Templeton Strong. "Colt," writes Strong two days later, "is the all-engrossing topic. . . . Poor creature. He's to be pitied, and if he knows of this last effort" to save him, "doubly to be pitied, for the agony of suspense, of a faint, an almost desperate hope, a shadow of uncertainty, is added to his miseries." The condemned man's spiritual adviser, father of one of the youthful diarist's best friends, "was with him today and is firmly convinced of his innocence." Yet the man must hang tomorrow. Specifically when? He would be allowed to name the hour: "Colt," so Strong was to learn, "flung himself on the bed and rocked there in agony for a moment or two, and then named 'sunset.' "

Rumors abounded. An attempt would be made to rescue him. The governor had reprieved the execution until early next year. The condemned man had bribed the sheriff, would escape in women's clothes, had been torturing himself by reading every word concerning the lurid affair that the numerous newspapers were printing . . .

The day of execution dawned. *"Last Act of the Tragedy,"* writes ex-Mayor Hone in his diary. "Among the òther transactions of this fatal day, the most extraordinary was Colt's marriage to Miss Henshaw, his kept mistress, which took place at noon." The man's ghostly confessor, Dr. Anthon, had performed the ceremony in the cell. But if the prisoner had "intended (dead as he was in the eye of the law) to wipe out the shame of his wretched companion and legitimize his child, the advice of his legal counselors was no better in this than in some other particulars of his case.

"Now," Hone goes on, "comes the dramatic incident of this romantic tragedy. An hour before the final one, he requested to be left alone, to perform his devotions uninterruptedly!"—having already prayed with fervor alongside Dr. Anthon for an hour or more. Colt was allowed his privacy. "A few minutes before four o'clock the sheriff opened his cell to bring him forth to execution. Dr. Anthon entered first, and the unhappy man was found lying on his cot, *dead*, with a small Spanish stiletto driven directly into his heart." Young Strong notes of the same event that the suicide had "had the resolution to *twist* as he did it, to make the wound more sure." But how had the knife come into Colt's possession? At an inquest soon after, "the sheriff and keepers, the brother of the deceased and his mistress all swore they knew nothing about it."

The case was closed at any rate, though some of the mob outside the Tombs, cheated of their spectacle, would maintain that the privileged Colt had not killed himself at all—rather had been spirited away and would someday reappear on the streets of the city.

Fifteen years afterward some were still saying so (and in "Bartleby, the Scrivener" Herman Melville would by then have alluded at some length to the still-famous murder). But for now, with the case disposed of, attention turned elsewhere as winter came abruptly to New York at the end of this present November 1842. The *Herald* was noting December 1 (day of the hanging aboard the *Somers* at sea): "STORM YESTERDAY.—A severe snow and rain storm set in yesterday morning about 10 o'clock. Snow fell till 7 o'clock in the evening, when it turned to rain, and the wind began to blow with great violence from the northeast. . . . There must have been a good deal of suffering all night on the coast, and a good deal of distress among the poor in the city. The winter has begun in good earnest. It bids fair to be a severe one. . . ."

Two weeks later, Thursday morning, December 15, the *Courier and Enquirer*, owned and edited by Commander Mackenzie's Tarrytown neighbor, J. W. Webb, was carrying on page 3 a story of routine interest to this community of merchants: "ARRIVAL OF THE U.S. BRIG SOMERS, FROM LIBERIA," including an innocent report of that African venture at resettlement: ". . . The colony was in a flourishing condition, the colonists more disposed than heretofore to devote themselves to agricultural pursuits." (Earlier those transported blacks had exhibited a tendency to subsist indolently by bartering American goods for ivory and gumwood and palm oil.) Sugar and coffee promise to become valuable staples. Recently arrived colonists are doing well, with few deaths. And "the most interesting news brought from St. Thomas," where the *Somers* had also anchored, "was of a small war that had broken out between the Spanish government and the Republic of Hayti." The article, seven paragraphs long, ends by assuring readers that the officers and crew of the brig have returned "in excellent health."

Not for another two days—not until the seventeenth—would the truth blare forth from all the local papers.

That Saturday morning, December 17, the *Herald* was headlining: "HORRIBLE MUTINY ON BOARD THE U.S. BRIG SOMERS—HANGING AT THE YARD ARM!" And the *Courier and Enquirer* began its lead story: "*Most atrocious Mutiny in a United States Man-of-War*— The astounding intelligence we are about to place before the public reached us to a certain extent in whispers on Thursday night. . . ." Now, two mornings later, after diligent inquiry, the editors have concluded that the details are substantially accurate, though communication with the vessel in question remains interdicted, and none of the officers who have come ashore will speak of the matter.

What had happened, nevertheless, was this: While the *Somers* was lying at anchor off the African coast, a midshipman aboard had led fifty of the crew in a mutiny. The twenty-five other crew members, with the remaining officers, "succeeded after a conflict with the mutineers, in which some of them were severely wounded, in suppressing the revolt and putting all the mutineers in irons." Following a drumhead court, the mutinous officer, Philip Spencer, son of the cabinet secretary, had been hanged with two of his confederates, not having been allowed ten minutes to write his father. "It has been extremely painful to us," the reporter adds, "to allude to the relationship the instigator of the revolt bore to the secretary of war. Heaven knows we would not add to the pangs which the conduct of such a son must cause a father, but it must come out, and it would have been a useless delicacy on our part to refrain from allusion to it."

For its part, Horace Greeley's recently founded (as of April 1841) but already influential *Tribune* printed that same Saturday morning a different version, admitting that "there are some portions of this account which lead us to suspect its entire accuracy, but we give it as it was told to us, upon authority which we deem most reliable." The *Somers*, the *Tribune* explained, had left St. Thomas and was two days out at sea when Commander Mackenzie had learned of a plot aboard to mutiny. "This was on the 7th of December. The captain immediately ordered all hands on deck, and ordered those of the crew who were opposed to him to go upon the forward deck. *Passed Midshipman* SPENCER, *son of John C. Spencer, our Secretary of War, the Boatswain's Mate, and the Master at Arms immediately led the way*, and were followed by thirteen apprentices and about sixty of the crew," which was reported to number "not far from four hundred." The mutineers, seventy-six of them by this account, "arrayed themselves upon the forward deck, without doubt supposing that they would be followed by a great proportion of the crew." Instead, they were instantly put in irons, and that same evening at a court-martial the three ringleaders *"were tried, convicted and sentenced, and the next morning* WERE HUNG AT THE YARDARM." The remaining mutineers, presumably to the number of seventy-three, were brought home shackled. The article takes pains to commend "the prompt, fearless decision and energy of Capt. Mackenzie."

As indeed did everyone else upon this initial disclosure of the terrifying ordeal—still only vaguely understood—that the *Somers* had passed through. (Yet another account, in *The New York Express*, described how the conspirators, aware that they had been discovered, had advanced on the commander in a body and demanded possession of the ship, as "young Spencer presented a pistol to his [Mackenzie's] heart. All this was at night, and the chief part of the crew were below when the officers on deck, not knowing the extent of the conspiracy, immediately closed the hatches and kept all confined who were below. The officers, after something of a struggle as we understand, overpowered the conspirators and, regaining complete possession of the ship, instantly caused the ringleaders to be tried by court-martial, and young Spencer, within ten minutes of the finding of the court, was hung at the yardarm, along with two of the men.") Having dealt successfully with a threat such as that—or the equally serious and overt threats of the other versions—the triumphant captain of the brig seemed entitled to the unreserved praise that was greeting him from every quarter during this first weekend home. The *Herald*, for instance—which soon would feel differently—now, Sunday, was groping for "language adequate to express our admiration of the conduct of Commander Mackenzie. The public voice has already pronounced a verdict of unqualified and unanimous approbation of that prompt, decided, and just act which visited with righteous punishment the chief participators in this hellish scheme." One conclusion seemed inescapable: "It has indeed been fortunate for the well-being of the naval service that on such a man as Slidell Mackenzie devolved the high responsibility of such a critical hour."

*   *   *

That first night back he had dispatched his clerk, the seventeen-year-old Oliver Perry, to Washington to deliver the captain's official report concerning recent events aboard the *Somers*, and to receive instructions from the secretary of the navy. Until such time as those instructions reached New York, Mackenzie and his subordinates would keep their own counsel. The commander did, the morning after dropping anchor, throw into irons Golderman, Warner, Van Velsor, Hamilton, Knevals, Gallia the Maltese steward, Sullivan, and the well-flogged Waltham, all eight of whom were transferred to the *North Carolina*, along with the four crew members (McKinley, McKee, Green, and Willson) who had remained manacled aboard the *Somers* since before the executions. Thus twelve men were imprisoned now in the receiving ship at the navy yard. As early as possible their captain had reported to the yard commandant—his brother-in-law Matthew Perry—and to the commander on the New York station, Commodore Jacob Jones. But to his own wife, for example, Mackenzie had at first confided nothing. When Mrs. Mackenzie was reunited with her husband, "she perceived that he looked dreadfully, and asked him at once 'What is the matter?' He turned her off by saying that he had had no sleep, and that they had experienced bad weather, etc., etc." And Charles King of *The New York American* "happened to see and have a long conversation with Commander Mackenzie on the day of his arrival without hearing from him one syllable, or hint of any kind, of the dreadful occurrence on board the brig."

How, then, was James Watson Webb's *Courier and Enquirer* as early as Monday morning able to appear on the streets with an astonishingly accurate account of the occurrence, detailed enough to fill nearly two columns of page 1? From what source had come all those facts so nearly in agreement with the captain's own lengthy, confidential account, just completed, that was not yet even in the hands of Secretary Upshur—an account that bore this present date of December 19 but that would not be made public for another ten days? The vessel had anchored Wednesday evening. Webb Friday had learned from Morris Robinson, Mackenzie's father-in-law, that although the captain "had been on shore with his family, not a word had escaped him referring to any difficulties which had occurred during his cruise." Over the weekend the editor had been out of town and thus was not responsible for the publication in his paper Saturday morning of the suggestion that young Spencer under sentence of death had not been allowed time to write his father. "From our knowledge of Captain Mackenzie's character, as also from our confidence in the source whence we received our information, we knew that there was not the slightest grounds for giving credence to such a rumor."

But for Monday morning's account, then, who was Webb's source, so well informed about everything that had happened aboard? The colonel would not say—only that what was published might be relied upon, and that neither the navy nor anyone else need "give themselves any unnecessary trouble to ascertain" how he had come by his information. He did later insist that no officer from the *Somers* had communicated with him. Had that other Tarrytown friend and neighbor, Commandant Perry, breached a confidence? Had Commodore Jones? As presented, the account was not only remarkably accurate but distinctly favorable to Mackenzie, who was reported to have accompanied his officers and crew to the chapel of the navy yard yesterday for divine services, "to return thanks to an all-wise Providence for their escape from the dangers to which they have been exposed." Made aware of those dangers, the most torpid member of New York's merchant class—and merchants formed the chief readers and support for Webb's newspaper—could appreciate the potential for harm that young Spencer would have posed had he succeeded in converting the fastest vessel in the service into a fleet privateer to hover off Sandy Hook and prey on commerce. "Sufficient is known already to establish beyond a question the necessity, imperative and immediate, however dreadful, of the course pursued by Commander Mackenzie, than whom a more humane, conscientious, and gallant officer does not hold a commission in the navy of the United States."

But sufficient was also known—after the *Courier*'s purported "semi-official" account of Monday—to raise preliminary doubts, in the pages of the *Herald*, for instance. James Gordon Bennett's *New York Herald* was an altogether different newspaper from Colonel Webb's *Courier*, with a different readership, drawn in large part from among the working classes. Those democrats would have less patience with naval ways—the hierarchical world at sea, autocratic captain, officers aft with their white gloves on, the enforced servility, floggings. Moreover, unlike the *Courier*, which resented the Virginian Tyler's desertion of Whig principles, and deeply resented such so-called Whigs as John C. Spencer who were supporting His Accidency Tyler's pursuit of policies injurious to the commercial East—unlike the Wall Street *Courier*, the penny-press *Herald* was at the time widely regarded as friendly to the administration in Washington. Views of the *Somers*'s case that the *Herald* was soon expressing differed accordingly from those of its rival. Already on Monday, Bennett's popular paper was taking note of a disturbing rumor circulating around town that one of the three men executed on the brig had professed his innocence to the last. And Tuesday morning, commenting on the *Courier*'s scoop of yesterday, editor Bennett stressed the absence from that account of any overt act of mutiny aboard ship, the absence of any plot other than one in embryo, the absence of any legally constituted court-martial aboard as required by naval law. "The officers," so the *Herald* concluded ominously, "would seem to have acted under a panic. . . ."

Nevertheless, most civic opinion of consequence, even after events aboard had been accurately related in the *Courier*, continued for now to support the decision that those officers had come to. Greeley's respectable *Tribune*, reprinting Webb's scoop Tuesday morning and commenting on the event that "has been the almost universal theme of conversation in this city," saw Captain Mackenzie's response in crisis as "prompt, efficient, and—every intelligent man must add—*humane* . . . We agree with the *Courier* that Congress should adopt some measures to signify, in a marked and emphatic manner, their sense of the gallant and most praiseworthy conduct of the commander of the *Somers* and the officers and seamen who remained faithful to his command." One thought more: "In looking at the transaction we trust regard will not be had merely to the wretches who suffered death for their crimes, but that others than the criminals will receive some sympathy and attention. There seems to be a very prevalent feeling just now to shed profuse and most pitying tears over the fate of every incarnate devil"—John C. Colt, for one—"who suffers at the hands of Justice and its minister the Law for his black and damning guilt; and it is with the greatest difficulty that the slightest consideration can be secured for the rights of society, the security of life, or the wrongs of those who have fallen victims to the spirit which destroys both. In this case we hope to see none of this mock philanthropy . . ."

At any rate the cause of the mystery about the *Somers* had been revealed, the mystery of why (as Philip Hone had noted in his diary) she had lain during the whole of Thursday in the bay and "nobody, not even the near relations of the officers, was permitted to visit her," why Lieutenant Gansevoort's own cousin and fellow officer in the navy had been forbidden to approach the vessel. Amid rumors the mystery had persisted until the news of the mutiny had broken Saturday morning. By Monday the *Courier*'s authoritative account had appeared, and Tuesday of that following week the *Herald* was expressing early doubts about proceedings aboard.

But by Wednesday even more serious doubts had emerged, and from another source, as Hone was recording in an entry of that date, December 21: "A statement is published in the Washington *Madisonian* signed S., which will occasion some revulsion in the public mind in relation to the melancholy tragedy on board the brig *Somers*." As a wealthy member of the ruling class who had made his money through trade, Hone sympathized with Slidell Mackenzie—protector of commerce—in the present developing controversy; but "S," whoever he was, made a formidable case for the opposition. Could "S" be John Canfield Spencer? The statement "is one of those strong, forcible documents for which he is celebrated: fierce in style, rigid in argument, and certainly presents the subject of his son's execution in a light somewhat different from that in which it was received at first. If," Hone goes on, "there exists any reasonable doubt of the absolute necessity for this awful exercise of power, Captain Mackenzie may wish sincerely that he never had been born to meet such a responsibility. A more dangerous opponent than John C. Spencer could not be found in the United States: stern, uncompromising, obstinate in temper, determined and energetic in action, and with talents equal to any effort which his feelings may prompt, or his duty may call him to execute."

Was the document in the *Madisonian* Spencer's? The secretary of war later denied having written it, but most people at the time assumed he did. Who else at Washington could have known so thoroughly details of Philip Spencer's brief life, and have discovered so promptly the contents of Mackenzie's dispatch to the secretary of the navy? That imperfect account of December 14, borne by the boy Oliver Perry, had reached the federal capital Friday evening of the preceding week. Secretary Upshur, according to the Washington correspondent of the *Herald* writing Monday, had been at a loss how to break the news to Mr. Spencer; "at last he sent for Mr. Morris, the son-in-law and private secretary of the Secretary of War, and through him the sad intelligence was communicated." If, under the circumstances, Mr. Spencer had asked to see Captain Mackenzie's report of events that had led to his son's execution, would a fellow cabinet officer have denied the request? Of Mrs. Spencer, the same correspondent wrote by the way: "The excellent mother of the wretched youth is quite beside herself. She was in feeble health, and this shocking event has made her quite delirious. Two physicians are constantly in attendance, and her ultimate recovery is even doubtful." How feeble her health was—"This will kill my poor mother"—is unclear; another account recorded the irony that shortly before receiving the awful news, Mrs. Spencer had "issued cards for a large party next Wednesday." As Secretary Spencer's fellow New Yorker Governor Seward was soon observing from Albany, "There are all manner of reports in Washington concerning the manner in which the parents receive this last sad blow"— this in a letter to his wife, in the course of which the governor had remarked upon the "calamity that has befallen the Spencers. Was ever a blow more appalling? I, of course, knew Philip only as friends know our children. I should as soon have expected a deer to ravage a sheepfold." (That qualified testimonial to the young man's apparent gentleness seems of particular interest.) "I know," the governor continues, "that Nature has given no firmness to resist the immediate shock to the mother, but time may heal and obliterate the wound. The card which Mr. Spencer has published"—referring to the document signed "S"—". . . shows that his iron nerves were proof." Indeed, within two days—Christmas Day it was—Seward had further corroboration of who had composed that remarkable document, and was passing that and other information on to an unnamed correspondent: "Weed writes from Washington that Mrs. Spencer is heartbroken, and her husband scarcely less. That article in the *Madisonian* was his. Weed says that the papers sent to Washington do not show a necessity for the execution, and that the conduct of Mackenzie, as ascertained from these papers, appears to have been cowardly and murderous. . . ."

In any event, the rectitudinous father and the scapegrace son would never now be able to make their peace with each other. Remorse was adding its portion to grief and anger. John Lorimer Graham, postmaster of New York City who at the time was in Washington, was writing anxiously as late as Christmas Eve day: "Our friend Spencer is stricken down. He wishes impartial but stern justice done in this matter. It is a case that will agitate the nation. . . . Mr. S has seen no one out of his own family but myself; I spent two hours with him today"—that is, on a day an anguish-filled week and more after the father would have learned of his son's harsh fate.

But in that interval "S" had composed the document challenging Mackenzie's as yet confidential version. "You would much oblige the Hon. J. C. Spencer," his son-in-law Henry Morris was promptly writing *The New York Commercial Advertiser*, "by publishing in your paper the article in the enclosed *Madisonian* . . ."

The article—that "strong, forcible" document as Hone called it, "fierce in style, rigid in argument"—reads:

> The friends of young Spencer, who was executed together with two seamen on the 1st inst., would have been content to abide the investigation which the laws of the country require in such cases, and would have trusted to that justice which our tribunals award to all entitled to the protection of the constitution and laws of the country. Various publications have, however, appeared in the New York papers and been copied into a paper of extensive circulation at the seat of government, giving versions of the transaction the materials for which, if not the versions themselves, were obviously furnished by some officers who had a hand in the bloody deed. This is evident from their containing some facts which could be known only to those officers—but so perverted, so exaggerated, and interspersed with so much surmise and so much downright falsehood, as to evince the deep anxiety felt to make sure of the first impression on the public mind. An awful responsibility rests on those officers, and above all on their commander. Without the least desire to render that responsibility more hazardous than it now is, it is still deemed an act of simple and bare justice to the memory of *the slain*, to say

that an examination of the papers transmitted by Com. Mackenzie shows these facts:

1st. That Acting Midshipman Spencer was put in double irons on the 26th of November, and the boatswain's mate, Samuel Cromwell, and Seaman Elisha Small on the day following, on a charge of intended mutiny.

2d. That no disorder of a mutinous character appeared among the crew for the four succeeding days; that the vessel was going with good breezes and in good weather towards the island of St. Thomas, where she actually arrived and took in supplies on some day between the 1st and 5th of December.

3d. That on the 30th of November, the opinion of the officers was required by Commander Mackenzie as to the disposition of the prisoners; that they appear to have examined thirteen seamen as witnesses to prove the alleged mutiny (and who are therefore supposed innocent of any participation in it), which examination was had, so far as the papers show, in the absence of the prisoners, and without giving them any opportunity to cross-examine the witnesses or to make any explanation or defense, or to procure any testimony in their own behalf. These officers, without even the form of a court, without even the obligation of an oath, and upon this ex parte secret information, united in the opinion that the safety of the vessel required that the prisoners should be put to death! How far this recommendation was influenced by the acts or fears of Mr. Mackenzie does not appear.

4th. That on the 1st of December, when every thing and person on board the vessel were perfectly quiet, after four days of entire security, the three persons were, by order of Mackenzie, hung at the yardarm at mid-day.

The allegation in some of the papers that it was proved to have been the intention of the mutineers to execute their project on arriving at St. Thomas is wholly destitute of any evidence. And had it been their design, it was effectually frustrated, so far as these prisoners were concerned, by their confinement. At St. Thomas, any of the crew might have been left, and the power of the officers of the vessel strengthened to any extent that was necessary.

The statement in the *Intelligencer*, copied apparently from *The New York American*, that Spencer violated an engagement formerly made to resign seems to have been deemed necessary to prejudice the public mind against him, that those who slew him might have a more favorable hearing. It is untrue. He did resign, and the secretary of the navy, on the recommendation of his commanding officer, considering the nature and circumstances of the offense (inebriation), restored his warrant with a strong admonition; and this was done without the solicitation of any of his friends. His age is represented in the same paper to have been over twenty. Had he lived, he would have been nineteen the 28th of January next.

As to the probability that such a mere boy—utterly unacquainted with navigation, brought up in the interior—would seriously endeavor to seduce to mutiny an old seaman who had arrived at the rank of boatswain's mate and who is represented to have been employed heretofore on board a slaver or to have been a pirate, an impartial tribunal before which *both sides* will be heard will determine.

The idea of the mutineers cruising off Sandy Hook to intercept the packets seems to have been thrown in for the special benefit of the merchants of New York. The papers, such as they are, contain no such information. The only account we have given by Spencer himself is, that *it was all a joke*. If it shall appear to have been the mere romance of a heedless boy, amusing himself, it is true, in a dangerous manner but still devoid of such murderous designs as are imputed, and if the execution of him and two seamen (against one of whom, at least, there is not yet a particle of evidence) should prove to have been the result of unmanly fear or of a despotic temper, and wholly unnecessary at the time to repress or prevent a mutiny—if all this can appear, it cannot be doubted that the laws will be vindicated. The laws of Congress prescribing the navy regulations forbid the taking of human life even by the sentence of a court-martial, before which all parties are heard, without the sanction of the President of the United States, or, if without the United States, of the commander of the fleet or squadron. This is believed to be the first instance in our history in which the law has been violated—the first in which prisoners, not of the enemy but of our own citizens, have been put to death in cold blood.

These remarks are made not to excite prejudice, but to repel the attempt to create it, and to enable the American people to see what mighty principles are involved in this unheard-of proceeding. Let justice be done. Let it not be denied because one of the victims was connected with a high functionary of government, nor because another is unknown and has not a friend or relation on the face of the earth. And let not wanton opprobrium be heaped upon the memory of the dead to justify the bloody deeds of the living.

S.

"There never was a more beautiful Christmas than this day," Philip Hone, agreeably distracted by the pleasures of the season, was having occasion to note in his diary that December. "Broadway from the Battery to Union Place has been an animated scene of new bonnets with happy faces under them, and little gentlemen and ladies bending under the weight of toys . . . and shops disregarding the injunction 'lead me not into temptation' . . . When I was in the Fulton Market on Saturday, I wondered where mouths could be found for the turkeys, geese, ducks, and chickens which I saw there, and today when walking up Broadway, I was tempted to exclaim, 'Where can ducks and chickens, turkeys and geese be found to fill all these mouths?' "

But Christmas, merry enough for the inoffensive Hone, for Slidell Mackenzie and his associates must have been anxious. The captain since coming ashore had spent much of his time at Commandant Perry's home in the navy yard, where he was kept busy responding to well-wishers and working on a final, lengthy statement of events on the *Somers*—his third account, after the one scribbled with a wretched pen at St. Thomas December 5, and the one of December 14 as the *Somers* was being piloted into New York Harbor, that second explanation transmitted to Washington under young Perry's care. But evidently Secretary Upshur had been less than satisfied to find so important a matter dealt with thus and entrusted to a seventeen-year-old. On the twenty-second the secretary had written Commander Mackenzie for a fuller account, indirectly making known to him that a more senior officer might fittingly bring it to Washington. Such a narrative, dated December 19, the literary commander had already completed—"a more detailed statement of the facts of the mutiny than I was at first able to communicate." Some thirteen thousand words long, this third version had on the twenty-first been put into the hands of Midshipman Rodgers, who by now would have delivered it to the navy department. Lieutenant Gansevoort likewise had left that same Wednesday afternoon for the capital, as the commander was prompt to assure Secretary Upshur by letter; he would be able to answer all questions concerning the affair.

Before leaving New York, however, the first lieutenant of the *Somers* had taken time to visit his family in Brooklyn, "almost by stealth, at 9 o'clock in the evening. He was then," as Gansevoort's mother wrote to her brother-in-law, "in such a situation from fatigue and exposure that I scarcely knew him. He had a violent cold, coughing constantly, very hoarse, his limbs so contracted that he walked like an infirm man of seventy. His eyes were red and swollen, and his whole face very much bloated. His back and sides were so sore from the strap and weight of the huge heavy ship's pistols that he could not raise himself erect. Having imprisoned so many of the crew, they were short of hands; and he, poor fellow," writes Gansevoort's solicitous parent, "did more than double duty" on the long voyage home.

"The evening of which I speak," she continues, "his first visit to us, he had not had even his coat off in four days. Mr. Upshur wrote to Mr. Mackenzie for Guert to proceed to Washington. He was here, and had just sent a note to Mackenzie saying that he was really sick, and that I had prevailed on him to remain and have medical assistance, which he would do, unless he"—the commander—"expressed a wish for him to return to the yard. Before his messenger got to Mackenzie, *his* dispatch to Guert arrived here, one a very friendly and confidential letter inquiring about his health, the other an official order. Nothing could stop him. He went, was sick one night at Philadelphia, but got there safe, had three interviews with the Secretary—*very satisfactory to Guert*—but this to *your ear only*.

"Commander Mackenzie and Guert seem well pleased with the officers composing the court. God grant," the mother of the first lieutenant concludes nevertheless, in terms that reveal her distressful uncertainty, "that all *is, and was* right."

The court that Mrs. Gansevoort referred to was a court of inquiry, ordered by the secretary of the navy to convene forthwith on the receiving ship *North Carolina* at the New York navy yard in Brooklyn, "to examine the facts connected with the recent alleged attempt at mutiny on board the U.S. Brig-of-War *Somers* . . ." Three officers composed the investigative body: Captain Charles Stewart as president, commander of the home squadron, Commodore A. J. Dallas, commandant of the Pensacola navy yard, and Commodore Jacob Jones, port captain on the New York station, to whom Mackenzie had reported on his return from the cruise. The judge advocate, charged with directing the presentation of evidence before the court, was the Honorable Ogden Hoffman, United States District Attorney for the Southern District of New York—himself a former naval officer who had served under Decatur during the War of 1812, and who had since become widely regarded as the outstanding criminal lawyer of his generation. (Hoffman was, incidentally, the brother of Matilda, betrothed to Washington Irving three decades earlier, child in her teens who had suddenly contracted consumption and died, leaving the bereaved lover to treasure her memory thereafter through a lifelong bachelorhood.)

The board met for the first time at eleven Wednesday morning, December 28. On hand at the navy yard were representatives of the New York press, making their way with officials and some ten or twelve private citizens the short distance from the wharf to the *North Carolina*. That ship of the line, once the pride of the fleet (fifteen years earlier, Matthew Perry had been serving as her first lieutenant in far-flung cruises, and on one occasion Slidell the traveler had elatedly watched her approach from shore at Gibraltar)—the ship was still kept in fine order, though her farthest voyaging now was to summer quarters nearby, at anchor in the Hudson off the Battery. This was the vessel to which young Spencer had reported scarcely more than a year earlier to commence his ill-fated naval career, the vessel aboard which Lieutenant Wilkes's court-martial had been held late last August while the *Somers* was preparing to sail. Marines would have been seen this December morning drilling on the quarter-deck, and boys would have been about, fewer than usual to be sure, as those with family nearby had been dismissed on Saturday for the holidays. Coming aboard, editor Horace Greeley of the *Tribune* did notice another twenty-five or so, apprentices at the naval school, receiving their two shillings each and liberty till sunset. He noticed in addition that arms on deck were burnished and well-arrayed, houses erected over the hatches for winter, half ports closed, belowdecks made "comfortable with stoves and abundant fuel." As always on receiving ships, smells of rum and tar and tobacco smoke and bean soup and bilge water pervaded the passageways, along which reporters and dignitaries were being led aft toward the captain's cabin, where, from eleven-thirty to four each coming weekday, the court was to conduct its business.

Inside the cabin Captain Mackenzie was sitting in full uniform at his assigned place, a man "of an amiable and pleasing rather than stern and commanding presence." Greeley's first impression was confirmed by the reporter for the *Herald*, who found the commander's appearance "decidedly prepossessing. His manner," readers of Bennett's paper would learn next morning, "was singularly composed and dignified, his entire demeanor indicative of calm but decided resolution." Present as well in the cabin were Commodore Perry, Lieutenant Henry Eld of the Polar Exploring Expedition as provost marshal, and some twenty others, officials and visitors. Commander Mackenzie was asking leave to be assisted by Mr. John Hone, attorney, great-nephew of the ex-mayor and husband of one of Perry's daughters—assisted not as counsel, but to take minutes of the proceedings.

That first day the captain's cabin was already crowded, though more people would come the second day, and still more thereafter. Indeed, before long everybody in town seemed bent on a visit to observe the proceedings firsthand. Early in the new year, for instance, Mr. Philip Hone passed an interesting two or three hours on board the *North Carolina*, after first calling on Commodore Perry at the navy yard. On that occasion, "the cabin," according to the diarist, "was filled with spectators and newspaper reporters, for the examination is conducted by the greatest publicity. I was received with flattering respect by the president and members of the court, who invited me to a seat at their table." From that enviable vantage point Hone had been pleased to observe that the inquiry was "characterized by the utmost dignity and decorum. The witnesses examined today were Mr. Leecock, the surgeon, and Mr. Rodgers, senior midshipman, the latter a fine, sturdy fellow, a sailor out and out. I was amused by his seamanlike reply of 'Aye, aye, sir,' on two occasions when requested by the judge advocate and commodore to raise his voice. The witnesses are made to give a narrative in their own words of the events attending the mutiny and execution on board the *Somers*, after which

questions are put to them in writing by Commander Mackenzie and oral-
ly by the judge advocate." By this time, a week into the hearing, the
commander (so Hone reports) "looks careworn and anxious. . . . God
send him a safe deliverance!"

The previous day another distinguished visitor had come aboard the
North Carolina, one much younger yet far more knowledgeable about
these matters than was Philip Hone. In his late twenties, the Bostonian
Richard Henry Dana, Jr., had journeyed to New York to deliver, before
the Mercantile Library Association, an evening lecture the chief purpose
of which, as the *Tribune* was reporting on the third, "was to insist that the
source . . . of all noble and heroic action is in the moral rather than in the
intellectual nature of man." Having discharged that task commendably,
young Dana had spent the morning of the fourth pursuing other matters,
specifically the subject currently of consuming interest as well in Boston
as in New York: the execution of Philip Spencer and two American
crewmen on the high seas.

First the visitor had called on a relative of Ogden Hoffman's at the
Customs House and "talked over the *Somers* mutiny and Captain Mackenzie." Then with a couple of friends he went down to the East River. "We
had," as he was soon describing the episode in a widely read letter, "a
fine, clear, cold day, and the Brooklyn ferry-boat zig zagged us across the
river to avoid the floating ice, and a lively sleigh took us to the navy
yard." The *North Carolina* lay moored a few rods from shore. "A little
wherry, in which were two sailors with the naval jacket and shirt collar,
was passing and repassing by a tow-line or guess-warp, taking passengers
off and on."

Dana would have observed such nautical details with a practiced eye.
Eight and a half years earlier, while an undergraduate at Harvard, this
member of a well-known family, son of a poet, essayist, and editor of *The
North American Review*, had for reasons of health interrupted his studies
and shipped aboard a merchant vessel bound via Cape Horn for distant,
foreign California. The college student had sailed, however, not as an
officer aft, but in the forecastle as a member of the rough, unlettered
crew. And he had made his way with those rowdies, scrambled aloft
with them in storms, got his health back, and struggled beside them in
the surf as they loaded the awkward cargo of hides aboard, gone on
liberties with them in the Spanish port hamlets of Santa Barbara, of Los
Angeles, of Yerba Buena in San Francisco Bay. One result of his remarkable adventure was *Two Years Before the Mast*, written from notes of the
voyage and published back East when the author was twenty-five. The
book was immediately a success, offering as it did a unique and authentic
view of shipboard life as experienced by those heretofore inarticulate
multitudes who went to sea without gloves on. Soon after, in 1841,
Dana, now graduated from Harvard and practicing maritime law in Bos-

ton, had composed *The Seaman's Friend*, filled with useful information—legal and otherwise—to ease the lot of the common sailor. In addition, much of the young attorney's professional work was becoming involved with fighting injustices against seamen, who were learning to seek him out in his office in the Old State House so that he might defend them from instances of official greed or brutality.

Dana's opinion of the *Somers* affair would be heard with great interest. That opinion, derived from this present visit, he would express in the pages of the *New York Evening Post* of January 13, 1843. "The marine on guard at the cabin door let us pass," he wrote in the course of preparing his readers to receive the conclusion he had reached, "and we found ourselves in the upper cabin, and in the midst of the grave and rather imposing assembly. A long table filled the middle of the room. On one side of it sat the three commanders who compose the court. Mr. Mackenzie sat at one end, Mr. Perry (the witness then under examination) stood at the other end; and opposite the court sat the clerk and Mr. Hoffman, the judge advocate," over near the stove. Spectators were on hand as well, as were reporters, who had been provided with a table of their own.

During his brief visit, Dana would study Mackenzie closely, "for this case is one which receives its complexion very much from the character of the chief actor." The results of that scrutiny were favorable to the captain, who showed "every mark of a calm, self-possessed, clear-minded man, and entirely free from any of that dashing, offhand, or assuming manner which sometimes attends the military button. I felt much confidence in him from the moment I had carefully observed him, and this confidence has increased by my being informed that he is more noted for conscientiousness, order, and thoroughness than for imagination or enthusiasm."

Aware that the testimony of Acting Master Perry would be reprinted tomorrow in the local papers, Dana had not stayed long at the hearing. He had preferred to spend time on the *Somers*, proceeding forthwith to where she lay moored alongside the larger vessel. That inspection impressed him forcefully: "I must say that no one ought to form an opinion upon the issue of this conspiracy without first seeing the *Somers*." Civilian notions founded upon a visit aboard a man-of-war were misleading, for here on the little brig—she looked like a pilot boat beside the *North Carolina*—was no "appearance of protection, defense, and imposing authority connected with the after end of the ship," no raised poop deck or elevated captain's cabin with windows facing forward, no armed marines at the captain's door and along the gangway, no "clear, roomy decks, a plenty of officers about, and the quarters of officers furnished with arms, and well guarded." No, the *Somers* was not at all like that. "You would hardly believe your eyes if you were here to see, as the scene of this dreadful conspiracy, a little brig with low bulwarks, a single narrow deck flush fore and aft, and nothing to mark the officers' quarters but a long trunk-house . . . raised a few feet from the deck to let light and air in below, such as you may have seen in our smaller packets which ply along the seaboard." Standing on the gun deck of the rakish little craft, Dana felt convinced that half a dozen resolute conspirators could have taken her at sea, officers below required to ascend through these same narrow companionways, where a couple of crewmen topside could easily have cut them down as they appeared, one at a time.

Though not permitted to go below himself, the visitor was persuaded as well that the vessel at sea, armed and provisioned and with more than a full muster aboard, would have offered no place other than the quarterdeck to put prisoners in irons. But you had to be here to know that—to know so much else besides. Obviously evidence afloat that had satisfied Captain Mackenzie and his wardroom would seem less convincing to landsmen after the fact and secure ashore. Dana, however, was certain now. "The crew were under some fear after the arrest, and would be careful not to do any overt act, or commit themselves at all, until they were ready to attempt the rescue. They would conceal every sign until the moment of the outbreak. If the officers had waited for that evidence, they would have waited just too long for their own safety, and for the prevention of dreadful crimes on the whole ocean." To be sure, those officers, including the captain, might have been willing to risk the contest rather than take life before it broke out. Personally they might have been willing to risk a great deal; "but they had also a solemn duty, as public officers, at all hazards, to prevent this vessel's becoming a pirate . . . and if, from over-humanity, or a fear of the consequences of an execution to themselves professionally or before the public, or from too much confidence in their own power, they had suffered the conspirators to prevail, and the dreadful consequences had come to our ears, not even the personal sufferings and death of these officers would have saved their memory from our reproaches."

Dana was certain now, as certain as he could be before all the facts were in, that Mackenzie's case was just. That certainty, publicly expressed, was widely noted, coming as it did from one who could not be charged, as he himself reminded his readers, "of inclining in favor of a despotic use of power at sea," from one indeed whose writings had already done much to bring attention to bear on cruelties against seamen afloat. Like many others, the commander currently under investigation read in the *Post* the opinion of the author of *Two Years Before the Mast*—and was grateful. Mackenzie with his wife soon called on a New York friend of the Boston writer to express the satisfaction that the letter had given him: "to use his own words, 'it was just the thing.'" He would like that friend to forward the captain's acknowledgments to the young lawyer returned to Boston, "and to beg that if any chance should bring you to the city, he might have the pleasure of seeing you."

Relaying the message, the friend of both had added a word about Captain Mackenzie's appearance when he called: "It is many years since I have seen him, and Time, which is the destroyer of beauty, has kindly mellowed his ugliness; and there is a simplicity and manliness about him which is very interesting now, when his name is in every mouth either for praise or blame."

Hone and Dana were but two of many who crossed the East River to the navy yard that January. "There never has been any case," the *Herald* asserted flatly on the twentieth, "whose examination has awakened such universal and pervading interest . . . It is the great topic of the day. . . . Immense crowds have visited the *Somers* and inspected her with all the closeness and interest of jurymen."

Among those crowds one other stands out: he, too, knowledgeable about naval matters—and the father of a schoolmate of young Spencer's at Geneva College. Writing his wife from Philadelphia on the tenth, James Fenimore Cooper noted that he like others had recently stood "alongside of the *Somers*, and saw the fatal yard at which Phil was swinging little more than a month since."

Editor James Watson Webb on the twenty-third of the month included in the *Courier* an item about "JAMES F. COOPER.—This somewhat notorious character is now in our city and, it is said, has openly avowed his determination to write a review of the *Somers* case which will 'annihilate Mackenzie.' That he will make the attempt no one can doubt who is at all familiar with the unforgiving nature of the man." Webb for one knew that nature well enough, having himself been hunted by it "from court to court with indictments" for slander. The editor proceeded to share with his readers a story lately come upon: "it is said that pending the session of the recent court of inquiry, Mr. Cooper remarked that the execution of the mutineers by Mackenzie was a cold-blooded MURDER! or some similar expression. Such is the story. If not true, we shall cheerfully correct the rumor"—better that than suffer through another libel trial—"but if true, it very clearly exhibits the feelings with which Mr. Cooper will undertake the task of *Reviewer*. He is a man of unquestionable talents," the colonel admitted, and for that very reason capable of writing a speciously able paper. "We therefore caution the public in advance that Mr. Cooper bears Mr. Mackenzie no good will." Indeed, in Fenimore Cooper, "that gallant officer has an enemy of no ordinary character to contend with."

By late January, when Webb was issuing his caution, the court of inquiry had completed its deliberations: an opinion was arrived at in secret session January 20 and forwarded confidentially to the secretary of the navy in Washington. Hardly anyone would be satisfied with that outcome. Even before the inquiry began, *The Boston Courier* had expressed the feelings of many when it questioned the disinterestedness of the court, though composed of three "honorable men"; for those three were "of the same profession as the officer who committed the deed. . . . To expect an opinion unfavorable to Commander Mackenzie would be to expect of human nature a degree of impartiality contrary to all experience."

The captain's enemies would be left unsatisfied at the conclusion of the court of inquiry. Nor would its termination satisfy Mackenzie himself, even though the court did unanimously exonerate him from all blame in what had transpired aboard the *Somers*. The public learned of the favorable judgment January 28 (birthday of the late Philip Spencer, who would have been nineteen). Yet well before the opinion had been arrived at, advisers had come to suspect that the commander had committed a tactical error in submitting his case to review by such an assemblage. "The friends of Mackenzie are desirous," wrote one such, "that a court-martial should immediately follow the court of inquiry, and they are now convinced that it would have been more judicious to have commenced with the court-martial. This course would have saved much future trouble."

Part of what was causing the captain trouble involved legal maneuverings by the father of one man hanged, and by the widow of another. Acting Midshipman Philip Spencer's bereaved father had dealt with his grief in seclusion more than a week at Washington. What emotions would have tormented him through that interval—having by then read the captain's rambling account: learned therein of a son's despair, face buried through a whole day in the grego, later his voice behind the black hood unable to give the command to fire? Finally, on the twenty-eighth of December, the secretary of war had resumed his seat in government, at what was described as "an affecting meeting" with his fellow cabinet members. But the elder Spencer was eager (so Postmaster Graham recorded the following day) to get Mackenzie into a civil court, where he would be tried for murder, with both sides being heard before civilians as jurors.

The possibility distressed the commander when he learned of it. Moreover, even while the court of inquiry was in progress, an attorney representing the widow of Chief Boatswain's Mate Cromwell had appeared January 12 before Judge Samuel Betts of the Federal District Court to apply for a warrant charging the captain of the *Somers* and his first lieutenant with willful murder on the high seas. (The lieutenant's mother had trouble of her own with such an application: "It seemed passing strange to me," she wrote Gansevoort's brother, "to have Guert, *honest and upright* as he is, keeping out of the way of the officers of justice; and the idea of his being taken up and lodged in prison under the charge of *Murder*—was it not awful? My blood chills when I write it, as coupling with the name of one of my beloved offspring.")

But in time Judge Betts was to deny the request made on behalf of Cromwell's widow, and another on behalf of Secretary Spencer, on the grounds that the naval court had prior jurisdiction. "Old Betts," the law-yer George Templeton Strong wrote in his diary when the second of those dismissals was handed down, "has decided that the civil courts have no jurisdiction over the *Somers* murder (we may as well call things by their right names). Confound him, I think his decision's right enough, but it's a pity that he should have accidentally gone right in this particu-lar case. . . ."

The judge's decision would not, however, be rendered for some weeks yet; and while he waited anxiously for it, Captain Mackenzie had addi-tional reasons to feel harassed. For one, the active bereavement of Mrs. Cromwell had awakened compassion. Moreover, friends of her husband, the dead petty officer, had come forward publicly to furnish a description of him different from what emerged in testimony at the court of inquiry. Some of those friends gave their names and addresses: Nicholas Code, 56 James Street; Joseph Murphy, 325 Water Street; James Carroll, 331 Water Street; Henry Harvey, who deposed for the newspapers that for fifteen years he had been well acquainted with Boatswain's Mate Crom-well, "since he was twenty years of age," and that the petty officer had been no pirate, but "an upright, honest, good-hearted, respectable man." Twenty-three New Yorkers signed one testimonial, all the signatories claiming to have known the deceased for many years, some professing to have sailed with him "and always found him a good sailor and compan-ionable man," obedient to those above him, kind and attentive to his inferiors.

That was not the Cromwell whose cruelty and hot temper the testi-mony of the *Somers*'s wardroom agreed on: the blaspheming boatswain's mate who would whip the boys "with all his might, as though it was pleasing to him to whip them." But then, the testimony of the *Somers*'s wardroom often had an all but unnatural consistency about it. One fact may help explain the consistency. Secretary Upshur, instructing Com-modore Jones on the New York station, had let it be known that he considered "of the utmost importance that the crew of the *Somers* should be so kept as to prevent the possibility of any improper tampering with them." To achieve that end, the crew (except for the twelve confined on the *North Carolina*) remained on the *Somers*, with the same officers over them under whom they had sailed during the fall. For himself, Captain Mackenzie had asked only one thing of the secretary of the navy: "that I may not be deprived of my command until proved to be unworthy of it." The request had been granted; while the court was deliberating, Macken-zie remained effectively in command of the very crew that testified. And in a number of instances their testimony had been sought out by First Lieutenant Gansevoort, asking around the vessel for any information that might help vindicate the course the captain had followed regarding the alleged mutineers. Officers and crewmen who did come forth were taken to the *Somers*'s wardroom or to Commodore Perry's home in the navy yard and coached on how to speak their piece in court. Under the circumstances, self-interest urged them to speak in their captain's favor. Some were liable to disciplinary action; others among the crew he was recommending for promotion. Among the officers, too: those officers who might be considered accessories before the fact if a court found Mackenzie guilty.

Many aboard the brig had much to gain by the commander's exoneration; for if that gentleman had asked for but one thing for himself—to retain his command during this trying interlude—he had asked the secretary of the navy for much on behalf of others. In closing his lengthy, official report from New York dated December 19, Mackenzie had felt "a pleasing yet solemn duty" devolving upon him: "to do justice to the noble conduct of every one of the officers of the *Somers*, from the first lieutenant to the commander's clerk." Consider, for instance, the behavior of Lieutenant Gansevoort during the ordeal. "Never since the existence of our navy," his superior had categorically assured the department at Washington, "has a commanding officer been more ably and zealously seconded by his first lieutenant." Such behavior deserved recompense. As for Purser Heiskell and Surgeon Leecock, the captain was unable to refrain from calling Secretary Upshur's attention to their "noble" conduct, to "the services which they so freely yielded beyond the sphere of their regular duties." In fact, it had seemed to Mackenzie invidious to particularize when all without exception had behaved admirably: "I respectfully request that the thanks of the navy department may be presented to all the officers of the *Somers* for their exertions in the critical situation in which she has been placed. It is true that they have but performed their duty, but they have performed it with fidelity and zeal."

And he had gone on. Though not of the wardroom, Mr. James W. Wales was deserving, too. Wales had received special mention in the commander's report. For having "rendered to the American navy a memorable service," the steward should be given a pursership—which would mean a substantial raise in pay—or at least "a handsome pecuniary reward." Sergeant Michael H. Garty should be promoted to a second lieutenancy in the Marine Corps. The commander had further recommended that Browning and Collins and Stewart and King and Anderson and Quartermaster Rogers and Dickerson all receive promotions. And he had concluded only after making one further, remarkable recommendation, on behalf of the young bearer of the earlier dispatch to Washington. "If I," wrote Slidell Mackenzie, "should be deemed by the navy department to have any merit in preserving the *Somers* from those treasonable toils by which she had been surrounded since before her departure from the United States, I respectfully request that it may accrue without reservation to the benefit of Nephew O. H. Perry, now clerk on board the *Somers*, and that his name may be placed on the register in the number left vacant by the treason of Mr. Spencer." For in a service top-heavy with officers, no midshipman's billet had been available when the brig had gone to sea. Now there was an opening. Commodore Perry's seventeen-year-old son—Mackenzie's nephew—he of the proud name Oliver Hazard Perry should fill it.

That recommendation had typified the complacency of the report to Secretary Upshur dated December 19, written soon after the *Somers's* return home while her captain was awash in public and private felicitations. But within two days of that date Mackenzie had read with dismay what "S" had published in the *Madisonian*. "S" he had recognized as Spencer, given prompt, full access to the commander's official dispatches delivered to Washington by Captain's Clerk Perry. Worse was to follow: "I have seen with severe pain from the papers," the captain would write Upshur in a different tone December 22, "that you passed the greater part of the day subsequent to the receipt of the dispatches from the *Somers*"—last Saturday it would have been—"in conference with the Secretary of War. I will not, sir, do you the injustice to ask that when my case comes under consideration, if it be necessary to seek counsel anywhere, it will not be of the Secretary of War." Have regard to that insidious portrait of young Philip Spencer that "S" had painted: a *mere boy* brought up in the interior, "utterly unacquainted with navigation": But it had been precisely the duty of the captain aboard the *Somers* to teach that "mere boy" navigation. Should not the father's own letters to that mere boy now be published, letters found among young Spencer's effects and (after copies were made) forwarded to Washington with Midshipman Rodgers? For those letters accused Philip Spencer of having stolen from home a pair of gold presentation spectacles, as well as a sum amounting to three hundred dollars. Those chilly letters contained a mother's judgment of her son as "a thief, a liar, and a villain." After the appearance of the article signed "S," with its attempt to gain sympathy for a "mere boy" and its talk of unmanly fear and a despotic temper on the quarterdeck, "I consider it due me," wrote Mackenzie indignantly to Upshur, "that this should also appear"—this correspondence from home found among the belongings of the hanged midshipman.

Writing in that new strain, the commander had begged leave "to introduce private matters into a public communication." He felt full confidence in the rectitude and protection of Secretary Upshur, all the more so from his own close association with the secretary's brother, with Lieutenant George Upshur of the navy, "to whom years ago, when I believed him to be on his deathbed and scarcely likely to see what I had written of him, I offered in the dedication of a work a public homage which I knew to be less than just and true, though it was pronounced to be fulsome." Beset by difficulties, Mackenzie was not unwilling to remind his superior of that earlier intimacy. For what was happening was infuriating: all the delicacy that had been exercised toward the late Midshipman Spencer's family was being met with slanderous imputations and threats of prosecution. "If I am arraigned before a civil tribunal," the beleaguered officer was soon complaining nervously to Secretary Upshur, "for a conscientious, though it may be esteemed by others a mistaken performance of my duty as commander of a national vessel on the high seas, though I apprehend no punishment and no dishonor, I shall still be subject to delays and vexation of every sort."

Nor was it long before threats to Slidell Mackenzie's ultimate vindication had issued from another source, nearer at hand. Those came from Captain Francis Gregory, commanding officer of the *North Carolina*. The morning after the returning *Somers* had dropped anchor in the East River, Captain Gregory had responded to a request from her commander to receive from the smaller vessel prisoners ironed on board for what could prove to be a capital offense. Arriving at the brig with his first lieutenant, the captain of the receiving ship had been displeased that mid-December morning by what he saw. To Commodore Jones, commanding the New York station, he was soon writing: "From my own observations and those of Lieutenant Hunt, who was employed on board the *Somers* several days, I am free to say that I have never known the crew of an American man-of-war so dirty and dejected in their personal appearance as hers were at the time of her arrival here." The untidy vessel had yielded up Mackenzie's prisoners for transfer to the *North Carolina* in double and treble irons, as Gregory remembered. "A note from Lieutenant Gansevoort accompanied them, enclosing a report from the master-at-arms of the *Somers* in which their offenses were stated to be 'mutinous conduct.' Shortly after their reception I," wrote the *North Carolina*'s captain, "inspected them personally, and considered them secure beyond the possibility of escape without the irons. I had them taken off. Wilson, Green, McKinley, and McKee had evidently suffered greatly from their confinement on board the *Somers*"—a confinement that had lasted by then two weeks and longer.

Now, at Commander Mackenzie's insistence, those four had been put in solitary confinement, each in a separate cabin on the orlop deck of the receiving ship, the spaces kept continuously lighted, the prisoners kept under continuous surveillance by armed sentries on the other side of openwork bulkheads. Eight other prisoners, arrested at quarters after the *Somers* had anchored in New York Harbor, were confined together in a messroom on the same deck of the larger vessel.

But the father of one of those eight, of George Warner, was by chance a long-standing friend of Captain Gregory's, and an altogether respectable gentleman: Samuel B. Warner, inspector of customs. The elder Warner was accordingly allowed to visit his son in the after cabin of the receiving ship. The equally respectable relatives of Seaman Charles Van Velsor were accorded the same privilege, all the more readily because both Van Velsor and Warner had earlier been regarded as worthy enough to be called to testify before the council of officers aboard the *Somers* at sea. Those summonses had encouraged Gregory in port to treat the two young men as prisoners at large, allowing them what amounted to the freedom of the ship.

Meanwhile, this same captain of the *North Carolina*, troubled by what he had seen of conditions aboard Mackenzie's brig tied up—her men crowded into damp quarters, in bad weather unable even to exercise— had written confidentially to the secretary of the navy and elicited an order from the department through Commodore Jones "to make a particular examination into the situation of the crew of the *Somers*." As Gregory later explained: "their treatment as regarded punishments came as I supposed within my supervision"; for he had been informed that, since the brig's return to New York, four of her apprentices had already at various times this winter been bound to the gangway and given twelve lashes each on their bare backs. "The log book of the *Somers*," as he noted, "had been on board this ship"—the *North Carolina*—"several days, lying in the wardroom and freely inspected by any of the officers who chose to do so." From there the captain presumed to have the document temporarily removed to a storeroom below, where a yeoman copied out its contents in secret. Information thus acquired was then summarized, on the seventh of January, for the benefit of Commodore Jones.

Punishments inflicted aboard the *Somers*, as Captain Gregory wrote to that member of the court of inquiry, "though not passing the bounds of the law, have been very frequent, and in the aggregate beyond all precedent within my knowledge." To be specific: "From the 3 of June last to the 10 December the log book of the *Somers* exhibits *two hundred and forty-seven punishments with cats and colts (247)*, in which *two thousand two hundred and sixty-five lashes* were inflicted on that crew of boys! (2,265), all within a period of six months and seven days." As only one example, the captain cited the case of Dennis Manning, fourteen years old, who during two months aboard the training ship, from September 22 to November 22, had been punished twelve separate times, receiving a total of one hundred and one lashes, *"fourteen with a cat, and eighty-seven with a colt."* So many lashes in sixty days across the back of a novice fourteen-year-old!

In the same outraged letter to his superior, Gregory was urging that

for their well-being the *Somers*'s crew be removed to more healthful surroundings. But his outrage did not stop there. It spilled over into conversations with civilian visitors aboard his vessel, with the result that before
mid-January local papers had got access to—and printed across their
front pages—a full tabulation of the recent and, to all appearances, shocking punishments inflicted aboard Mackenzie's training brig.

The commander of the *Somers* had been unprepared for such revelations. He felt incensed, of course, reading *The New York Standard*, and at
a loss to know how reporters had got their hands on such confidential,
prejudicial information. But soon there was delivered to Mackenzie a
note signed mysteriously "R T," a note deploring the effect on a tender-
hearted populace of those recently published statistics from the *Somers*'s
log; "with me, however," wrote the unidentified correspondent, their
publication "has had a different effect, by convincing me of the necessity
of being more strict with the Boys in the observance of the Rules for the
maintenance of discipline than with old seamen, even to the frequent use
of the *Cat*, they being placed in the navy as incorrigible for their vicious-
ness on shore . . ." The citizen would have those wretched boys at sea
whipped more vigorously still; should the commander desire to know
who his correspondent was, and who his friends were, and how the log
of the *Somers* had been made public, he might call and announce himself
at 25 White Street this very evening.

The commander did—it was January 16—call on the public-spirited
informant, a certain Robert Taylor, from whom he learned that he had
no friend in Captain Gregory. The captain of the *North Carolina* (as it
transpired) had given the *Somers*'s logbook to young Warner's father, "at
his particular request," and Mr. Warner in turn had given the facts contained in the logs to the papers.

The letter signed "R T" was sent with notations to Washington. Before
long, Mackenzie was having the honor to write again to Secretary Upshur, this time to request the reason in the first place for the secretary's
directive of December 30, in which he had authorized an investigation of
the well-being of the men of the brig. "I did not," wrote the commander,
"conceive that the order . . . to Captain Gregory had reference to anything beyond the health of the crew of the *Somers*, and the manner of
rendering any invalids on board her more comfortable." By examining
the logbook and publishing his findings, had not the officious Gregory
exceeded his instructions, usurping the business of the court of inquiry?

Though Secretary Upshur conceded as much (stopping short of identifying who had occasioned the order), that unauthorized interference had
damaged the commander's reputation further. Nine days later Mackenzie
had cause to pen yet another fretful letter to the department, this time
expressing his earnest desire to have those prisoners of his—wandering
unironed about the receiving ship—transferred from there to confine-

ment ashore in the navy yard. That much he managed to bring about. During Captain Gregory's absence from his vessel, Commodore Jones did order the twelve crewmen delivered over to Captain Matthew Perry, who saw that they were put back in double irons and confined in a cellar under the payhouse. Marines on guard over them henceforth denied all visits, even from members of the prisoners' families.

The commander subjected to investigation in New York had been writing almost constantly since his return from the African cruise: summaries, protests, clarifications, solicitations, expressions of gratitude. But of all that he had set down, what served him least well was that detailed account of the mutiny dated December 19, an account that his own legal counsel would come to regard as "a diabolical document"—judgment uttered along with the hope that something might "winnow Mackenzie's brain of the notion that he is a lawyer as well as a sailor and historian." The document in its entirety, all thirteen thousand words (from which much of this present narrative of the cruise is drawn), had been read aloud during the opening days of the court of inquiry and thus had become public property. The *Herald* promptly labeled it "a singular mixture of folly, silliness, and"—offended by what appeared to be three cheers sounded to God on a notable occasion—"blasphemy." Fenimore Cooper perusing the document thought that he had "never read a more miserable thing in my life." Mackenzie had actually included in the course of it "one of the prayers he read to his crew. To crown all he admits he told Spencer that he would not be hanged if he got in, on account of his father's influence, and he actually recommends his nephew" to fill the vacancy that the execution created. The favorably disposed Philip Hone, having studied the commander's account, concluded, "well would it have been for him if it had never seen the light. 'Oh that mine enemy should write a book!' was the vindictive exclamation of some such person as the Secretary of War. . . . Here is a document ten times longer than was necessary, written without consultation with any judicious friend . . . And here, instead of a concise, manly statement of his proceeding on the discovery of the mutiny, the necessity which, in his judgment, existed for his summary exercise of power, and his regret that he had been called upon to adopt measures so painful to his feelings, we have a long rigmarole story about private letters discovered on the person of young Spencer, orders to blow out the brains of 'refractory men,' religious ceremonies, cheers for the American flag, and conversations with the accused, in one of which he said to Spencer that 'he hung him, because if he took him to the United States he would escape punishment, for everybody got clear who had money and friends' —a national reproach which, even allowing it to be true, came with a bad grace from an officer of the American navy."

To be sure, Mackenzie had apologized for that "indiscreet expression. But," wrote Hone in his diary, "in the name of all that is wonderful, why should he stigmatize himself by relating such a conversation in a document which will be carried on the wings of the wind to the most distant part of the earth?" The diarist hazarded a guess as to why. Hone sensed that much in the document suggested pride of authorship in one who in times past had written "a clever book" on Spain—thus one who in this instance would, regrettably, have "disdained to take advice in regard either to the matter or the manner of the narrative. . . ."

Philip Hone, like many others, had read Mackenzie's official account attentively. So had Fenimore Cooper—more closely than had the anonymous writer for the *Herald*. Cooper was aware that the commander after the hanging had not ordered his crew to give three cheers to God, as the press averred, but rather to sing a hymn and, as it were, thus figuratively to cheer God as they had earlier literally cheered the flag. Blasphemy was not one of the offenses that was leading the novelist to describe the captain's account as "a medley of folly, conceit, illegality, feebleness, and fanaticism." What he did find objectionable about the revelations will emerge, but meanwhile the sympathetic Richard Henry Dana, Jr., had been attempting to deal with that suggestion from Mackenzie that had distressed Cooper and Hone and so many other readers, the suggestion that Philip Spencer had been put to death because the boy would have gone free if brought back to New York. Such a motive for the act would have turned execution into murder. What the commander had in fact been trying to do, according to Dana, was console the young criminal— "an indifferent consolation, to be sure, but the best he could offer." A piratical son's disgrace, insofar as it attached to an honorable father, was less this way—atoned for through hanging—than if that father had been enabled to follow a parent's instinct and use "the power of wealth and station" back home "to screen his son and thus injure himself." Or so Dana offered as his own explanation of the commander's ill-judged admission.

Such matters as those—the extent of Spencer's guilt and Mackenzie's, the interview on the booms, the Greek lists, the carrying away of the mainmast, the rush aft, the council of officers, the last hour of the condemned, the cheers, the burial, the prayers—had been for much of January "the one table-talk" in the city: "the theme of the boys at the corners, of the hackmen in the street, of servants and masters, of the grave and the gay, the busy and the idle." But even such brightly thrilling topics as those had been dulled through repetition in the course of testimony by successive witnesses reported in full during the lengthy court of inquiry. "Is it not time to sum up?" the *Herald* was asking as early as the ninth. The inquiry extended a number of days longer, however, until beyond mid-January; and with its findings still not made public, the secretary of the navy was already acceding to Commander Mackenzie's request by ordering the convocation of a naval court-martial to follow immediately on this same *North Carolina*. That second court—different officers sitting in judgment now—would be meeting, as had its predecessor, aboard in the captain's cabin, on February 1.

All the evidence was to be sifted through again. Yet the two courts meeting at the same place to consider identical evidence differed in significant ways. For the court-martial, Captains Stewart and Jones and Dallas were replaced by what amounted to a jury of twelve officers with their president, Captain John Downes. At the inquiry, Judge Advocate Hoffman, despite an awesome reputation as a criminal lawyer, had handled witnesses tenderly; he was replaced at the court-martial by a young Baltimore attorney bent on cross-examining those same witnesses with appropriate rigor. And the earlier court's investigative duties had been enlarged to include a commitment to reach a legal verdict by the end of the court-martial, thus deciding the guilt or innocence of a defendant now formally charged on five counts: of oppression, cruelty, conduct unbecoming an officer, illegal punishment, and murder on board a United States vessel on the high seas.

Even so, Mackenzie was better off before this tribunal than he would have been in a civil court. Secretary of War Spencer recognized as much, and in the early days of the trial attempted to place in the courtroom representatives to take part in the proceedings on behalf of the late midshipman's family, "to examine and cross-examine the witnesses who may be produced, by propounding such questions as may be approved by the court." Those distinguished emissaries—attorneys B. F. Butler and Charles O'Connor—respectfully submitted to that body that such a course on behalf of the Spencers was proper, considering the nature of the investigation and "the interest naturally and justly felt therein by those for whom they appear." But the request was denied; the two lawyers retained by young Spencer's family would not be permitted to participate in the proceedings.

As for the judge advocate, William H. Norris was working from disadvantages that would further benefit the defendant. The Maryland attorney—"a young man and little known in his profession even in Baltimore" —saw his role in this case not as that of a prosecutor, but rather as that of a judge in England in olden times, when defendants were put on trial without the privilege of counsel. In other words, he would discover the truth wherever it lay, and thus meant to interrogate all witnesses— friendly to Mackenzie or unfriendly—with the same thoroughness. But because he had only recently been appointed and was at a distance from his office and lawbooks, Norris had not yet been able to acquaint himself with numerous aspects of the case. Nor had the Navy Department furnished him with a list of witnesses. Nor had he had the opportunity "of conversing with any of the witnesses, of whose names he is even entirely ignorant," so he told the court upon his arrival, "except by rumor in respect to a few of them." Thus, among the judge advocate's first acts was a request to delay proceedings in order that time might be provided him to prepare his case by meeting with the officers of the *Somers*.

The time was granted, but it proved unproductive. Throughout their interviews in Mr. Norris's room at the Astor House, Midshipman Hayes and Acting Midshipman Tillotson, for example, politely declined to cooperate with him. "All the officers and crew of that brig," he had occasion soon to complain in court, "were furnished by the Department for witnesses at my selection. With neither"—crew nor officers—"have I had any opportunities of conversation. I have never sought any with the crew"—though why not is unclear; later he would, and to good purpose. The officers for their part had shown themselves uniformly uncommunicative, frankly regarding the judge advocate as an adversary. Accordingly, "my duties to the case compel me," as Norris was required to admit at the court-martial, "to offer these gentlemen wholly in the dark as to their disposition and acquaintance with facts, except as shown in the record of the court of inquiry."

Considering handicaps he was laboring under, he did manage to elicit significant testimony from witnesses he cross-examined. Would Mr. Hayes please to answer this question? From the time of Acting Midshipman Spencer's arrest until his execution, did the commander of the *Somers* or any other officer of the brig conduct an investigation into the guilt of the accused "in the presence of said Spencer, so that he might confront the witnesses, so that he might cross-examine them, so that he might offer vindicatory proof, so that he might object to the reception of mere hearsay and belief or other illegal evidence as competent legal evidence against him?"

Mr. Hayes's answer: "None that I know of, in his presence."

Other witnesses confirmed that. Yet, as Judge Advocate Norris reminded the court, "the officer or seaman who chances to be in a single ship is not without prerogatives." Ashore and on trial for wrongdoing, he may be executed only if the sentence is approved by the President of the United States. Attached to a squadron, he is entitled to a trial before a court-martial, and in a capital case his sentence must be ratified by a vote of two-thirds of the court and approved by the commodore. But "his connection with a single ship does not outlaw him." True, no court can be organized on board: "trials, as such, Commander Mackenzie had no right to institute, the law confining that privilege to higher officers than the commander of a single ship." Still, the "ordinary care and prudence" of the commander himself, exercising "reasonable judgment, caution, and firmness," must be allowed to serve as the protection for anyone accused of a crime in that isolated, seaborne world. And "it is the duty of prudence and ordinary caution, first, to bring the offender if possible to port, where the privilege of the law may be afforded him. Second, if that is impossible, to afford him an opportunity to hear the charge, examine the testimony, and confront the witnesses; and a most serious and overwhelming necessity would needs have to be shewn to dispense with this due care."

Did such an overwhelming necessity exist on the *Somers* in late November 1842?

The judge advocate was cross-examining Purser's Steward Wales. Yes, he and Midshipman Spencer had been friendly. Wales guessed he was as close to the acting midshipman as any officer aboard—would provide the segars and tobacco that the midshipman drew from the ship's store. The judge advocate asked: When young Spencer broached the conspiracy on the booms that fateful November evening, did he really do it that abruptly, without "any crafty inquiries as to the state of your feelings as to the commander and officers, and to sound you as to how you would like the life of a pirate?"

Wales reaffirmed that the plan had been broached exactly as he had testified at the court of inquiry: the catechism of three questions, the oath, the revelation.

"Now, sir," asked the judge advocate pointedly, "had you never indulged in any mutinous conversation before?"

That would have accounted for such abruptness—for the superfluousness of any exploratory probings. But no, sir, Wales protested stoutly on the stand, he had not—"not with him nor with anyone else."

The witness himself had estimated that an hour had gone by after Small had left them on the booms that night and before his talk with Spencer had ended. Assume that the midshipman had been playing a trick. "What would have been your predicament, Mr. Wales, had Small, when called off from the conversation, divulged what was going on on the booms to an officer?"

An extremely awkward predicament at the least—Wales himself might even have swung, and Small be alive and commended now—though the purser's steward was professing not to know the answer to what the judge advocate had asked him.

Another question: During the extended time that Spencer and Wales had conversed clandestinely that night—upward of two hours—"did he tell you the names of any of these your future associates, and of whom you were to be third officer? Did you ask him for their names?"

No, Wales had never asked that obvious question of the mutineer.

"When Mr. Spencer told you he intended to make a scuffle some night when he had the midwatch, run with his associates to the mainmast, call

Mr. Rodgers, and throw him overboard, did you tell him that it would be likely to rouse the men and prevent him from going on with his plan—which he told you was to open the arms chest and distribute them to the men, and station the men at the hatches, and proceed in person to the cabin to murder the commander and the officers in the wardroom and steerage, and of slewing the two after guns round so as to rake the deck, and to call up the crew to select those to be thrown overboard—considering he had but twenty associates in a crew of one hundred and twenty men and boys?"

But to that lengthy question defense counsel objected. It would have been legitimate if designed to discredit the witness. Wales, however, had already testified that he had played along with Spencer that night in order to learn more of his plan, so that witness must now of course answer in the negative. "As an argument," counsel for Mackenzie admitted, "the question is exceedingly harmless, but as a precedent it is significant and dangerous." And an argument it was. "It is a question merely in form, but in reality and intent an argument, brief it is true, but doubtless to be followed by others of a similar tenor." The real object of the question was not to elicit a fact—the answer being already known—but rather to entrap the witness and prejudice the defense of the accused by suggesting the impracticality of the mutineer's plan.

The question would not be allowed. The judge advocate accordingly posed a similar one. "Did Mr. Spencer give you," Mr. Wales, "any explanation how he was to contrive to get his twenty men to be on deck at midwatch, so as not to expose them to the resistance and outcries of such others as were on duty, not in the scheme?"

No, sir, was the answer; but then Wales was no sailor. This bookkeeper only a few months at sea (who despite that had been promised the berth of third officer in the pirate ship) was no sailor, and thus was unfamiliar with watch lists and stations.

"What," asked the judge advocate, "did you mean we should understand by stating the change of manner of Cromwell to the boys in the course of the cruise?"

"I should judge," answered Wales, "he meant to bring as many over as he possibly could, to get the good will of the boys."

"Was it not a part of Mr. Spencer's plan to throw the smaller boys overboard as useless consumers of biscuit?"

"That is what he said he would do."

Then why would the mutineers bother to curry favor with the boys if they meant to throw them overboard?

Wales had no answer for that either. Nor was he sure when first he had mentioned that the mutiny was scheduled to take place before the brig arrived at St. Thomas. And yet wasn't that information crucial? If the mutiny was to occur when Messrs. Rodgers and Spencer had the midwatch, and within the ten days or so that lay between the vessel's present position and her arrival at the Danish West Indies, didn't that identify the very night it had to break out? But to the council of officers meeting on board—if their minutes were to be trusted—neither Wales nor anyone else had mentioned the fact. Was it not true, asked the judge advocate, that the earliest mention of the mutiny's occurring before St. Thomas had been made by Wales after the *Somers* had returned to home port?

The purser's steward didn't remember. The record would have to show.

Question: "When did Commander Mackenzie first inform the crew of the projected mutiny?"

"I believe," answered Wales, "after the arrest of Cromwell and Small."

By then Midshipman Spencer would have been in irons in plain view on the arms chest a full twenty-four hours. Question: "Was Mr. Spencer a favorite with the crew?"

"Yes, sir, he appeared to be so."

"Do you think it a mutinous indication that, being so, crews should gather in knots and talk as to the cause of his confinement, not having had the cause explained, and seem dissatisfied?"

But Wales didn't see "why they should be secret about it, and separate when an officer approached them, and go to another part of the vessel and still continue to converse in a low tone of voice."

"Is it," the judge advocate persisted dryly, "the habit of naval seamen to be heard by officers discussing such matters?"

To which question the landsman could only answer lamely, "I don't know." . . .

First Lieutenant Guert Gansevoort had taken the stand. On learning of the mutiny and reporting it to his captain Saturday morning, the lieutenant had been instructed to observe Midshipman Spencer closely throughout the day.

Question: "Was Mr. Spencer on the 26th of November till the time of his arrest engaged in the usual duties of an officer of his station?"

"I believe," answered the first lieutenant, "that he was engaged in the usual duties of his station except when in the foretop . . ."

"Was he on duty when he was in the foretop?"

"No, sir."

"Have you not seen other young officers in the foretop when not on duty?"

"Yes, sir, I have."

What, then, was suspicious about the acting midshipman's behavior that day? Yet "you say that when asked your opinion on the 26th of November by Commander Mackenzie as to what you would do in his place, you said you would bring that young man (meaning Mr. Spencer)

aft and iron him. Had the purser's steward have come to you with a like
story in respect to any other officer but Mr. Spencer"—say, one of those
two nephews of the captain's on board, Matthew Perry's sons, or Mr.
Rodgers, whose uncle had married a daughter of Commodore Perry's, or
young Deslonde, brother of the wife of the captain's brother and formerly a guest at Mackenzie's Tarrytown home—"would you," Mr. Gansevoort, "have determined on such a course before any announcement to
him of what Mr. Wales had reported?"

The lieutenant insisted, though it hardly answered the question: "I
would have confined any officer if I had the same cause for suspecting
him."

Consider the Greek lists, discovered in Spencer's locker the night of
the arrest. "Count if you please," Mr. Gansevoort, "and say how many
names are among the doubtful, how many to be kept nolens volens."

The lieutenant confirmed that ten were listed as doubtful, eighteen to
be kept whether willing or not.

And only four were down as certain, one of whom was Spencer himself, another being McKinley, a third being an unidentified Andrews,
and the fourth being the blameless Wales. "When you saw Mr. Wales's
name on the list found in Mr. Spencer's locker, did you conclude that it
was put there without Mr. Wales's authority, or put there after the conversation on the booms?"

"I supposed," the lieutenant answered, "it was put there after the conversation on the booms, and without his authority."

But if so, "what was there in the paper to excite alarm?" Did Mr.
Gansevoort—seeing on the updated list two at the most for certain—
really believe that the acting midshipman "had any matured plot with
twenty men of the crew of the *Somers?*"

Yes, sir, he did, both from what Wales said and from the looks of the
crew. "My alarm was not excited by the paper, but from the manner of
those that were on that paper, and the manner of those that were not on
it."

Question: "Did you ever ask Mr. Spencer when he had put down
Wales's name?"

"No, sir, not to my recollection."

Had he asked Mr. Spencer how far the plot had advanced—farther
than those on the *John Adams* and the *Potomac?*

No, not that the lieutenant recollected.

Inside Mr. Spencer's razor case had been found another list, containing
the names George A. Brest, Frederick Wells, and Edward Roberts, none
of whom were aboard the *Somers*. Had the first lieutenant while interviewing the prisoner asked him to identify those names?

No, he didn't recollect ever doing so.

Had he asked Mr. Spencer when the scheme was broached to Small?

Not that the lieutenant recollected.

Did he ask him which of the crewmen listed had been spoken to, which ones had been set down on the list without their knowledge?

Not that he recollected.

Question: "As the commander had instructed you to find out all you could . . . how is it you put none of the preceding matter of inquiry to Mr. Spencer?"

Gansevoort answered that the prisoner had not shown "much of a disposition to communicate at any time"—though earlier he had testified about Spencer's willingness to tell him whatever the captain wanted to know.

"If you made none of these inquiries of Mr. Spencer, what did you do in pursuance of the commander's instructions to find out from Mr. Spencer what you could as to the mutiny?"

The lieutenant answered, feebly, that he had "inquired among the crew forward. . . ."

"Did you tell Small that Mr. Spencer had told you that E. Andrews"—that unidentified name on the Greek list, down as certain—"was Small's genuine name?"

"I don't recollect. I am not positive as to that, but I think not."

Did you or anyone in your hearing before the execution "ask Small how much he knew of Mr. Spencer's plot? Who were engaged in it, and when it commenced?"

"No, I did not ask him, and no one that I heard, to my recollection."

"When was Mr. Spencer first given to understand there was no intention to take him to the United States?"

"I believe on the morning of his execution."

"Were Mr. Spencer, Cromwell, and Small notified that an investigation was to be held?"

"Not that I know of."

"During the time the investigation was going on before the council of officers, was Mr. Spencer, Cromwell, and Small informed of it, and desired to state if they had any questions to put? Or was the evidence in particular of any witnesses reported to them, or either of them?"

Mr. Gansevoort didn't know that anything of that sort was done.

"From the time of his arrest to the time of his execution, did any officer apply to the commander or yourself for permission to explain to Mr. Spencer his situation, and what was contemplated in respect to him, that he might afford him any friendly services to take care of his rights?"

The lieutenant didn't recollect anyone's having done so.

"Was anything of the like kind asked or proposed by any of the crew in respect to Cromwell and Small?"

"Not that I know of." . . .

Acting Master Matthew Perry, Jr., at twenty-one years of age third in seniority aboard the *Somers*, was called to the stand. "Do you know," he was asked, "whether the relatives and friends of Commander Mackenzie were cautioned by him after the coming aboard of Mr. Spencer to be wary of an intimacy with him?"

"I don't remember," the master answered tentatively. "I have a slight recollection of something being said about it."

But if so, then the new arrival would have had to find his friends elsewhere than in the wardroom or steerage. About Mr. Spencer's familiarity with Boatswain's Mate Cromwell, "is it an unusual thing," the judge advocate was asking the witness, "for young officers to inquire the history and adventures of the experienced seamen and to talk with them on such topics in their watches?"

Mr. Perry granted that he had "known it to be done by the young officers, in such tone that others might hear them."

Question: "When did Mr. Gansevoort first consult you as to the propriety of executing Mr. Spencer, Cromwell, and Small, and what did you tell him?"

"He asked me during the day before the council of officers was held." The council was held on the thirtieth. "I told him that I did not think we could take charge of any more prisoners with safety to the vessel, and if necessity required more to be taken"—as almost certainly would be the case—"the first three ought to be disposed of, that is, put to death."

"Did you not swear before the court of inquiry that this conversation with Mr. Gansevoort was on the 28th of November"—not the twenty-ninth, as now suggested?

"I may have done so. I don't remember. If I did so, it was correct. . . . I do not mean to be positive as to dates except when I refer to the log-book."

But that would have been two full days before the council had met to conduct its impartial investigation, three long days before the prisoners were told they were not being taken home. So early had their fate been decided, for other officers had been polled at the same time and agreed with Perry. And had the first lieutenant in polling them phrased the question to provoke a particular response? "How many," asked the judge advocate, turning to another subject, "would compose the knots of people you have seen collected on the deck after the arrest of the prisoners?"

"Three or four." Lieutenant Gansevoort testifying had estimated the number at up to fifteen.

"On what deck would these knots be?"

"On the spar deck"—that is, topside.

"Can not the conduct of people on the spar deck be more readily observed than in any other place of the vessel allowed the men?"

By the officers, yes, Acting Master Perry confirmed.

Tuesday evening, November 29, the master as officer of the deck had

had occasion to give an order, "Some of you lay aft." In response, many more crewmen had rushed down the quarterdeck than were needed. Yet Mr. Perry had known—as did everyone else on board—that "this was a time when you must not disobey orders, a time when you might lose your life for it."

Question: "Knowing of this previous order, how could you have been surprised that an indefinite direction to a body of men, 'Some of you come aft,' should bring each man that heard it?"

"Because," the witness answered, "during the same time they had disobeyed other orders, had to be told two or three times."

The questioning moved to the council of officers. "Did you or not," Mr. Perry, as a member of the council "hear Wales testify that Mr. Spencer had told him that the mutiny was to break out before the arrival of the *Somers* at St. Thomas?"

Referring to the council minutes, the witness found there "no mention made of such fact. Therefore, I conclude it was not made."

"Was it discussed in the council of officers as to whether the vessel could be carried into St. Thomas or any nearer port?"

It was, but Master Perry for one had insisted at the time "that I would rather go overboard than go into St. Thomas for protection—that I would never agree to a thing of the kind . . ."

But why had he said that? Why would he not agree to such a thing?

"Because I thought it would be a disgrace to the United States, the navy, and particularly the officers of the brig. My reasons were that if an American man-of-war could not protect herself, no use in having any. . . ." Here was no milky-hearted officer (and Bennett's *Herald*, commenting within the week on that bit of testimony, inevitably raised the question of what constituted the greater disgrace: the seeking of help in a foreign port, or "the hanging of three human beings, unarmed, in irons, without trial"). Despite Perry's unequivocal views on the matter, the judge advocate was proceeding to question this acting master—as navigator and log keeper aboard—about distances of the *Somers* from island ports shortly before the execution. How far to Antigua? To Barbados? To Martinique? With that, the defense intervened, placing a statement on record:

"To save the time of the court and spare the judge advocate the trouble of the laborious investigation on which he proposes to enter as to the distance of the *Somers* from various West India islands at the time of the discovery of the mutiny, Commander Mackenzie takes occasion to mention that the idea was never entertained by him of seeking protection against his crew in any foreign port, from any foreign power whatever, or from any foreign ship in port, or at sea, or anywhere, save in a port of the United States, or under the guns of an American man-of-war—it being his deliberate opinion that a naval commander can never be justi-

fied in invoking foreign aid in reducing an insubordinate crew to obedience." Moreover, "his views in this particular were well known at the
time to the first lieutenant of the *Somers*, were shared by him, and by him
communicated to others of the officers."

But might not defense counsel be permitted now to interrupt this interrogation of members of the *Somers*'s wardroom by calling to the stand
crewmen whose testimony would establish the guilt of Boatswain's Mate
Cromwell? Since the brig's return, Commander Mackenzie had grown
alarmed at defections among his crew. Two in particular, whose evidence
had seemed crucial at the court of inquiry, had since absented themselves
without leave from the infirmary in the navy yard. One had been overtaken in Philadelphia, but the other—an Englishman—was still at large,
probably out of the country by this time. The commander was eager to
make his case against Cromwell in court before any others of the crew
absconded.

William Neville, second captain of the foretop, was accordingly called
to the stand. He remembered during the cruise having seen Mr. Spencer
on the berth deck by the forward storeroom showing a sheet of paper to
the boatswain's mate. The front of the paper contained what had looked
to Neville like letters in a foreign alphabet; on the back were what
seemed to be geometrical figures (one of the Greek lists was known to
have been set down on a page torn from a geometry textbook). Could
there be doubt, then, that the executed boatswain's mate had been privy
to Mr. Spencer's plot—was involved in the mutiny even though his name
appeared nowhere on that list?

But the judge advocate questioned Neville closely as to exactly where
he had been standing that day on the berth deck, then reproduced the
positions and movements of the three men involved—of Neville, Cromwell, and Spencer. In doing so, he was able to establish that the seaman
could not have seen both sides of the paper the midshipman was holding.
One side perhaps, but not both. And in any case, where and when had
the foretopman first mentioned that he had seen Mr. Spencer and Cromwell so engaged?

"Aboard the *Somers*," answered Neville, "after we came in."

"Whom did you first tell?"

Lieutenant Gansevoort. "He was inquiring round the brig if anybody
knew anything about it. I wrote it off and sent it in."

So Commander Mackenzie would not have possessed Neville's evidence at the time he had determined to execute Cromwell. Indeed, much
of the evidence presented at the court of inquiry and the court-martial
would not have been known in the captain's cabin when the executions
took place, and thus could not have contributed to justifying the hangings. A civil court might arguably have barred such testimony—Wales's
recollection of Cromwell's slighting remarks about his wife, Mr. Tillot-

son's recollection of Spencer's expressed desire to seize a vessel in sight, much more that was recollected and reported only after the cruise was done. Yet the court-martial—another advantage for Mackenzie—made no distinction between evidence in the captain's possession when he had decided to execute three men, and evidence uncovered only later, after diligent inquiries among officers and crew back in New York.

The present testimony from crew members, by the way, was raising an awkward matter concerning how the four surviving prisoners on board had been treated between the time of the execution December 1 and their arrival home two weeks later. Among those four was Willson, sailmaker's mate. With Mr. Spencer and Cromwell and Small buried at sea, Willson had been set to work—"tied to a bolt in the side of the vessel"—making sou'westers for the officers in anticipation of bad weather after St. Thomas. And for the prisoners, Willson had been ordered to fashion body bags out of topgallant-steering sail covers. Finished, those four bags were laid on deck, and the prisoners put feet first inside them. But when? Anderson and Garty (both recommended for promotion in the captain's official report) insisted that the bags had been used only after the weather had turned cold along the Eastern Seaboard of the United States, only in daylight and stormy sailing, with blankets inside and the strings loosely drawn about the prisoners' shoulders, a bight taken round with a half knot and not even tied. The four bagged seamen, in fact, were more comfortable in the cold and wet than anybody else on board; at night they had been routinely removed from the bags and led below.

The prisoners themselves told a different story. McKinley on the stand insisted that he had first been put into a bag two days after the execution, even before the vessel had reached St. Thomas. It was nighttime in those subtropic waters, and the bag had been pulled around him and over his head and tied. "After a while the bag got very hot. Whoever was the officer I don't know. I told him I was smothering. I could not breathe. He came back with the orders that I could not have it untied. I turned myself round as well as I could and got my mouth to the opening of the bag and stayed so till morning."

Green and McKee, called to the stand, would confirm McKinley's version of when and how the bags had been used. But did the prisoners find them comfortable when not tied over their heads? No, sir, McKinley insisted. They were either hot or cold, cold after St. Thomas as the vessel beat northward off the Atlantic seaboard: his bag "would get full of rain water up to my knees . . ."

This witness's case is of particular interest, his being the only name besides Spencer's and Wales's and the unidentified Andrews's to appear among the roster on the Greek list as certain. Had he known his name was on that list? No, sir, he had not. Had Mr. Spencer ever spoken to him about a mutiny? No, sir. Born in Boston, McKinley, now twenty-one, had been a waiter at Howard's Hotel in New York before signing aboard the *Somers* as a landsman, cot boy to the purser. But Commander Mackenzie had early been impressed by the young man's "courage and alacrity," on an occasion when he had leaped to rescue a crewman fallen overboard while the vessel lay moored in Wallabout Bay; during the forthcoming cruise the landsman might show himself to have the stuff to become a sailor. There was talk of that. And on the cruise itself, was not McKinley in the role of wardroom servant "regarded as a good boy"? The judge advocate would put the question to Purser Heiskell. Answer: "He was. I regarded him as attentive." Indeed, that dirk of Willson's, the one found in his sail bag that Commander Mackenzie had judged to be "of no use for any honest purpose . . . fit only to kill": "Can you tell me where the knife of Willson, or dirk, came from?" The purser would explain that McKinley ashore in Monrovia had seen the dirk for sale "and wished me to pay for it or to give him the money to pay for it." So the weapon fit only to kill turned out to be "a present to a serviceable boy" from an officer—a present that McKinley had later sold to Willson for a dollar of grog money. And Lieutenant Gansevoort, who incidentally had praised Boatswain's Mate Cromwell's indispensable skills early in the voyage, had apparently been impressed by McKinley as well. In the wardroom after Monrovia and before the mutiny was discovered, the first lieutenant, with Mr. Leecock and Mr. Heiskell present, "asked me if there was nothing I wanted": pea jacket, shoes, stockings? No, only a leave of absence to visit friends when the brig got back to New York. McKinley had everything else he desired. To which Lieutenant Gansevoort had replied that "I was a 'damned sight better off than he was.' " But that was what made Tyson's testimony implausible, testimony to the effect that that lounging seaman had overheard McKinley and Willson by the after gun plotting to jump ship at St. Thomas and join a slaver. McKinley had no wish to jump ship, having Lieutenant Gansevoort's promise of leave to see friends when they reached home. Yet after Mr. Spencer had been arrested, the cot boy's name was found on the Greek list as certain, "and I saw Mr. Gansevoort watching, chasing, and following me all round the vessel," so that to Browning and others of his messmates McKinley had said "that I expected to be put in irons before a week."

He was. "On the 30th of November, at morning quarters, I was arrested. The commander put Willson in irons. When he was put in irons, the commander cried, 'Send McKinley aft.' I went aft. The commander and Mr. Gansevoort held pistols at my head and told me to sit down. Mr. Gansevoort told King, the gunner, to stand by to knock out their brains if they should make a false motion. I was put in irons then. . . . Mr. Gansevoort ordered me to get on all fours and creep round to the larboard side, as I could not walk." A month and more would pass, two months, and the prisoner would still be in irons, confined onshore—though lucky for that matter to be alive, having burst into tears on deck the fatal afternoon, under the hooded, swaying forms at the yardarm overhead, when the captain had told him at last that he "could find nothing" against the cot boy, so that for now his life would be spared . . .

Midshipman Rodgers had been called to the stand. The midshipman was protesting that any change of course, for Martinique or any other island, would have been a "tacit confession" by the officers "of their own weakness. . . . I think the moment land was made with these prisoners on board, it would have been a signal to take the vessel."

How many might have joined in such an uprising? the judge advocate asked.

About two-thirds of them, Rodgers thought, or even three-fourths, "including all the elder portion but the petty officers."

But did the midshipman really mean to suggest that as many as that were Spencer's accomplices?

"I mean they were willing to join in his rescue, and knew of the plan."

Still, "of all that crew, large and small, have you known one on oath, or otherwise, to admit to this hour that he knew of Mr. Spencer's plan?"

"No, sir," Rodgers conceded.

That business concerning Mr. Spencer's having inquired, shortly before he was arrested, about the accuracy of the rate of the ship's chronometer, an inquiry apparently by one bent on taking over the vessel: was it not true that on the previous day Mr. Spencer and Mr. Rodgers had made a bet of a bottle of brandy concerning the brig's arrival time at St. Thomas? Yes, that was so. And might it not thus be that the bet was on Spencer's mind when he had sought to determine how reliable the chronometer was? As for brandy, had Mr. Rodgers, by the way, seen other officers besides Mr. Spencer giving brandy to the crew? Yes, he had seen Browning and Stewart, drenched while performing ship's tasks, "go down in the wardroom wet and cold," where Lieutenant Gansevoort had given them each a drink . . .

On the stand now was Purser Heiskell, reading Midshipman Spencer's account to the court: one comb 15¢, sheeting $2.76, pair of shoes $1.10, one mattress $4, sugar 50¢, tea 50¢, buttons 10¢, ½ lb thread 45¢, one scrub brush 25¢, two bars soap 60¢ . . .

The purser had recorded the minutes of the council of officers that had met to decide the fate of the mutineers. Judge advocate: "Are those minutes made with a pencil?"

"Yes, sir."

"Why was this, in so grave a matter?"

"I do not know that I can give any particular reason. There were no lawyers there."

"Was any portion of this testimony revised or corrected after the execution, by the witnesses or any one of them?"

"I am not positive. Some of these corrections were made after the examination. . . ."

"Was any proposition made to apprise the three executed persons of a pending investigation and to offer them assistance and counsel to see that nothing but truth should be against them?"

"Not that I am aware."

"Did the officers pass any cautions to each other not to signify their opinions in the hearing of witnesses?"

"Not that I remember." To the contrary, it would be established that some of the examining officers had made no effort at all before witnesses to hide their settled conviction of the prisoners' guilt.

"Were any of the witnesses asked before the council of officers as to the carrying away of the mast, or as to the rush aft, as indicating an insubordination on board, or did any of them testify as to either of these matters?"

"I don't recollect," said the purser, "that the question was asked." Both incidents, then—of which Commander Mackenzie's report and the testimony of Gansevoort and others had made much—would seem to have acquired sinister meanings only some time after they had occurred, perhaps even after the executions. Small's yank on the weather royal-topgallant brace that was said to have shattered the mast, with the intention of creating confusion by knocking a boy aloft overboard: about that presumably ominous event the defense would have formally to admit at the court-martial "that in the entry made on the 27th November in the logbook relative to the carrying away of the topgallant mast, it is not stated that it was carried away by design." Nothing in the logbook at the time suggested alarm. "It is further admitted that there is no entry in the logbook of any rush aft having been made by the crew that day."

An additional bit of information emerged in the course of the purser's testimony. This concerned a question that the council of officers on board had put to successive witnesses to determine their opinion of what should be done with the prisoners. How had the question been phrased?

"The general question," Mr. Heiskell answered the judge advocate, "was, whether they thought the vessel would not be safer with those persons made way with—that is, killed; to the best of my belief, these were the words."

And a leading question if ever there was one . . .

Young Oliver Perry took the stand, seventeen-year-old captain's clerk who had delivered Commander Mackenzie's early dispatches to the Navy Department in Washington. Before the execution, while the commander had been interviewing Spencer in irons beside the arms chest on the *Somers* through that final hour, Perry had been standing between the binnacles, four or five feet away. "Do you know," he was asked now, "whether Mr. Spencer wrote home to his friends?"

"No, sir."

"Did you not say," the judge advocate persisted, "in the presence of the secretary of the navy and other gentlemen, that you were of the impression that Mr. Spencer did send a written message home?"

If so, that was an admission damning to Captain Mackenzie's cause, inasmuch as no such letter had ever been delivered to Secretary and Mrs. Spencer. "At the time of the execution," answered Perry, "it was my impression he did send a message home. The captain was copying something."

"State the conversation that then passed between the commander and Mr. Spencer."

"I did not hear any of it. I thought he was writing a letter home to his parents, and did not try to hear it."

"Did Mr. Spencer take the pen and try to write?"

"I did not see him."

"Did you hear the commander tell him he would write for him?"

"No, sir."

Here Mackenzie rose from his seat at the table, the chair where he had sat patiently through long days for two and a half months. Abruptly the captain rose, interrupting the examination to approach the judge advocate and demand of him:

"Why do you ask this question, about Mr. Spencer's not being able to write in irons? He declined to write."

"Yes, sir, but I am told," replied the judge advocate, "he afterwards dictated to you what to write."

"He said he did not wish to write," the commander insisted.

"Yes, sir, but I am told he afterwards dictated to you what to write."

"Yes, he did."

"Then," the judge advocate repeated for clarification, "he did dictate to you what to write?"

"Yes, he did. The substance of it is in my report—my official report."

The judge advocate turned to the court. "There is no use of further examination on the point," he said, "as Captain Mackenzie admits that Mr. Spencer did dictate to him what to write."

"Yes, sir," Mackenzie repeated, facing the president of the court.

But the accused had made a concession that would have to be retracted a week later, March 17. In the interval he fell ill; on three successive days, March 14, 15, and 16, word from the yard surgeon and Dr. Lee-cock was read to the court: the defendant, "in consequence of severe indisposition," was unable to attend. The court was in adjournment thus until the seventeenth, at which time Commander Mackenzie again addressed the matter of Mr. Spencer's utterances at his final interview.

Much time had passed since that fatal, sunlit noon at sea, much time even since the penning of the captain's official report of December 19. In his recent illness he had had leisure to look over the imperfectly recollected report, which was discovered to contain—among various comments, questions, confessions, and musings—only one brief message from Spencer to friends back home: "Tell them I die wishing them every blessing and happiness. I deserve death for this and many other crimes." But to deal with this matter once and for all, Captain Mackenzie would now produce the very document that he had transcribed at the arms chest beside the ironed midshipman. In court he swore that it was "the only memorandum or writing of any description made by him on that day, while in communication with Mr. Spencer."

The document survives: a disturbing and affecting scribble on three pieces of paper. As notes for an hour-long interview it seems brief. It reads, indeed, as though recollected after the event, rather than transcribed in the course of the talk. The second- and third-person voices employed hardly suggest dictation. Parts are illegible, not surprising under the circumstances, though the present writer, familiar with Mackenzie's penmanship, finds this specimen uncharacteristically impenetrable at points, as did the editor of the courtroom proceedings, who was reduced to publishing the contents of the memorandum with numerous ellipses to indicate what he could not decipher. One wonders how young Spencer, given the paper to read over, had been able to make much of it. Incidentally, the boy is recorded early on as having admitted to deserving death "for this and other sins," though Mackenzie's official report changes the crucial word to "crimes." Such imprecisions are troubling; much about the document—that record of human anguish, desperation, and resolve—may trouble readers these hundred and forty years later. It reads in its entirety:

> When asked if he had any message to send. None that they would wish to receive. Afterwards that you die wishing them every blessing and happiness. You deserved death for this and other sins. That you felt sincerely penitent and only fear of death was that your repentance might be too late. Many that he had wronged but did not know how reparation could be made to them. Your parents most wronged. Excused [*crossed out, and illegible word or words* ("Think not"?) *written above*] himself by saying that he had entertained same idea in John Adams and Potomac. But had not ripened it into. Do you not think that a mania which should. Certainly. Objected to manner of death. Requested to be shot. Could not make any distinction between him and those whom he had seduced. Justifiable desire at first to save others. Cromwell. The last words he had to say and hoped they would be believed that Cromwell was innocent. Admit-

ted it was just that no distinction should be made. Asked that his face might be covered. Granted. When he feared that his repentance might not be in season, I referred him to the story of Penitent thief. Tried to find it could not. Read the bible. The Prayer book. Did not know what would have become of him if succeeded. Makes no objection to death but objects to time. Reasons. God would consider shortness of time. Offences. Pictured to him a [*one word illegible*]. Many sins. Dies praying God to bless and preserve. I am afraid this may injure my Father. God who was all merciful as well as all wise could not only extricate the difficulty growing out of shortness of time and from the abundance of his mercy forgive. Be the death of my poor Mother. Do you not think she would have felt worse if instead of dying you had succeeded in undertaking. Horrors here others in course of piracy. Cut off by Cromwell. Passing to gallows. Met at pump well. Asked for Mr. Wales. Mr. Wales I beg you to forgive me for having tampered with your fidelity. Mr Wales much affected. Are you not going too far? are you not going too fast Sir. I think sir you [*blank*] The best service he could render his Father was to die. Small said Shipmates "give me quick and easy death." Knot, toggle, shift knot, asked leave to give word. Granted. Took station on trunk to see all parts. Waited. Waited. Prayer. "Shall I die?" Browning of opinion only then began to think he really was going to die. He kept such good heart. Small up. Suffocated. Told him in scarcely audible whisper to tell Commander he must give the word himself. Preparations live coal match—keep passing them up so as to have [*two words illegible*] perpetually there. Cromwell and Spencer meeting. No Notice of each other. Spencer as calm as at any moment of life. Wales. Small. Asked forgiveness no by God Mr Spencer can't forgive you. You betrayed me [*those three words crossed out*]. Consulted him Mr Wales so both together. Forgive me Small for leading you into this trouble—We shall soon be in the face of God Almighty then see. You must forgive me Small. I told him to be more generous. He softened. I do forgive you Mr. Spencer. Shook hands. May God Almighty forgive you also. Small on hammocks asked leave to address the ship's company. Now boys &c Now Brother Topmates give me a quick death. Run me up smartly. Do not let there be any interval between word & firing. Asked 1. lieut. if firing with lock. match. Open arm chest & get wafers. Ordered live coals to be passed up from galley. "Stand by" "fire!" instantaneous. Shotted gun. Arrangements. Conversation about coffin. Beating to call. Gan't asked about covering face. No hangmen. You others [?] nothing to do with requirements [?] of business and as done in secure seamanlike manner. The starboard rope string stitched to the [*one word illegible*] of [*one word illegible*]. [*One word illegible*] a strain, hooks moved ["moored"?]. Tail chocks well secured. Roll. S. Small stept up. Cromwell overboard. Rose dripping to yard arm.

Mackenzie's notes of those fatal hours were introduced in court as late as March 17. By that time the attention of much of the American populace had been diverted elsewhere. Weeks before, as long ago as February 25, Philip Hone had mentioned in his journal that "the court-martial at Brooklyn on the *Somers* case drags along its tedious length so slowly . . . that the public here appears to have lost all interest in the matter, and you scarcely hear an inquiry made as to its progress or the probability of its termination. . . . The interest of the protracted affair has given place in the public mind to new subjects . . ."

One such subject was nothing less than the impending end of the world. According to the numerous followers of William Miller, sixty-year-old Long Island farmer and interpreter of the Bible, the end was due most likely during the approaching month of April. After pondering the Book of Revelations, Miller had constructed elaborate charts that persuaded some fifty thousand people that he had found there unequivocal proof of the Second Coming of Christ very soon in the clouds of heaven, with Judgment Day accompanying—within the present year, likely in April 1843. On the evening of this same day in March when Mackenzie's notes were placed in the court record, young George Templeton Strong was observing that over New York City the comet "that the Millerites are in such a stew about shone out in great glory tonight." Its nucleus was below the horizon, but the tail streamed gorgeously upward nearly to the zenith, like "a long riband of pale transparent light." The local scene offered other confirmations. On the twenty-first of March, four days later, Strong comments on the "fine weather, but most unseasonably cold. Another 'sign,' the Millerites say it is, and I suppose a most superb meteor I saw on Saturday night was still another. It was a most beautiful sight, sailing slowly down the sky, the meteor itself like a large ball of bright bluish flame and the broad train behind it red and scintillating. It lasted nearly half a minute, I think, and I could scarcely believe at first that it was not some sort of rocket running the wrong way."

More mundanely, the papers in mid-March were carrying news that Secretary of State Daniel Webster had announced his forthcoming retirement from Tyler's cabinet. And before the month was out a fund-raising dance—"one of those political jollifications"—had lured much of New York society to support the presidential ambitions of Henry Clay. As for the naval court-martial, some were now suggesting that the judge advocate had been protracting its length to gain time for Mr. Spencer's allies to pursue their efforts to have Mackenzie indicted in a civil court. In early March, Strong had noted that those allies were exploring every path toward that end—and "may they succeed," he adds, "for if ever there was a case of cold-blooded lynching, that *Somers* tragedy was one." For his part, Mr. Hone felt differently—and was pleased to record later that month that all such efforts had failed. Judge Betts of the United States Circuit Court handed down his ruling that civil courts could not lawfully take cognizance of the case; the judge advocate might therefore (Hone thought) just as well let the court-martial end, surrendering his emoluments of ten dollars a day expenses and ten additional dollars for every fifteen pages of evidence amassed. Indeed, on the twenty-first, Mr. Norris did inform the court of his unwillingness to protract proceedings further; but for that, he would have called to the stand "every unexamined member of the *Somers* crew to prove that no plan of mutiny was known to any but Wales before the arrest . . . If any witness can be named to prove the contrary, he offers to call him."

No such witness came forward. The defense would sum up tomorrow.

On the following morning, March 22, 1843, the chapel in the navy yard, to which the court for convenience had been transferred from the *North Carolina* more than a month before, "was filled at an early hour by anxious spectators, including a large number of ladies." Among those latter were Philip Hone's daughters, and Hone himself was on hand, to hear Counselor Griffin present his summary defense of Commander Mackenzie during an uninterrupted hour and a half. "Never was an audience more attentive": as for the ex-mayor and journalist, attending too, he found himself entirely persuaded by the force of Griffin's facts, here marshaled all together for the first time in order to prove that beyond doubt a mutiny had existed aboard the *Somers*, that Spencer, Cromwell, and Small were its indisputable ringleaders, and that the size of the vessel and the ever mounting disloyalty of much of the crew made impossible the bringing home of those plotters for trial. But "suppose," the defense counselor hypothesized in a peroration so eloquent that Hone was moved to transcribe much of it verbatim into his journal:

> suppose that the execution had not taken place; that the unconfined malcontents had risen and released the prisoners; that the mutiny had triumphed, and the brig been turned into a piratical cruiser; that the faithful of the officers and crew had been all massacred, except the commander alone; that, from a refinement in cruelty, the pirates had spared his wretched life and sent him on shore that he might be forced to wend home his solitary way and become himself the disgraced narrator of what would then have been indeed "the tragedy of the *Somers*."

> With what a burst of indignation would the country have received his narrative! How would the American press, with its thousand tongues, have overwhelmed him with exclamations and interrogatories like these: "You were seasonably urged, by the unanimous voice

of your trusty officers, to save their lives, the lives of your faithful seamen, and the honor of your country, by the timely execution of these malefactors, who deserved to die and whose immediate death was imperiously demanded by the exigencies of the case. Why did you not heed the counsel, the earnest counsel of your associates in authority, your constitutional advisers, with whose opinion your own, too, concurred? You did not because you *dared* not. You faltered in the path of known and acknowledged duty because you wanted moral courage to tread it. On you, in the judgment of conscience, devolves the responsibility of those murders, which you might and ought to have prevented. On you recoils the disgrace of that flag which never sustained a blot until it was committed to your charge."

To finish the picture, permit me to fill up another part of the canvas. Suppose that the *Somers*, now turned pirate, while cruising off our coast had been permitted by Heaven in an evil hour to capture some vessel plying between this and Europe, freighted with the talent and beauty of the land. The men are all murdered, and the females, including perhaps the new-made wife and maidens just blooming into womanhood, are forced to become the *brides of pirates*. A universal shriek of agony bursts from the American people throughout all their vast domains, and the wailing is echoed back from the whole civilized world. And where then could the commander of the *Somers* have hidden his head, branded as it would have been by a mark of infamy as indelible as that stamped on the forehead of Cain!

The case of the *Somers* [Counselor Griffin persisted] may form an epoch in our naval history. Should the course of the commander be approved by his country, mutinies in our ships of war will probably hereafter be of rare occurrence. But should this court, or the high tribunal of public opinion, pronounce sentence of condemnation on the course which he felt himself bound to pursue, it is respectfully yet solemnly submitted that the sentence will be the signal for the general prevalence of insubordination in our navy. The means and subjects of mutinous excitement are always at hand. Filled with men of mixed national character, crowded with spirits as turbulent as the element on which they dwell, the ship's berth deck ever abounds in materials of combustion, which a single spark may ignite. The commander must quench the flame, even if it is sometimes done by the sacrifice of life. . . ."

The defense had completed its summation. In cases before courts-martial "it is not the duty of a judge advocate to sum up the facts" unless specifically requested to do so; in this instance Mr. Norris is spared that "painful and arduous labor." The court is cleared of all but its member officers. They hear the lengthy testimony reread during five days that follow. On March 27, the judge advocate presents a legal statement to guide the court during its deliberations toward a finding. The finding is reached the following day.

JOHN CANFIELD SPENCER.
The likeness was made in 1843, during the New York politician's service
in President Tyler's cabinet in Washington.

THE *SOMERS*.
A lithograph, by Nathaniel Currier, issued in early 1843.

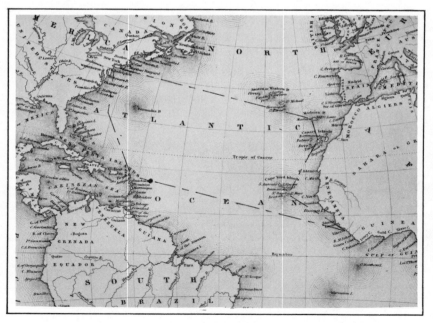

THE VOYAGE OF THE *SOMERS*.
The track is superimposed on a map from an atlas of 1841. The dot east
of the Virgin Islands shows the ship's position, at 58° W, on
December 1, 1842.

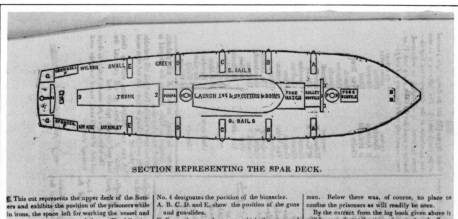

SECTION REPRESENTING THE SPAR DECK.

This cut represents the upper deck of the Somers and exhibits the position of the prisoners while in irons, the space left for working the vessel and the entrances to the rooms below. The following will sufficiently explain the whole:

No. 1—Just behind F. M., the foremost represents the place of the bitts. The whole space behind this to M. M. the mainmast, to the dotted lines at the sides is occupied by the launch cutters, and over them the booms, spare spars, sails, &c.

No. 2—Is the entrance to the steerage from deck, and the space to 3 is occupied by the trunk raised about two feet from deck, in which are two skylights.

No. 3 is the entrance to the 'Cabin, and from 3 to 4 is the only clear passage across decks.

No. 4 designates the position of the binnacles.

A. B. C. D. and E. show the position of the guns and gun-slides.

F. F. are the arm-chests on which Spencer and Cromwell were kept after confinement. The places of the other prisoners are marked by their names.

G. G. Roundhouse—the top being on a level with the bulwarks.

H. The wheel and fixtures.

It will be seen from these engravings that the only space in the vessel where prisoners could be kept was that which those in confinement occupied. After having disposed of the officers on deck the entrances from below by which officers could have come up could easily have been guarded by two men. Below there was, of course, no place to confine the prisoners as will readily be seen.

By the extract from the log book given above it will be seen that at the time of execution the Somers was four days sail from St. Thomas, and there was reason to fear that her arrival might have been retarded by adverse winds.

The following are the ages of the Officers and Men on board:

Officers, of 20 and upwards	8	Men, of 19 and upwards...	1
" 19	1	" 18	18
" 17	1	" 17	20
" 16	2	" 16	20
Petty Officers, of full age...	3	" 15	16
Cooks and Stewards, of do	8	" 14	5
Men, of 20 and upwards...	5	" 13	3
Spencer, Cromwell and Small			3

Total number of the Crew.....................120

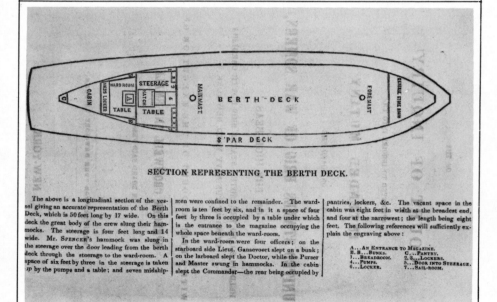

SECTION REPRESENTING THE BERTH DECK.

The above is a longitudinal section of the vessel giving an accurate representation of the Berth Deck, which is 50 feet long by 17 wide. On this deck the great body of the crew slung their hammocks. Mr. Spencer's hammock was slung in the steerage over the door leading from the berth deck through the steerage to the ward-room. A space of six feet by three in the steerage is taken up by the pumps and a table; and seven midshipmen were confined to the remainder. The ward-room is ten feet by six, and in it a space of four feet by three is occupied by a table under which is the entrance to the magazine occupying the whole space beneath the ward-room.

In the ward-room were four officers; on the starboard side Lieut. Gansevoort slept on a bunk; on the larboard slept the Doctor, while the Purser and Master swung in hammocks. In the cabin slept the Commander—the rear being occupied by pantries, lockers, &c. The vacant space in the cabin was eight feet in width at the broadest end, and four at the narrowest; the length being eight feet. The following references will sufficiently explain the engraving above:

A...An Entrance to Magazine.
B. B...Bunks.
1...Breadroom.
4...Pumps.
6...Locker.
C...Pantry.
2, 3...Lockers.
5...Door into Steerage.
7...Sail-room.

THE DECKS OF THE SOMERS.

Like the sketch of Mackenzie, these illustrations are from the flimsy newspaper pamphlet published at the conclusion of the court of inquiry.

ABEL PARKER UPSHUR.
Secretary of the navy and secretary of state in John Tyler's
administration. Upshur's brother was at one time Slidell Mackenzie's
closest professional friend.

JAMES GORDON BENNETT, SKETCHED FROM LIFE.
"An ill-looking squinting man," as Philip Hone called him, an
"impudent disturber of the public peace"—and one of the great figures
in the history of journalism.

RICHARD HENRY DANA, JR.
The photograph was taken in the early 1840s, when the subject was
in his mid-twenties and already famous as the author of *Two Years
Before the Mast.*

CHARLES SUMNER IN 1846.
Two years earlier Sumner had published his eloquent defense of
Mackenzie; within five years he would undertake his lengthy and
controversial service as United States senator from Massachusetts.

HERMAN MELVILLE IN 1885.
The author was sixty-six. Three years after the photograph was taken,
he began his final imaginative work, *Billy Budd*.

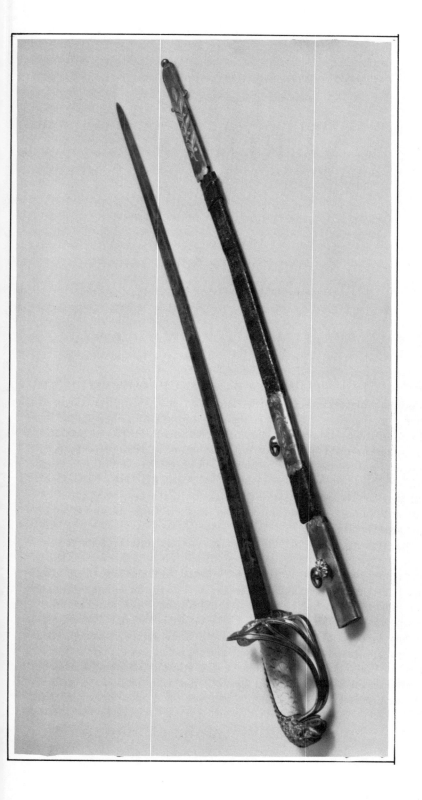

SPENCER'S SERVICE SWORD.

This is the weapon, now at the naval museum at Annapolis, that, according to Commander Mackenzie, the acting midshipman "had forfeited the right to wear."

VERDICT

TWO OF THE FIVE CHARGES—UNNECESSARY CRUELTY
and conduct unbecoming an officer—had been dropped in the course of
the trial. To the three charges remaining—oppression, illegal punishment, and murder—the court-martial returned a verdict of not proven.

"The agitation of the public mind in relation to the trial of Commander
Mackenzie is put to rest by the promulgation of the decision of the court-
martial," Philip Hone recorded in his diary April 10, 1843. "The character of the navy is sustained and the majesty of the laws vindicated by
the full and honorable acquittal of the accused from all the charges
brought against him."

But that was not quite so. Though others would interpret the results
the same way, "honorable" was not quite so. Those others included a
brilliant young Boston lawyer, Charles Sumner. In the course of the trial
Sumner had been approached by Alexander Slidell Mackenzie's counsel
to write publicly on behalf of the embattled officer—and friend of Sumner's own good friend Longfellow. The Bostonian had had "no misgiv-
ings of any kind" about doing so: "I should write about Mackenzie as a
labor of love." But when his substantial defense of the captain's course
appeared in *The North American Review* that summer, it made the same
assumption about the verdict that Hone had made in his diary earlier;
indeed, Sumner's defense repeatedly stresses the honorableness of the
acquittal.

What the future senator and abolitionist (then in his early thirties) had written provoked in response the first of a series of three letters to *The Boston Courier* by one less partial to Mackenzie's conduct: William Sturgis, wealthy and respected merchant, shipowner, and veteran of many years at sea as captain on vessels trading with China. Of the account of the verdict in the *North American*, Sturgis observed that "the words *honorably acquitted* are given in italics to mark the importance which the reviewer [Sumner] attaches to them, and he subsequently twice speaks of the *honorable* acquittal of Commander Mackenzie." But "the decision of the court-martial as officially given was something very different from an *honorable* acquittal." Sturgis proceeds to clarify: "It is given, in the *Madisonian* of April 13th, upon each of the charges and specifications that it 'is not proven,' and 'the court do therefore acquit Commander Alexander S. Mackenzie of all the charges and specifications preferred against him by the Secretary of the Navy.' It is added: 'As these charges involved the life of the accused, and as the finding is in his favor, he is entitled to the benefit of it, as in the analogous case of a verdict before a civil court; and there is no power which can constitutionally deprive him of that benefit. The finding, therefore, is simply *confirmed* and carried into effect, without any expression of approbation on the part of the President, no such expression being necessary.'

"In colder language," Sturgis concludes, "an acquittal could hardly be expressed."

For unlike the verdicts of civil courts, verdicts of courts-martial if favorable to the defendant are often accompanied by commendations: a later captain of the *Somers* (no less a figure than Raphael Semmes) was, for example, commended after an inquiry into his conduct aboard that same ill-fated vessel. As for the present instance, President Tyler, by declining to make a gesture that might seem to condone the behavior of him who had executed the son of a cabinet secretary and friend, had doubtless been willing enough to avoid any further offense to John Canfield Spencer.

Meanwhile, Commander Mackenzie, in receipt of the verdict at his farmhouse near Tarrytown that spring of 1843, had been vexed to read a newspaper report professing to have penetrated the secrecy veiling those recent deliberations on his fate. According to the report, the verdict had been by no means unanimous: no fewer than "seven out of twelve were of opinion that the charges, or some of them, had been proved." Having digested that unsubstantiated disclosure, the commander was writing his counsel from Tarrytown April 18 "to consult as to what is best to be done with regard to the libel of the *Journal of Commerce*. If by bringing a suit against him"—presumably the editor of the paper, Gerard Hallock—"the entire secret of the voting of the court could be ascertained I should be glad. I do not believe that more than two at the most voted against me on any charge, and I am inclined to think that there was only one, and he not of sound mind. . . ."

As it turned out, both the editor and the officer were wrong. Mackenzie did have friends among those twelve who had sat in judgment, and might thus have felt some confidence about how the vote had gone. As Fenimore Cooper had observed privately a month or two earlier, "neither Turner nor Page should have been on the court. They are both honest, but their feelings are too much interwoven with the family of Mackenzie to judge impartially. Turner is, to all intents and purposes, one of the Perry family"—Captain Daniel Turner had been third in command at the Battle of Lake Erie—"and Page was John Slidell's second in his duel with Price. He has ever since been much caressed by the Slidell connection." Moreover, at least one officer, Captain Robert Stockton, had (as the novelist remarked elsewhere) refused at the outset to serve on the court, giving as his reason that his mind was made up: he would have voted to hang Mackenzie. So the ill-disposed may have removed themselves at the start, while the well-disposed toward Mackenzie remained. In any event, counsel for the commander meant to institute a suit for libel against the editor of the *Journal of Commerce* and thus secure examinations from among the various members of the court to discover just how they had voted on the several charges.

The examinations, of Captain Isaac McKeever and Commodore Downes at Boston, revealed that the vote had been "nine in Captain Mackenzie's favor to three against him"—neither as sweeping a vindication as the commander had presumed, nor as feeble a one as the *Journal of Commerce* had published.

At the trial, Counselor Griffin's closing defense had made its appeal not only to the court, but also to "the high tribunal of public opinion." Yet like the court, public opinion in the aftermath declined to render a unanimous verdict. Griffin's defense, by the way—that eloquent summation—had been promptly published in octavo as a thirty-page pamphlet, copies of which the exonerated commander was soon finding himself autographing for well-wishers. In fact, the article by Charles Sumner that appeared in Boston some months later, in July 1843, was ostensibly a review of the published defense—a review that aspired to place Mackenzie's exoneration on even firmer ground than Griffin had sought to do.

For Counselor Griffin had been mistaken, so Sumner thought, in basing his defense on establishing two facts: that a mutiny had existed aboard the *Somers*, and that the persons executed had been parties to that mutiny. In Sumner's opinion, the guilt of Spencer, Cromwell, and Small was irrelevant; any effort at the trial to prove their guilt had been effort misspent, only widening the field of inquiry "beyond the requirements of law." The law, so Sumner insisted, would have been satisfied to know "that the Commander, in taking the steps that he did towards the suppression of the mutiny, acted in good faith, even supposing subsequent knowledge may have made it evident that he erred in judgment." The vessel had, after all, been placed in what amounted to a state of war during the climactic days of late November. "It was as if the enemy were at the gates, or rather already within the walls of the city." Under those harrowing circumstances common law would protect such a person as the captain, given judicial authority, if he acted sincerely and conscientiously, "even though grievous error may have occurred" from the exercise of that authority. Consider, for instance, the case of the officer who, "in the heady current of battle," with his own arm strikes down the soldier seeming to shrink from his post. Or consider the many historical instances of "extraordinary military punishment, under peculiar circumstances," wherein an example must be made even though the real offender is impossible to identify.

As for the *Somers* affair, "the legality of the means employed by Commander Mackenzie in suppressing the mutiny may be judged by the answer to the simple question, whether, under the circumstances of the case, he acted honestly, to the best of his judgment, and without any corrupt motive or wilful thought." Of course an *apparent* necessity must have existed to provide reasonable grounds for resorting to such extreme measures for quelling the mutiny. But all the defense had been obliged to show, according to Sumner, was that such did exist. And to determine if it did, "we are to banish from our minds all knowledge or impressions derived from recent results or evidence. We are to carry ourselves back to the morning of December 1st, 1842, and to the actual point of time when the execution took place. We are to put ourselves in the position of the commander: to scan the countenances of the crew, to note the signs of disaffection, to breathe the atmosphere of distrust. We are, with him, to examine the narrow accommodations afforded by the brig, and to consider the difficulty of preventing communication between the prisoners and the crew. And finally, with him we are to listen to the unanimous recommendation of his officers that Spencer, Cromwell, and Small should be put to death." Indeed, it would seem to Sumner to be "trifling with human testimony to say that the ship was not at least in *apparent* danger, when all the officers join in testifying to its existence."

Legal precedent that the lawyer-reviewer was able to cite supported the actions of the captain aboard, stipulating (again) only that those actions had to have been taken in good faith. Was there any doubt of that? As for historical precedents, which Sumner cited also—in considerable detail—they taught "at least one lesson, which the faithful commander should not forget except on peril of the highest misfortune." Mutinous acts aboard the *Bounty*, at Spithead, at The Nore, on the *Hermione*, on the

Essex in the Marquesas all underscored that such outbreaks of indiscipline and terror "may be sudden, unexpected, and overwhelming, even among a crew that has given no previous sign of disaffection." If he had failed to act, the captain of the *Somers* might have imperiled his command, with all the dire consequences to commerce and to the innocent and fair on the high seas that Sumner's pen proved as able to evoke as had Griffin's in the defense's peroration. "Honor, then, to the commander," the reviewer concludes with some fervor, "for the courage and promptitude he displayed and the service he has rendered to his country! He has done more than gain a battle, and deserves more than the homage of admiration and gratitude with which we greet the victor returning from successful war. We thank him, and the country thanks him, that he did not hesitate; that, just and firm of purpose, with a soul full of tenderness, he did not allow the sacred regard for human life, nor the wicked machinations of conspiracy, nor the fear of civil tongues at home to shake his solid mind."

Others at the time were comparably fervent in recording their approval of what the captain had accomplished. From Cambridge, Longfellow wrote his old friend: "The voice of all upright men—the common consent of all the good—is with you. Of course you have seen Sumner's article in the *North American*. I have not yet seen it, but hear it spoken of by all as very able, and as putting your defense upon stronger and more unassailable grounds than even your own legal advisers did.— You will see more and more, my dear Mackenzie, how strongly you are supported in this quarter for maintaining the right at any sacrifice." Indeed, from that very quarter had already come a request that the commander sit for his portrait, which would be prominently displayed for the edification of New England's various citizenry. Nearly four hundred of those—"the most eminent citizens of Boston"—had, moreover, signed a statement on parchment commending the gallant officer's "noble and heroic conduct," the statement transmitted to Tarrytown "in an elegant silver case, with an envelope of morocco." Tarrytown itself had assembled as one and passed a resolution: "That we cordially welcome back . . . our fellow-citizen . . . That we regard with sincere pleasure his acquittal . . ." And farther south, at the tip of Manhattan, New Yorkers had published their own letter, "signed by three hundred merchants and others of our most respectable citizens," so Hone recorded that spring: a letter "addressed to Commander Alexander S. Mackenzie, expressing their approval of his conduct in the unhappy affair of the mutiny on board the *Somers*, and their congratulations on his honorable acquittal by the court of inquiry and court-martial. His answer"—bearing the date May 6, 1843—"to this high compliment is much better written, and in better taste," says Hone, "than his unfortunate statement made to the government on his arrival. . . . The merchants," the diarist adds, "have raised a sum of money by subscription to pay the lawyers' fees and other charges attending the trials; but this fact is delicately kept out of view in the correspondence."

So Slidell Mackenzie's friends and supporters stood by him, not only through the long ordeal but after it had officially ended. In our own time he has had his supporters as well, and some formidable ones. There was a tradition in the navy through the latter part of the nineteenth century of avoiding discussion of the *Somers* affair, though one old navy man, Robert C. Rogers, writing in 1890 of an event by then nearly a half-century into the past, did not scruple to give as his opinion that Spencer had been guilty all right—an opinion of more than passing interest, coming from one who when young had known the offending midshipman in Rio. Looking back, Rogers recalled that he had not been surprised when news of the execution reached him, though now, nearly fifty years afterward, he did wonder if young Spencer had had to be hanged so promptly—and would it not have been sufficient to make an example of the midshipman alone, thus sparing the other two?

In the present century, Rear Admiral Samuel Eliot Morison, another navy man, has shown no reluctance to address the *Somers* episode, or to take a firm stand on the issues it raises. Morison treats the cruise and its consequences in a chapter of his splendid biography of Matthew Perry (1967). There the troublesome Spencer emerges as "a prototype of what nowadays is called a 'young punk,' " and his scheme to seize the ship and convert her into a pirate, however fantastic it might now sound, is judged to have been practicable at the time. "*Somers*," writes Morison, "could outsail anything afloat except her sister ships, overhaul any merchant-man, and overpower any vessel smaller than a frigate. And she would have been far more difficult to catch than CSS *Alabama* in the Civil War or the German raiders of the two world wars." Drawing as it does on a vast knowledge of both the steam and the sailing navies—the iron and the wood—Morison's opinion commands respect. To support it, he quotes approvingly a stern fact that Captain Mackenzie would have known and that Admiral Chester Nimitz a century later recalled to the Pacific Fleet in World War II: "The time for taking all measures for a ship's safety is while still able to do so. Nothing is more dangerous than for a seaman to be grudging in taking precautions lest they turn out to have been un-necessary. Safety at sea for a thousand years has depended on exactly the opposite philosophy."

What, asks Morison, was the captain aboard the *Somers* to do? Disci-pline was disintegrating. St. Thomas lay at least a week away. The vessel was small, vulnerable. The officers were exhausted. "What was Macken-zie to do, with this sinister plot simmering, and no possible help from anyone outside the ship? What might not happen in a sudden squall at night?" The historian grows warm about those—"the malignant and the sentimental"—who would depict the commander as "a savage martinet, a

sadist, or a coward who preferred hanging innocent men to taking risks."
And he tellingly assembles character references from people who knew
Mackenzie. Matthew Perry himself, for one, had soon after the return of
the *Somers* written, December 27, 1842, from Brooklyn to his congressman at Washington: "You know the character of Mackenzie well, and
you know that he would not hurt the hair of a man's head unless from
stern necessity. His conduct is borne out by everyone in this quarter.
The clergy, judges, lawyers, women and children all praise him and his
officers for having crushed in the bud a most diabolical scheme of rapine
and murder." Perry, incidentally, goes on in the same letter to address
another aspect of the case: "So far as my two sons have been concerned
in this melancholy affair, they have my unmeasured approbation, and
they would have been spurned by me if they had acted otherwise. *No
man is fit for the Navy if he is not ready at all times to interpose his life in the
preservation of the integrity of the American flag and the safety of the vessel
entrusted to his and their charge. . . .*"

Such was the caliber of the commander's adherents. Of his various
critics, at the time and later, Morison retrospectively takes most sternly
to task James Fenimore Cooper, in particular for a lengthy "Review of
the Proceedings of the Naval Court Martial," which the novelist had
published in New York in 1844, a year after the trial had ended. In that
review, so Morison charges, Cooper "used every argument good or bad to
prove Mackenzie to be a jittery, incompetent martinet. He sneered that
Somers was more of a 'family yacht' than a man-of-war, and boasted how
he himself could have handled the situation better. Cooper flattered himself that his tract would 'finish' Mackenzie as a naval officer, which it
certainly did not. It should have finished Cooper as a competent authority on naval affairs."

Whether all that is just may appear. We turn, then, to the background
of the document in question, bearing in mind as we do a different opinion expressed by still another twentieth-century navy man, by Rear Admiral Livingston Hunt, who in 1925 authoritatively recapitulated, from
the vantage point of eighty-some years later, both the commander's ordeal and the reactions it provoked. "There is," Hunt concluded, "no
article or review called forth by this remarkable trial more analytical,
more illuminating as to technicalities, than the eighty-page review of it
by James Fenimore Cooper," a review that the admiral judges to be "masterly in its keenness of observation of the motives behind the various acts
of the chief persons of the drama."

Fenimore Cooper had read the notice that James Watson Webb earlier,
at the conclusion of the court of inquiry, inserted in *The Morning Courier
and New York Enquirer*, the item of January 23, 1843, warning readers
about the novelist's avowed determination to review the *Somers* case in

order to "annihilate Mackenzie." A letter to Bryant's *Evening Post* in early February contained his reply to that accusation. Cooper did admit that "there is, certainly, a grave collision between Captain Mackenzie and myself in our characters of historians. That gentleman has had his say; it remains to hear me." The reference is to their dispute concerning the Battle of Lake Erie, about which Slidell Mackenzie had written against the Naval History in the pages of the *North American* and in his life of Oliver Perry. "I have several times," so Cooper reminds his readers, "announced an intention to publish my side of this case, and this was the very moment when I expected to lay it before the world. I do not wish *now*"—with Mackenzie's court-martial just beginning—"to publish what I may have said on the subject of this controversy, but I will add that, while last in New York, I acquainted several friends of my determination *to defer it, until the investigation of the affair of the* Somers *had terminated!* I presume that Mr. Webb, like others who fetch and carry"—rumors or whatever—"has made a material mistake in his facts. I certainly have no recollection of having made the remarks he quotes, in connection with the mutiny, while, as certainly, I have often said something very similar to it in relation to the other affair. . . ."

So it was "the other affair"—the controversy between historians over Lake Erie—that concerned Cooper publicly at this time; for the present he had no intention of writing about the *Somers* case. Now it happened that the very day—January 23—on which had appeared Webb's newspaper item, a disabled seaman in an old sailor's home on Staten Island had composed a letter to the novelist. "Sir," it began, "Excuse the liberty I take in addressing you, but being anxious to know whether you are the Mr. Cooper who in 1806 or 1807 was on board the ship *Sterling*, Cap. Johnson, bound from New York to London, if so whether you recollect the boy *Ned* whose life you saved in London dock on a Sunday, if so it would give me a great deal of pleasure to see you. . . ." The same Cooper it was indeed, James Cooper, now James Fenimore Cooper in his mid-fifties, who as a fractious adolescent expelled from Yale those many years before had been sent by his exasperated father to sea to learn some discipline. The novelist promptly answered his old shipmate's letter, and soon was in correspondence with Captain Johnston as well—all those memories of youth flooding back—writing the captain of the *Stirling* who last had been seen bringing his schooner up the Delaware after a year-long Atlantic voyage. Now, as Ned had divulged, the merchant captain was living in retirement in a seaport town in Maine. "To my great surprise," Cooper wrote him at Wiscasset, "I got a letter a few days since from Ned Myers, acquainting me not only with his own, but your existence . . . I was eighteen the day we entered the Capes of the Delaware on our return passage. I thought you then about seven and twenty, which will make you about sixty-four now. . . ."

To those greetings, accompanied as they were by cordial accounts of Cooper's present life and family, Captain Johnston responded in early April. "You have a very correct idea of my age," he confirmed. "I was born March 9th, 1779, and wanted two days of sixty-four when I received your letter." The captain's health was still good, and he had spirits enough, so he assured his former crewman, to take charge of a vessel if need be—and "I think I could manage a ship's company without hanging any of them at the yardarms. . . ."

That allusion from distant Maine to the current story of national interest. And meanwhile, would certain similarities have failed to occur to Cooper as thoughts of his own youth at sea were being awakened and mingled with considerations of events aboard the *Somers?* Two sons of prominent fathers, both with dismal college careers interrupted, both sent to sea in hopes of reformation. And James Cooper had come back—sailed up the Delaware to Philadelphia and was now living out a rewarding life at Cooperstown with his beloved Sue and their four daughters and son, about whom he could boast with a father's pride to his former captain, old John Johnston of Wiscasset, Maine. Indeed, to that son, Paul Cooper, schoolmate at Geneva College of the late Philip Spencer, the proud father had only recently, January 28 (by chance Phil Spencer's birthday), been writing amply enough to show how closely he had been following testimony at the just completed court of inquiry: ". . . Three men *certain* did not make a formidable mutiny—but, there were *nine* doubtful. The doubtful were sure to join the strongest side. But four of these doubtful were marked as likely to join before the rising. Well, that makes but seven in all, and surely a brig of 266 tons could hold seven, or seventeen, or seventy prisoners if necessary. Suppose she had taken a pirate. What should she have done with the crew? Hang them, by way of precaution? . . ." And he had passed on to Paul news of an encounter with "a person in Albany, whom I took to be an employee of John C. Spencer, that had been at Geneva obtaining testimony as to Phil's character. He told me it was not so very bad. I told him, in answer, that I had received the worst accounts of it. He then told me that [a] letter desiring Phil to call on the writer before the *Somers* sailed, and signed 'Eliza,' had been found in Phil's trunk. This letter was sent to Washington with an endorsement on its back, to say that it was a *proof of his dissolute habits &c.*" But in fact, the letter "was written by a female relative, who had already given poor Phil—and wished still to give him—good advice!"

All this time, as far as the public prints were concerned, the novelist was maintaining a discreet silence, beyond conceding, in that answer to Webb in the *Post* of February 3, "that my opinion" of the *Somers* case "has undergone a material change with the change of testimony." For like almost everyone else, Cooper at the start felt favorably disposed toward Mackenzie in his ordeal. But disturbing facts had emerged during the court of inquiry. Now, having scrutinized accounts of court sessions carried in New York papers, the novelist privately, February 5 (as the court-martial was getting under way), addressed a long analysis of the case to his close friend Commodore William Shubrick, USN. "I have postponed answering your last letter," he began, "under the impression that you might be on Mackenzie's court, and a desire not to say anything that might have an appearance of wishing to influence your opinion. As you escape, I can now write freely."

Shubrick's own letter, dated from Norfolk a month earlier, January 6, had raised the subject of the *Somers:* "Let me know what you think of it." So Cooper did, declaring right off that by this point in the proceedings he regarded the affair as "one of the most discreditable events that ever occurred in the service, since it exhibits a *demoralized quarterdeck.* I can find no necessity for the executions, and certainly nothing like substantial *proof* against Cromwell. I have serious doubts whether this man had any connection with Spencer's mad schemes at all." For not only is the name of the boatswain's mate nowhere on the Greek lists, and not only did Spencer solemnly and repeatedly assert his innocence, and not only did Cromwell himself reaffirm that innocence to the last. The testimony against him, as Cooper reads it, is "confined to half-comprehended and contradictory dialogues, all of which he might have satisfactorily explained, had an opportunity been allowed him. Why was not this opportunity given him?" Furthermore, some of that testimony "is downright wicked. Thus, at first he was severe with the boys, then mild. This is to show that at first he follows his nature, afterwards the policy of a mutineer. When Mackenzie wishes to justify himself from the coltings, however, he shows that he reproved Cromwell for his severity, about the time the man changed his system! His obedience is tortured into a proof of guilt. Again, at one time he changes his treatment because he had enlisted in the mutiny; at another, the mutiny was planned before the brig sailed," the boatswain's mate having been reported to have predicted mutiny in a Bowery saloon last summer. As for the way he was arrested on board, "was ever such sign of apprehension before exhibited in an American man-of-war?" The quarterdeck is clear of all but officers, all armed; as the unsuspecting Cromwell descends the rigging, the first lieutenant points a cocked pistol in his direction—and the gun goes off! The lieutenant next orders the mate aft to be ironed; there the captain tells him he will be taken home and tried. And all this "without one single *act* of revolt on board!" In the course of making the arrest, by the way, Commander Mackenzie demands of the prisoner whether he did not communicate with Mr. Spencer last night. Cromwell answers: "It was not me, sir; it was Small"—a remark interpreted at the time as further implicating the little sailmaker, who himself is thereupon promptly ironed. But isn't it likely that Cromwell misunderstood the question—

thought the reference was to the notorious conversation, *two* nights earlier, on the booms between Spencer and Wales, which Small had been
summoned to join? Isn't Cromwell, before Small's arrest, "fancying he
has been taken by mistake"?

Cooper raises other points in his letter to Commodore Shubrick. He
asserts, for one thing, that "it is a mistaken idea that the discipline of the
navy is involved in supporting Mackenzie. Nothing good can be connected with the maintenance of error. But suppose this execution had taken
place, as an example, on board another vessel, and Spencer's mutiny
existed as is now believed. Would the men be as likely to submit to be
ironed, as these men were ironed, if they believed themselves liable to be
hanged without a trial? I think not. You make men desperate by resorting
to such desperate expedients." And more: "That the Department has
favored Mackenzie I take to be indisputable. Why was he left in command of the brig, containing all the witnesses? Every officer should have
been taken out of her the instant she arrived, or the men transferred
beyond their influence. Then Mackenzie's letter! It asks for promotion of
two-thirds of the witnesses! The world cannot show a parallel to such
stupidity, or such corruption. The letter is damnable." Shubrick had
reported that opinion at Norfolk in early January was decidedly in the
captain's favor; but now, a month later, his friend Cooper farther north
professes to have conversed with eleven high-ranking naval officers,
"every man of whom is dead against him. I sustained him *at first;* but it
was on very different facts from what have since appeared."

Those later facts the novelist would continue to ponder as the court-
martial unfolded through March. By early April, with the verdict
reached, he had journeyed to New York again, where he managed, presumably on April 6, to have his reunion with Ned Myers after all those
years. He found the seaman crippled from a shipboard fall, his sailing
days behind him. For all that, the meeting was a success. So gratified
with it was the famous author that he invited Ned to Cooperstown for
what turned out to be a five months' stay—this although that same spring
and summer of 1843 may have been the very busiest of all the busy
periods in Cooper's industrous and prolific life. His satirical romance—a
better book than its title: *The Autobiography of a Pocket Handkerchief*—was
appearing serialized in issues of *Graham's Magazine* in January, February,
and March. In May and June that same periodical published the next in
his continuing series of lives of naval officers, this one of Oliver Perry.
Issues of July and August contained the life of John Paul Jones. In September would appear a novel of the American Revolution, *Wyandotté*,
which the writer had been working on all but simultaneously with another full-length work, and an unusual one, derived over the spring from
conversations with his shipmate from the *Stirling*, set down as nearly as
possible in Ned's own words; that work would be published in Novem-

ber as *The Autobiography of Ned Myers*—profits to be shared with the sailor whose life Cooper had saved off a London dock thirty-some years earlier.

One other work appeared this same fruitful year, 1843. In June was published at Cooperstown a pamphlet entitled *The Battle of Lake Erie, or Answers to Messrs. Bruges* [sic], *Duer, and Mackenzie*. The work had been ready to print for a long while; but delays had arisen first from the ultimately successful suit settled a year ago against editor William L. Stone over matters discussed in the pamphlet; then further delays were caused by Mackenzie's embroilment in the *Somers* affair. Now, however, with the formal verdict of that latter trial rendered, Cooper at last felt free to submit to the public his long-promised argument against those polemicists—the legislator, the college president, and the naval captain—who had challenged the accuracy of his treatment in the Naval History of the Battle of Lake Erie. Richard Henry Dana, Jr., was in New York that June, on the nineteenth, and called upon the popular novelist Catharine Sedgwick: "Speaking of Mackenzie, she says Cooper told her he was about publishing a pamphlet in which he should not leave enough of Mackenzie to put between his thumb and finger." For after all, as the pamphleteer reminds his readers in the course of his argument, "No man has had a larger share in injuring both Com. Elliott and myself than Capt. Mackenzie . . ."—"myself" injured by an unbalanced review and that hasty book of special pleading on Oliver Perry that together had drastically hindered sales of Cooper's own careful and comprehensive naval survey nearly a decade in the making.

Much of the pamphlet on Lake Erie recapitulates yet again nautical details of the battle—respective positions of vessels, wind directions, orders given, maneuvers taken—but the author proves himself unable to resist weaving into his completed text some references to current matters. Thus he charges Mackenzie the historian with being able to see only "one side of a question. He is a man of prejudice and denunciation, and he accuses, less under evidence than under convictions. Were he inspired, this last might do well enough; but as he is only a man, and quite as often wrong as right, fearful consequences have followed from his mistakes." The charge has expanded beyond the historian to include the naval officer. More specifically, in order to show the workings of his adversary's mind, Cooper alludes to the *Somers* outright, to Midshipman Spencer's claim to have enlisted "about twenty" conspirators aboard, an estimate that Wales reported to his captain. "Upon this Capt. Mackenzie distinctly tells the court of inquiry he had reason to infer that *at least* twenty men and boys were engaged in the mutiny. Nine hundred and ninety-nine ordinary minds in a thousand would have said '*at most*' for Capt. Mackenzie's '*at least*.' Who ever heard of a conspirator's *underrating* his force to a recruit?—who but Capt. Mackenzie?"

It bears repeating: such ungenerous observations were ostensibly included to enlighten readers about the mental processes of Mackenzie as naval historian. That they should be included at all in a pamphlet on the Battle of Lake Erie may be accounted for only in the light of Cooper's state of mind in the spring of 1843—youthful memories awakened and court testimony before him—and a long-simmering grievance that he felt toward one whose misrepresentations of the past (lies, as they seemed) had cost the scrupulous naval historian at Cooperstown a large portion of the livelihood he had counted on for his family. Such feelings of exasperation led him on, for instance, to excoriate Mackenzie's abiding tendency to accept dubious evidence, on historical questions as elsewhere. "Sad experience may teach Capt. Mackenzie that it is miserable testimony to *hear* it said 'That the d——d fool is on the larboard arm-chest, and the d——d rascal on starboard'—that there is really such a thing as 'evidence' in this world, and that wise men seek it, and intelligent and just men like to get it on *both* sides before they make up a judgment." Nor did Cooper stop with that. "There is a rumor, now very prevalent in this country"— and no less prevalent for this repetition of it—"that Capt. Mackenzie proved himself a coward in the affair of the post-boy who was assassinated in Spain, and it has grown out of the supposed qualities that he manifested on board the *Somers*. I do not mention this," the author hastens to add, "because I think Capt. Mackenzie merits either accusation—for in this I honestly think gross injustice is done him—but to give him tangible proof of the value of 'rumor.' I make no doubt he was right in taking the course he did in Spain, nor do I think he was influenced by fear in its abject sense in the affair of the *Somers*. . . ."

The concession about the captain's courage would be more convincingly developed at a later time, but what Cooper would stress here is that "calumny"—against Boatswain's Mate Cromwell as against Commander Mackenzie—"may be refuted and rebuked, but it is never wholly effaced." Assuredly through repetition it is not. In any case, by this time the pamphleteer seems scarcely less interested in the *Somers* in mid-Atlantic than in the *Lawrence* on Lake Erie. In fact, he has by now, by June, determined to review the *Somers* affair. To Shubrick in another letter that resolution has already been expressed, in late March, even as Mackenzie's court-martial is nearing its end: "I take it for granted he will be acquitted," Cooper writes. "I shall wait for the record, when I intend to give the whole proceedings a close and searching review. To this my mind has been made up within the last few days. . . ."

That the historian would resolve to review so crucial an episode in the annals of the navy seems logical enough; nor is it surprising that before long his intention came to the notice of partisans of John C. Spencer. That fall, Cooper was approached by Secretary Spencer's son-in-law. "Upon consultation with my friends," Henry Morris wrote from Washington, "they all agree with me that you are the only person in the country who possessed the peculiar information, knowledge, and ability to place before the public in a strong, distinct, and true light that horrid affair; and we are therefore extremely anxious that you should undertake the task."

As the addressee had already determined to do—no doubt in part because he was uniquely possessed of just those qualities Morris recognized, no doubt also—at least at first—because of his personal involvement with the captain of the *Somers* these several years. "Mackenzie deserves exposure," Cooper had written Shubrick darkly, "and he shall get it." But as his examination of relevant facts proceeded through summer and autumn, the called-for exposure spread beyond any one person's transgression. The whole naval system, Cooper came to feel, demanded treatment of the case in order that false doctrine should be rectified and misapprehensions of national import corrected.

In short, the novelist had grown indignant at what he took to be official complacency regarding the implications of the *Somers* affair. The commander's own character might by that time, by the autumn of 1843, have seemed to Cooper of no more than passing interest—merely a clinical instance of moral obliquity. But concerning the executions, "the very circumstance that the power of the government was the agent in the act renders the case more grave."

So the target had widened beyond "poor Mackenzie," who was daily losing ground in any case, as Cooper assured his wife from Philadelphia, September 17: "An old seaman, of the name of Sturgis, is writing against him under his own name. Three letters have appeared," including a first one in answer to Sumner's review in the July *North American*. That same September day that he wrote his wife, the novelist expressed himself directly to William Sturgis at Boston: "Sir: I have read your letters in the *Courier* with great interest, and being somewhat of a seaman myself, can appreciate their justice. Your third letter I hold to be one of the simplest and best arguments, on the point it treats of, that can be written. . . ."

The point treated in Sturgis's third letter, of September 13—the others had appeared August 4 and 5—concerns those crewmen whom Mackenzie had kept in irons for weeks after his vessel's return to home port. "When it was made public that twelve men had been brought home in the *Somers* charged with such grave offenses" as being overtly mutinous through intentionally missing muster, disobeying orders, uttering seditious expressions, and the like, "was there a man in the United States," the Boston merchant asked readers of the *Courier* rhetorically, "who doubted but they would be brought to trial?" After all, four of them—McKinley, McKee, Willson, and Green—had been kept in irons on board since before the executions, their guilt asserted by their captain in unqualified terms; McKinley, for example, had been judged at the time of his arrest to be the most formidable conspirator on the vessel. Moreover, the alleged acts of insubordination committed by those four and the eight later arrested had been "open and apparent, witnessed by the officers and others, and as capable of proof—*had they actually been committed*— as the execution itself." No wonder that during the court-martial the secretary of the navy had written Judge Advocate Norris (February 15) to prefer charges against whoever might be implicated by emerging testimony. Thereupon, the judge advocate had consulted with Captain Mackenzie, then reported back to Washington, on the twenty-second, that the commander at this time proposed to prefer charges against one person only of those confined, "a person by the name of Wilson."

Yet no such charges were forthcoming. Indeed, some of the prisoners of the navy yard had already been released. And while arguing against those releases, an attorney in the United States court in the district of New York had come to a conclusion that William Sturgis in Boston could not have known of, expressed as it was in private correspondence, from Attorney William Watson to R. H. Dana, Jr.: "I must say from an examination of those boys" from the *Somers*, "all of whose discharges on writs of habeas corpus I have had to oppose, I do not believe a soul of them had any hand in it." The attorney had added, somewhat ambiguously: "I say to you *in confidence* that they [the defense? the navy?] are very willing to let the boys go—the opposition, by instructions, not being very strong. . . ."

Were those instructions from Mackenzie? Soon the secretary of the navy would return to the matter, this time in late March, on the twenty-fourth, as the court-martial was nearing its end. A letter from Secretary Upshur to Commodore Downes, president, contained directions to keep the court in session until any others whom it might be necessary to charge had been arraigned. That letter was read aloud the last day the court sat, April 1, after which the judge advocate submitted that "so far from hearing of any intention to prefer charges, it is believed that Commander Mackenzie has no such design. It is certain none are presented"— and, in fact, the commander at that very time had retired to his home in the country, thirty miles north, near Tarrytown.

Yet why, after so long confining those twelve boys and men—eighteen to twenty-three were their ages—why, after keeping them under guard through weeks and weeks of that winter, did their captain let them go? Admiral Morison suggests that the commander came to feel that there had been enough of punishment. Yet twelve men and boys had been kept in prison, some for two months and longer, with no charges ever filed against them, whereas the captain himself, charged with murder, had been allowed to go and come at will. Besides, as Cooper insists, it was Mackenzie's duty to prosecute mutinous crewmen; he "had every inducement of duty and self-respect to demonstrate the truth of what he had officially reported. . . ."

There had been, says Morison, enough of punishment. Does it not seem more probable that despite some forty days of court testimony, as well as earlier, detailed testimony at the court of inquiry, nothing had been found to warrant charging any one of the twelve? And if so—as Sturgis observes: "if no offense could be discovered which would subject the offenders to a trial before a court-martial, what becomes of all those charges of mutinous conduct which compelled the commander to put three helpless prisoners to death?" For this, then—for nothing—were twelve men and boys—"felons," as Mackenzie had branded them: "felons leagued in a conspiracy for murder and piracy"—for nothing more than this were they kept in irons through weeks and weeks, then turned loose at last, friendless, powerless, stigmatized. And "even now," as Sturgis reminds his readers in September, six or seven months later, "a large portion of the community are not aware that they have been released from arrest and suffered to go about their business, without any apparent intention on the part of anybody to bring them to trial."

The "old seaman," engaged in lucrative commercial pursuits at Boston, had earlier—as he explains in writing to the *Courier*—been four times around the world in vessels smaller than the *Somers*, and had had constant intercourse with sailors through half a century. What Sturgis had learned of those generally unlettered solitaries led him to feel troubled when he considered the twelve from the brig turned loose to make their way as best they could, charges of "felon," of "mutineer" not proved, yet not officially effaced from the record of their lives.

Other aspects of Captain Mackenzie's case troubled the former shipmaster. "Can any man familiar with nautical matters think it necessary to resort to mutinous intentions to account for the carrying away a topgallant-mast in the shive-hole, with the royal, royal steeringsails, topgallant staysail, and skysails set, and the braces leading forward?" No, Sturgis insists: "It is altogether gratuitous to impute to design that which can be satisfactorily accounted for from ordinary causes. The mast was undoubtedly carried away by the press of sail and weight of the boy"—of Gagely, aloft on the main-royal yard. As for the rushes aft, of course the crew hurried aft when generally ordered. Not to do so would have been disobedience, and at a time when every officer was armed. Moreover, if the men had rushed aft to seize the vessel, why had they not done so? Why didn't they seize her? Sturgis quotes Dana for his own purposes: "The crew were under some fear after the arrest . . . They would conceal every sign until the moment of the outbreak." Precisely—and hence those rushes down the quarterdeck must have been innocuous. As for the

uniformly corroborative testimony of the men before the council of officers on board, anyone expressing disbelief or making light of the present
danger "might have found himself an object of suspicion"—and been the
fourth one hanged.

But with such a crew of malcontents as later testimony describes,
could the *Somers* have gone into action? During the court-martial Captain
Mackenzie had, through questioning, repeatedly made the point that the
vessel with its mutinous crew was not prepared to uphold the flag if
challenged. Could she have? Doubtless not honorably, the Boston merchant concedes; "and those who believe that in time of profound peace it
could be necessary to hang three prisoners to 'clear ship for action' may
find perhaps, in this belief, a justification of the commander." Sturgis
himself found no such justification, there or anywhere else in the evidence that had emerged. "It seems to me," he concluded in explaining
what had occurred aboard the brig-of-war, "Commander Mackenzie and
his first lieutenant were *panic-struck*." Not that either lacked personal
courage. But in the course of the voyage, "unaccustomed and unmeasur-
able danger" had diseased their imaginations, making innocent happen-
ings sinister.

In writing his private letter of appreciation to the Boston merchant,
Cooper at Philadelphia developed a couple of points that Sturgis had
alluded to publicly in the *Courier*. In the case of Cromwell, did Captain
Mackenzie hang the man on circumstantial evidence without ever once
questioning him about those circumstances? Cooper came back to that.
"If he *did*, and I believe he did, that single act stamps his conduct and his
character. What just man would correct a child, discharge a servant, on
circumstantial proof, without a hearing?" Moreover, that business of the
mast's being carried away—"the turning point in the whole affair," the
point at which the commander felt his fears of conspiracy confirmed:
could it have been anticipated? A boy aloft, an order from aft—and a
decision taken in a matter of seconds to seize the vessel in the confusions
that would follow a mast split and a crewman hurled overboard. "Small
was on the bitts, within ten feet of the brace, probably nearer, and ten
seconds are quite sufficient for all he did"—reaching the brace in response to an order and yanking on it. "In this brief space, the man in
quick physical movement, *must* this deep plot have been laid!" But how
much easier and more reliable would have been any number of alternative plans. You prepare your men to move on the vessel with the cry in
the darkness of "Man overboard!" Then some night you throw over a
billet of wood, or get a boy into any one of fifty situations outboard and
tip him into the sea under the pretense of helping him. "It is a libel on the
common sense of Cromwell to suppose he could not have devised a hundred better expedients than that Capt. Mackenzie attributes to him . . ."

And something ought to be said, Cooper adds in this letter to Sturgis that ends with the hope that "we shall hear farther from you"—"Something ought to be said of the atrocious principle that a man-of-war is to hang a citizen before she will ask a foreign state to receive her prisoners." It would have redounded to the credit both of the captain—would it not?—and of his country if Mackenzie had gone ashore at Guadeloupe, hunted out the governor, and explained: " 'I command a vessel of war, without marines. A mutiny exists, and I must either leave the ringleaders here, or hang them at sea, without legal process. I belong to a government of laws. The ship I command is commissioned to enforce, and not to violate these laws. My country is tender of the life and liberties of the meanest citizen, and I prefer the self-mortification of asking your assistance to robbing an American citizen of his rights in so grave a matter.'

"The man who does not feel this moral truth," Cooper declares, "is not worthy to hold an American commission. . . ."

Despite urging by the eminent novelist, William Sturgis would offer no further public letters on the mutiny after those three in the *Courier* in the late summer of 1843. Through the fall that followed, Fenimore Cooper went on considering his own review of the same events, and by mid-November was writing it: the review would have been "soon finished had the record of the court-martial arrived. I expect it soon, however," he told his son Paul at Geneva. And the record must have come in good time, because by early 1844 his detailed examination of the case was being printed, to be bound right in with the official transcript of the court-martial. Posterity would get the two together; that much, at any rate, had John C. Spencer managed.

His lengthy consideration of the matter had led the naval historian to formulate a theory to explain events during six crucial days aboard the brig. "My theory is this," Cooper had written Shubrick in December. Wales's story was essentially true. Gansevoort, told of the conversation on the booms, had overreacted, became a "wonder monger." Cromwell was hated by others of the petty officers, so intensely that they had made a bugbear of him in the crisis: "Had not Cromwell been in the brig, I think no one would have been hanged." False alarms and ridiculous episodes had succeeded each other: part of a mast carried away, the so-called plotting aloft, Cromwell's arrest, the rush aft, and the like—all in the wake of Wales's story, but without one act of resistance or loggable instance of insubordination to give them weight. Yet more episodes had produced more reactions, until a point had been reached where a mutiny was required in order to explain steps the officers had taken—in order, indeed, that the officers might escape ridicule for the state that they had let the vessel get into, with prisoners cluttering the decks and armed guards prowling and suspicion everywhere.

That was Cooper's theory of where thoughts of hanging had come from. He had set it down in his review, which was finished now—though publication was to be delayed. For with the transcript and review in type, John Canfield Spencer had personally intervened, postponing publication because of a disaster that occurred at just that time, in late February 1844.

This is what had happened. The Captain Robert Stockton who had refused to sit on Mackenzie's court because he would have voted to hang the man had been at work at the Philadelphia navy yard directing construction of the first screw steam warship in the U.S. Navy, the *Princeton*. Cooper had referred to the project, most recently in that letter to Shubrick December 9: "Stockton seems to have succeeded surprisingly well. . . . I shall wait with some anxiety until the ship gets her armament in." By February she had got it in, including one mammoth wrought-iron gun, the Peacemaker, of which the captain was particularly proud, a weapon weighing over 27,000 pounds that could throw a 225-pound projectile as far as three miles. On the twenty-eighth, in the Potomac off Alexandria, a social gathering of some three hundred and fifty gentlemen and ladies had assembled aboard the new vessel: dignitaries and their wives, including the President, every cabinet member but Mr. Spencer, various army and navy officers, senators, representatives, "and all the distinguished persons resident and visiting at Washington." Thus complemented, the vessel was to pass a gala afternoon cruising downriver beyond Mount Vernon and back to where she had started from.

At four, on the return trip, the two hundred ladies aboard were still at their "sumptuous collation" below, but many of the gentlemen had gone topside to watch the Peacemaker exercised yet a third time at a demonstration firing. By chance, President Tyler at the last minute was detained to hear out a song begun as he was approaching the ladder to ascend; so that when the world's largest naval gun was fired, and when the breech of the overheated weapon exploded and hurled jagged fragments of hot iron into the horrified crowd above decks, he was out of harm's way. Some were not so lucky. Eight had no luck at all that day. Lying burned and wounded about the blood-strewn decks when the smoke cleared were Captain Stockton himself, Senator Thomas Hart Benton, and nine others; and killed—most of them instantly—"under the most shocking circumstances," were not only two seamen, and President Tyler's body servant, and the newly appointed secretary of the navy, Thomas W. Gilmer, and David Gardiner, New York state senator, and Virgil Maxcy, recent chargé d'affaires at The Hague, and Commodore Beverly Kennon, USN—not only those seven, but also the former secretary of the navy and Webster's successor as secretary of state, Abel P. Upshur.

Abel Parker Upshur: June 17, 1791–February 28, 1844. In the immediate aftermath of that gentleman's horrible death, his fellow cabinet officer, John C. Spencer—now secretary of the treasury in Tyler's fluid administration—was unwilling that Fenimore Cooper's analysis of the *Somers* affair appear. "In New York," wrote the novelist to his friend Shubrick April 12, "I ascertained the review was delayed by Mr. Spencer on account of Mr. Upshur, on whom I am a little severe. In my opinion he was a humbug"—Upshur was, that former judge of the Virginia general court, for having shown Mackenzie favoritism by leaving him and his officers free to tamper with witnesses during the inquiry and trial. Of the dead nothing unless good; but this judgment of character was expressed in confidence to an intimate friend, by one who was not given to playing the hypocrite under any circumstances.

About this time, during the spring of 1844, there appeared in New York yet another negative evaluation of Mackenzie's captaincy of his brig-of-war. With Sturgis's letters and Cooper's forthcoming review, it was one of three such notably effective statements by contemporaries. *The Cruise of the "Somers,"* a pamphlet a hundred and two pages long, is often credited to Cooper himself; for some of the arguments it presents do duplicate his, and the anonymous author is, like Cooper, obviously at home at sea. But this unnamed contributor to the national debate tells his readers that he was on a voyage to foreign parts while Sturgis's letters were appearing the previous summer, and thus had not seen them when he wrote his pamphlet. That does not describe Cooper. Nor is the tone of the pamphlet Cooper's polemical tone, for on occasion it reaches a shrillness that the novelist would not have permitted himself in public argument. Moreover, various points developed in *The Cruise of the "Somers"* had not been made elsewhere, and would not be found in Cooper's review.

The latter, for instance, judges the story told by Purser's Steward Wales to have been essentially true—that account of the dog-watch, oath-sworn conversation on the booms. But the author of *The Cruise* disagrees. Indeed, toward Wales the anonymous critic is particularly harsh. What right, he asks, had the officers on board *"to take for granted every syllable that was told them against Mr. Spencer by Wales, this man marked 'certain' on the paper they so much depend upon as evidence of the conspiracy?"* What proof was there, what proof is there, that Wales was not one of the guilty, if any were guilty? On Spencer's Greek roster, Cromwell's and Small's names did not appear, not even among the doubtful. But Wales's name was there, and among the certain. Had it all been a joke, then, a game between Wales and Spencer that got out of hand? Whatever, the list must be taken whole or not at all; either it told the truth or didn't—and it had Wales among the certain. Accordingly, the commander should have scrutinized the purser's steward with all suspicion, and Acting Midshipman Spencer should have been given an opportunity, long before the execution, to confront his accuser. Instead, Wales was trusted on faith;

he was allowed to swagger about the decks armed—even on occasions of record brandishing his pistol at crew members, threatening them—and left routinely to guard prisoners put in irons solely on his evidence. Moreover, his captain now minimized whatever those earlier differences had been between him and Wales, and in his report would recommend that for the young man's services he be promoted from purser's steward, at $216 a year and with no rank, to purser, at about $1500 a year with quarterdeck rank. What motive, asks the anonymous pamphleteer, did the self-important informant have to mitigate his testimony? None whatever—and every motive to persist in the course he had set himself.

The author of *The Cruise of the "Somers"* reminds us that this was a picked crew; the captain himself had chosen his men from among those on the receiving ship, and had replaced a number of them after returning from the shakedown to Puerto Rico in June. Spencer, he further reminds us, tried before the September sailing to get transferred from the *Somers* to the *Grampus;* he sailed reluctantly, then, and with a wardroom cautioned to keep him at a distance. As for the cruise of the brig itself, even the outbound passage saw much flogging of those homesick greenhorns; taking note of the liberal use of colt and cat, the pamphleteer does not wonder that discipline deteriorated after Madeira, though he stresses that no mention of the fact occurs in the logbook, and that Captain Mackenzie fifty days later, when first informed of the mutiny November 26, seemed unaware of deterioration, commenting incredulously to his first lieutenant that the vessel appeared to be in good discipline. The author notes, too—of a ship where punishment was abundant—the neglect to punish Cromwell for insubordination on more than one occasion. Is not that a sign, he asks, of a timid quarterdeck, one likely to panic?

The mutinous disposition of the crew before the revelations of November 26 seems to the anonymous author to have been exaggerated subsequently in any case, in order to justify the reactions of officers to Wales's story. That story is told aboard a vessel in the northeast trades, with a fair wind for her all the way to St. Thomas. "There was, in consequence, no extraordinary stress of weather to be apprehended on her passage thither, no extremity of suffering and danger growing out of any possible coldness of weather." In addition, it was a time of peace; "there was not the remotest chance of meeting a hostile vessel." And under such benign circumstances had young Spencer been boasting to none other than the master-at-arms—the lone marine aboard—that he and six more like him could take the vessel. "Would any man in his senses," asks the anonymous author, "have come with this species of bravado to such an individual as Garty, if he had the slightest intention of committing the alleged crime?"

But Spencer had talked to Garty, and to Wales too, and Wales had told the officers, and Spencer was arrested. Next day the mast broke, and the captain saw with alarm that some of the alleged conspirators seemed to be out of station aloft among the wreckage. Who was up there? Anderson for one, but he was a trusted petty officer whose name did not appear on the Greek lists, one of seven petty officers armed by the captain the morning of the execution. How conspire with Anderson in earshot? Who else was up there? Cromwell was, but Cromwell's name was not on the Greek lists either, and as chief boatswain's mate he should have been up there. And Small, as captain of the maintop, belonged up there too—nor was Small's name on one Greek list, though it did appear on the second sheet of Greek characters, the one presumably assigning mutiny stations. And after supper the same men had gone aloft again, with Willson and Golderman and the innocent Gedney, some to pursue their plotting, as the captain assumed. Or had they simply gone back to finish the job?

The job done, Cromwell descending the mainmast after dark is arrested; and yet "not a single fact had been brought forth against him." He was not on the mutiny list, and scarcely a syllable in Wales's long story even so much as referred to the chief boatswain's mate. (In this connection, Cooper had written William Sturgis that the senior officer on the court of inquiry, Commodore Stewart, had told him—Cooper—that the only real evidence against Cromwell had been a seaman's testimony that he had seen Mr. Spencer showing the boatswain's mate the Greek papers; yet the judge advocate had exposed that evidence as having been reported to the officers only after the *Somers* had got into home port, and thus it could have formed no part of the captain's deliberations at sea.)

Cromwell is arrested for whatever reasons, and so is Small. A couple of more days pass, and sometime before nine in the morning of November 30, Mackenzie writes his wardroom a letter seeking counsel. The letter refers to "a crew which has so long and so systematically and assiduously been tampered with by *an officer*." But is not that prejudging? Is not evidence of such tampering precisely what the council should be charged with uncovering?

The tendentious letter is delivered. By then, morning muster has come and gone, a muster at which four other crewmen have been arrested. And do not those arrests further urge a course on the council, that council composed in large part of officers already predisposed—in the event of other prisoners being taken—to hanging the three they are called upon to judge?

They meet and hear witnesses, thirteen crew members including some who must have borne grudges against Cromwell for his floggings in the line of duty. The witnesses are those only whom the council chooses to hear, including none of the accused, and none who might speak on behalf of the accused. And what the council hears is for the most part not facts but opinion, supposition, hearsay: "I thought him guilty . . ." "I think they are the main backers . . ." The evidence, moreover—such as it is—is taken down in pencil, on loose sheets of paper, and at least in some instances corrected after the executions. For the captain did execute the three accused, having made up his mind to do so no matter what the council recommended—and rather than carry them to port in the West Indies, to English Harbor, Antigua, say, which at the time lay some two hundred and fifty miles off, maybe thirty-six hours away, less than the distance between Detroit and Buffalo.

Rather than being set ashore for transshipment home to be tried, three lives, the anonymous author asserts, were "laid in the scale against a foolish professional vanity." Three human beings. The author's indignation, a year and more after the event, wells up at the thought: "The transactions on board of the *Somers*," he feels, "present an instance in which the public condemnation is imperatively called for. Though the principal perpetrator of them has safely passed the ordeal of a court-martial—to the wonder of all who have read the testimony—the blood of the slain cries from out the deep, and sooner or later will be heard, no matter what attempts may be made to stifle it. Life is too valuable to be taken as it was on board the *Somers*, and to let those who took it continue to occupy posts of honor and profit in the service of the people. . . ."

Fenimore Cooper's "Review of the Proceedings of the Naval Court Martial," the final document to be considered, appeared later that same year, 1844. Besides repeating some of the points made by Sturgis and the anonymous writer in *The Cruise*, the "Review" also develops publicly thoughts that its author had been expressing in private to friends and family during the preceding twelve months and longer. One of the most judicious of his twentieth-century biographers, James Grossman, has contrasted the result with that earlier argument, *The Battle of Lake Erie*, in which Cooper had unfairly handled his literary enemy Mackenzie. In this later work, Grossman finds the historian "at his very best polemically," so that the resulting "Review of the Proceedings" emerges as "a masterpiece of quiet sanity." For throughout, the author is in control—of his facts and of his tone, coolly dissecting the various specimens of testimony as he concedes what he can to Mackenzie and his officers.

He grants, for example, that the captain of the *Somers* "did no more than his duty" when he arrested young Spencer—though, as Cooper adds, "the *manner* of the arrest was a little too melodramatic for the practice of a man-of-war." He grants that "Mr. Spencer and Small were, to say the least, extremely indiscreet . . . That these two men engaged in a *seeming* plot, resembling the one described, we hold to be proved, though we greatly question if an attempt would ever have been made to carry it into serious execution." Cooper grants, in addition, that "the case of the mast-rope, and of the tramping aft might justify Mr. Gansevoort in believing a crisis had come, *under his previous impressions*, though we think the impressions themselves to have been insufficiently sustained. The conduct of Mr. Gansevoort," he adds, *"always allowing for his impressions, was spirited and good."* Indeed, the author expresses his pleasure at being able to say so, as a longtime friend of Gansevoort's lawyer uncle in Albany, Peter Gansevoort (that benefactor of the Melville family). Finally, the naval historian concedes that fear was not likely the dominant motive for Mackenzie's behavior. "We distinguish," he does say, "between the exaggeration of danger, and the unmanly dread of meeting it." But neither the captain's reluctance to go into port, nor the dilatory progress of his council of officers, nor the execution itself suggests to Cooper any unmanly dread of meeting danger, even if all three do suggest want of judgment. He elaborates: "We suppose the tendency of the commander to regard one side of a question suddenly took the direction of magnifying this mutiny. We think it evident Mr. Gansevoort had a strong disposition that way from the first. We believe the opinions of the two to have influenced all the rest of the quarterdeck. . . ."

Poor judgment, then; not fear. But to return to the arrest. It was unwise at the start, according to Cooper, "to arrest Mr. Spencer in so public a manner, and then to place him on the quarterdeck in full view of the crew. We entertain no doubt that much the greater portion of the ominous conversations, groupings, shakings of the head, and strange looks, which seem to have awakened so much distrust aft, had their origin in the natural wonder of the crew at seeing an officer in this novel situation —and he, too, not only a favorite forward, but one who was known to be the son of a minister of state." Would not the captain have shown better judgment to send for Spencer and question him in his cabin, incarcerating him there if need be? In fact, the procedure of arrest—at quarters with the crew mustered forward, the midshipman's sword ostentatiously removed, his person searched—"strikes us as failing in judgment on all points, and somewhat in generosity. Were there any real danger, such an exhibition would be apt to inflame and excite to action the remaining conspirators, whereas the quiet disappearance of the young man might have left them in some of that doubt and uncertainty which seems to have been such a source of uneasiness aft, as respects the conduct of the crew." Better the other way around: certainty stirs energy, whereas "there is nothing more demoralizing than doubt . . ." Yet the commander's course had led those contrasting moods to harbor exactly where they should not have been: doubt aft, certainty forward. Incidentally, "we feel great difficulty in believing that Captain Mackenzie would have pursued a similar course, had one of those connected with him 'by blood or alliance' been accused by such a narrative as that of Wales."

Iron Spencer if need be, in the captain's cabin, under guard, but quietly. For that matter, "what judge of human nature can suppose that a man of forty, possessed of authority, could not have got complete control of the feelings of a lad of nineteen by means of kindness and judicious representations, more especially of one who manifested the disposition to repentance and confidence that it is acknowledged young Spencer manifested a day or two later?" Then too, something was owing to the father's station, and to the extraordinary character of the revelation—by Wales's word alone—that had accused the son. Yet Mackenzie had chosen to arrest the midshipman publicly and place him in irons in full view on the quarterdeck. And the crew had thereupon gathered in knots topside.

But of course they had. "The *Somers* had one hundred and twenty souls on board her—at least thirty more than she should have had—and it is scarcely possible that, with her boats stowed, and one third of the deck reserved for officers, one hundred men could be on her remaining deck without being in what is called knots." For that matter, the ingenuousness of the men in gathering and talking under such circumstances indicates innocence; "we should have considered a contrary course as affording much the strongest proofs of conspiracy. . . . Those who really had anything to conceal at such a moment would be very apt to act with caution." Similarly, all that obvious intimacy between Cromwell and Mr. Spencer that had preceded the arrest, the hours of private talk that so many had noticed as extending over days and days: no doubt the two had talked of piracy, and slaving, and sailing off the northwest coast; but "the first thing thought of by men who seriously had determined on such a plot as this is assumed to have been would be to foresee the necessity of avoiding any *appearance of an intimacy*." In the same vein, "the dullest intellect" among that crew gathering after Mr. Spencer's arrest would understand the necessity, if an attempt to seize the vessel were imminent, "of feigning even unusual obedience . . . rather than awaken suspicion by betraying disaffection."

Yet the seamen had collected together about the decks that first night, remarking their favorite in irons aft, then had mustered next morning, which was Sunday, presumably expecting to be informed of the reasons for those extraordinary events of the evening before. They were not then informed. The captain did, however, inspect the crew, possessed as he was by that time of the Greek lists and the opinions of his first lieutenant and trusted petty officers. In particular, he observed the demeanor of Cromwell and Small. And the conclusion drawn from those observations, as expressed in the official report, provides what Cooper judged to be an "extraordinary specimen" of the captain's reasoning powers. Mackenzie had reported that both sailors "were faultlessly clean; they were determined that their appearance in this respect should provoke no reproof." Yet sailors on men-of-war are required, as the novelist reminds us, under pain of punishment to be faultlessly clean at Sunday inspections. What if they had been dirty? As for their bearing, Mackenzie set down that Cromwell stood straight, muscles braced, eyes fixed, battle-ax

grasped resolutely. Small, by contrast, looked more fearful than dangerous, shifting his weight from side to side, passing his battle-ax from one
hand to the other, darting his eyes irresolutely about—"but never toward
mine." Here, then, as Cooper points out, "were two men who manifested
guilt, according to Captain Mackenzie, by directly contrary deportment.
In order to escape his distrust, a man must be neither firm nor irresolute;
look frightened, nor look determined; hold his battle-axe quiet, nor pass
it from hand to hand; stand erect with his muscles immovable, nor shift
his weight from leg to leg; look steadily but indifferently across the deck,
nor let his eyes wander . . . Evidence like this, of the judgment that was
brought to bear on this important case, awakens reflections of the most
painful character."

To be sure, that faculty of judgment might have surprised others more
than the novelist. "We have had," he confesses, "some occasions for
understanding the mind of Captain Mackenzie, and we ascribe more to
its peculiarities, perhaps, than total strangers and severe judges might be
disposed to yield." Consider, as another example of that mind at work,
its reaction to the affair of the mast, which broke the same Sunday, in the
afternoon, and which event, with the subsequent muster of alleged plotters aloft, confirmed, in the captain's words, "the existence of a dangerous conspiracy." Mackenzie adds as a matter of moment that, with the
men in the rigging, "the eye of Mr. Spencer traveled perpetually to the
mast-head, and cast thither many of those strange and stealthy glances
which I had heretofore noticed": further indication of conspiracy brew-
ing. Those adjectives—*strange, stealthy*—at least one reader found offensive, as he found offensive such overprecise details from the captain's
official account as Browning's salute before reporting, at the execution,
that the hooded Spencer could not gather strength to give the order to
fire. "Nothing is more apparent," Cooper remarks of such effects, "than
the fact that Captain Mackenzie in his report intended to favor the world
with a fine and memorable description, one that should be quoted in after
ages for its thrilling incidents and graphic beauty." It was unprofessional
for all that, author betraying naval officer that way. And as for the prisoner's behavior when the mast broke, "can anything be more violent than
the inference as to Mr. Spencer's motive" in looking upward? "He was at
sea, seated on an arm-chest, in irons, with nothing to do, and nothing but
the vacant ocean to gaze at outward." Orders are given to rig sails. In
doing so, "a mast is carried away in full view of him, and it is thought
extraordinary that he sought the very natural relief of gazing at what was
going on . . . !"

What was going on could hardly have included plotting in any event,
with some among the hands up there untainted by even a suspicion of
guilt, others too far from their mates to converse, and Cromwell at work,
at least according to Acting Master Perry's subsequent testimony in

court. Nevertheless, apprehension aft had increased from that moment onward, so much so that Cromwell and Small were promptly arrested; and later that same night, when men had rushed down the quarterdeck in the darkness—at Mr. Rodgers's order, as it turned out, and with Browning wielding his colt to hurry them on—the first lieutenant had drawn a pistol in alarm and hastened along the trunk house to meet them. But concerning that tense interlude, "Mr. Gansevoort admits himself it was all a mistake," Cooper reminds us, "and is rejoiced he did not fire."

Suppose, however, the matter had ended after the egregious rush aft. Suppose the *Somers* had proceeded home without further mishap, but with Mr. Spencer and the two crewmen still in irons. The prisoners at the New York navy yard are led off the vessel and later released, as twelve others subsequently arrested aboard have been released. "What would have been the gossip of the service?" Think about it. Though the case might have been generally forgotten in a fortnight, naval officers and enlisted men alike would have remembered and gone on wondering. No, the officers in mid-Atlantic needed a situation of sufficient gravity to justify their actions. Only a mutiny could justify what they had done so far—and were yet to do and think: arming the loyalists, conferring with trusted petty officers, those later arrests, the rationale concerning the vessel's size and the guards' exhaustion and the nights that favored a rescue.

But was mutiny in the offing? Nothing on the Greek lists indicates that those whose names appeared there had been apprised of the fact. All denied it except Small, whose voice had been silenced, and Wales. "It is," writes Cooper, "one of the remarkable features of this transaction that, Mr. Wales and Small excepted, no one has been disposed to betray the confidence of Mr. Spencer. With so many in irons and menaced with the gallows, not a man has been found willing to come forward, under the impulses of either contrition, fear, or cupidity, to reveal the secrets of this formidable conspiracy!" It is, the reviewer supposes, "probably the only case of the sort on record"; for "all experience shows that state's evidence is seldom wanting in an affair in which many are implicated." In fact (though Cooper could not have known this), Commander Mackenzie had earlier written in confidence to Secretary Upshur from New York as the court-martial was about to begin, January 29, 1843: "My expectation was, and I believe I had the honor of announcing it to you on my arrival here, that by secluding these prisoners entirely and keeping them wholly free"—the irony! he is referring to the twelve under marine guard —"keeping them wholly free from being approached or influenced in any sinister manner, that such as you might be disposed to offer a pardon to might at a proper moment be induced to come forward with a complete confession." Not a man had come forward despite the captain's expectation, and despite whatever might have been offered; not one of those examined under oath during the inquiry and subsequent trial—no one but Wales—had been tempted to confess knowledge of a mutiny, and this, too, in spite of the natural tendency of all of us "to be of importance in moments of excitement, to know something, to have something to tell . . ."

Only Wales would admit to having been recruited by Spencer. Captain Mackenzie and his first lieutenant had needed a mutiny, however, and were able to convince themselves they were threatened by one. The novelist clarifies his interpretation: "We do not wish to say that they were frightened in the abject sense, but their minds were in that condition in which they were most disposed to exaggerate." Dana's opinion to the contrary notwithstanding, the officers exaggerated risks that the size of the vessel would submit them to if mutiny should break out. Cooper had been aboard the brig himself. "The size of the *Somers* was, perhaps, as near as possible to that which was most desirable for her officers in the event of such a conflict. Had she been much smaller, all her officers and petty officers might not have been able to act together, and thus have lessened their efficiency; while had she been much larger, there might have been too much to defend or to avoid for so small a party. . . . It is merely the old fact that a small body can defend a defile against an enemy that would overwhelm it in a plain." As for the risks from sailing at night, the captain and his second-in-command had exaggerated those too: "There was no necessity for darkness, every man-of-war possessing means of lighting her decks." And the exhaustion of the officers, who at the executions would not have been able to last two days longer without relief: "what was there," asks Cooper, "to cause all this exhaustion? These gentlemen were in watch and watch; so are thousands of others daily. We have ourselves, at a tender age too, been watch and watch for weeks and weeks, and had our rest broken night after night." What was so tasking about duty on the *Somers* that her officers at their first crisis should be on the point of collapse? In any case, as Cooper proceeds to demonstrate, she could have reached a West Indian port within the allotted two days from December 1, had she altered course promptly; but even holding course, "we have a better opinion of the physical powers of these gentlemen," he writes, "than they seem to have themselves." As for the plaint that the officers, burdened with weapons, were half dead on their feet, the solution seemed ready at hand: Captain Mackenzie should have let them sit down.

He might have done more. He might have relieved matters by stretching a line midships abaft the mainmast, then posted an order that no crewman on pain of death pass it unless called by name. "That would have prevented anything like a surprise of the quarterdeck; did that fail, Mr. Spencer's own alleged expedient, that of two of the quarterdeck guns pointed forward, loaded with canister, would have rendered the quarterdeck of so *small* a craft as inviolable as a sanctuary." There were, incidentally, all the officers but Spencer himself, as well as at least seven loyal petty officers, and doubtless some of the smaller boys available to handle the brig; fewer than that number compose the crew of merchant vessels that have sailed around the world. "I have been myself," writes Cooper, recalling the *Stirling*, "one of eleven hands, officers included, to navigate a ship of three hundred tons"—somewhat larger than the *Somers* at 266—"across the Atlantic Ocean; and what is more, we often reefed topsails with the watch."

A rope strung midships would have forestalled all attempts at rescue. But was such a rescue contemplated? As affirmative evidence, officers cited the prisoners' lack of concern as they sat in irons at the arms chests port and starboard. To Cooper, that unconcern argued the other way. What would have caused the prisoners worry was the thought of a rescue attempt; at the first sign of such, his guard would have shot the giant Cromwell down for sure, and Spencer too—all three captives most likely, long before their mates could have reached them and removed their irons. "On the other hand, what had they to fear in their present situation? Mr. Spencer declared, it is said, he intended to run away as soon as he got home, and with a father who was a cabinet minister, he could not have apprehended much for his life. There had been no overt act of mutiny, and the whole affair, without the executions, would not have been remembered, probably, but a week or two after the brig got in." For his part, Small had confessed, and so might look forward to mercy. Cromwell is to be presumed innocent. What did the three have to fear, then, jaunty as they may have acted in their irons?

Indeed, what had the prisoners to fear on that vessel cruising westward, assured as they were of being taken home for trial? Meanwhile, unknown to them, a trial of sorts was already under way below. The captain had convened a council—to advise him, or to sustain his course of action? Mackenzie's letter to his officers sounds rather as though he has already reached a verdict; the ambition of the author may again have let us into the secrets of the commander. Moreover, while the officers are assembling, Lieutenant Gansevoort approaches the unsuspecting Spencer at the arms chest with questions designed to confirm the midshipman's guilt. So Gansevoort himself later testified; and "what man," asks Cooper, "who confessedly commenced an inquiry with such an object, ever failed of seeing something to corroborate his previous opinions?" It was pathetic: "a youth of nineteen"—eighteen, in fact—"ironed hands and feet, destroying himself in the confidence of penitence, while his admissions were borne away to a secret conclave that only waited for testimony to pronounce its doom, and to obtain the 'CONCURRENCE' of a commander who had drawn up the programme of the executions hours before that doom was rendered!"

Other testimony would be brought before the council, and "a more precious set of depositions was probably never flouted in the face of justice." Opinion and hearsay. Cooper had learned a lot of law in the course of arguing his numerous libel trials. Of the testimony of the crew of the *Somers* at sea, "nine-tenths of their matter," he concludes, "would be rejected in the loosest court in Christendom." Not that it made much difference. The record is clear that at least four of the officers—and they among the most senior—had for two days been persuaded that the prisoners must hang if more were taken. More had been taken. As for the surgeon and the purser, the two landsmen on the council of seven would have needed "unusually decided characters to venture opinions opposed to those of the sea-officers"; and the remaining members of the group were very young. Such a gathering "must have been more than human if their inquiries were not quite as much directed to obtaining confirmation of what they already believed, as to obtaining the truth."

Thus, their unanimity appears less surprising than it would under different circumstances. After all—and here is part of what was later to offend Admiral Morison (though Cooper seems hardly to be sneering as he says it)—the *Somers* "was sent to sea with too much the character of a family yacht to come within the usual category of a regular cruiser." It was true; the captain was related by blood or marriage to most of his officers, and so would have exerted an even more disproportionate influence on those young gentlemen than usual. And even under usual circumstances, "so generally is the influence of military supremacy appreciated that it is a standing law of courts-martial to oblige their junior members to deliver their opinions first, commencing with the youngest and ascending according to date of rank." No such niceties were observed aboard Mackenzie's brig-of-war.

"We conceive," writes Cooper, "and have maintained ever since the leading facts of this case have been accurately known to us, that the instant the commander of the *Somers* foresaw a probable necessity for executing the prisoners, it became his duty to stand for the nearest available port." The nation was profoundly at peace. No foe threatened. Whatever orders the captain was sailing under, he had sworn to uphold a higher one: that no person shall "be deprived of life, liberty, or property without due process of law." To spare three lives for trial, he should at once have made for port.

Yet a doctrine was apparently current aboard that the *Somers* would be disgraced if she sought aid abroad at such a time. Cooper dismisses so deluding a doctrine out of hand: "we all know it is not true that a man-of-war will not seek protection in a friendly port in grave emergencies. It is done constantly, in peace or in war. Protection is sought in this way from the elements, from the horrors of starvation, from enemies, and why not from mutineers?" Still, no officer (it was said) would have let fear lead him to order a course change. To that, Cooper submits that "it must have been a strange set of officers who did not understand the difference between going into port *in order to avoid the necessity of hanging men without a trial*, and of going into port out of apprehension of the crew." But the mutineers at large might nevertheless have taken heart at the course change, misinterpreting it as a sign of fear aft. To that objection, the reviewer notes that the officers were armed to the teeth in any case, and a slight change of course—all that would have been needed if done promptly, and with the free wind that was—would have gone unnoticed; minor adjustments in compass headings are made all the time at sea. Besides, what evidence suggests that the alleged conspirators were poised to attack? One of them was said to be Waltham; "if Waltham was flogged on the 28th and 29th, the brig running northwest by west three quarters west, we fancy it felt to him very much as it would had the brig been running west by north three quarters north." And during those floggings on whatever course, no coconspirators had moved to help him. "As for the opinion that at sight of land, the disaffected would certainly have attempted a rescue, we will ask if that is as reasonable as to anticipate the same consequences from the sight of the gallows?" For even around noon on the first, and with two hours elapsing thereafter, with the crew mustered, with the ropes to hang the prisoners rigged, with their hooded forms standing under those ropes, with more minutes passing and men at the whips to haul, no rescue was attempted.

Mackenzie should have stood for port. "If the prisoners could be hanged, they could certainly be transshipped. There always existed the ample excuse of sending the men home, in the month of December, under cover, in preference to leaving them exposed to the elements on the deck of their own brig." But the captain had chosen to do otherwise, had held his course for St. Thomas as he was receiving the opinion of his officers' council and moving at once to carry the sentence into effect.

Before proceeding, though, he had talked at length with Mr. Spencer at the arms chest. Mackenzie's brief memorandum of that interview is couched in large part in the third person. How had those two occupied the hour or more they had spent together? Did they converse further than is recorded; and if so, what did they say? Did Spencer dictate—as young Perry had thought—matter taken down in the first person? If so, where is it? Was what he said the lies that the captain was later reported to have charged the young man with dying with: "He said he was satisfied that the young man had been lying to him for half an hour before his death . . ." Question to Surgeon Leecock by the judge advocate: "Did you hear any statement that Mr. Spencer had been telling the commander falsehoods before he died?" Answer: "I think I did hear some such observation as that." And McKee and Green both testified at the court-martial that the captain had addressed the crew to that effect after the execution: "this young man died with a lie in his mouth." Nor will it do to discredit the testimony of those two witnesses on the grounds that both were alleged conspirators. By that logic, an officer under investigation could, to enjoy impunity throughout his trial, first put in irons any witness he feared. No, the testimony of those two (both of whom were subsequently released without any charges brought against them) appeared to Cooper quite as plausible, to say the least, as did the defense's testimony in denial; it is, after all, the kind of fact "not likely to be invented."

From start to finish errors of judgment. "But the most inexplicable part of the conduct of Captain Mackenzie," according to this reviewer of the record, "is the extraordinary manner in which he kept aloof from all investigations into the fact." From first to last he did. "Why did he not demand the particulars of a plot of which the existence was admitted? Or did Mr. Spencer give any particulars, and were these the falsehoods he had been telling?"

In summary, the naval historian returns to root causes. "Want of judgment, and a disposition to view one side of a case so intensely as to forget it may have another, lie at the root of this matter . . ." In the very conception of the cruise, in the presumption that boys can govern boys, Cooper finds want of judgment. The captain had, for example—and entirely extralegally—elevated his seventeen-year-old nephew and clerk, Oliver Perry, to acting midshipman for the length of the voyage; that lad would thus serve as officer of the forecastle over the bewhiskered veteran Cromwell, twice his age. And when the crisis arose, "very young officers were given pistols, and went about the decks in a way to excite feeling among the crew. We have in evidence several instances in which menaces of putting portions of the crew to death were used, and it is probable many more occurred." Under such circumstances, who could be surprised that, after prisoners were taken, the conduct of crewmen became willful? That was how any innocent man might have acted—though, to be sure, plotters "would have had a direct and obvious interest in pursuing another course."

To one of those prisoners taken, by the way, not a single evidential question had been put; of Cromwell "it almost seems that there was a fear he might exculpate himself." Yet the chief boatswain's mate had been acting openly throughout the voyage, laying little restraint on his temper, making no effort to hide the fifteen dollars Mr. Spencer had given him early on. When he got to Madeira, he would send that money to his wife so she could buy coal for the winter; that was what Cromwell had told Garty. On what grounds, then, may we doubt the man's affection for her, to whom his thoughts had turned first when his fate was announced —"God of the universe, look down on my poor wife"—and again at the very last: "Tell my wife I die an innocent man"? Until proof is offered to the contrary, says Cooper, the boatswain's mate "has just as good a right to be placed in the category of those who have friends and home as pledges of their conduct as Captain Mackenzie himself."

Indeed, above all other instances perhaps, Mackenzie's poor judgment was manifested in his dealings with Samuel Cromwell. In the official report, the captain gives the department and the public reason to think that that petty officer had held a secret interview with Spencer the night of the twenty-sixth, after the latter's arrest. Yet he "does not even *attempt* to prove any such thing in subsequent investigations." Did you not communicate with Mr. Spencer during the night? "It was not me, sir; it was Small." By such a denial—no doubt to a question misunderstood in any case—was the little sailmaker "pointed out by an associate to increased suspicions." So Mackenzie explains, thinking to have furnished cause why Small, too, was put in irons shortly thereafter; but "here Cromwell's guilt is *assumed* as an additional reason for arresting Small!" For whether or not the two were "associates" was precisely what needed to be established.

"As for the attempt to drag in a particular speech of Cromwell's"— about his indifference at sea to his wife's chastity back home—"in order to show his general indifference to virtue . . . we can hardly trust ourselves to write about it. It was unknown to Captain Mackenzie when he hanged the man, in the first place. Then, such language is common in the mouths of common sailors, and passes for mere bravado. We have heard it often, almost verbatim, and from men whom we know felt differently. The excuse for thus harrowing the feelings of a woman who may have been perfectly innocent, nay, who is said to be respectable, was to destroy the sympathy of the public in the fate of her husband! If Captain Mackenzie could not destroy this sympathy by his evidence of guilt, what sort of case had he?"

And what sort of case had he if, on the morning of the execution, Mr. Spencer's solemn assertion of Cromwell's innocence could "stagger" the commander? The accused midshipman had been ready to tell all, had admitted his own failings, had said not a word on Small's behalf. Cromwell, on the other hand, he had repeatedly said was innocent. Nor had Wales more than mentioned the boatswain's mate in his story as he originally told it. Nor was the man's name anywhere on the Greek lists. "It is pitiable, pitiable," writes Cooper feelingly, "to see on what evidence all these strong corroborating circumstances are set aside."

Cromwell is hanged with the others. And while their bodies sway aloft, the captain bids the new chief boatswain's mate mount the pump well and draw a moral from an earlier episode. Collins tells the men that aboard another vessel he had served on, he alone among the crew had been entrusted with knowledge of a keg of money hidden in the run, and had proved worthy of that trust; Cromwell had once heard the story and said, "Had the case been his he would have run away with the keg." But there swings Cromwell now, and here stands Collins with his boatswain's pipe . . .

"We are of opinion," writes Cooper of the incident, "had Collins told his story of the doubloons to one hundred sailors, quite fifty would have made some such idle remark as this attributed to Cromwell. On shore, even, it would have been made by thousands who would not dream of performing what they said." So what kind of judgment of sailors is this that Captain Mackenzie brings to bear, he who presumes that three bottles of wardroom wine—for revealing the location of which the steward Waltham was flogged to the legal limit—three bottles would be sufficient to inflame twenty conspirators to attempt a rescue? "Those who (though KNOWN to be very guilty) were considered to be the least dangerous were called out and interrogated," the captain had reported of a muster at quarters in the course of the crisis. "Now," says Cooper, who provides the emphasis, "this statement is true or untrue. If true, why has not Captain Mackenzie done his duty, and preferred charges against wretches KNOWN TO BE VERY GUILTY? If untrue, what is the value of his report?" "Wilson having failed in his attempt to get up an outbreak in the night . . ." the captain writes in his narrative, quietly assuming Willson's guilt as he does so—"and yet," says Cooper, "we are astounded with the fact that no attempt has been made to punish the man." McKinley's name was on the Greek list among the certain; but rather than suspecting the accuracy of a list that, after all, had Wales certain too, the captain sets down his judgment: McKinley was among the certain "beyond a doubt correctly." "Well, this man McKinley, after remaining weeks and weeks in irons, was discharged by habeas corpus, because imprisoned without any charges. . . . The strongest case of guilt among the surviving conspirators, one THAT ADMITTED OF NO DOUBT, is allowed to pass unpunished, even unprosecuted."

Against all mitigating evidence, Commander Mackenzie had acted, then returned with his vessel and three fewer aboard than had sailed from home port. To answer questions of the department, he had thereupon detached an ill-equipped youth bearing dispatches. The captain had, moreover, virtually asked to retain command of his brig—"a new proof of that officer's weakness of judgment," though the request should have brought the whole subject to Secretary Upshur's mind; it seems to Cooper extraordinary that one who had been a practicing judge did not foresee the importance of immediately removing from the *Somers* all who had advised the execution. It was equally extraordinary "that Captain Mackenzie, when he wrote his report, knowing that a court of some sort or other must sit on him, did not comprehend the nature of the indiscretion into which he was falling" when he recommended, before the matter had been investigated, that men who would necessarily be witnesses in the case "be preferred to situations that would give them competencies for life . . ." Indeed, "it is just as fair to assume that the tempting hopes he places before his own witnesses produced their results as to suppose that Cromwell was bought by . . . fifteen dollars to desert a wife he evidently loved, and to enter on a life of murder and rapine."

Of a piece, at sea and onshore. To what, then, should finally be ascribed the calamity of events on the *Somers*? For to Fenimore Cooper it was nothing less than a calamity, "to have a deep reproach rest on the justice and principles of a country." His country. All is traceable, he says a final time, "to a disposition in Captain Mackenzie to regard things as he has at first conceived them to be, and to act under his *convictions*, rather than under *the authority of evidence*." And he ends: "God alone can say how far any selfish feeling was mixed up with the mistakes of this terrible transaction. The act was, unquestionably, one of high moral courage, one of the basest cowardice, one of deep guilt, or one of lamentable deficiency of judgment."

Months earlier, with the court of inquiry just finished and the court-martial still to come, Bennett's *New York Herald* had reached its own conclusions about the case. "There is only one way in which Captain Mackenzie can be justified," it editorialized as long ago as January 19, 1843. "Captain Mackenzie and his officers acted at the time under *a species of insanity* produced by panic, a vivid imagination, and the spirit of the age all working together." The mad spirit of that age of Transcendentalism, Fourierism, Millerism, Mormonism, Abolition, jingoism: "everything is running riot—perfectly wild." Young Spencer longs to be a Red Rover; for his part, Mackenzie "is fired with the idea of being a patriot of the old Roman order, and hence gives about a hundred boys, in a short cruise, two thousand colts, cats, or cowhides, and hangs up three individuals, without trial or evidence, merely to enforce order and preserve discipline. Madness all—madness all . . ."

In his official report the officer had written, "I freely meet that ordeal to which my conduct will undoubtedly be subjected, trusting to that consciousness of rectitude in my bosom which has never for one moment forsaken me, or wavered in the slightest degree."

Never? Before his execution, Acting Midshipman Spencer had asked his captain: "Have you not formed an exaggerated estimate of the conspiracy? Are you not going too far? Are you not fast? Does the law entirely justify you?"

A reply of sorts Mackenzie had returned at the time, by repeating the prisoner's "catechism." Apparently he had answered the youth by posing to him Spencer's own questions to Wales: Do you fear a dead man? Could you kill a man? Are you afraid to die?

Within the pages of the official report occurs a later, perhaps more satisfactory answer:

"In the necessities of my position I found my law, and in them also I must trust to find my justification."

EPILOGUE

SOME YEARS LATER SLIDELL MACKENZIE'S WIFE, who alone might have been aware of it, recorded her observation that for only performing his duty her husband had paid a heavy toll privately. What he had done in executing mutineers was done, she affirmed, "at the price of a personal suffering such as few could know because few have the capacity so keenly to feel . . ."

Even so, the commander had been exonerated publicly by the court-martial that met for the last time April 1, 1843. On that same day was published in the *Courier and Enquirer* evidence of acute personal suffering experienced by another of the officers aboard the *Somers;* for "last evening at six o'clock"—Sunday it was—the ship's doctor, Passed Assistant Surgeon Richard W. Leecock, alone in the steerage of his vessel as it lay moored alongside the *North Carolina*, had placed the muzzle of a pistol above his right eye. He had fired, and thus ended a life for whatever reasons. The papers attributed Leecock's suicide to "a settled melancholy and a partial derangement induced by a long and severe attack of the yellow fever, which he contracted on a former voyage to the coast of Africa in the U.S. schooner *Shark*." From the *Shark* the surgeon had come aboard the *Somers*, had been aboard that vessel since her commissioning the previous spring. Now, with the trial at the navy yard ended at last, he would put to sea one final time, this time aboard the schooner *Mary*

Jane, which delivered the remains of the twenty-eight-year-old medical officer April 12 to his native Norfolk for burial.

Following a tradition to the taste of that earlier age, we might in concluding pursue a little way the fates of others among the principal participants and observers of the *Somers* affair. "At the termination of the court-martial," writes Mrs. Mackenzie, "my husband was allowed to return to his home," to rural Tarrytown. "He remained at home until the summer of 1846"—and we have glimpsed him there, receiving congratulations of friends and fellow citizens amid more tangible evidences of support: funds from consequential New Yorkers to help defray legal expenses; from grateful Boston merchants a parchment scroll in a silver case, and a portrait commissioned, and a bust by Henry Dexter; from Philadelphia a presentation sword with diamond-studded hilt (gift of local gentlemen and ladies); from Baltimore a pair of gold epaulets for the commander, paid for by subscription, "as a tribute of respect for his firmness and ability as an officer, and his character as a man." Young Dana, to whom Mackenzie had earlier sent a copy of Griffin's defense, wrote from Boston to Tarrytown April 16: "Among the numerous congratulations which you have received and are receiving I am unwilling to have no place"— and proceeded to assure his correspondent of the "strong *enthusiasm* in your favor" that had developed among local representatives of the educated classes, to whom "you were (you must excuse me the indelicacy of a direct compliment to a stranger) a hero, and not a hero of the sword, but the hero of a moral conflict." Already, during the trial, Longfellow had written, suggesting that his friend visit Cambridge when his ordeal was over, and the poet would write again during the months ahead. The first of those supportive letters had, by the way, awakened in Mackenzie a hope, expressed even as the court-martial was in progress, that Longfellow might "one of these days" (would Cooper not have seen this as further evidence of poor judgment?) take hold of the *Somers* case and turn it into poetry, "under some other name and with the scene thrown into the past. It seems to me," wrote Mackenzie, "a fruitful theme." And he had gone on, in that letter to the poet of mid-February, to recall how the previous June he had formed a plan to cruise along the East Coast of America in his new training brig. "I proposed it to the Navy Department, intending if it was acceded to, to entice you on board the *Somers* and explore with you some of those scenes which you had indicated as favorable for locating a novel of the sea. Instead of going there I went to the coast of Africa, and you know the result . . ."

But of that notorious result, Longfellow was to assure his friend in July (as already mentioned) that "the voice of all upright men—the common consent of all the good—is with you." In confirmation, that same month

had appeared in *The North American Review* Charles Sumner's able defense
of Mackenzie's course, the reading of which caused its subject, August 9,
to yield to "a strong desire to write to you"—to Sumner directly—"to
express the great satisfaction I had derived from your flattering view of
my efforts to do my whole duty to my country on that trying and mo-
mentous occasion. . . ."

A few days earlier, as summer was passing on, the commander at
Tarrytown had been granted additional comfort from the visit of a mentor of Sumner's, the remarkable Dr. Francis Lieber. Born in Berlin in
1800, Lieber had fought at Waterloo as a schoolboy, had enlisted in the
cause of Greek independence, had served as a tutor in Rome, had been
expelled from his native Prussia for his liberal views, and in his late
twenties had come to the United States, where he had founded and edited *The Encyclopaedia Americana*, to which Mackenzie in the 1830s contributed articles on naval subjects. Now a distinguished professor of political
economy in South Carolina, the foreign-born visitor was on a trip east, in
part to explore possibilities of an appointment to the Harvard faculty.
For the present, however, "here I sit," Lieber was writing his wife from
Tarrytown, August 3, "Cpt. and Mrs. Mackenzie in the room, at a window which looks upon the noble Hudson, down nearly to N. York . . ."

The letter home from the Mackenzies' sitting room furnishes a vivid
enough glance at the commander among his family and friends—court-
martial behind him—to quote at length. On the last day of July, from the
foot of Chambers Street in Manhattan, "at three o'clock Mackenzie and I
started in one of those smaller steamboats for short routes"—the steamboat *Telegraph*—"to Tarrytown. Mrs. Mackenzie could not go with us,"
Lieber explained, "because her boys were not quite well. In Tarrytown
we found Mackenzie's plain, country wagon, stopped at the p. office . . .
and in the evening arrived at Mackenzie's plain, simple, comfortable,
neat farm-house, where we made ourselves very comfortable according to
a very detailed memorandum of his wife's: what to give me, what to do,
what to look after."

That evening the two gentlemen had talked together "very freely and
frankly" about the *Somers* affair, reading over relevant documents ("I saw
the original letter in a fine silver box the Boston people sent him"), and
on Tuesday had paid a visit to Mackenzie's sister, Mrs. Matthew Perry.
The commodore was away: "he commands at present the squadron on
the African coast; his wife, an exceedingly good-looking grandmother, I
believe of not more than forty at the utmost"—she was forty-six—"re-
sides here, where they have built a beautiful cottage on the bank of the
river, near Mackenzie's. Here we took tea with some women and girls,
and then walked home—smoked, saw a fine moonlight view of the river
from a hill, and turned in."

The following morning Lieber had given over to writing down his opinion of "Cpt. Mackenzie's Case," then dined, swam, visited the Perrys again, and returned to the little farmhouse on the Beekman acres to meet his hostess at last, arrived from Manhattan with her children. Mrs. Mackenzie "was formerly a great belle, but is wholly free of all coquetry, a fine, a good woman who stood by her husband in his late trials with advice and love." Up from Manhattan with her had come the sculptor Dexter to do that bust for the New England merchants, a work of art that in time would find its way to the Boston Athenaeum. Now, this present morning, on the third, Lieber "read a good many papers of Mackenzie's. (The letters of young Spencer, found with him, I read on Monday evening"—that first night in. "A greater villain and deeper dyed scamp probably never lived. He robbed his father repeatedly . . . The letters of the mother are shocking to read—full of the deepest distress. The father begins one [of] his letters: 'Philip' and signs it 'Spencer.' . . .)—At this moment Mackenzie is sitting for the sculptor, Mrs. Mackenzie reading my views of the *Somers'* Mutiny. . . ." Probably, their visitor concluded, he would set off for the East next day. And when he did leave, Francis Lieber took with him to Cambridge feelings of love for his host: "I cherish him. He is neither lively, nor bright in conversation; very quiet, yet so kind and mild, so true and unaffected, that one cannot help liking, nay cherishing him, especially when with all this one remembers his unswerving will. I am very much gratified with my visit. . . ."

Others would be similarly impressed as they met the commander for the first time on his own visit to Boston and Cambridge, in company with his brother John Slidell, the following month. From there, in mid-September, Charles Sumner was writing Samuel Gridley Howe: "Mackenzie is here. I like him very much. He is a modest and unassuming man, with a countenance expressive of firmness and courage. Anyone who sees him must believe in his complete justification. I took him to Longfellow's yesterday"—the thirteenth, with William Sturgis's hostile third letter appearing that day in *The Boston Courier*, exactly one year after the *Somers* had sailed from New York—"they were old companions in Spain." Dana, meeting the commander for the first time a few days later, found him "unusually interesting," a gentleman who "creates a feeling of personal affection towards him in those whom he meets. Such was the impression he produced upon me, and I find he made a similar impression upon all who fell in with him during his stay here." Assuredly the visitor did upon Cornelius Felton of Harvard, Greek scholar who would one day become that university's president. "His calmness, self-possession, gentleness, and refinement of manner are the admiration of everybody that has met him," wrote Professor Felton enthusiastically, and went much further: "In my opinion, Mackenzie is one of the greatest men now living among us"—an officer in line to become "the Lord High Admiral, or anything he pleases, when our government comes in . . ."

Next fall, that was: in November 1844, when a national election would decree that His Accidency John Tyler was soon to be replaced, God willing, by the true Whig Henry Clay. Meanwhile, Mackenzie must remain without command at Tarrytown, composing his biography of Stephen Decatur and overseeing yet another edition of his popular life of Oliver Perry. By then—and though many had spoken in the captain's favor—he had perforce attended to one voice decidedly disapproving, to Fenimore Cooper's, in that pamphlet on the Battle of Lake Erie published over the summer to answer complaints brought by Messrs. Duer, Burges, and Mackenzie. On its opening page the commander would have read how Cooper "has not sought this discussion. It has been forced on him by his assailants, who must now face the consequences. For years the writer has submitted in comparative silence to a gross injustice in connection with this matter, not from any want of confidence in the justice of his case or any ability to defend himself, but because he 'bided his time,' knowing when that should arrive, he had truth to fall back on." The time to present Cooper's account of the truth proved to be this summer of 1843; and Mackenzie having read the account, which he found to be "more than a hundred pages of special pleading, sophistry, and venomous abuse," resolved to answer it. To the fifth edition of his life of Oliver Perry the commander accordingly attached an appendix, dated from Tarrytown, November 1843, containing a lengthy reply. The appendix, of fifty-five pages, impugns Cooper's seamanship, implicitly (and unjustly) accuses him of exploiting Mackenzie's troubles for his own political ends—to recommend himself to the Democrats as a likely head of the navy department—and dryly takes note of the "abundant allusions to the case of the *Somers*" that "enrich" what purports to be an argument about Lake Erie. Cooper "has 'bided his time!'" writes Mackenzie with level scorn. "Let any one consider the coincidence of circumstances under which the first insolent announcement of his pamphlet was made, and observe how completely it calls up the image of the assassin lurking in ambush, and watching to take his enemy unawares. . . ."

If the commander later penned a response to Cooper's detailed and even more devastating review the following year of the *Somers* case and the court-martial, none has survived; perhaps he spared himself the annoyance of reading it. During that year he did go on with his biography of Decatur; "after that task is accomplished," he was explaining to a correspondent June 20, 1844, "I hope to find myself with leisure and, what is equally necessary, with inclination enough to address myself earnestly to the task of preparing a history of our Navy . . ."

Yet another such history—to correct Cooper's?—unless President Clay should in the near future call on the captain to serve as "Lord High Admiral." It was not the Whig Clay, however, who won the presidential election in November, but rather the dark-horse candidate of the Democrats, James Knox Polk. One beneficiary of that succession turned out to be Mackenzie's older brother John Slidell, affluent attorney who had been serving as representative from Louisiana to the federal legislature.

An epilogue provides hardly the space to describe events leading to the Mexican War—or the war itself, in which both Slidell and his brother played parts. Northern fears were that the impending annexation of Texas would enlarge the boundaries of slavery. The Southerner Tyler approved of annexation; and when the people elected as his successor Governor Polk of Tennessee on an expansionist platform, Tyler proceeded in the final, lame-duck days of his presidency to interpret that result as a mandate to bring annexation about. (That the President did annex Texas was enough, by the way, to drive his secretary of the treasury back into private life. Twice denied a seat on the Supreme Court by a hostile Senate, the New Yorker John C. Spencer retired from national office in 1844 over the annexation question, returning to his home state to resume the practice of law. His wife survived only a year or two the death of their son Philip; Spencer himself, as a private citizen, lived on until 1855, dying in his sixty-eighth year.)

The annexation of Texas in 1845 caused Mexico to sever relations with the United States. Polk, assuming the presidency in March 1845, moved to reestablish diplomatic contact in order to negotiate a settlement of differences between the two nations. The new President had learned that the Mexican government would receive an envoy; as his negotiator he chose John Slidell. The loyal Whig Philip Hone in New York professed to know why. Not so much that Slidell, in his early fifties, was an agreeable gentleman, an able lawyer, an excellent Spanish scholar. The appointment was made, wrote Hone in his diary, "as a reward for frauds practiced in New Orleans by which the vote of the state was gained for Mr. Polk . . ." In any case, John Slidell as envoy extraordinary and minister plenipotentiary would be sailing for Veracruz—indeed, arrived there November 30, 1845, preparatory to proceeding overland toward the Mexican capital.

Meanwhile, back home that same autumn, an outcome was brought about in no way related to Mr. Slidell's mission, though closely related to the experience of Slidell's brother aboard the brig-of-war *Somers*. The recent sensational court-martial of Commander Mackenzie had directed attention nationwide to conditions in the navy. To be sure, knowledgeable people had been aware of those conditions for years. Slidell Mackenzie himself—and in that troublesome review in 1839 of Cooper's *Naval History*—had stressed the importance (scarcely inferior in importance, he wrote, "to the creation of the rank of admiral," which did not then exist and which Cooper had been urging) of establishing "a naval academy for the education of midshipmen. . . . At all times," Mackenzie explained in *The North American Review* of October 1839, "our ships of war are representatives of our country, in every quarter of the globe; it is chiefly by the worth, intelligence, and courtesy of their officers that an estimate can be formed of the nation that sends them forth." Too often those officers were drunken, hot-tempered ne'er-do-wells—and that had been written three full years before the commander first shook the hand of Acting Midshipman Spencer, reporting aboard his brig at Brooklyn. In fact, Mackenzie writing in 1839 could remind his readers that "our ideas of a naval academy . . . are unchanged since we expressed them ten years ago in this journal. . . ."

Thus, some at least had been aware for a long time of the need for an institution to train aspiring naval officers, a need far more generally acknowledged after the late fall of 1842 and those mournful events on the *Somers. The New York Tribune* was commenting, for example, January 26, 1843: "We trust recent occurrences have aided to arouse the public mind to the necessity of a Radical Reform in our Navy—a Reform which shall strip that arm of the Public Service of some of its revoltingly aristocratic features and assimilate it in some slight degree to the genius of our Free Institutions." For as of now, a midshipman has "a warrant for tyranny over and abuse of the helpless slaves of this atrocious system. He has no experience, a boy's judgment, passions, and caprices; he is usually the son of some rich or eminent man, and has served a full apprenticeship to doing nothing or doing mischief; he is often put into the Navy because his temper is ungovernable or his vices disgraceful . . ."

Reviewing Cooper's History, Mackenzie had found occasion to redescribe his own decade-old vision of an academy, where likely youths of thirteen would be admitted to "some healthy, isolated situation, with the sea in sight," and for three or four years would study such subjects as math, navigation, and naval architecture, while learning shiphandling and gunnery during interspersed cruises that would "furnish an invaluable groundwork of professional education to our officers": freshmen on deck, sophomores aloft, juniors as petty officers, seniors in steerage and wardroom rotating the duties of captain. Such an academy would replace those ill-conceived asylums at the several naval stations and do away with the current "abortive and worthless" schools aboard ship, where youngsters played tricks on the hapless schoolmasters, whom senior officers disparaged.

So sensible a proposal would seem to have been irresistible. After all, West Point, founded in 1802, had been training leaders for the army through four decades. Yet only in the wake of the *Somers* affair was public opinion finally sufficiently bestirred to accept the need for a comparable institution to train officers of the navy. And with the Democrat Polk's election to the Presidency, that needed reform was brought about at last. The new secretary of the navy, George Bancroft, managed to secure Fort Severn, an obsolete army base on Windmill Point at Annapolis, Maryland, to which were ordered cadets from the now disbanded naval asylums in Boston, New York, Norfolk, and Philadelphia. What amounts to the charter of the United States Naval Academy is contained in Bancroft's letter to Commander Franklin Buchanan of August 7, 1845. When the new academy opened its doors two months after that date, Buchanan was serving as its first superintendent; its second was to be Mackenzie's close professional friend Commander George P. Upshur.

Late fall of 1845. John Slidell is proceeding from Veracruz inland to undertake negotiations with the Mexican government on behalf of his country. But various affronts and delays make it clear that the Mexicans will not receive Polk's envoy, who by early May has returned home with war between the two nations all but inevitable. Back at Washington the rejected minister is soon writing Andrew Jackson Donelson, nephew of Old Hickory, May 13, 1846: "It has always been to me a source of deep regret not to have had some evidence under the hand of our good old chief"—Jackson himself, who had died the year before—"of his approbation of the cause of my brother in the affair of the *Somers*. Would you, my dear sir, have any objection to state what you know on this subject? I intend in a few days to make an appeal to the President"—to Polk, Young Hickory, that other Tennessean—"for the employment of my brother, and such a document would have great weight with him."

Slidell's appeal would be answered; President Polk would summon Commander Mackenzie from Tarrytown to serve his country, as Washington Irving was to discover upon his return to America, to Tarrytown, this same year. Irving, we remember, had been abroad since the spring of 1842 as Tyler's ambassador to Spain. But with a new administration in office the ambassador's term at Madrid had come to an end, after a final visit to Paris and London. Incidentally, in that latter capital the sixty-two-year-old Irving had met another political beneficiary of Polk's victory. Gansevoort Melville, Herman's older brother, who had labored faithfully for Governor Polk during the recent campaign, was experiencing his reward as secretary of the legation under the ambassador to the Court of St. James's, Irving's good friend, Louis McLane. January 6, 1846: "While quietly writing, to my surprise our Minister to Madrid, Washington Irving, walked in, lamenting Mr. McLane's absence from town. He is just from Paris. He sat down and we soon fell into an interesting conversation which lasted two hours . . ." January 7: "10 a.m.— Washington Irving and Mr. Jno. Murray the publisher breakfasted with me . . . At 12 Mr. M went away, and I read to Mr. Irving various parts of the first ten chapters of Herman's forthcoming book. He was very much pleased—declared portions to be 'exquisite,' said the style was very 'graphic' and prophesied its success. This delighted me." The forthcoming book was the younger Melville's first, *Typee*, an account of some weeks spent among natives of the Marquesas after he and a mate had jumped ship in the Pacific in 1842 during a whaling cruise. What the ever generous Irving had done for Slidell Mackenzie some fifteen years earlier he was doing now for Herman Melville: recommending a first book by an unknown American to the attention of the House of Murray. January 16: "Saw Mr. Murray on the same subject. Mr. Irving had spoken to him most favorably of the book." February 3: "Washington Irving read the Preface and Appendix to *Typee* in the office today and expressed himself highly pleased. . . ."

What, one wonders, had been Irving's thoughts all this while concerning sensational news about his neighbor Slidell Mackenzie that had been dominating public attention three years before? Which side in the national dispute had the great author taken? At that earlier time, Irving as ambassador had been deeply involved in diplomatic maneuverings at Madrid on behalf of his government. Many of his letters from the Spanish capital survive; and it comes as a surprise to discover that during the trial, early in 1843, he makes no extant mention, even in private correspondence, of Mackenzie's ordeal. Irving did write home about occurrences at Tarrytown that his family had shared with him—indignantly, for example, about the reneging by a young acquaintance on an engagement to one of his nieces. And names of other neighbors enter his correspondence —though not a word about Alexander Slidell Mackenzie. To be sure, the ambassador had been busy: "I have been much occupied of late by various concerns," he wrote from Madrid at the time of the trial. Events surrounding those endless struggles for power in the peninsula "have been thickening upon us so as to require incessant attention among diplomatic agents to collect correct information for their respective governments." No doubt; yet one suspects that discretion, in one temperamentally averse to controversy, accounted as much as preoccupation for Irving's politic silence.

Despite that silence, we may infer what the ambassador's opinion was. For one thing, he would have shared a community of interest with his neighbor James Watson Webb. The two gentlemen had known each other a long time, had dined together, corresponded. Tarrytown's historian Edgar Mayhew Bacon, who as a boy knew the then elderly Webb, assures us that the newspaper editor was a "really great friend" of the much befriended Irving. And Webb's views were repeatedly in print. Perry was a close friend too; and one of Irving's nephews-in-law (yet another close Tarrytown friend) was Moses Grinnell, wealthy builder of clipper ships, one not likely to have much sympathy for aspiring pirates. Such Whig opinions from valued associates—plus trust in and fondness for Mackenzie himself—would have disposed the author overseas in the captain's favor.

We may thus confidently assume that Irving supported the course that Mackenzie had followed aboard the *Somers*. In fact, substantiation is implicit in a letter of 1846, not long after the ambassador's return from Spain, and five years after one on a May day to his then recently married niece Sarah Storrow that was quoted earlier. By this later time Washington Irving was back at Tarrytown for good. Again he was writing to Paris from Sunnyside, again to Sarah—though now in the autumn—and again of a call on various neighbors. His favorite niece was now to learn that "a day or two since I drove with your uncle"—Irving's brother Ebenezer—"and two of the girls to make my visit to the Mackenzies, Perrys, and Creightons." That last-named was the family of the rector of Christ Church, Tarrytown. "Mackenzie has improved his farm greatly," Irving writes, "and has rendered the house much more respectable in appearance than I had supposed it capable of being." All would have seemed by then, in October 1846, nearly four years after the mutiny, pretty much back to normal. "He is likely," however, continues Irving, "to have a poor man's fortune, a house full of children. He has four already: two boys and two girls." Mackenzie himself "was absent on business, being in active employment at present on confidential matters connected with the Mexican War. I am glad"—and here is where a loyal friend's opinion of events aboard the *Somers* emerges obliquely—"I am glad he has the confidence and countenance of Government, which he well merits."

The commander's employment on confidential matters had taken him to Havana in early July. Ostensibly the Spanish-speaking Mackenzie was there to check on privateers, but in fact he was holding secret negotiations with the exiled leader Santa Anna, whom President Polk had been encouraged to believe might sue for peace with the United States if he were allowed to regain power in Mexico. The Home Squadron in the Gulf had been blockading Mexican ports; might Santa Anna be permitted to pass through the American blockade and land at Veracruz, in order to lead a coup that would establish a government committed to ending a war already three months old?

Details of the scheme were worked out. Before the end of summer the wily Mexican general had fulfilled his ambitions and was once more on his native soil, hailed as a hero and given control of the army. But rather than end the war, Santa Anna proceeded to wage it all the more vigorously. Mackenzie himself, his own part in negotiations in Cuba successfully concluded, had meanwhile sailed from Havana for home, and from there later to join the blockading American fleet, now effectively under the command of his brother-in-law Commodore Matthew Perry.

Among vessels serving in the blockade of Veracruz that fall was the brig-of-war *Somers*. Perry himself was soon charged with writing the secretary of the navy, December 12, 1846, that "the *Somers* had been performing the most active blockading duties for several months, exposed to every vicissitude of weather, and the *John Adams*, Commander McCluney, had been ordered to take her place. Her long and arduous cruise would have ended today or tomorrow . . ." But at ten in the morning four days ago, on the eighth, while pursuing a sail that was attempting to run the blockade, the brig had been hit by a heavy squall. "We were still under topsails, courses, jib, and spanker," her then captain, Lieutenant Raphael Semmes, would explain in an official report. "I was myself standing on the lee arms chest"—on a larboard tack, and thus where Boatswain's Mate Cromwell had sat in irons through four nights and three days four years earlier—"having just passed over from the weather quarter, and with my spy-glass in hand . . ." The crew was in the act of shortening sail when the squall struck. "It did not appear to be very violent, nor was its approach accompanied by any foaming of the water or other indications . . . But the brig being flying-light, having scarcely any water or provisions, and but six tons of ballast on board, she was thrown over almost instantly, so far as to refuse to obey her helm . . ." All at once the overrigged *Somers* had been tossed on her beam ends, water pouring into the hatches and scuttles. Semmes had ordered masts to be cut away; the crew, struggling to the weather bulwarks, had begun to do so. "But as this was a forlorn hope, the brig filling very fast, and her masts and yards lying flat upon the surface of the sea, I placed no reliance whatever on their efforts." She would go down—within ten minutes had sunk to the bottom, with a loss of thirty-nine of the seventy-six officers and crewmen then aboard.

To the last an ill-fated vessel. Semmes himself, a swimmer, along with a Lieutenant Parker, had been saved by reaching an arms chest grating afloat on the water.

A court of inquiry would exonerate the vessel's captain from any blame in the sinking. Raphael Semmes, in fact, would go on to become one of the most famous of naval heroes of the nineteenth century, although in another navy, one formed a decade and more later by the Confederate States of America, for which he brilliantly commanded the bark-rigged cruiser *Alabama* in a succession of raids on Union commerce through much of the Civil War.

Semmes was but one of many names from the Mexican War destined to become famous in that later conflict; McClellan, Lee, Jackson, Meade, Grant, Jefferson Davis were others. First, however, there was to be an interlude of uncertain peace: the decade of the fifties between the two slaughters. In New York April 8, 1850, as the decade began: "I dined on Saturday," wrote that capital diner Philip Hone, "with Mr. August Belmont, the agent of the great house of Rothschilds, at his splendid mansion in the Fifth avenue." Belmont had five months earlier married a daughter of Matthew Perry; the guests this particular evening "were Washington Irving, Commodore Perry, Edward Jones, Rev. Dr. Wainwright . . ." Three months later, with peace persisting, at fashionable Saratoga Springs Mr. Richard Henry Dana, Jr., and his wife were taking the waters. There on Sunday, July 21, they encountered Mr. and Mrs. John Slidell: "Talked with Mr. Slidell about his brother." And within two days at that upstate New York spa the Danas were meeting another old acquaintance, Lieutenant Guert Gansevoort.

That same year—or early in the year following—back on Manhattan occurred one further encounter, a particularly pleasant one to record. After the New York house of Harper's had rejected young Melville's first manuscript, George Palmer Putnam had published an American edition of *Typee* with great success. Moreover, Putnam had lately been issuing the collected works of Washington Irving in a uniform edition, a venture that had brought that famous author, now well into his sixties, financial security at last. And the same energetic publisher was also producing a comparable edition of the works of James Fenimore Cooper, fellow New Yorker whom Irving had steadily admired, though with little enough reciprocation. "One day," Putnam later remembered, "some time after I had commenced a library edition of Cooper's best works, and while Irving's were in course of publication in companionship, Mr. Irving was sitting at my desk"—presumably in the new offices at 10 Park Place, for this would have been in 1850 or early 1851. Irving's back was to the door "when Mr. Cooper came in (a little bustlingly, as usual), and stood at the office entrance talking. Mr. Irving did not turn"—not recognizing the voice and not wanting to intrude—"and Cooper did not see him." After a moment the publisher obeyed an impulse. "Mr. Cooper," he announced stoutly, "here is Mr. Irving"; and as the latter rose, "Cooper held out his hand cordially, dashed at once into an animated conversation, took a chair, and, to my surprise and delight, the two authors sat for an hour, chatting in their best manner about almost every topic of the day and some of former days. They parted with cordial good wishes"—at the end of a visit that would prove to have occurred "not many months" before the novelist's death, at Cooperstown, September 14, 1851. Irving would chair the committee that arranged a memorial service for Cooper, at which Daniel Webster would preside and Bryant deliver the eulogy. Another author, recently turned thirty-two and at the height of his fame, would be invited from Pittsfield in the Berkshires to New York to participate. Unable to do so, Herman Melville sent a letter to acknowledge that Cooper's works had exerted "a vivid and awakening power" on his own mind—a mind recently engaged in conceiving and writing *Moby-Dick*, even then in the presses and to be published before year's end.

The Slidells would have been enjoying their visit to Saratoga Springs when Dana encountered them there in 1850; in August of the following year they had returned, and this time the Louisiana politician found himself face-to-face with Charles Sumner, newly elected to the United States Senate from Massachusetts. At the meeting, Slidell behaved with marked reserve, and soon after declined an invitation to a dinner at which the Northern senator was to be present. Later in the month he wrote to Sumner, by then at Newport, to explain his behavior. Slidell did express his gratitude for the "chivalrous and zealous advocacy" of his brother Slidell Mackenzie's cause that Sumner had prepared for *The North American Review* seven years before; but, he went on, he found an embarrassment in entering into relations with one whose hostility toward Slidell's section of the country, toward the South, was so pronounced. Sumner, in fact, was by then an outspoken Free-Soil Democrat, and the awkwardness of his meeting with the Louisiana gentleman, soon to be a member of the Senate himself, was an ominous indication of differences that before long would tear the nation apart.

For now, though, peace. Early in 1852 orders reach New York for Commodore Matthew Perry. He is fifty-seven, has never in that long time sailed in the Pacific, has never even seen it—and has no desire for further sea duty unless to return to the Mediterranean, given "the present state of discipline of the Navy." Perry's reference is to the recent abolition of flogging aboard naval vessels, a reform brought about in part by such writings as Dana's and Melville's, in part by the urging of such officers as Captains Stockton and David Conner and Uriah Levy. But Perry is one of many who disapprove of the reform. He obeys his orders for all that, and in November 1852, sails on the *Mississippi* from Norfolk bearing a letter, in a rosewood box with gold fittings, from President Millard Fillmore to the ruler of Japan, island empire that has been closed to foreigners for over two hundred years.

Seven months after his departure, Perry anchors in twenty fathoms south of Edo—modern Tokyo—with Mount Fuji magnificently in sight beyond pine-tufted hills, as crews aboard junks in the bay gape in astonishment at those seaborne intruders: two strange vessels belching black smoke, and two sailing vessels in tow. By March 1854, at Yokohama, the sailor-diplomat Perry has signed with the emperor's representatives a treaty that prepares the way for establishing normal relations between Japan and the outside world. A stunning achievement, boon for the now continental nation that the commodore represents, brought about with no loss of life and without awakening either the hostility or the resentment of the Japanese. On the contrary, even to our own time Matthew Perry continues to be held in the highest esteem by descendants of those island people who once, on the third day of the sixth month, sixth year of Kaei, July 8, 1853, had stared in wonder toward four black vessels, two seemingly on fire, moving at nine knots in a calm to anchor just south of Tokyo Bay . . .

By 1856, the year after Perry's return from his successful cruise, Charles Sumner had established himself as a leader of one faction in the United States Senate, where John Slidell was serving too. That May the Massachusetts abolitionist delivered in the chamber yet another scathing oration against slavery and against those states that supported so inhuman an institution. Southern senators were attending his hours-long speech with sullen resentment—his sarcasm, the eloquent satire, the stinging allusions. Two days later, in the early afternoon with the Senate just adjourned, Sumner sat at work at his desk in the rear of the chamber. Quarter past one, Thursday, May 22, 1856. Some twenty people were lingering in or near the hall. When he heard his name spoken the senator glanced up from his writing. A tall, handsome gentleman stood on the other side of the desk. "I have read your speech over twice carefully," the gentleman was saying. "It is a libel on South Carolina and Mr. Butler, who is a relative of mine." And without waiting for a reply, the stranger —he proved to be Mr. Preston Brooks, member of the House—lifted his gutta-percha cane and brought it down with full force on Sumner's bare head.

Eyewitnesses would reconstruct what happened next. That first blow had stunned and blinded the senator. It was followed by a succession of other blows equally powerful, maybe as many as ten, as twenty, while the blinded victim, pinioned by his chair and desk, moved instinctively to defend himself. He bent his head and, as the blows fell, wrenched the desk from its floor fastenings. Staggering to his feet, he swayed forward, throwing his arms about convulsively, as his assailant seized him by the collar and continued the beating with full strength until the substantial cane broke, and Sumner fell bloodily to the floor at the edge of the aisle.

Senator Slidell had been conversing with Senator Stephen Douglas and others in an anteroom of the chamber when a messenger burst in with news that someone was violently caning Mr. Sumner in the main hall. As he later testified, the senator from Louisiana received the information "without any particular emotion. For my own part I confess I felt none . . . I am not particularly fond of scenes of any sort. I have no associations or relations of any kind with Mr. Sumner; I have not spoken to him for two years. I did not think it necessary to express my sympathy or make any advances towards him. . . ."

To passionate defenses of the "peculiar institution," to ever louder cries for abolition, to squatter sovereignty in those new territories wrested from Mexico, to free-soil settlers and old John Brown, to Bleeding Kansas had the Compromise of 1850 that had begun the decade yielded. Not for three and a half years was Charles Sumner recovered enough to resume his seat in the Senate, and by then, by late 1859, old John Brown of Osawatomie had led his handful of troops to Harpers Ferry. The irrepressible conflict that another senator, Seward of New York, had foreseen was about to begin.

Civil war that overwhelmed the nation altered the lives of all its citizens, including those who survived from the days of the *Somers* affair: Slidell and Captain Wilkes and Semmes and Seward and Webb and Dana and Strong and all the others. The nation that emerged on the other side of the war was a different nation, with new concerns. But from time to time, as the century pressed on toward its end, would be recorded some recollection or retelling of an increasingly distant episode that had occurred on a United States naval training brig in the early 1840s.

One such appeared in the autobiography of Thurlow Weed, published soon after the death of that celebrated public figure in 1882. Weed, born before the century began, had lived a long and colorful life: early on as a founder of the Anti-Masonic party, an organizer of the Whigs, power behind Seward's election as governor of New York. An Albany newspaper proprietor and editor (sued in good time by Fenimore Cooper) and a political opponent of John C. Spencer's, Weed had been active for half a century in state and national politics. A chapter of his posthumously published memoirs deals with the *Somers*. How long after the events themselves had he written the chapter? Specific days are sometimes faultily recollected—though not so much as to discredit the remarkable story altogether. Would he have made up such facts? Would memory have served him so poorly?

The editor remembers having passed through Manhattan late in 1842, soon after the brig-of-war had returned to home port. "The *Somers* arrived in New York about the 20th of December," he writes. "I reached New York on my way to Washington on Sunday morning, the *Somers* having arrived on Saturday." The preceding Wednesday she had come in, in fact, the 14th—though Saturday had been when the story of the mutiny had broken in all the newspapers. "There was," Weed continues, "a midshipman on board whose warrant I had obtained, and who was a sort of protégé of mine. Immediately after breakfast I went to the navy yard to see him. Commodore Perry informed me that Captain Mackenzie had gone with his officers to church, but that as soon as they returned he would ask Captain Mackenzie to give Midshipman Tillotson leave to come to the Astor House."

Consequently young Tillotson had joined his sponsor for dinner on Broadway that afternoon. Though instructed not to converse about the case, which a court of inquiry would soon be investigating, the sixteen-year-old did mention in passing that he had been on deck with the captain at sea while the council of officers was sitting below in judgment on Spencer and the two other prisoners. According to Weed, the acting midshipman remembered that "Lieutenant Gansevoort, who presided, came on deck twice during the trial and conferred with Captain Mackenzie. . . ."

The editor records that he left New York for Washington that Sunday evening, after his dinner with Tillotson—but might the departure have been somewhat later? Leaving Sunday would have put him in Philadelphia late that same night or Monday to spend the evening. At Philadelphia "I met Passed Midshipman Gansevoort, a cousin of Lieutenant Gansevoort, who was first officer on board the *Somers*. Both of these

officers were from Albany, where I had known them in their boyhood."
That Guert Gansevoort's cousin, Passed Midshipman Hunn Gansevoort,
would be in New York himself a few days later is verifiable, so it is not
implausible that within a week after the brig had anchored, he would
have been dining with Thurlow Weed in Philadelphia, where his own
vessel (the *Grampus*) lay. "Of course," writes Weed, "the *Somers* affair
formed the staple of our conversation. He informed me that his cousin,
on his way to Washington with the official dispatch, passed the previous
evening with him at that hotel, and at a late hour, and after much hesitation, he had made a revelation to him which he thought proper to make
to me as a friend of them and their families."

The revelation is extraordinary. Is it true? Guert Gansevoort could
hardly have been in Philadelphia Saturday or Sunday evening, as he
would have had to be if Weed's chronology is insisted upon. He was
most likely in Brooklyn; nor did the first lieutenant carry either of Mackenzie's dispatches to Washington. Captain's Clerk Perry had set out
from New York with the earlier dispatches the previous Wednesday
night, immediately after the *Somers* had dropped anchor, and delivered
them to the navy department Friday. Weed's supper with Hunn Gansevoort in Philadelphia, as he remembers it, was early the following
week; yet not until Wednesday of that week was the captain's more detailed account dispatched from New York, in the hands of Midshipman
Rodgers. We do recall, however, that the first lieutenant had been ordered to the capital at the same time as Rodgers, to answer whatever
questions the dispatches might bring forth. And his mother is authority
for the lieutenant's having delayed at Philadelphia. Suffering from the
effects of his recent shipboard ordeal, he had been visiting her in Brooklyn when the orders from Mackenzie came; "nothing could stop him. He
went, was sick one night at Philadelphia, but got there safe," to Washington.

Has Weed merely confused dates, in an account otherwise sound? He
says that Hunn Gansevoort had spent the previous evening with his cousin Guert, who late in their talk together, after some hesitation, made a
shocking disclosure about what had gone on aboard the *Somers*. The
council of officers had completed examining the various witnesses. "I,"
the first lieutenant is supposed to have told his relative in Philadelphia,
"went on deck and informed Captain Mackenzie that the testimony was
not as strong as had been represented to him, and that I thought from the
indications the court did not attach much importance to it." But Mackenzie had responded "that the witnesses had not been thoroughly examined, and directed me to recall them, and put certain interrogations to
them, a copy of which he handed to me."

With that unusual directive the first lieutenant had complied, though
without eliciting any new information. Thus, even after additional testi-

mony, comments among the council satisfied Gansevoort that his fellow officers were not prepared to convict the prisoners. He returned topside and reported his opinion to the captain. Thereupon Mackenzie is said to have remarked "that it was evident these young men had wholly misapprehended the nature of the evidence, if they had not also misapprehended the aggravated character of the offense, and that there would be no security for the lives of officers or protection to commerce if an example was not made in a case so flagrant as this. It was my duty, he urged, to impress these views upon the court." Gansevoort had accordingly gone below once more and done so. And only in that way had he managed to obtain "a reluctant conviction of the accused." But the officer and relative to whom alone he had later confided that startling information—and who was sharing it in turn with Thurlow Weed over supper in Philadelphia— "sailed," Weed tells us, "the next day in a United States brig which, with all on board, was engulfed at sea." Passed Midshipman Hunn Gansevoort was, in fact, aboard the USS *Grampus* that departed Philadelphia if not next day, then soon, for Norfolk, out of which port she sailed that March, never to be heard from again.

There is a sequel. "In the following summer, at Boston," Weed writes, "in visiting the United States seventy-four-gun ship *Ohio*, I encountered Lieutenant Gansevoort and invited him to dine with me at the Tremont House. At dinner the sad fate of his kinsman was spoken of, when I remarked that I had passed the evening with him previous to his sailing from Philadelphia, adding that we sat gossiping over our hot whiskey punch into the small hours. The lieutenant, with evident surprise, asked, with emphasis, 'Did he tell you that I passed the previous night with him?' I answered in the affirmative. He said, 'What else did he tell you?' I replied, with equal emphasis, 'He told me all that you said to him about the trial of Spencer.' Whereupon he looked thoughtful a moment, then drank off his champagne, seized or raised the bottle, again filled his glass and emptied it, and, without further remark, left the table."

Seven years passed before Weed next saw Guert Gansevoort; and when he did, the interval "had told fearfully upon his health and habits." Toward the end of his life—Gansevoort died, retired with the rank of commodore, in 1868—the officer had been stationed at the Brooklyn navy yard, "a sad wreck of his former self," according to Weed, whom he frequently visited—"always moody, taciturn, and restless. In my conversations with him I never again referred to this affair, nor do I know that he ever spoke of it to others. But I do know that a bright, intelligent, highly principled, and sensitive gentleman, and a most promising officer of the navy, spent the best part of his life a prey to unavailing remorse for an act the responsibility of which belonged to a superior officer."

How much of this is reliable? Assuredly Gansevoort after leaving the *Somers* served aboard the receiving ship *Ohio* at Boston, and was serving there in 1844, so that Weed might well have dined with him that summer at the Tremont House. Indeed, the lieutenant was on hand on the *Ohio* in October to greet his first cousin Herman Melville (whom he resembled: "looks very much like Herman; we all noticed it"), when the latter returned from those three years of sailing in the Pacific that would be shown to have provided most of the subjects for the great writing career about to begin. And the following April (1845), an Albany uncle with influence was soliciting consideration from the then secretary of war: "My nephew, Lieutenant Guert Gansevoort of the Navy, is now and has for about nineteen months been in the receiver ship *Ohio* of Boston." What the lieutenant desired was sea duty. "He is esteemed an excellent officer," wrote his uncle Peter Gansevoort, "and has always preferred active service. . . ." The subsequent record of the applicant (who would get his active service) was not, however, unblemished. There was Captain David Farragut's decision at Mare Island, California, in 1856, to suspend Commander G. Gansevoort for being intoxicated at eleven in the morning, and to order Lieutenant Middleton to succeed him in command of the *Decatur:* "I was not surprised to hear of the circumstances," wrote Commodore Mervine of that action, "having long known indirectly that his habits in this respect are bad . . ." But Melville himself, following his cousin's naval career as it unfolded, always spoke well of Guert— during the Civil War, for example, rejoicing to learn that he was then commanding the *Roanoke:* "he is brave as a lion," Melville wrote, "a good seaman, a natural-born officer, and I hope he will yet turn out the hero of a brilliant victory . . ."

Guert never did. And he seems never again to have spoken of his role in the *Somers* affair. In a poem composed late in life Melville referred to one "Tom Tight":

> Tom was lieutenant in the brig-o'-war famed
> When an officer was hung for an arch-mutineer,
> But a mystery cleaved, and the captain was blamed,
> And a rumpus too raised, though his honor it was clear.
> And Tom he would say, when the mousers would try him,
> And with cup after cup o' Burgundy ply him:
> "Gentlemen, in vain with your wassail you beset,
> For the more I tipple, the tighter do I get."
> No blabber, no, not even with the can—
> True to himself and loyal to his clan. . . .

Such verses were what Herman Melville had been writing when he wrote at all now. That great career flourishing in the 1840s and early fifties had ended prematurely. Some of his war poems did appear in the sixties, though scarcely anyone read them. Then a virtually unbroken silence. The author had moved his family from Pittsfield to New York City in 1863, and for twenty years thereafter had uncomplainingly filled the routine duties of inspector of customs at dockside, each morning making his way the eighteen or twenty blocks crosstown to the Hudson, then back at the end of the day to his brick-and-brownstone home on East Twenty-sixth Street. At sixty-seven, all but forgotten, the once illustrious Melville, who long ago had lived among the cannibals and written about it, finally resigned from the prosaic chores of the customs house, unambitiously content with the obscurity that had enveloped these latter days.

Not everyone had forgotten him, though. A Professor Archibald MacMechan of Halifax wrote November 21, 1889: "Although a stranger, I take the liberty of addressing you on the ground of my ardent admiration for your works. For a number of years I have read and re-read *Moby-Dick* with increasing pleasure on every perusal; and with this study, the conviction has grown up that the unique merits of that book have never received due recognition." Professor MacMechan wanted to set the virtues of Melville's works before the public. Toward that end, he would appreciate any particulars of the author's life and literary methods.

The answer seems to have come from the very edge of the grave. "Your note gave me pleasure," Melville responded December 5, "as how should it not, written in such a spirit. But you do not know perhaps that I have entered my eighth decade. After twenty years nearly as an outdoor Customs House officer, I have latterly come into possession of unobstructed leisure, but only just as, in the course of nature, my vigor sensibly declines. What little of it is left I husband for certain matters as yet incomplete, and which indeed may never be completed. . . ."

On his desk, ocher-colored pages of a manuscript in progress carried a notation dated the previous year: "Friday Nov. 16, 1888. Began." Began a sea tale in prose, the first such that Melville had undertaken in more than thirty years. What had provoked the old man to resume thus? Poems he had written lately were about the sea; and that March he had made a final, brief voyage, as a passenger to Bermuda and, aboard the SS *Trinidad,* on to St. Augustine and home. He would doubtless by then have looked over the autobiography of Thurlow Weed, friend of the Melville family, that had been published earlier in the decade. Moreover, on May 1, 1888, in *The American Magazine* had appeared a retelling, by Lieutenant H. D. Smith, of "The Mutiny of the *Somers.*" For whatever reasons, half a year from that date this former customs inspector, now retired, was evolving into a full-length story a poem he had earlier written about a mutineer.

Captain Mackenzie decades before had urged his friend Longfellow to take hold of the subject of the *Somers*—that "fruitful theme"—and turn it into poetry, under some other name, set in some previous time. Melville sets his own prose tale of a hanging at sea in the past, in the English navy, during the French revolutionary era and soon after historical mutinies had occurred at Spithead and the Nore. Thus the execution aboard the English seventy-four takes place in wartime, mutinies having recently been attempted in the fleet. Is the author suggesting circumstances under which a decision such as that made by Captain Mackenzie and concurred in by Lieutenant Gansevoort might have been justified? A member of the ship's company must be hanged in any case, though our sympathies are with him, and though he is as popular on board his vessel (isolated as it is from the squadron) as Seaman Small, according to what Tillotson had told Thurlow Weed, had been on his. "You are right, sir," Small had exclaimed to his captain before the historical execution on the *Somers*. "You are doing your duty, and I honor you for it. God bless that flag and prosper it!" And the saintly Billy Budd, with the rope around his neck, utters a strikingly similar sentiment: "God bless Captain Vere"—for performing a duty for the larger good despite that sensitive officer's personal reluctance to do so.

On the manuscript, those seven- by six-inch sheets of glazed paper: "Revise—began March 2, 1889." The upstairs study on Twenty-sixth Street faced bleakly north. Within, a bearded old man was bent over the great mahogany desk, before the four shelves of dim leather books above which hovered dusty plaster busts nearly at ceiling level. Nearby were the narrow grate, his small iron bedstead. On April 19, 1891, he would write on his manuscript: "End of Book."

> . . . Just ease these darbies at the wrist,
> And roll me over fair!
> I am sleepy, and the oozy weeds about me twist.

Five months later, on September 28, 1891, Herman Melville died, aged seventy-two. At the time of his death the manuscript of *Billy Budd, Sailor* lay with other papers in his desk, to be found by survivors. His wife bound all such into neat bundles and put them in a trunk for safekeeping. Not until 1921 did the scholar Raymond Weaver gain permission from Melville's granddaughter to examine what had been stored away. The late masterpiece that he found among the author's papers is now generally judged to rank second only to *Moby-Dick* in the Melville canon.

On that marvelous late story the *Somers* had exerted her influence. "Not unlikely," Melville had written of the tense mood among officers at the drumhead court aboard his fictional *Bellipotent*, "they were brought to something more or less akin to that harassed frame of mind which in the year 1842 actuated the commander of the U.S. brig-of-war *Somers*, under the so-called Articles of War, articles modeled upon the English Mutiny Act, to resolve upon the execution at sea of a midshipman and two sailors as mutineers designing the seizure of the brig. Which resolution was carried out though in a time of peace and within not many days' sail of home. An act vindicated by a naval court of inquiry subsequently convened ashore. History, and here cited without comment. True, the circumstances on board the *Somers* were different from those on board the *Bellipotent*. But the urgency felt, well-warranted or otherwise, was much the same. . . ."

He who most acutely had felt that urgency in life—Alexander Slidell Mackenzie—had been granted only a few more years of existence after the *Somers* came home. In 1846 Mackenzie had published his biography of Stephen Decatur, and in that same year had served his government as emissary to Santa Anna in Cuba. At year's end, December 10 (the *Somers*, all unknown to him, had sunk in the Gulf two days before), Mackenzie was writing from the United States Hotel in Boston to Longfellow across the river in Cambridge: "I have just . . . received orders to go to West Point when my duty here is accomplished, which will be tomorrow." The commander was proving guns for the navy at Charlestown. "But I will contrive to postpone duty to pleasure at least so far as to go to you tomorrow, Friday . . ." Accordingly, in Longfellow's journal December 11 appears an entry: ". . . Could not go to the Whist Club. But Slidell Mackenzie came, and passed the night"—at Craigie House, where the poet was engaged in writing *Evangeline*—"and we talked of the old and the new. A very good fellow, with very sound sense and great love of literature."

The following April, from aboard the USS *Mississippi* (vessel that would later carry Perry to Japan), Commander Mackenzie, back serving his country in the Gulf of Mexico, was sending his friend some patriotic odes come upon in the newspaper, knowing Longfellow's "voracious craving for national poetry of any sort." Mackenzie had acted as interpreter at the recent surrender of Veracruz, would command artillery at the forthcoming attack on Tabasco. His final naval service would be as captain of this same steamer *Mississippi*, which returned to America in April 1848, with peace at hand.

But by then, as Mrs. Mackenzie notes, her husband's health was much impaired. Again he retired to Tarrytown with his family, and there he set to work on the manuscript (never published) of his tour in Ireland, long in the past—a tour taken fourteen years earlier. After mornings spent at that literary labor, he would indulge himself in solitary horseback rides. "At last one day, as related by old people who lived here then, the horse," says Tarrytown's historian Edgar Mayhew Bacon, "came home and halted as usual in front of the door, and whoever came to take the animal to the stable found Mackenzie in the saddle, dead." He had succumbed to a heart attack. The date was September 13, 1848—six years exactly since the *Somers* had weighed anchor at Wallabout Bay to begin her fateful cruise.

At his death, the commander was forty-five years old.

As for Washington Irving, that great author would live another decade and longer, nearby at Sunnyside—he who had been born in the final year of the American Revolution surviving until the very eve of the Civil War, long enough to suffer at the last through weeks and weeks of an asthmatic indisposition that tormented his rest in his seventy-seventh year. "One of his favorite books during his long illness," according to Irving's devoted nephew in attendance through those grim, closing months of 1859, "was Slidell's *Year in Spain*. He read it again and again. Its graphic pictures seemed to carry him back to pleasant scenes, and out of himself. . . ."

No further references to Mackenzie the naval officer survive among Washington Irving's papers; but the spirit of the young lieutenant whom he had known in Madrid was with the world-beloved author to the end. For to the very last Irving relished *A Year in Spain*. "When reading to him," the nephew goes on, "as we did constantly to produce sleep"—on the sofa in the parlor at Sunnyside, or upstairs in the withered old gentleman's modest bedroom—"we always avoided it, as we found it excited his imagination and roused rather than soothed": that book of travels that would guide an aged mind restlessly back to its unenfeebled prime, to those sun-flooded days in Madrid when Washington Irving was still on his far-flung wanderings, when Slidell Mackenzie was young still—and scarcely tested—long before either had sought out a haven at Tarrytown.

NOTES

Within citations generally, punctuation, spelling, and capitalization have been altered as appropriate to conform to current usage; in all cases, diction and syntax have been left unchanged. Full titles of the sources to which the notes refer appear on pages 291–296.

Epigraph. *Proc CI*, 30, 18, 32, 28, 30, 27, 25.

PROLOGUE

PAGE
3   "The society of the Americans." Longfellow to his father, 3–20–1827. Longfellow, *Life*, I 108. Longfellow arrived in Madrid March 6 and left for the south of Spain in early September.
3   "The unhappiest of my life." [Slidell], *Year in Spain*, I 93. The account of the robbery and murder, from which citations in the text are taken, is at 88–98.
6   Spectacle "of deep and painful interest." Same, I 336. Citations from 336–53.
7   "Fidelity of a Flemish picture." Irving, Review, 320.
8   "Countryman . . . in search of instruction." [Slidell], *Year in Spain*, I 355. The trip is described at 355–413. Cf. Longfellow's account in letters to his mother and sister; Longfellow, *Life*, I 110–16.
9   "A youthful, kind, and happy spirit." Irving, Review, 320–21.

SLIDELL

10   "Best street . . . in America." Mason, "Diary," 8.
11   "Topsy-turvy rantipole city." Irving, *Oldstyle, Salmagundi*, 186–87, 211.
11   "A man of great intelligence." Duyckinck, *Cyclopaedia*, II 361. The citation that follows is from the same source, same page.
11   Slidell's family. See Barrett, *Old Merchants*, 257 ff, and Willson, *Slidell*, 9. On the future Louisiana politician see Willson's work and Sears's. Price, who died in 1840, was to be involved in other duels; Haswell, 346–47.
11   "Not at all precocious." Duyckinck, II 361.
12   "A chicken gets his breakfast." [Slidell], *England*, I ix.
12   "The last halloo." [Slidell], *Year in Spain*, I 30. Irving's juvenile letter is in Irving, *Oldstyle, Salmagundi*, 8–11.
12   "A distance of five hundred miles." Slidell Mackenzie, *Perry*, I 132. The battle and its context (including preparations aboard the *Lawrence*) are described at 132–261. On Lake Erie see also Paullin's *Documents* (including quotations here from Perry and Commodore Barclay), and Dutton's *Perry*, 144–81.
14   "The courage . . . of a single man." Henry Adams, *History*, VII 126. Cf. "The splendour of this victory dazzles the imagination. It was gained by a portion of an inferior squadron over another every way superior, and throughout the action concentrated in its force. It was gained, more eminently than any other naval victory, by the exertions of one individual, a young man of twenty-seven, who had never beheld a naval engagement." Slidell Mackenzie, *Perry*, I 258–59.
14   "Perry on his periodical visits." Slidell Mackenzie, *Perry*, II 96, 242. The biographer's "exaggeration even reaches to the stature of his hero, who he says was of the 'loftiest.' This is pretty well for a man who was about five feet ten!" J. F. Cooper to W. B. Shubrick, 4–13–1841. Beard, *Letters and Journals*, IV 148.
15   Slidell's earliest days at sea. Slidell Mackenzie, *Perry*, II 107–10, 144–45. A letter in Captain Perry's handwriting, from Port Mahon, 3–6–1816, to Commodore John Rodgers, survives as confirmation of the rigors of the just completed voyage: "I had one of the most boisterous passages across the Atlantic that you can conceive—a continued gale from the time I left Nantucket Shoals drove us in fourteen days within a hundred miles of Cape St. Vincent; here I lost my maintopmast, and a gale coming on with great violence from the westward compelled me to lie to for two days. Still, I made a passage in twenty days from port to port." Library of Congress, Naval Historical Foundation Collection, Rodgers Family papers (Series I).
16   "He daily visited them." Slidell Mackenzie, *Perry*, II 144–45.
16   "Letters written at sixteen and seventeen." Duyckinck, II 361.
17   "The *age of piracy*." *Niles' Weekly Register*, 10–20–1821; quoted in Philbrick, *Cooper and Sea Fiction*, 88. Other citations to the end of the section are also in Philbrick. Concerning West Indian duty at this time see Calkins, "Repression of Piracy." Allen, *Our Navy*, gives additional instances, from contemporary reports, of horrifying piratical outrages, along with a vivid account of the arduousness of naval duty in the Caribbean, "in the small schooners and in open boats—in a severe climate—exposed to the heat of a tropical sun by day and to the not less dangerous dews and exhalations at night. The vessels themselves, from their size, were destitute of suitable accommodations, and the operations in which they were engaged"—in pur-

suit up jungle rivers and the like—"necessarily imposed incessant fatigue and constant exposure" (p. 54). On Irving's brush with pirates see Irving, *Letters,* I 145–48.

18 "Confined on board a small vessel." Slidell Mackenzie, *Perry,* II 199.

18 "Died Oliver Hazard Perry." Same, 224. Slidell's appointment as lieutenant is dated 1–13–1825; Callahan, *Officers,* 344.

19 "My motives for going to a country." [Slidell], *Year in Spain,* I 5. Citations that follow are from the preface, v–vi, vii.

19 "He has been robbed." Irving to Mrs. Thomas Wentworth Storrow, 5–5–1827; Irving, *Letters,* II 232–33.

19 "Determined to return home." Slidell to Longfellow, 7–7–1827. Houghton Library, Harvard University.

20 "I enclose the charts." Irving to Slidell, 12–1–1827. Houghton Library.

20 "From the same intelligent source." Irving, *Columbus,* III 307 (Appendix XVI).

20 "Perpetrate a book." [Slidell], *England,* I ix.

20 "The land of literature." Irving to Slidell, 2–16–1828. Houghton Library.

21 "I am going to the country." Slidell to Longfellow, 6–30–1828. Houghton Library.

21 "This wonder of wonders." Slidell to Longfellow, at Paris, 2–15–1829. Houghton Library. (Table Rock, on which Slidell and thousands of other tourists had stood, broke loose and plunged into the abyss June 25, 1850.)

21 "Difficulty in getting a publisher." Irving, from Puerto Sta. Maria, to Slidell, 10–22–1828. Houghton Library. The letter thanks Slidell "for the pains you have taken to give me an account of the success of my life of Columbus" in America.

21 "Explore the Antarctic region." Slidell to Longfellow, at Paris, 2–15–1829. Houghton Library. For problems in getting the Polar Expedition organized, see Mill, *Siege,* 212–13. Discussions of the expedition are in *Proceedings of the American Philosophical Society* (Philadelphia), issue for June 1940. For Wilkes as Ahab, see Jaffé, "Portrait of Ahab."

22 "Soon to be great doings." Slidell to Longfellow, 2–15–1829. Houghton Library.

22 "The reign of King MOB." Quoted in Parton, *Jackson,* III 170. The crowds at the inauguration, "like the inundation of northern barbarians into Rome," are described at 169–72.

22 "It makes me . . . very melancholy." Longfellow, from Bowdoin, to Slidell, 10–15–1829. Houghton Library. Longfellow reached New York 8–11–1829 and went on to Boston six days later; Thompson, *Young Longfellow,* 146. He returned to New York for a visit with Slidell the following month; "I saw so little of you here in September," Slidell, in New York, was writing "My Dear Don Enrique" at Bowdoin, 11–17–1829. Houghton Library.

23 "My feeble and untutored efforts." Slidell to Longfellow, 11–17–1829. The citation that follows, from aboard the *Brandywine,* is from a letter of Slidell's to Longfellow dated New York, 2–20–1830. Both letters are at Houghton Library.

23 "Terrible cutting and slashing work." Irving to Slidell, 3–5–1831. Houghton Library. Citations that follow are from the same letter. The history of the various editions of *A Year in Spain* and an examination of the changes that Irving made in the American text appear in McClary, "British Edition." McClary points out that apparently the publisher Murray never paid Slidell so much as a farthing, nor did Irving receive anything for his efforts. McClary, 374. *A Year in Spain* was soon translated into Swedish.

24 "The fashionable book of the day." Quoted in Duyckinck, II 361. See also Pierre Irving, *Life and Letters*, II 450, quoting a letter to Irving's brother in New York, in which Washington Irving requests that Slidell's father (whom the expatriate author obviously knew) be furnished with copies of the book and of the favorable review in the *Quarterly*, "with my kind regards."

24 "Scrupulously honest man." Letter in the *New York Evening Post*, 1-11-1843. The correspondent mentions that the elder Slidell "was, at one time, wealthy; but before his death, lost his property and became the secretary of an insurance company." (Hence his naval son's impecuniousness, as noted by Irving in a letter quoted later in the text, page 31.)

24 "He felt all to be well." Reverend Manton Eastburn to Slidell, undated letter (1832) at Houghton Library.

24 Awaken more public passion. "No case of the century, prior to the assassination of President Lincoln, aroused as much interest and passion." Morison, *"Old Bruin,"* 160.

24 "Never slept out of a ship." [Slidell], *England*, I 62. The seven citations that follow are from the same source: I 21, xiv, xvi, II 107, I 212, II 237, 118 ("oculist"). During his dreary stay in England, Slidell was led at one point to reflect on "my inimitable friend, Geoffrey Crayon [Irving]; and would have given the world, in that moment of despondency, for one of his quiet unwritten jokes, or one friendly pressure of his hand." I 150-51. Notes from Irving to Slidell, reprinted in Irving, *Letters*, show that the two had renewed their friendship after Irving's return to America in 1832, and before Slidell's departure for England (III 773, 775).

26 "Service . . . of some difficulty." [Slidell], *England*, II 218.

26 "Joven anglo-americano teniente." [Slidell], *Spain Revisited*, I 375. The six citations that follow are from the same source: I 195, 196-97 ("my native city"), 353-54, 365, 367 (execution and reaction). Irving strongly recommended Slidell's new book on Spain to the publisher Murray: "It is capital. As minute and graphic and faithful as his *Year in Spain*, and, in my mind, superior in some respects." 2-24-1836. Irving, *Letters*, II 859-60. Murray declined, however, to publish the book; like *An American in England*, it was brought out by Bentley (the English publisher of Fenimore Cooper's works).

27 "Manners of Ireland." [Slidell], *England*, II 238-39. The author's papers, including this manuscript, are either dispersed or no longer survive. Somewhere, to be sure, may be a trunk containing the account of the trip to Ireland, the manuscript of Slidell's journey from Seville to Granada, a copy of a pamphlet he wrote from the Brazil station in the 1830s (one of those latter may be among the Charles H. Davis papers), as well as material— copies of Philip Spencer's letters and the like—mentioned at later periods of this naval officer's far-ranging life. Of Slidell's three sons, two died in the nineteenth century; the third, Rear Admiral Morris R. Mackenzie, lived on at Morristown, New Jersey, until his death in 1915. That had been the town to which the admiral's mother had moved soon after his father's death. Had she taken her husband's papers with her? Did her youngest son, who grew up in Morristown and retired there in old age, retain the papers and manuscripts? "The surrogate's office at the Morris County Court House has a copy of [Morris Mackenzie's] will. His heirs are so numerous, most of them in Europe, that the surrogate's office stated that it would be necessary for someone to copy the information. We regret that we do not have the time to do this for you" (letter from a reference librarian at

the Joint Free Public Library of Morristown and Morris Township, New Jersey, 4–2–1957, answering a query about Ranald Mackenzie). Admiral Morris Mackenzie left his personal effects to Captain Raymond Perry Rodgers, USN, who died in the 1920s. Through one of the numerous Rodgerses someone with patience and luck may yet locate the manuscripts and papers of Alexander Slidell and, using them, write the detailed biography that the present work does not aspire to be.

27 "Thraldom of a . . . man-of-war." [Slidell], *Spain Revisited*, dedicatory letter, I iii–vi. The citation that follows is from the same letter.

28 "Increased and increasing happiness." Slidell Mackenzie to Longfellow, 6–10–1843, responding to news of the poet's impending marriage. The citation that follows is from a letter to Longfellow dated 7–13–1843. Both at Houghton Library. (Mrs. Mackenzie's age is based on the 1850 census for Morris Township, New Jersey, where she reports that she is thirty-five.)

28 General Grant's opinion of Ranald Mackenzie. Cited in Wallace, "Border Warrior," 22.

28 "The circle of my unambitious hopes." [Slidell], *England*, I 125.

29 "Apollo of the press." Crouthamel, *Webb*, 81. For Webb's eventful life, see Crouthamel's study and Andrews's. (The editor moved from Long Island to Tarrytown in 1838.)

29 Slidell's name-change. The petition, in Slidell's handwriting, is dated aboard the U.S. ship *Independence*, Portsmouth, England, 7–1–1837; the request was granted 1–5–1838. Historical Society of Pennsylvania.

29 "I got the *Dolphin* under way." *Proc CI*, 28–29. On Brazil at this time, see Haring, *Empire*.

30 "Their lives upon the sea." Duyckinck, II 361.

30 "Disgustful surroundings." [Slidell], *England*, II 143. The two citations that follow are from the same source, same page.

30 Irving's visit to the Mackenzies. Irving to Sarah Storrow, 5–3–1841; Irving, *Letters*, III 88. Morison points out that officers in the nineteenth-century navy "enjoyed no great social status," and that their meager pay and the uncertainty of their career (most were discharged at the end of hostilities) made them poor catches as husbands. Morison, *"Old Bruin,"* 51.

31 "Digging . . . in a new garden." Mackenzie to Longfellow, 4–23–1841. The citation that follows is from an earlier letter to Longfellow, also from Tarrytown, dated 2–28–1840. Both at Houghton Library.

32 "March in with a more lofty step." Longfellow, from Cambridge, Mass., to "My dear Slidell," at Tarrytown, 5–31–1840. Houghton Library.

32 "Menaced with the high displeasure." Mackenzie to John Gorham Palfrey, editor of *The North American Review*, 3–29–1841. Houghton Library.

32 "A cure for Sue's eyes." Cooper to his wife, 1–29–1837. Beard, *Letters and Journals*, III 256.

33 "A rum time of it." Cooper, *Ned Myers*, 19.

33 "Button on to those waters." Cooper to Daniel Dobbins, 5–20–1843. Beard, *Letters and Journals*, IV 384. Perry's achievement at the Battle of Lake Erie "awakens no admiration in the breast of Mr. Cooper, of that individual whose peculiar notions of chivalry, when himself an officer in the American navy, indicated the near approach of war with England as a fit season for abandoning the service of his country." Slidell Mackenzie, *Perry*, II 276. Mackenzie, by contrast, had (according to Duyckinck's account, based on information furnished by Mrs. Mackenzie) cut short his own stay in Europe in the 1830s to return home, at a time of tension between America and

France, in order to put his professional skills to the service of his country. As it happened, the crisis had passed before his country was required to call on those skills. Duyckinck, II 361; Catherine Mackenzie, Biographical Sketch, 4.

34 "The value of a good wife." Cooper to Horatio Greenough, 7–1–1838. Beard, *Letters and Journals*, III 328.

34 "Testimony of their high respect." Quoted in Beard, *Letters and Journals*, I 84.

35 "A very 'castle of a man.'" Irving to Rufus Griswold, 9–18–1851; *Memorial of Cooper*, 7.

35 "The aristocracy of Great Britain." Cooper, *Critical Essays*, 140. Waples attributes Cooper's dislike of Irving to the latter's Toryism; Cooper's irritation at being called the American Scott arose, she plausibly maintains, from the same source. Waples, *Whig Myth*, 57.

35 "All enthusiasm about this book." Quoted in Beard, *Letters and Journals*, IV 306–7. On Cooper's opinion of Irving see also Williams, *Irving*, II 54–57 and *passim*.

36 "What I think of *them*." Cooper to Rufus Griswold, 8–7–1842. Beard, *Letters and Journals*, IV 306. The Reverend Mr. Griswold was at the time the twenty-six-year-old editor of *Graham's Magazine;* later he would serve as Poe's executor and the vilifier of his name. But for now Griswold was professionally close to Cooper. His magazine published, in October 1842, disagreeable and inaccurate charges of literary self-promotion against Irving, then abroad in Madrid as American ambassador. Given the timing, could Cooper have been innocent of involvement, either directly or indirectly, in the episode? See Pierre Irving, *Life and Letters*, III 264–73.

37 "Feelings of regret, pity, contempt." Outland reprints the entire review. Outland, "Libels," 69–77.

37 "A notorious huckster woman." *Courier & Enquirer*, 4–14–1841; quoted in Outland, "Libels," 222.

37 "A series of libellous falsehoods." Cooper to W. C. Bryant, for the *Evening Post*, 11–22–1838. Beard, *Letters and Journals*, III 350–51.

38 "I have beaten every man." As paraphrased in Bryant, "Discourse," 62; Cooper to J. Hunt, Jr., 2–28–1843, printed in the *Cincinnati Gazette:* ". . . depend upon it, sir, I shall beat him [Greeley] again, as I have every man I have sued who has not retracted his libels." Quoted in Waples, *Whig Myth*, 234–35.

38 "A hook into the nose." Bryant, "Discourse," 62. Outland's "Libels" recounts Cooper's quarrels with the press in lively detail.

39 "This book will not disappoint you." Cooper to Richard Bentley, 12–6–1837; Beard, *Letters and Journals*, III 302. See same, I 140, quoting Cooper's farewell speech to the Bread and Cheese Club, 5–29–1826, before his departure for Europe: ". . . if there be a man in this community who owes a debt to the Muse of History, it would seem to be the one who now has the honor to address you. No writer of our country has invaded her sacred precincts with greater license or more frequency. Sir, I have not been unmindful of the weight of my transgressions in this particular, and I have long and seriously reflected on the means of presenting an expiatory offering before the altar of the offended Goddess. . . ."

39 "Never worked half as hard in my life." Cooper to James DePeyster Ogden, 1–30–1839. Beard, *Letters and Journals*, III 366. The three citations from Cooper's letters that follow are from the same volume: 427 ("first and

last," 9–27–1839); 437 ("$500 a year," 10–19–1839); 430 ("best hit," 10–5–1839). All three letters are directed to Mrs. Cooper.

40   "Unfair account of . . . Lake Erie." [Slidell Mackenzie], "Cooper's *Naval History*," 450. About a third of the review, twelve of the thirty-five pages, concerns Lake Erie; fifteen of the remaining pages concern the need for reforms in the navy.

40   "I'll tell you." Elliott, "Address," 9, note.

40   "Almost superfluous to speak." Slidell Mackenzie, *Perry*, I 275. The Perry side of the quarrel is documented in Mackenzie's biography, which includes correspondence in 1818 between the contending officers; II 161–79. A concise examination of the controversy as a whole is in Lounsbury, *Cooper*, 208–30.

41   "Merit my warmest approbation." Perry to Elliott, 9–19–1813; Slidell Mackenzie, *Perry*, I 286 (source prints "meet" for "merit"). The three citations that follow are from the same source: I 288 ("elated with our success"); II 166 ("humiliating"), 168 ("pretending to be sick," from Newport, 6–18–1818).

41   "Epistolary blackguardism." Elliott, from Norfolk, to Perry, 7–7–1818. Slidell Mackenzie, *Perry*, II 169.

41   "Able to exculpate yourself." Same, 171.

42   Holmes's poem. "Old Ironsides" was originally published 9–16–1830, in the *Boston Daily Advertiser;* Holmes was then twenty-one.

42   Perry's version. The account is that of Purser Samuel Hambleton, in his journal, as related to him by Perry on the evening of the battle. Slidell Mackenzie, *Perry*, I 250.

43   Elliott's version. Elliott, "Address," 7–9. The unattributed apology (by Russell Jarvis) that was published in the wake of events of 1834 is entitled *A Biographical Notice of Com. Jesse D. Elliott, Containing a Review of the Controversy between Him and the Late Commodore Perry . . .* (Philadelphia, 1835).

43   "Elliott was a very odd fish." Morison, *"Old Bruin,"* 49.

43   "Machinations and falsehoods." Matthew Perry to Cooper, 3–13–1839; Cooper, *Correspondence*, I 386. For one, Perry's Tarrytown neighbor James Watson Webb had announced in the *Courier & Enquirer* of 1–26–1839 that the part of Cooper's work dealing with Lake Erie "is, we understand, to be dictated by Elliott; and if so, the fame of the gallant Perry will doubtless be blackened and injured to the full extent that two such congenial spirits can detract from it."

44   "Not in a fit state." Cooper to John Holmes Prentiss for the *Freeman's Journal*, 7–2–1839. Beard, *Letters and Journals*, III 411.

44   "The quarrels of the Navy." Cooper to *Freeman's Journal*, 7–2–1839. Beard, *Letters and Journals*, III 407. The two citations that follow are from the same volume: 388 ("disgrace the service," to W. B. Shubrick, 6–14–1839) and 386 ("petty quarrels," to James DePeyster Ogden, 6–11–1839).

44   "Doctor Grant Champlin Perry." Slidell Mackenzie, *Perry*, I iii.

45   "Inconsistency, and love of paradox." *New York Commercial Advertiser*, 6–8–1839. Continuations of the review appear in issues of June 11, 14, and 19.

46   "A loser of several thousands." Cooper to William Gilmore Simms, 1–5–1844; Beard, *Letters and Journals*, IV 438. The four citations that follow are from the same volume: 357 ("into the fire," to John Beauchamp Jones, for the *Madisonian*, 2–4–1843); 345 ("much belied," to Rufus Griswold, 1–10/18–1843); 187 (*"want* of controversy," to David Conner, 11–7–1841); 206 ("a precious fellow," to W. B. Shubrick, 12–7–1841).

47 Elliott lectures. Elliott, "Address," 12, 14–15.
47 "Stone has libelled me." Cooper to Jesse Duncan Elliott, 6–19–1842; Beard, *Letters and Journals*, IV 294. The citations that follow and end the chapter are from the same volume, 298.

THE *SOMERS*

48 Mackenzie's promotion. He was made a commander 9–8–1841; Callahan, *Officers*, 344.
50 "Born to rule the seas." Quoted in Philbrick, 260. I am indebted to Philbrick's stimulating work for numerous insights concerning the role that the navy played in American life early in the nineteenth century.
52 "I gave him my hand." Mackenzie's narrative; *Proc CM*, 196. The three citations that follow are from the same source, same page. On Gansevoort and Melville, see Anderson, *South Seas*, 16–17.
53 "Haughtiness of his manner." Proctor, "Spencer," 307. The John Duer who aided Spencer in revising the statutes of New York State would become Mackenzie's uncle by marriage, the gentleman to whom that naval officer would dedicate *The American in England*, and one of the attorneys who would serve as Mackenzie's defense counsel in his later court-martial. Butler, too, would have a small role to play in the trial, on Spencer's side; see page 183 of the present text.
53 Philip's two brothers. During Mackenzie's forthcoming ordeals in naval courts, efforts were made to show that Philip Spencer's brothers were dissolute. Mackenzie himself, in an unpublished letter to Lieutenant Oscar Bullus dated 6–3–1843, at the New-York Historical Society, suggested that one brother, Ambrose, was at this very time engaged in piracy in the Gulf of Mexico; and Francis Lieber reported that another "forged the father's name and was actually all ready to be put on trial." But see the letter by "W" (Thurlow Weed?) to the *National Intelligencer* of 12–24–1842, identifying young Ambrose as a practicing lawyer and John C. Spencer, Jr., as not "an inmate of the Sing Sing prison," as some in the press were then charging, but rather an "exemplary, estimable, and virtuous" member of the ship's company aboard a naval vessel commanded by his uncle in the Mediterranean. Hayford, *Somers*, 179, 13. That John, Jr., was indeed aboard the *Columbus* is confirmed by Parker, *Recollections*, 17. On the elder Spencer's daughter in maturity, see the charming entry in Adams, *Memoirs*, XII 60–61 (6–20–1844).
53 "A high-toned courtesy toward the bar." Proctor, "Spencer," 311. The citation that follows is from the same source, 309.
54 "Very quick to learn." Testimony of I. H. McCollum, a classmate of Spencer's at Geneva College. Quoted in Chaille, "Philip Spencer," 74.
54 Descriptions of J. C. Spencer: "Quick-rolling" quoted in *Dict. Am. Biog.*: "John Canfield Spencer." Adams, *Memoirs*, XI 335–36 (3–10–1843). Other citations in Proctor, "Spencer," 307, 305.
55 "Free from personal vices." Proctor, "Spencer," 325. The citations that follow, concerning Spencer's bride, are from the same source, 312, 313. "Keen sarcasm" from Proctor, 329; pamphlets mentioned at 317.
56 "A man of extraordinary capacity." Tyler, *Letters and Times*, II 397.

56 "Severe and ardent labor." Proctor, "Spencer," 334–35.
57 "Struggling with all his strength." Greene, *Broken Seal*, 95. Sightings of Morgan at 235. Valence's confession quoted at 296–99.
58 "Concealment of the most atrocious crimes." Greene, *Broken Seal*, 241.
59 "The nation's pledge of protection." Same, 237.
59 "A universal excitement." Adams, *Memoirs*, VII 345 (10–25–1827).
59 "Your own blood will run." Proctor, "Spencer," 342.
60 "I am practically disavowed." The text of Spencer's letter of resignation is in Greene, 280–86. *A Narrative of the Facts* provides a contemporary account of the Morgan affair, hostile to Masonry. For the occurrence as viewed by a twentieth-century writer partial to Masons, see Mock, *Morgan Episode*.
60 "Have my throat cut across." Spencer, "Portrait of Masonry," 20. Spencer's seven-page attack on the order, signed "PHOCION," is dated 2–20–1832.
60 "Blasphemous mockeries of order." Spencer, "Portrait of Masonry," 20. The quotations that follow to the end of the section are from the same source, 23.
61 "Stern and darksome thought." Samuel B. Judah, *The Buccaneers* (1827), I 214–15; quoted in Philbrick, 301.
61 "Bitter, relentless fate!" *Ramon*, 110. The three citations that follow are from the same source, same page.
62 "Sick of these terra firma toils." Melville, *White-Jacket*, 428.
62 "Religious example and culture enough." R. C. R., "Reminiscences," 25.
62 "His manner was remarkably good." Quoted in Chaille, "Philip Spencer," 74. In later life Paul Cooper recalled that young Spencer was "by far the best declaimer I have ever heard with the exception of one or two men whose reputation is national." Same.
62 "A participant in the cider disturbance." The college records were examined by a Professor Charles D. Vail; the results are given in Chaille, 75. The three citations that follow are from the same source. Another classmate of Spencer's at Geneva had occasion later to remember the young man, whom he had boarded with during the winter of 1838–39, as possessed of "little force of character. He was easily led into schemes of mischief, but I do not remember any in which he was a leader. He was entirely wanting in self-respect. His deportment was unpleasant; he was very irascible, though more of a talker than a doer. His word could not be depended upon. I then regarded him in a somewhat humorous light, to be laughed at rather than positively hated, and this was his general estimation among his fellow students." George Duyckinck, from New York, to Alexander Slidell Mackenzie, 1–12–1843. Rare Books and Manuscripts Division, New York Public Library.
63 "Remains there with his name in it." *Proc CI*, 45. Andrew Dickson White saw the inscribed volume, "shown as a great curiosity," eight years later, when he attended the college briefly as a student. White's recollections of Geneva make the place sound appalling. He witnessed, for example, lecturers being pelted with boots and brushes and the like, and "even the president himself, on one occasion, obliged to leave his lecture-room by a ladder from a window, and, on another, kept at bay by a shower of beer-bottles." White explains that the authorities of the college "could not afford to expel or even offend a student, for its endowment was so small that it must have all the instruction fees possible, and must keep on good terms with the wealthy fathers of its scapegrace students." About forty young men attended while he was there, in 1849, "the majority of them, sons of wealthy

churchmen, showing no inclination to work and much tendency to dissipation." White, *Autobiography*, I 18–20.

63 "Murderous stories and tales of blood." *Proc CI*, 45. The citation that follows is from the same source, same page.

63 Refusing "to be bound or held." McCollum's testimony, quoted in Chaille, 74.

64 "A fixed, staring look." *New York Evening Post*, 1–7–1843.

64 "Pirate, freebooter or buccaneer." I. H. McCullom's recollection, quoted in Van De Water, 30.

64 Spencer at Union College. The acquaintance was James Lafayette Witherspoon; citations are from his recollections, quoted in Chaille, 75.

64 Craney's account of Spencer. Citations in the section are from Dana, *Journal*, I 150–52 (4–25–1843), and an anonymous article in the *New York Tribune* of 12–21–1842, almost certainly by Craney himself. Incidentally, the captain of the *North Carolina* at the time was Captain Francis Gregory, not Perry, who was commandant of the navy yard. Young William Parker, who joined the *North Carolina* in the fall of 1841, describes life aboard the receiving ship in Parker, *Recollections*, 2–5. Among his messmates was Spencer; "I remember him as a tall, pale, delicate-looking young man of perhaps nineteen years of age. . . ." One who had become acquainted with Spencer aboard the whaler loading at Nantucket during the summer confirmed the young man's delicacy of appearance, and insisted later that he had given "entire satisfaction to the officers and owners" during his couple of weeks there. Moreover, Spencer had endeared himself to his shipmates as well, "by his amiable disposition and acts of kindness." It was generally known that the new member of the whaling crew was the son of the secretary of war, according to the same source, who concluded, "The fact is he was a very delicate, affectionate looking youth, and in his *most* 'ferocious moments' could not have scared any man who could lift a fifty-six pound weight." Letter to *The Boston Courier*, 12–27–1842.

68 Craney's earlier dismissal from the navy. Hayford, *Somers*, 163, note. Hayford's casebook relating to the *Somers* affair is a valuable resource; documents in it have been judiciously selected and scrupulously transcribed. (A *passed midshipman*, incidentally, was a warrant officer who had passed an examination after sufficient time at sea, and was consequently in line to be promoted to a lieutenancy when a vacancy in the overcrowded ranks occurred; indeed, he was qualified to do a lieutenant's duties, and was paid $750 a year, as compared with the $400 annual payment to a midshipman. The insignia of a passed midshipman placed a star within the gold lace on the collar. The rank was abolished in 1862. Benjamin, 104.)

68 Spencer's letter to Commodore Perry. National Archives, 826.

68 Rogers and Spencer in Rio. R. C. R., "Reminiscences," 24–29. The author had been made a midshipman in 1839 and resigned from the navy, as an acting master, in January 1854; Callahan, *Officers*, 472.

70 "I did it considering it my duty." National Archives, 831. Citations that follow to the end of the section are from the same source: Spencer to Morris, 834; "Return to the U. States," 832; letter to his brother, 833; Upshur to Spencer, 838 (8–6–1842); Spencer's orders, 836. The fullest account of Upshur's life is in R. G. Adams, "Upshur."

72 Dickens on New York in 1842. Dickens, *American Notes*, 91–111. On the dinner for Dickens, see Tuckerman, *Hone*, II 118–19, and Pierre Irving, *Life and Letters*, III 184–85.

74 "Mr. Accidental President Tyler." Nevins, *Hone*, II 563, 561. Both Hone and the editor Webb have been credited with applying to the new party the name *Whig*, to suggest opposition to encroachments of the executive; specifically, of President Jackson. See Waples, *Whig Myth*, 35. Webb's exasperation with Tyler would hardly have been assuaged by the President's refusal to appoint him postmaster of New York City, a position that Webb had coveted and expected.

75 "The most astonished man in . . . New York." Pierre Irving, *Life and Letters*, III 176.

75 "The secret of Irving's appointment." Beard, *Letters and Journals*, IV 252 (3–22–1842).

75 "Somers is ready." Cooper to Rufus Griswold; same, IV 301.

76 "A watchword in the American Navy." Cooper, *Naval Officers*, I 122.

76 *"He will be demolished."* Cooper to Jesse Duncan Elliott; Beard, *Letters and Journals*, IV 295.

76 "As broad as the charges." The retraction is reprinted in Cooper, *Correspondence*, II 486–87.

76 "A good deal of fun." Cooper, from New York City, to Mrs. Cooper, 6–28–1842. Beard, *Letters and Journals*, IV 297.

77 "His sleepless industry." Tyler, *Letters and Times*, II 398.

77 "Respectability and éclat." *Courier & Enquirer*, 12–10–1842.

78 "Fifty-six closely printed pages." *New York Herald*, 9–7–1842.

79 "Perpendicular threads." [Slidell], *England*, I 24. The newspaper items have been drawn from issues of the *Herald* and *Tribune* for early September 1842.

VOYAGE

The narrative of the voyage and mutiny emerges from two sources: from testimony after the cruise by personnel of the *Somers* before, first, the court of inquiry and, second, the court-martial. In this and the following chapter, where the text makes clear who is speaking, I have not taken space to locate citations by *Proc CI* or *Proc CM* (Proceedings of the Court of Inquiry or of the Court-Martial). In such obvious instances, a given quotation will be seen to appear in that speaker's testimony before one of the two courts. Mackenzie's own version of events is contained for the most part in his extended account to the secretary of the navy, dated December 19, 1842, read into the record at the court of inquiry (and imperfectly reported by the press), then reprinted in *Proc CM*, 194–211. The notes here refer to that document as "Mackenzie's narrative."

82 "Those *children*." Mary A. Gansevoort (the first lieutenant's mother) to Peter Gansevoort, 1–2–1843, quoting her son. Leyda, *Melville Log*, I 161.

82 "Some very small." Wales's testimony; *Proc CI*, 18.

83 "Sail from New York so full." *Proc CI*, 43. Testimony of Commander Joshua R. Sands, under whose supervision the vessel was fitted out. Dimensions of the *Somers* from this source, and from Sands's testimony before the court-martial, *Proc CM*, 150.

83 Shipboard routines. Melville's *White-Jacket* describes in detail life aboard an American man-of-war during this period. To evoke routines at sea, I have borrowed from that rich source, as well as from such contemporaneous works as [Henry James Mercier's] *Life in a Man-of-War*, Charles Nordhoff's *Man-of-War Life*, and Dana's *Two Years Before the Mast*.

85 The colt. At the court-martial Gansevoort testified that punishment with the colt (unlike the cat) was through the clothing, not on the bare back; *Proc CM*, 59. This was usual in the navy. A training ship would, of course, see that the salutary effects of all sorts of punishment aboard were maximized.

85 Of "good character." Punishments aboard the brig are taken from the *New York Herald* for 1–14–1843. The *Herald* was one of several papers that reprinted appropriate notations from the log, surreptitiously made available to the press after the *Somers* had returned home. Alongside some of the names of those punished, such evaluations as "good character" were entered not by a member of the *Somers*'s company but by someone who had known individuals of the crew earlier aboard the receiving ship *North Carolina*. (In some instances the names and punishments as given in the *Herald* are all but illegible on the microfilm. I have done what I could to reproduce them accurately—and stand by the general representation of those punishments as reliable.)

86 Opinions ashore of Mackenzie. Lieber's quoted in Morison, "*Old Bruin*," 145. Sumner's to Dr. Samuel G. Howe, 9–14–1843; Pierce, *Sumner*, II 270. Felton's to Lieber, 9–17–1843; quoted in Hayford, *Somers*, 181. Dana's in his journal, 9–19–1843; Dana, *Journal*, I 218.

86 "A strict and exacting commander." Slidell Mackenzie, *Perry*, II 126. (Source reads "exact" for "exacting.")

86 "Dishes from his own table." Wales's testimony; *Proc CM*, 26–27.

86 "Slight and trivial complaints." Leecock's testimony; *Proc CI*, 30.

87 Cromwell's attack on Sears. *Proc CM*, 118–19 (Joseph Sears's testimony); *Proc CI*, 37 (Thomas Dickerson's testimony).

87 "Terrible little boys." Melville, *White-Jacket*, 374. (The term *midshipman* arises from the location aboard that such aspiring young officers occupied, amidships, to carry the captain's orders from aft forward to lieutenants commanding the various guns.)

88 Citations from the articles of war. *Proc CI*, 6.

89 "Continually intimate with the crew." Mackenzie's narrative; *Proc CI*, 9.

89 "Damned old humbug." *Proc CI*, 17, 31 (Wales's and Rodgers's testimony).

89 *He* could accommodate them." Wales's testimony; *Proc CI*, 19.

89 "Making music with his jaw." Mackenzie's narrative; *Proc CM*, 196.

91 "*Your time's damn short.*" Dickerson's testimony; *Proc CI*, 37.

92 "Wine of a rare value." Mackenzie's narrative; *Proc CM*, 195.

93 "Too much work out of the crew." Wales's testimony; *Proc CI*, 18. Mackenzie prided himself on his ability to work crews efficiently. By his own account, he had, when a young man of twenty (in 1823, before serving with Commodore Porter in the Caribbean), taken a furlough from the navy to assume command of a merchant vessel, "solely for the purpose of engaging in more responsible professional duties than my rank enabled me to perform in the Navy, and of learning the art, but little understood on board a man of war, of accomplishing a great deal of work with an inconsiderable force of men." Mackenzie to George Bancroft, secretary of the navy, 8–19–1846. Massachusetts Historical Society, Bancroft papers.

95 Punishments at the Canaries. As recorded in the *Somers*'s log and published subsequently in the *New York Herald*, 1–14–1843. References to punishments later in the chapter draw on the same source.

95 "Fresh from private life." *Proc CI*, 28. The question was posed by Commander Mackenzie.

97 Small's "carelessness of duty." Acting Master Perry's testimony; *Proc CM*,

67. If Small, like his officer crony, had been and would be careless in discharging his duties, the same could hardly be said of Midshipman Spencer's father, who at this very time was writing (October 19) from Washington to nine "friends of the administration" in western New York, in order regretfully to decline an invitation to visit them for the purpose of explaining his position in the present unpopular administration: "my duties at the seat of government forbid an absence so protracted as would be required to perform a journey" of such distance. But the letter, soon published as a thirty-page pamphlet, proceeds deftly to defend the secretary's reputation, "which is the property of my children, and to some extent of my country . . ." Spencer, "Correspondence," 5, 28.

99 Liberia. Details are drawn principally from Lugenbeel, *Sketches*, and Furbay, *Top Hats*. Morison it is who credits Perry with choosing the site for Monrovia; Morison, *"Old Bruin,"* 66. Knox gives then Lieutenant, later Captain, Robert Stockton the credit; Knox, 145.

101 "A very usual thing." Edward English's testimony; *Proc CM*, 85.

104 "A damned sight of humbug." Midshipman Hayes's testimony; *Proc CI*, 33.

105 "Marks pricked in his arms." *Proc CI*, 26. Many aboard the brig availed themselves of Green's aptitude. He tattooed on Garty's arm an eagle, on Warner's a ship, on McKinley's a female pirate with an American flag, on Wales's "a sort of free-mason's coat of arms." *Proc CM*, 219. By this time, incidentally, Spencer had abandoned his journal, which was to be kept by all midshipmen and submitted for the captain's perusal on Sundays; Tillotson noticed "that he had not written in it for some time, and I spoke about it, and he said, 'Damn the journal.'" *Proc CI*, 34.

MUTINY

See the clarification on page 272, at the start of the notes to the preceding chapter.

106 "So monstrous, so improbable." Mackenzie's narrative; *Proc CM*, 195.

106 "Converse on their joint duty." Same, 194.

106 Wales's reply to Spencer's questions. The purser's steward furnished his crucial testimony on numerous occasions: to Heiskell, 11–26–1842, the morning after Spencer had approached him, again to the council of officers aboard ship, 11–30–1842 (reprinted in *Proc CM*, 155–57), yet again at the court of inquiry, 12–30–1842 *(Proc CI*, 15 ff), finally at the court-martial, 2–6–1843 *(Proc CM*, 10 ff). The different versions contain discrepancies. The present account is taken principally from his testimony to the court of inquiry. (Before joining the *Somers* soon after her launching in the spring, Wales had been bookkeeper "for several years" for the New Bedford [Mass.] *Mercury*, according to the *Courier & Enquirer* of 12–26–1842; he was thus new to the sea.)

108 "My doubts vanished." Mackenzie's letter to the court of inquiry, 1–18–1843; Shufeldt, "Letter," 129. Having served in Commodore David Porter's squadron in the Caribbean, Mackenzie would have been well acquainted with that officer's experience with the only other approximation of a mutiny in the United States Navy. In 1813, in the Marquesas in the South Pacific (setting later of Melville's *Typee*), Porter had brought the *Essex*

NOTES TO PAGES 109-120 / 275

into Nookaheva Bay and was off the ship. In his absence several crewmen had talked of refusing to hoist anchor and sail from such a paradise—either that or seize the vessel a day or two under way and return to port. Back aboard, Porter made short work of the dereliction, exposing the ringleader and sternly driving him ashore. With that, disaffection ceased. Contrasts between the event and events surrounding the present mutinous conduct aboard the *Somers* are evident—as are the responses—yet the salutary effect of Porter's prompt action in the earlier incident could hardly have failed to visit Mackenzie's mind. For the Marquesas "mutiny," see Hunt, " 'Essex.' " Four later incidents of insubordination in the navy, in the 1970s—each racially motivated—are considered in Ryan, "*Constellation* Flare-up."

109   "Reading some piratical stories." Mackenzie's narrative; *Proc CM*, 195.

111   "Did not wish to do anything hastily." Gansevoort's testimony; *Proc CI*, 20.

111   Additional troubling information. Mackenzie's narrative, *Proc CM*, 195; Wales's testimony, *Proc CI*, 16.

111   Rodgers's "speedy and violent death." *Proc CM*, 196. This young man can be evoked rather more clearly than some of his shipmates. A member of a distinguished naval clan, Henry (Hal) Rodgers is recalled as a boy in a vivid family memoir quoted in Paullin, *Rodgers*, 368–82. He was serving as a lieutenant aboard the sloop-of-war *Albany* when the ship sailed from Aspinwall, Panama, September 29, 1854, enroute to New York; the *Albany* was never heard from again. Letters from his mother to members of the family during that latter, sad period are in the Rodgers Family papers at the Library of Congress.

112   Wales's earlier differences with the captain. Wales was not on trial, of course; neither court pressed for an explanation of what those differences were. "Did you have any difficulty with Commander Mackenzie at Porto Rico, and what was it?" "I had a difficulty, but decline explaining it." *Proc CM*, 23.

113   The arrest. The account draws primarily upon Mackenzie's narrative and Gansevoort's testimony. Here the captain's adjectives describing Spencer's manner at the arrest—"deferential," "smiling," "unmoved"—are relied upon, although it is worth noting that Gansevoort "thought Mr. Spencer appeared confused. He said 'No—it was all a joke.' " *Proc CI*, 20. On Small's interrogation at the arrest, see Midshipman Egbert Thompson's testimony; *Proc CM*, 185.

113   "Appeared willing to submit." Wales's testimony; *Proc CI*, 16.

114   "No suspicious collections of individuals." Mackenzie's narrative; *Proc CM*, 197.

114   "The two oldest and most useful." Same, 196.

116   "*I'll pay you for this before long.*" Gansevoort's testimony; *Proc CI*, 21.

116   "God damn the jib." Gansevoort's testimony; *Proc CM*, 54.

117   Cromwell and Small at inspection. Mackenzie's narrative; *Proc CM*, 198.

117   "Playing them false." *Proc CI*, 16. Wales's early version, before the council of officers aboard ship within five days of the event itself, makes no mention of Cromwell except once in passing, as a crony of Spencer's. *Proc CM*, 155–57.

118   Church service. Mackenzie's narrative; *Proc CM*, 198.

118   "Health, activity, intelligence and spirit." *Proc CM*, 162.

118   "One of the best . . . apprentices." Mackenzie's narrative; *Proc CM*, 198. The account of the shattered mast that follows is Mackenzie's.

120   "The season of danger." Mackenzie's narrative; *Proc CM*, 199. The descrip-

tion of Cromwell's arrest follows Gansevoort's testimony. In one perhaps telling detail the captain's version of the same event differs from it: "as his [Cromwell's] voice was heard in the top descending the rigging, *I met him at the foot of the jacob's-ladder* surrounded by the officers, guided him aft on the quarter-deck, and caused him to sit down . . ." (italics added). Mackenzie's narrative; *Proc CM*, 199.

121 "All the officers . . . armed." Gansevoort's testimony; *Proc CI*, 21.

121 "Pointed out by an associate." Mackenzie's narrative; *Proc CM*, 199.

123 "Not right to put them in irons." *Proc CI*, 37.

124 "Crimes of considerable magnitude." Mackenzie's narrative; *Proc CM*, 199.

124 "Mumbling out threats." Dickerson's testimony. *Proc CI*, 37.

124 "Suppressed indignation." Melville, *White-Jacket*, 489. The citations that follow are from the same source. Melville's book is an account of his cruise as a seaman aboard a man-of-war, on his way home from adventures afloat and ashore in the South Seas. Leon Howard surmises that young Melville would have first heard of the *Somers* affair among sailors' gossip at Callao, Peru, in 1843. Howard, *Melville*, 82–83. In *White-Jacket*, the author alludes twice to the *Somers*, in chapters 70 and 72. Melville, *White-Jacket*, 659, 668–69.

125 "Excitement to the conspirators." Mackenzie's narrative; *Proc CM*, 199.

126 Jörgen Iversen. Zabriskie, *Virgin Islands*, 4.

127 "No tobacco." Mackenzie's narrative; *Proc CM*, 200.

127 Mackenzie's letter of clarification. The letter is reprinted in Shufeldt, with an explanatory note (and at *Proc CI*, 46–47). Boatswain's Mate Browning concurred emphatically with one point in the letter; he did not believe "Spencer was seaman enough to sail the brig without the assistance of Cromwell and Small. I do not think he knew a dozen ropes aboard of her." As for the other sailors, "there were none more capable of taking charge of that brig than I am of a balloon." *Proc CI*, 36.

128 The captain at nineteen. Thus Duyckinck, following Mrs. Mackenzie: "At 19 he took command of a merchant vessel to improve himself in his profession" (II 361). Mackenzie himself said twenty: "At the age of twenty I received a furlough and took command of a merchant ship, in which I made three voyages, solely for the purpose of engaging in more responsible professional duties than my rank enabled me to perform in the Navy . . ." Mackenzie to George Bancroft, secretary of the navy, 8–19–1846. Massachusetts Historical Society, Bancroft papers.

128 "Dismay and confusion on board." Shufeldt, 129.

130 "The most dangerous man." Gansevoort's testimony, quoting Dickerson; *Proc CI*, 21.

131 Weather entries in the *Somers*'s log. Log entries from Nov. 26 through Dec. 1 are given in National Archives, 808.

131 "His spirits gave way." Mackenzie's narrative; *Proc CM*, 200.

132 "I considered the imminent peril." *Proc CI*, 11 (source reads "unharmed" for "unarmed").

133 "Another such should not be passed." Mackenzie's narrative; *Proc CM*, 202.

135 Spencer "eloquently" asserts Cromwell's innocence. *Proc CM*, 204.

136 "Made up my own mind." Mackenzie, from Charlotte Amalie, to Upshur, 12–5–1842. National Archives, 803.

136 "The only effectual method of bringing them back." Shufeldt, 130.

136 Mackenzie's letter to his officers. *Proc CM*, 201.

137 Testimony before the council of officers. Minutes of the council begin at

National Archives, 387, *Proc CM*, 151. (Citations in the text are from the former source.)

137 "Bundle after bundle." Howard's testimony; *Proc CI*, 40.

138 "Their fellow-creatures should live." Mackenzie's narrative; *Proc CM*, 201. Robert Rogers reminds us (R. C. R., "Reminiscences," 25) that under the best of circumstances "young people of a steerage afloat are neither disinterested nor impartial [toward each other], warped by professional jealousy and rivalry . . ." Aboard the *Somers*, where many officers were connected by "blood or alliance" and all had been discouraged at the start of the cruise from associating with Spencer, the difficulty of judging him fairly would likely have been increased.

138 "Anxious to know the result." Gansevoort's testimony; *Proc CI*, 22.

138 "Without interruption and . . . food." Mackenzie's narrative; *Proc CM*, 202.

138 "The vessel in danger." Gansevoort's testimony; *Proc CI*, 22.

138 The officers reply. *Proc CM*, 202.

139 Mackenzie addresses Spencer. *Proc CM*, 203. The words are very slightly altered from the source, in order to make the speech direct by converting third person to second. Young Oliver Perry testified that Spencer, on first hearing his doom, got down on his knees for half a minute, then returned to the campstool. *Proc CM*, 190.

140 "Small looked at me and smiled." Green's testimony; *Proc CM*, 218.

140 "What is that?" McKinley's recollection; *Proc CM*, 180.

140 "Cromwell is innocent." Mackenzie's narrative; *Proc CM*, 203.

141 "Is it not strange?" Lewis Benedict, from Washington, to Thurlow Weed, 2-25-1843; quoted in Hayford, *Somers*, 133.

142 "An extreme and erroneous opinion." Mackenzie's narrative; *Proc CM*, 204.

145 "The stars and stripes." [Slidell], *Year in Spain*, I 30.

146 "Tell the officers to overlook this." Deslonde's testimony; *Proc CM*, 176. The midshipman acknowledged that Cromwell's tone as he uttered the words was "anxious and entreatful."

146 "Cromwell's last words." *Proc CM*, 207. Commentators of the time—and later—professed to be mystified by the identity of Lieutenant Morris. Who he was seems clear enough: "I recall a conversation bearing upon the *Somers* tragedy which I overheard between my father and his early friend, Thomas Morris, when their indignation was boundless. The latter's son, Lieutenant Charles W. Morris, U.S.N., had made several cruises with the alleged mutineer Cromwell" and had found him "a well-disposed and capable seaman." Gouverneur, *As I Remember*, 93 (1911).

147 Belongings of the doomed midshipman. National Archives, 845. Mackenzie's letter ordering the inventory of Spencer's possessions is at 322.

147 "Nothing in such a spectacle." [Slidell], *Year in Spain*, I 353. Recurring motifs of such an episode at sea are suggested in *Ramon, the Rover of Cuba*, where that precursor of penny-dreadful heroes stands up to a threatened mutiny: "The old sailors and all who were not of the nine leading conspirators were for throwing these worthies overboard, but I insisted on a free pardon for all but Patricio. I directed the old sailors to try him by a court of inquiry after their own fashion and dispose of him as they found him guilty or innocent of originating the whole plot, which I think extended much farther than to the nine who appeared in the business, as I should have found to my cost if I had exhibited the least symptom of fear. The trial lasted about five minutes. Patricio was condemned by acclamation, and strung up to the yardarm as soon as his sentence was pronounced.

There has never been a sign of discontent among my men since." *Ramon*, 75.

149 "Risen to the command." Mackenzie's narrative; *Proc CM*, 201.

152 "Not so much on deck." *Proc CI*, 44.

152 "With a wretched pen." Mackenzie to Upshur, 12–5–1842. National Archives, 805. The letter from Charlotte Amalie is at 797–806.

153 Mackenzie's second letter to Upshur. 12–14–1842. Same, 920.

TRIAL

154 Hone's diary entries. Nevins, *Hone*, II 604 (Cooper), 608 (duel), 610 (reservoir), 620 (prizefighting), 637 (Yankees), 624–25 (water celebration), 635–36 (Colt).

156 The Colt murder case. In addition to New York newspapers of the time, see Sutton, *Tombs*, 64–80, for a retelling of the murder and events surrounding it. Among Colt's close friends—and with him near the end—were (in addition to his brother) John Howard Payne, author of "Home, Sweet Home" and earlier a collaborator with Washington Irving as playwright, and Lewis Gaylord Clark, editor of *The Knickerbocker*, to which Irving was a contributor. Adams had printed a work on accounting that the bookkeeper Colt had written; New York newspapers of the period contain recurring advertisements for "COLT'S BOOKKEEPING . . . *A practical work upon a plan entirely new.*—The accounts which form the basis of the science are classed under Five Divisions, with definite explanations after the forms of grammar and arithmetic. . . ." *New York Herald*, 2–28–1840 and elsewhere.

156 "Moving heaven and earth." Strong, *Diary*, 189 (11–15–1842). George Templeton Strong had graduated from Columbia College in 1838, in the same class as Hone's son, Philip, Jr. Other citations from Strong's diary relating to Colt are at 190–91; citations from Hone's diary are in Nevins, II 635–36.

158 News of the *Somers*'s return. The text indicates newspaper sources and dates of citations. Rumors flew through the days immediately after the brig had arrived home. One such reported in the *Herald*, 12–21–1842, was to the effect that, "about two weeks since," it was thought in Albany that the *Somers* had foundered at sea with all hands lost, news that a New York merchant was supposed to have received from a vessel out of St. Thomas; now such information was believed to have been disseminated by a crony of the mutineers in order to explain the planned disappearance of the ship. Similarly, the *Tribune* the same day was recalling an incident "some two or three weeks ago, just as our paper was going to press." Two military-looking types had come into the publication office and asked whether "we had received any account of the loss of the *Somers*, saying that they had heard such a report at the barge office, whither it had come from the Custom House." But "we could not learn that the report had been received or even heard of" at the Customs House.

159 Account in *The New York Express*. Quoted in Hayford, *Somers*, 3.

160 " 'What is the matter?' " Dana, *Journal*, I 118–19 (1–4–1843). In the entry Dana describes Mrs. Mackenzie, whom he was meeting for the first time, as "a sensible and rather handsome woman."

160 "One syllable, or hint of any kind." *Courier & Enquirer*, 12–22–1842.

160 The *Courier*'s account of Monday. Allusions to Morris Robinson and to Webb's absence from town are included in that article of 12–19–1842.

"Neither Alexander Slidell Mackenzie, or any officer or man of his vessel, has either directly or indirectly communicated one word, syllable or sign to this paper." Courier & Enquirer, 12–28–1842.

161 "Acted under a panic." New York *Herald,* 12–20–1842: "The plot was merely *in embryo.* This was a conspiracy, but nothing had been done in pursuance of it . . ."

162 The *Tribune's* opinion. *New York Tribune,* 12–20–1842.

162 "Nobody . . . permitted to visit her." Nevins, *Hone,* II 640. Hone specifically mentions a brother of Gansevoort, but more likely the naval officer forbidden to approach the *Somers* was Gansevoort's cousin, Hunn Gansevoort, then in New York: "I am here with your brother [Guert] attending the court and shall remain until it adjourns . . ." Hunn Gansevoort, at the Astor House, to Stanwix Gansevoort, on the *Erie,* 1–7–1843. Leyda, *Melville Log,* I 161.

162 "A statement is published." Tuckerman, *Hone,* II 165.

163 "He sent for Mr. Morris." *New York Herald,* 12–21–1842.

163 "A large party next Wednesday." Same, 12–20–1842.

163 "A deer to ravage a sheepfold." Seward, *Autobiography,* 640–41. Secretary Spencer's undated reply to Seward's letter of condolence is given at 646: "I ought sooner to have acknowledged your kind and feeling note of sympathy in the horrible calamity which has overtaken me and my family. I now do so, with my grateful assurances of the consolation it has afforded; but Mrs. S— and myself are well aware that we must look to a higher than human source for that balm which only can heal the wounds of our bleeding hearts."

163 "Weed writes from Washington." Same, 641.

164 "Spencer is stricken down." John Lorimer Graham, from Washington, to Silas M. Stilwell, 12–24–1842. Rare Books and Manuscripts Division, New York Public Library.

164 "Oblige the Hon. J. C. Spencer." Undated note to Colonel William Leete Stone, "Editor NY Com. Adv.," in Rare Books and Manuscripts Division, New York Public Library.

164 The article by "S." The letter was widely reprinted, as, for example, in *The Boston Courier* of 12–23–1842 (the text followed here).

166 "Never was a more beautiful Christmas." Nevins, *Hone,* II 641.

167 "A more detailed statement." Mackenzie's narrative; *Proc CM,* 194.

167 "I scarcely knew him." Mary Ann Gansevoort to Peter Gansevoort, 1–2–1843. Hayford, *Somers,* 69–70.

168 "To examine the facts." *Proc CI,* 5.

169 Coming aboard the *North Carolina. Proc CI,* 5. Details of the receiving ship are from that source, from the *New York Herald,* 12–29–1842, from Benjamin, 52 and *passim,* and from Parker, *Recollections,* 2–4. Walt Whitman describes the navy yard—its boom derrick, the rows of thirty-two pounders, the pyramids of balls, the sentries, the surrounding walls of dull yellow brick—as the place appeared a few years later, in "A Slaver"; Holloway and Adimari, *New York Dissected,* 113.

169 Hone visits the court of inquiry. Tuckerman, *Hone,* II 170–71 (1–5–1843).

170 "Talked over the *Somers* mutiny." Dana, *Journal,* I 117 (1–4–1843). Dana's letter to the *Evening Post* of 1–13–1843 is reprinted in Adams, *Dana,* I 51–57. The letter had been requested by Catharine Sedgwick, a novelist and friend of Dana's, Cooper's, and Mackenzie's: "Of course it will not appear who your correspondent is. I have an invincible aversion to women

appearing before the public when they can help it." Catharine Maria Sedgwick, from New York, to R. H. Dana, Jr., 1-5-1843. Massachusetts Historical Society, Dana papers.

172 " 'It was just the thing.' " Mrs. Robert Sedgwick to R. H. Dana, Jr., 1-23-
1843. Massachusetts Historical Society, Dana papers.

173 "The great topic of the day." New York *Herald*, 1-20-1843. By this time
events aboard the *Somers* had been dramatized, "and brought out in defiance
of all good feeling and taste, at the Bowery Theatre, New York." Hayford,
Somers, 111.

173 "Saw the fatal yard." Cooper, from Philadelphia, to Mrs. Cooper, 1-10-
1843. Beard, *Letters and Journals*, IV 340.

173 "An enemy of no ordinary character." *Courier & Enquirer*, 1-23-1843.

174 "Impartiality contrary to all experience." *Boston Courier*, 12-27-1842. The
verdict of the court of inquiry appears in National Archives, 685.

174 "A court-martial should immediately follow." Charles Davis to Charles
Sumner, 1-12-1843. Houghton Library, Sumner papers. Davis had sailed
with Mackenzie, to Russia and Brazil, aboard the *Independence* in the 1830s.

174 "An affecting meeting." John Lorimer Graham, from Washington, to Silas
Stilwell, 12-29-1842: "Mr. S. has returned to his office and yesterday
resumed his seat at a cabinet meeting which is said to have been an affecting meeting . . ." Rare Books and Manuscripts Division, New York Public
Library.

174 "Was it not awful?" Leyda, *Melville Log*, I 162-63 (1-29-1843).

175 "Call things by their right names." Strong, *Diary*, 200 (3-21-1843).

175 Friends of Cromwell come forward. New York *Herald*, 12-24-1842; the
editors include the testimonials on behalf of the boatswain's mate "without
any remark."

175 Whip "with all his might." Wales's testimony; *Proc CI*, 19.

175 "Improper tampering with them." Upshur to Jacob Jones, undated in
source ("on the eve of the court-martial"); the letter is quoted in Van De
Water, 184-85.

175 "Not be deprived of my command." Concluding sentence of Mackenzie's
narrative; *Proc CM*, 211.

176 "A pleasing yet solemn duty." Same, 209.

177 "In conference with the Secretary of War." National Archives, 897.

177 "A thief, a liar, and a villain." Same, 846.

178 "Delays and vexation of every sort." Mackenzie to Upshur, 1-7-1843;
same, 692.

178 Captain Gregory writes about the *Somers*. Gregory to Jones, 1-7-1843,
National Archives, 768; Gregory to Upshur, 1-21-1843, same, 761. Both
Van Velsor and Warner were examined before the council of officers
aboard the *Somers* and later by the court of inquiry in New York. *Proc CI*,
38-39. One of the other prisoners, the tattoo artist Benjamin Green, from
aboard the *North Carolina*, had meanwhile written his mother in Maine a
letter dated 12-19-1842. The letter was subsequently reprinted in the
newspapers, with the notation that Green was "of a very respectable
family" in Portland. "On our passage," he wrote, "the most dreadful sight
I ever saw was a Midshipman and two seamen who were hanged for mutiny at the yard-arm. Midshipman Spencer was about 22 years of age. Samuel Cromwell and Elisha Small were the men; one was said to belong to
Boston and the other to New-York, but I think they were not Americans.
Cromwell has left a wife and children in Brooklyn. There have been twelve

boys and men sent on board the North Carolina, and I am one; but I hope you will not be uneasy about it, for I knew nothing about it until it happened. Mr. Gansevoort, our first lieutenant, told me there was nothing against me more than suspicion." Quoted in Hayford, *Somers*, 7.

180 The note from "R T." National Archives, 782.
180 "Rendering any invalids . . . more comfortable." Mackenzie to Upshur, 1–15–1843; National Archives, 775. Mackenzie's letter to Upshur of 1–24–1843 is at 862.
181 "A diabolical document." Theodore Sedgwick, from New York, to Charles Sumner, 7–6–1843. Houghton Library, Sumner papers.
181 "A singular mixture of folly . . ." *New York Herald*, 12–31–1842.
181 "Never read a more miserable thing." Cooper to Mrs. Cooper, 1–4–1843; Beard, *Letters and Journals*, IV 337.
181 Hone on Mackenzie's report. Nevins, *Hone*, II 641–42 (12–29–1842).
182 "Folly, conceit . . . and fanaticism." Beard, *Letters and Journals*, IV 337.
182 "An indifferent consolation." Adams, *Dana*, I 57–58.
182 "The one table-talk." *National Intelligencer*, 1–5–1843; quoted in Hayford, *Somers*, 70.
182 "Is it not time to sum up?" *New York Herald*, 1–9–1843. The court of inquiry sat from Dec. 28 to Jan. 19. Captain Stewart summed up the verdict on the twentieth: "That Commander Mackenzie under these circumstances was not bound to risk the safety of his vessel, and jeopardize the lives of his crew, in order to secure to the guilty the forms of trial, and that the immediate execution of the prisoners was demanded by duty and justified by necessity." Further, the court was of opinion that throughout the ordeal the officers had been "prudent, calm, and firm, and that he and they honorably performed their duty to the service and their country." National Archives, 689–90.
183 "To examine and cross-examine." *Proc CM*, 8–9. The petition was received and read to the court Feb. 4.
183 "Little known . . . even in Baltimore." W. B. Shubrick to J. F. Cooper, 3–10–1843. Cooper, *Correspondence*, II 498.
184 "Conversing with . . . the witnesses." *Proc CM*, 163–64. "It appears by the record . . . that the proceedings were so much hurried that the judge advocate was not prepared to open when the court-martial convened." Cooper, "Review of . . . Proceedings," 273. Was the haste, as Cooper implies, in order to keep the matter under naval jurisdiction and thus forestall Mackenzie's arrest by civil authorities?
184 "Offer these gentlemen . . . in the dark." *Proc CM*, 164.
184 The judge advocate interrogates Mr. Hayes. *Proc CM*, 9–10. Interrogation of other witnesses may be readily located in *Proc CM*; accordingly, I have not taken space to cite page numbers when witnesses' identities are clear.
184 "Not without prerogatives." Same, 34–35.
191 What constituted the greater disgrace. *New York Herald*, 2–24–1843.
191 "To save the time of the court." *Proc CM*, 72.
192 The defense produces witnesses. Same, 79 ff.
193 "Tied to a bolt." Acting Master Perry's testimony; *Proc CM*, 74.
194 "Courage and alacrity." *Proc CM*, 183.
194 "Fit only to kill." Mackenzie's narrative; *Proc CM*, 201.
195 "Nothing" against the cot boy. McKinley's testimony; *Proc CM*, 183.
196 "No entry in the logbook." *Proc CM*, 226.
197 Mackenzie protests the interrogation of Perry. *Proc CM*, 172 (3–9–1843).

197 "Severe indisposition." National Archives, 461; *Proc CM*, 188–89.

198 "The only memorandum or writing." *Proc CM*, 191. "And this deponent further saith, that the latter portion of the said paper . . . ending with the words, '*my father*,' and beginning with the words, 'God who was' was written by him subsequent to his said conversation with Mr. Spencer, but within a very short time thereafter, and for the purpose of keeping alive his recollection of the facts" *(Proc CM*, 192–93). The admission means that less than half of the brief document was set down during that hour and longer when the commander was observed to be writing beside the prisoner just before his execution.

198 Mackenzie's notes of his interview. National Archives, 199.

200 "Drags along its tedious length." Tuckerman, *Hone*, II 174.

200 Strong on the Millerites. Strong, *Diary*, 198 (3–17–1843). The citation that follows is from the same source, 199 (3–21–1843).

200 "Political jollifications." Nevins, *Hone*, II 653 (3–21–1843).

201 "A case of cold-blooded lynching." Strong, *Diary*, 198 (3–6–1843).

201 "Every unexamined member." *Proc CM*, 223 (source misreads handwritten "crew" as "even").

201 The chapel "filled at an early hour." Tuckerman, *Hone*, II 178–80.

201 Griffin sums up. *Proc CM*, 240–42 (paragraphs inserted). The summation begins at 228. (Attorney Griffin had for many years been a law partner of George Templeton Strong's father, and thus emerges as a character, not always appealingly, in the vigorous pages of young Strong's diary.)

202 "It is not the duty." *Proc CM*, 246.

VERDICT

204 The verdict. Two-thirds were needed to acquit; a vote of seven for acquittal and five against would have sufficed. The verdict is given as an appendix in *Proc CM*, 245 ff. At 227–28 appear the judge advocate's reasons for abandoning the fourth and fifth charges. (In *White-Jacket* [1850], alluding to the "recent" instance of the *Somers* affair, Melville quotes Blackstone's Commentaries: "If any one that hath commission of martial authority doth, in time of peace, hang, or otherwise execute any man by color of martial law, this is murder; for it is against Magna Carta." Melville, *White-Jacket*, 669.)

204 "The agitation of the public mind." Nevins, *Hone*, II 654.

204 "A labor of love." Charles Sumner, from Boston, to Theodore Sedgwick, 1–1–1843. Houghton Library, Sumner papers.

205 "The words *honorably acquitted*." Sturgis, *Letters*, 106–107. On Sturgis, see *Dict. Am. Biog.* and Loring, "Memoir" (material on the *Somers* letters at 452–55).

205 "Seven out of twelve were of opinion." Quoted, from the *Journal of Commerce*, in *Niles' National Register*, LXIV (7–1–1843), 276.

205 "Bringing a suit against him." Mackenzie to Theodore Sedgwick, 4–18–1843. Houghton Library.

206 "Neither Turner nor Page." Cooper to W. B. Shubrick, 2–5–1843. Beard, *Letters and Journals*, IV 362. On Stockton, same, 413 (Cooper to Mrs. Cooper, 9–22–1843).

206 "Nine in . . . favor." *Niles' National Register*, LXIV (7–1–1843), 276. Three members had voted Mackenzie guilty on every charge, acquitting him only "of moral or personal malice." Sturgis, 114.

206 "The high tribunal of public opinion." Griffin's summation; *Proc CM*, 241.

206 "Beyond the requirements of law." Sumner, "Review," 237. Other citations from Sumner's review at 236, 228 ("enemy . . . at the gates"), 229 ("error"), 236 ("heady current"), 231 ("legality"), 234 ("banish from our minds"), 235 ("trifling"), 213 ("sudden, unexpected"), 239-40 ("Honor, then"). Sumner's point concerning the irrelevance of the conspirators' guilt or innocence had been addressed by the judge advocate during the trial: "Such a course of reasoning would justify the killing of one man because he was mistaken for another." *Proc CM*, 258. As for "the most important document" of the whole affair, Mackenzie's lengthy official dispatch of 12-19-1842, Sumner doubts "if ever a good cause . . . received greater detriment from any single document or circumstance," especially because of the captain's recorded talk with Spencer before the execution, and his recommendations for promotions afterward. "It was not with triumph that he should have presented himself before his country; rather with humility and sadness, for he had taken the life of a citizen." The reviewer does note that the document was said to have been "prepared in great haste, and under the pressure of anxiety and care" (p. 240).

208 "The voice of all upright men." Longfellow to Mackenzie, undated (before 7-13-1843). Houghton Library.

208 "The most eminent citizens of Boston." *Niles' National Register*, LXIV (7-8-1843), 296.

208 "We cordially welcome back." Same, 133 (4-29-1843).

208 "Signed by three hundred merchants." Nevins, *Hone*, II 655 (5-11-1843). A newspaper clipping giving the merchants' letter and Mackenzie's response is among the John Gwinn papers (Box 3) at the Library of Congress (Gwinn was a member of Mackenzie's court-martial): ". . . Your judgment forever sets at rest the suspicion, if such has, indeed, been sincerely entertained, that my acquittal by the Naval Court of Inquiry and Court Martial was in any degree owing to the professional sympathy of my brother officers, and not wholly to the intrinsic justice of my defence, and the irresistible evidence on which it rested. When I look at the names of those who have subscribed the letter before me, and reflect on their standing and position, their capacity of forming a sound judgment, their admitted intelligence, and unsullied probity, I cannot but regard the opinions it expresses as conclusive evidence that the judgment of the Navy is ratified by the verdict of my country. . . ."

209 Rogers's opinion of the *Somers* affair. R. C. R., "Reminiscences," 27. The reticence of other officers at the time and later is exemplified by William Parker, who was aboard the *Columbus* at Genoa when news of the *Somers* affair arrived. It created much excitement, he tells us, because the captain of the seventy-four was Spencer's uncle, and the captain's clerk was his brother. But, Parker continues in his *Recollections* (p. 17), naval officers wouldn't discuss it at the time, and he doesn't propose to now (c. 1885).

209 Morison's opinion. *"Old Bruin,"* 154, 161. The chapter on the *Somers* is at 144-62.

210 "The hair of a man's head." Quoted in Morison, 158-59 (Perry to Aaron Ward, 12-27-1842).

210 The opinion of Rear Admiral Hunt. Hunt, " 'Somers,' " 2097. In his own analysis of the case, the admiral concludes that only a "reasoned certainty" of an impending rescue attempt could have justified execution. "There is nothing in the evidence to prove that such a rescue was even meditated, or if attempted, could have succeeded" (p. 2093).

211 "It remains to hear me." *New York Evening Post*, 2–3–1843.

211 "Excuse the liberty I take." Cooper, *Correspondence*, II 490–91.

211 "A letter a few days since." Cooper to John Johnston, 3–4–1843; Beard, *Letters and Journals*, IV 374. The captain's reply, dated 4–5–1843, is given in the same source, 375–76.

212 "Hang them, by way of precaution?" Cooper to Paul Cooper, 1–28–1843. Same, IV 350.

213 "I can now write freely." Same, 357 (2–5–1843). A portion of Shubrick's letter that solicits Cooper's opinion is given at 363.

215 "Between his thumb and finger." Dana, *Journal*, I 168.

215 "Injuring both Com. Elliott and myself." Cooper, *Lake Erie*, 49. Other citations at 58 ("one side"), 59 *("at least* twenty"), 95 ("Sad experience," "rumor").

216 "A close and searching review." Cooper to W. B. Shubrick, 3–25–1843. Beard, *Letters and Journals*, IV 379.

217 "You should undertake the task." Henry Morris to Cooper, 10–27–1843; quoted in Beard, *Letters and Journals*, IV 336. The four citations that follow are from the same volume: 379 ("Mackenzie deserves exposure," to W. B. Shubrick, 3–25–1843); 405 ("Government was the agent," to William Sturgis, 9–17–1843); 409 ("Three letters"); 405 ("best arguments").

217 "When it was made public." Sturgis, *Letters*, 121 (Letter II). The citation that follows is from Letter III, 127.

218 "A person by the name of Wilson." W. H. Norris to A. P. Upshur, 2–22–1843. *Proc CM*, 245.

218 "Willing to let the boys go." William Watson to R. H. Dana, Jr., 2–22–1843. Massachusetts Historical Society, Dana papers.

218 "Mackenzie has no such design." *Proc CM*, 244. Upshur's letter to Downes (3–25–1843) is on the same page.

218 "Every inducement of duty." Cooper, "Review of Proceedings," 314.

219 "What becomes of all those charges?" Sturgis, *Letters*, 122. Other citations at 127 ("felons leagued"), 121 ("suffered to go"), 118 ("topgallant-mast").

219 "The crew were under some fear." Adams, *Dana*, I 55. Hunt, writing later, turns another of Dana's points against its author. About those narrow companionways aboard, which had led Dana to conclude that a handful of mutineers could very well gain mastery over officers and men below as they emerged on deck one at a time: why doesn't that work both ways? The officers above, quelling the mutiny, could easily manage a large number of mutineers below decks, obliged as they would be to ascend singly. Hunt, " 'Somers,' " 2091.

220 "An object of suspicion." Sturgis, *Letters*, 124. The two citations that follow are from the same source: 124 (" 'clear ship' "), 122 *("panic-struck")*.

220 Cooper's letter to Sturgis. 9–17–1843. Beard, *Letters and Journals*, IV 405–8.

221 "I expect it soon." Cooper to Paul Cooper, 11–9–1843; same, 425. Citations that follow are from the same volume, 429 ("My theory," and "her armament," to W. B. Shubrick, 12–9–1843). The *Princeton* was the first warship built with the propelling mechanism entirely underwater, safe from shot. On the *Princeton*, see Church, *Ericsson* I 117 ff (Ericsson designed both the *Princeton* and the ironclad *Monitor)*, and on the disaster, [Benton], *Thirty Years' View*, II 567–69.

222 "All the distinguished persons." Nevins, *Hone*, II 687 (2–29–1844).

222 Their "sumptuous collation." [Benton], *Thirty Years' View*, II 567. Benton was aboard the vessel and on deck at the time of the explosion. The sena-

tor's memoirs contain, by the way, an extended account of the *Somers* affair (II 522–62), fashioned, as he says (562), from Cooper's review and the official record of the trial. The Missouri democrat's impatience with the aristocratic pretensions of the navy is abundantly on view throughout.

222 "Under the most shocking circumstances." Nevins, *Hone*, II 687.

223 "He was a humbug." 4–12–1844. Beard, *Letters and Journals*, IV 451. As the new secretary of the treasury, Spencer took pains to see that regulations of the Coast Guard, for which his department was responsible, were reformed in a way that would prevent any such occurrences as had happened aboard the *Somers*. Earlier regulations were silent on procedures for developing charges against suspended officers. Regulations issued under Spencer's signature as secretary of the treasury contain a section (chapter XV) on "Suspension and Arrest": "When the commanding officer shall suspend or continue the suspension of an officer, he shall call upon him for an explanation of the complaint made against him, and a list of persons to be questioned, and shall promptly institute an inquiry into the circumstances, in order to regulate his further proceedings. . . ." *(Rules and Regulations for the Government of the United States Revenue Marine*, issued November 1, 1843 [Washington, 1843], pp. 21–22. Cf. *Instructions to Officers in the United States' Revenue Cutter Service*, October 3, 1834, p. 3.)

223 *"Take for granted every syllable." Cruise*, 30. Other citations at 19 ("stress of weather"), 19 ("hostile vessel"), 69 ("bravado"), 44 ("not a single fact").

225 "I thought him guilty . . ." Testimony before the council of officers is reprinted in *Proc CM*, 151 ff.

226 "A foolish professional vanity." *Cruise*, 6. The citation that ends the section is at 8–9.

226 "A masterpiece of quiet sanity." Grossman, *Cooper*, 190. Webb had earlier reminded his readers that "Mr. Cooper is the very last man in the United States who should condemn Mr. Mackenzie, he having by his writings done more to foster a taste for *Piracy* than any other person in it." *(Courier & Enquirer*, 1–23–1843.) The editor's reference is to such seaborne romances by Cooper as *Red Rover* (1828) and *The Wing-and-Wing* (1842).

226 "No more than his duty." Cooper, "Review of Proceedings," 279. Other citations at 279 ("the *manner*"), 299 ("a *seeming* plot"), 296 ("Gansevoort"), 343 ("unmanly dread"), 343 ("magnifying this mutiny"), 279 ("arrest Mr. Spencer"), 280 ("quiet disappearance"), 280 (" 'blood or alliance' "), 280 ("disposition to repentance"), 280 ("knots"), 280 ("a contrary course"), 302 ("avoiding . . . *intimacy*"), 290–91 ("feigning . . . obedience"), 281 ("extraordinary specimen"). Cooper's opinion that some consideration had been owed young Spencer because of his distinguished father was one not shared by Captain Mackenzie: "The circumstance of Mr. Spencer being a son of a high officer of the government, by enhancing his baseness in my estimation, made me more desirous to be rid of him [before sailing from New York]. On this point I beg that I may not be misunderstood. I revere authority; I recognize in the exercise of its higher functions in this free country the evidence of genius, intelligence, and virtue. But I have no respect for a base son of an honored father. On the contrary, I consider that he who by misconduct sullies the lustre of an honorable name is more culpable than the unfriended individual whose disgrace falls only on himself. I wish, however, to have nothing to do with baseness in any shape; the navy is not the place for it. . . ." *Proc CM*, 196.

228 "Faultlessly clean." Mackenzie's narrative; *Proc CM*, 198.

229   "Two men who manifested guilt." Cooper, "Review of Proceedings," 281.
229   "The mind of Captain Mackenzie." Same, 338.
229   "The existence of a dangerous conspiracy." Mackenzie's narrative; *Proc CM*, 198. The citation that follows is from the same source, same page.
229   "A fine and memorable description." Cooper, "Review of Proceedings," 283. Other citations at 283 ("more violent"), 296 ("all a mistake"), 334 ("gossip of the service"), 277 ("disposed to betray").
230   "Keeping them wholly free." Mackenzie to Upshur, 1–29–1843. National Archives, 942.
231   "To have something to tell." Cooper, "Review of Proceedings," 318. Other citations at 334 ("disposed to exaggerate"), 276 ("size of the *Somers*"), 277 ("lighting her decks"), 291 ("a tender age"), 292 ("physical powers"), 277 ("inviolable as a sanctuary"), 292 ("what had they to fear?"), 324 ("his previous opinions"), 339 ("a youth of nineteen"), 288 ("a more precious set"), 287 ("more than human"), 286 ("a family yacht"), 287 ("military supremacy"), 294 ("nearest available port").
233   "Due process of law." Fourteenth amendment to the Constitution.
233   "Protection in a friendly port." Cooper, "Review of Proceedings," 270. Other citations at 295 ("strange set of officers"), 296 ("Waltham was flogged"), 296 ("the gallows"), 271 ("exposed to the elements").
234   "The young man had been lying to him." McKee's testimony; *Proc CM*, 215.
234   "Telling the commander falsehoods." *Proc CM*, 220.
235   "Died with a lie in his mouth." Green's testimony; *Proc CM*, 218.
235   "Not likely to be invented." Cooper, "Review of Proceedings," 327. Other citations at 329 ("inexplicable part"), 332 ("root of this matter"), 297 ("given pistols"), 297 ("obvious interest"), 330 ("exculpate himself").
235   "Look down on my poor wife." McKinley's testimony; *Proc CM*, 180.
235   "I die an innocent man." Mackenzie's narrative; *Proc CM*, 207.
236   "Friends and home as pledges." Cooper, "Review of Proceedings," 311.
236   "Does not even *attempt* to prove." Same, 319.
236   "It was not me, sir." Mackenzie's narrative; *Proc CM*, 199.
236   "Cromwell's guilt is *assumed*." Cooper, "Review of Proceedings," 319. Other citations at 311 ("a particular speech"), 312 ("pitiable, pitiable").
237   "Would have run away with the keg." *Proc CM*, 207.
237   "His story of the doubloons." Cooper, "Review of Proceedings," 323. Other citations at 322 ("VERY GUILTY"), 321 ("Wilson"), 314 ("This man McKinley"), 310 ("a new proof"), 304 ("competencies for life"), 304 ("murder and rapine"), 279 ("a deep reproach"), 279 ("his *convictions*"), 343 ("lamentable deficiency of judgment").
238   "That consciousness of rectitude." Mackenzie's narrative; *Proc CM*, 210. The citations that follow to the end of the chapter are from the same source, 205, 203.

EPILOGUE

240   "A personal suffering." Catherine Mackenzie, Biographical Sketch of Her Husband, 13. Rare Books and Manuscripts Division, New York Public Library.
240   Leecock's suicide. *Courier & Enquirer*, 4–1–1843; *Tribune*, 4–1–1843.

241 "Allowed to return to his home." Catherine Mackenzie, Biographical Sketch of Her Husband, 13–14.

241 "As a tribute of respect." *Chicago Express*, 4–20–1843; quoted in Hayford, *Somers*, 160.

241 *"Enthusiasm* in your favor." R. H. Dana, Jr., to Mackenzie, 4–16–1843; Massachusetts Historical Society, Dana papers.

241 "A fruitful theme." Mackenzie to Longfellow, 2–20–1843. Houghton Library.

241 "The voice of all upright men." Longfellow to Mackenzie, undated (before 7–13–1843). Houghton Library.

242 "A strong desire to write to you." Mackenzie to Charles Sumner, 8–9–1843; Houghton Library, Sumner papers. Sumner's answer is in Box 3 of the Rodgers Family papers (Series I), Naval Historical Foundation Collection, Library of Congress. Dated from Boston 8–17–1843, the letter reads in part: "My dear Sir, On my return last evening from a journey with Longfellow and his new happy wife, I found your most flattering letter of August 9th. I do not deserve such thanks. It is very little that I have been able to do; it is nothing, compared with your deserts; but even this nothing has a value in my eyes, if it is not entirely unacceptable to you. I have never doubted the courage, the justice, the magnanimity displayed by you in the *Somers*, or the necessity of the sacrifice you ordered. . . . You will have true occasion for pleasure in knowing that Judge Story, the first living jurist, approves of your conduct throughout and, without hesitation, affirms the entire *justice* of the execution. . . . On the top of the Catskills we all talked of you (Lieber was of the party), and I began to enjoy in advance the pleasures of your acquaintance and the privilege of admiring Mrs. Mackenzie. . . ."

242 The visit of Francis Lieber. Lieber to Mrs. Lieber, from "Near Tarrytown, Capt. Mackenzie's Farm," 8–3–1843. Hayford, *Somers*, 178–79. (Original is in the Huntington Library, Pasadena.) The pedestal of Dexter's bust of Mackenzie remains at the Boston Athenaeum, but the bust itself has been missing for a quarter of a century, and no picture of it seems to have survived.

243 "A modest and unassuming man." Sumner to Dr. Samuel G. Howe, 9–14–1843. Pierce, *Sumner*, II 270.

243 "A feeling of personal affection." Dana, *Journal*, I 218 (9–19–1843).

243 "The Lord High Admiral." C. C. Felton, from Cambridge, to Francis Lieber, 9–17–1843. Hayford, *Somers*, 181–82. (Original in Huntington Library.)

244 "Truth to fall back on." Cooper, *Lake Erie*, iii.

244 "Sophistry, and venomous abuse." Slidell Mackenzie, *Perry*, II 271. The two citations that follow are from the same source, II 326–27.

244 "A history of our Navy." Mackenzie to J. G. Palfrey, 6–20–1844. Houghton Library.

245 Spencer's retirement. President Tyler late in his administration had twice proposed Spencer for the Supreme Court, but for political reasons the Senate blocked the nomination both times. In retirement, the former secretary revealed a lingering animosity toward the President he had served, on one occasion referring to him publicly as "weak and wayward." Tyler seems to have ascribed the judgment to his own refusal to intervene in the *Somers* affair. "When Capt. Mackenzie arrived and reported the case," Tyler wrote, "a naval court was ordered for his trial and a thorough investigation

of the whole case. There never was assembled in this country a more dignified or able naval court. Its sentence acquitted Capt. Mackenzie, and I
could do nothing but approve the sentence. If it had ordered Mackenzie to
be shot, I would not have interposed to save him. Spencer, then still Secretary of War, was very urgent with me to set aside the trial, and to order
another for the slayer of his son. But I answered that it would be contrary
to the general rule of law that, when a man had been once fairly tried and
acquitted, he should be tried again upon the same charges and evidence."
Tyler, "Letters," 174–75.

245   "A reward for frauds practiced." Nevins, *Hone*, II 759 (4–4–1846). On the
Mexican War, Justin Smith's account is the classic work—and one of the
great works of American historical scholarship; Bill's is a popular, vividly
written narrative; Bauer's is a recent, comprehensive treatment of the subject.

245   "Creation of the rank of admiral." Slidell Mackenzie, review of "Cooper's
Naval History," 455. The five citations that follow are from the same source,
455–56.

247   "A source of deep regret." Quoted in Sears, *Slidell*, 75. Since the time of his
trial, Mackenzie, according to his wife, had passed his days principally at
Tarrytown. We catch a glimpse of him in New York City in the summer of
1845, calling on an English traveler: "One morning I was agreeably surprised by a visit from Lieutenant [*sic*] Mackenzie, whom I had known in
England, and whose very pleasant 'Year in Spain' had afforded me much
gratification.—Time had somewhat changed his appearance, but had left
his frank and courteous manners ever the same. He once had spent a winter's day at our fireside in Cheshire, and we had charmed the hours by
turning over the pages of Audubon. . . ." Maury, *Englishwoman*, 220–21.

247   "Washington Irving, walked in." Leyda, *Melville Log*, I 202 (1–6–1846).
Citations from Gansevoort Melville's journal that follow are in the same
source, 202–204 (2–3–1846).

248   "Much occupied of late." Irving, from Madrid, to Irving Paris, 1–10–1843.
Irving, *Letters*, III 459–60.

248   A "really great friend." Quoted in Griffin, *Westchester County*, I 347.

249   "Make my visit to the Mackenzies." Irving to Sarah Storrow, 10–18–1846.
Irving, *Letters*, IV 99. On Mackenzie's mission to Cuba, see Polk, *Diary*, III
290–92 (1–8–1848) and Reeves, *Diplomacy*, 299–308.

249   "The most active blockading duties." M. C. Perry to John Y. Mason, secretary of the navy, 12–12–1846. Quoted in Semmes, *Service*, 94. Aboard the
Somers in the Gulf shortly before she went down was Robert Rogers; he
relates details of her latter days, as well as traditions aboard concerning
ghosts of the mutineers in the rigging and the like. R. C. R., "Reminiscences," 36.

250   "Standing on the lee arms chest." Semmes, *Service*, 95.

250   "I dined on Saturday." Nevins, *Hone*, II 890.

250   "Talked with Mr. Slidell." Dana, *Journal*, I 398–99.

251   "Mr. Cooper came in." Putnam, *Memoir*, 264.

251   "A vivid and awakening power." Melville's letter is in *Memorial of Cooper*,
30.

252   "Chivalrous and zealous advocacy." Pierce, *Sumner*, III 480.

252   "The present state of discipline." Quoted in Morison, *"Old Bruin,"* 272.

253   "I have read your speech." Pierce, *Sumner*, III 470. The citation that follows ("without any particular emotion") is from the same source, 480.

254 Thurlow Weed's account. Weed, *Autobiography*, I 515–19. Guert Gansevoort may, of course, have traveled to Washington earlier than Wednesday in a trip not on record, returning to New York before making a second journey at midweek. In 1842, the trip from New York to Philadelphia took Dickens between five and six hours; from Philadelphia to Washington took him a little over twelve hours. Dickens, *American Notes*, 112, 130–33.

255 "Nothing could stop him." Mary Ann Gansevoort to Peter Gansevoort, 1–2–1843. Quoted in Hayford, *Somers*, 69–70.

257 "Looks very much like Herman." Augusta Melville to Allan Melville, 8–11–1841. Leyda, *Melville Log*, II 120.

257 "Always preferred active service." Peter Gansevoort, from Albany, to William L. Marcy, 4–2–1845. Same, II 194–95. The two citations that follow are also from Leyda: II 522 ("habits in this respect") and 652 ("brilliant victory," Melville to Thomas Melville, 5–25–1862).

257 "Tom Tight." From "Bridegroom Dick" (1876). Melville, *Poems*, 212.

258 "Read and re-read *Moby-Dick*." The letter is quoted in Leyda, *Melville Log*, II 817. Melville's reply is at 818.

258 "Friday . . . Began." Melville, *Billy Budd*, 7 (editorial material).

259 "God bless that flag." Mackenzie's narrative; *Proc CM*, 206.

259 "God bless Captain Vere." Melville, *Billy Budd*, 123. The definitive Hayford and Sealts edition, here cited, contains at pp. 28–29 a discussion of similarities and differences between the *Somers* incident and the one imagined in *Billy Budd*. For a suggestion of another possible source for Melville's story, see Morison, *"Old Bruin,"* 458 (notes to chapter XII).

259 "Roll me over fair!" Melville, *Billy Budd*, 137. The citation that follows is from the same source, 113–14.

260 "Orders to go to West Point." Mackenzie to Longfellow, 12–10–1846. Houghton Library.

260 "Slidell Mackenzie came." 12–11–1846. Longfellow, *Life*, II 66–67.

260 "Craving for national poetry." Mackenzie, aboard the USS *Mississippi* at Anton Lizardo, to Longfellow, 4–29–1847. Houghton Library.

260 "Mackenzie in the saddle." Griffin, *Westchester County*, I 349. The obituary in the *New York Herald* of 9–14–1848 reads: "Died, in Westchester County, State of New York, on the 13th inst., Commander Alexander Slidell Mackenzie, U.S. Navy, aged 45. The officers of the Army and Navy, and his friends generally, are invited to attend his funeral, from St. Mark's Church, city of New York, on Friday, the 15th inst., at 3½ o'clock." Longfellow sent his condolences to the widow 10–30–1848: "Dear Mrs. Mackenzie, I have been often prompted by my feelings to write to you and as often checked by the thought how very intrusive all words of consolation are in any deep affliction. . . . But the Angel of Death has lately visited our fireside also [his daughter Fanny had died September 11], which seems to give me the right to say to you how deeply I have felt for you in your bereavement. Console you I cannot. I can only mourn with you. I can only assure you how much the memory of your husband is honored among us by all who knew him personally and by many who knew him only by name. . . ." Houghton Library. At her husband's death Mrs. Mackenzie took her family of five young children to live with relatives in Morristown, New Jersey. The youngest was born the year his father died; he would grow up to become Rear Admiral Morris Robinson Mackenzie (1848–1915). Of the two older sons, Alexander Slidell Mackenzie, Jr. (1842–1867) would rise to the rank of lieutenant in the navy and die during a punitive shore raid

against natives on Formosa (Taiwan). The eldest, Ranald Mackenzie (1840–1889) would make for himself an outstanding record at the head of his class at West Point, during the Civil War, and in the latter part of the century in the West, where he was the most successful of the cavalry officers engaged in Indian wars.

261 "One of his favorite books." Pierre Irving, *Life and Letters*, IV 312.

SOURCES

The list comprises only those books, articles, newspapers, and collections from which citations have been taken or to which the notes refer directly.

Adams, Charles Francis, ed. *Memoirs of John Quincy Adams: 1795–1848*. 12 vols. Philadelphia, 1874–77.
_____. *Richard Henry Dana*. 2 vols. Boston, 1890.
Adams, Henry. *History of the United States of America* . . . 9 vols. New York, 1891–96/1962.
Adams, John Quincy. "Letters Addressed to William L. Stow, Esq. . . . upon the Subject of Masonry and Anti-Masonry," to which is added "A Portrait of Masonry," by John C. Spencer. Providence, 1833.
Adams, Randolph G. "Abel Parker Upshur." In S. F. Bemis, *The American Secretaries of State and Their Diplomacy*. Vol. V, 67–124. New York, 1928/1963.
Allen, Gardner W. *Our Navy and the West Indian Pirates*. Salem, Mass., 1929.
Anderson, Charles Roberts. *Melville in the South Seas*. New York, 1939.
Andrews, George H. *Biographical Sketch of James Watson Webb*. New York, 1858/1869.
Barrett, Walter [Joseph A. Scoville]. *The Old Merchants of New York City: Second Series*. New York, 1863.
Bauer, K. Jack. *The Mexican War: 1846–1848*. New York, 1974.
Beard, James Franklin, ed. *The Letters and Journals of James Fenimore Cooper*. 6 vols. Cambridge, Mass., 1960–68.
Benjamin, Park. *The United States Naval Academy*. New York, 1900.
[Benton, Thomas Hart]. *Thirty Years' View*. 2 vols. New York, 1854–56.
Bill, Alfred Hoyt. *Rehearsal for Conflict: The War with Mexico, 1846–1848*. New York, 1947.

Boston Courier, The. A complete set for the period is on microfilm at the Boston Public Library.

Bryant, William Cullen. "Discourse on the Life, Genius, and Writings of J. Fenimore Cooper." In *Memorial of James Fenimore Cooper.* New York, 1852, pp. 39–74.

Calkins, Captain Carlos Gilman. "The Repression of Piracy in the West Indies, 1814–1825." *United States Naval Institute Proceedings* 37, no. 4 (December 1911): 1197–1238.

Callahan, Edward W. *List of Officers of the Navy of the United States . . . from 1775 to 1900.* New York, 1901.

Chaille, W. Jackson. "Philip Spencer." In *The Chi Psi Story,* edited by H. Seger Slifer and Hiram L. Kennicott. Ann Arbor, 1951, pp. 74–79.

Church, William Conant. *The Life of John Ericsson.* 2 vols. New York, 1911.

Cooper, James Fenimore. *The Battle of Lake Erie, or Answers to Messrs. Bruges* [sic], *Duer, and Mackenzie.* Cooperstown, N.Y., 1843.

____. *Early Critical Essays (1820–1822).* Edited by James F. Beard, Jr. Gainesville, Fla., 1955.

____. *Lives of Distinguished American Naval Officers.* 2 vols. Philadelphia, 1846.

____. *Ned Myers, or A Life Before the Mast. Works,* Vol. 33. Mohawk Edition. New York, 1899.

____. "Review of the Proceedings of the Naval Court Martial," in *Proceedings of the Naval Court Martial in the Case of Alexander Slidell Mackenzie . . .* New York, 1844, pp. 263–344.

Cooper, James Fenimore. *Correspondence of James Fenimore-Cooper.* 2 vols. New Haven, 1922.

Crouthamel, James L. *James Watson Webb.* Middletown, Conn., 1969.

The Cruise of the "Somers"; Illustrative of the Despotism of the Quarter Deck . . . with an Appendix Containing Three Letters by Hon. William Sturgis. 3d ed. New York, [July], 1844. (The first edition, without Sturgis's letters, appeared in March 1844.)

Dana, Richard Henry, Jr. *The Journal of Richard Henry Dana, Jr.* Edited by Robert F. Lucid. 3 vols. Cambridge, Mass., 1968.

____. *Two Years Before the Mast.* Edited by John H. Kemble. Los Angeles, 1964.

Dickens, Charles. *American Notes for General Circulation.* Vol. 19, *Works.* London, 1874.

Dictionary of American Biography. New York, 1928–37. Entries on Benjamin F. Butler, Lewis Gaylord Clark, Charles H. Davis, William Alexander Duer, Jesse Duncan Elliott, Ogden Hoffman, Francis Lieber, Charles O'Conor, John Gorham Palfrey, William Branford Shubrick, Richard Somers, Ambrose Spencer, Robert Field Stockton, William Sturgis, and others.

Dutton, Charles J. *Oliver Hazard Perry.* New York, 1935.

Duyckinck, Evert A., and George L. *Cyclopaedia of American Literature.* 2 vols. New York, 1866.

Elliott, Jesse D. "Address of Com. Jesse D. Elliott, U.S.N., Delivered in Washington County, Maryland, to His Early Companions . . . on November 24th, 1843 . . ." Philadelphia, 1844.

Furbay, Elizabeth. *Top Hats and Tom-Toms.* Chicago, 1943.

Gouverneur, Marian. *As I Remember: Recollections of American Society During the Nineteenth Century.* New York, 1911.

Greene, Samuel D. *The Broken Seal; or, Personal Reminiscences of the Morgan Abduction and Murder.* Chicago, 1873.

Griffin, Ernest Freeland, ed. *Westchester County and Its People*. 3 vols. New York, 1946.

Grossman, James. *James Fenimore Cooper*. New York, 1949.

Haring, C. H. *Empire in Brazil: A New World Experiment with Monarchy*. Cambridge, Mass., 1958.

Haswell, Charles H. *Reminiscences of an Octogenarian* . . . New York, 1896.

Hayford, Harrison, ed. *The Somers Mutiny Affair*. Englewood Cliffs, N.J., 1959.

Henderson, Daniel. *The Hidden Coasts: A Biography of Admiral Charles Wilkes*. New York, 1953.

Historical Society of Pennsylvania. In addition to a letter from Simon Cameron to John C. Spencer (1–29–1843), eloquent in its outrage over Mackenzie's behavior aboard the *Somers*, the society has the petition to the New York legislature, dated 7–1–1837, in which Slidell "prayeth that he may be permitted to assume his maternal name of Mackenzie and be hereafter known as Alexander Slidell Mackenzie, in order to qualify himself to inherit property."

Holloway, Emory, and Ralph Adimari, eds. *New York Dissected* (newspaper articles by Walt Whitman). New York, 1936.

Houghton Library, Harvard University, Cambridge, Mass. Various holograph letters of Alexander Slidell's, Longfellow's, and Irving's. All but four citations here may be located through the card catalog under Mackenzie, Alexander Slidell. The exceptions are in the Sumner papers: Charles Davis's letter to Charles Sumner of 1–12–1843, Theodore Sedgwick's to Sumner of 7–6–1843, Sumner's to Sedgwick of 1–1–1843, and Mackenzie's to Sumner of 8–9–1843.

Howard, Leon. *Herman Melville*. Berkeley, 1951.

Hunt, Livingston. "The Attempted Mutiny on the U.S. Brig 'Somers.' " *United States Naval Institute Proceedings* 51, no. 11 (November 1925): 2062–2100.

———. "The Suppressed Mutiny on the 'Essex.' " *United States Naval Institute Proceedings*, November 1933, 1547–52.

Irving, Pierre M. *The Life and Letters of Washington Irving*. 4 vols. New York, 1863–64.

Irving, Washington. *Letters of Jonathan Oldstyle, Gent.; Salmagundi*. Edited by Bruce I. Granger and Martha Hartzog. Boston, 1977.

———. *Letters of Washington Irving*. Edited by Ralph M. Aderman, Herbert L. Kleinfield, and Jenifer S. Banks. 4 vols. Boston, 1978–82.

———. *Life and Voyages of Christopher Columbus*. 3 vols. New York, 1828.

———. Review of *A Year in Spain*. *The Quarterly Review* (London) 44, no. 88 (Feb. 1831): 321–42.

Jaffé, David. "The Captain Who Sat for the Portrait of Ahab." *Boston University Studies in English* IV, no. 1 (Spring 1960): 1–22.

Knox, Dudley W. *A History of the United States Navy*. Rev. ed. New York, 1948.

Leyda, Jay. *The Melville Log*. 2 vols. New York, 1951.

Library of Congress. Rodgers Family papers, Naval Historical Foundation Collection. John Gwinn papers.

Longfellow, Samuel, ed. *Life of Henry Wadsworth Longfellow* . . . 3 vols. Boston, 1899.

Lounsbury, Thomas R. *James Fenimore Cooper*. Boston, 1883.

Loring, Charles G. "Memoir of the Hon. William Sturgis." *Proceedings of the Massachusetts Historical Society: First Series* VII (Aug. 1864): 420–73. (Material on the letters about the *Somers* at 452–55.)

Lugenbeel, J. W. *Sketches of Liberia: Comprising a Brief Account of the Geography, Climate, Productions, and Diseases of the Republic of Liberia.* Washington, D.C., 1850.

McClary, Ben Harris. "Washington Irving's British Edition of Slidell's *A Year in Spain." Bulletin of the New York Public Library* 73 (1969): 368–74.

Mackenzie, Alexander Slidell. See Slidell Mackenzie, Alexander.

Mackenzie, Catherine. Biographical Sketch of Alexander Slidell Mackenzie. This untitled manuscript, seventeen pages long, was written after Mackenzie's death by his widow, at the request of Evert Duyckinck, for use as the basis for the entry on the sailor-author in the *Cyclopaedia of American Literature.* Rare Books and Manuscripts Division, New York Public Library.

Mason, Jonathan. "Diary of the Hon. Jonathan Mason." *Proceedings of the Massachusetts Historical Society: Second Series* II (1885–86): 5–34.

Massachusetts Historical Society. Bancroft papers. Dana papers.

Maury, Sarah Mytton. *An Englishwoman in America.* London, 1848.

Melville, Herman. *Billy Budd, Sailor (An Inside Narrative).* Edited by Harrison Hayford and Merton M. Sealts, Jr. Chicago, 1962.

———. *Poems. The Works: Standard Edition.* Vol. XVI. London, 1922–24.

———. *White-Jacket. In Redburn. White-Jacket. Moby-Dick,* notes and chronology by G. Thomas Tanselle. New York, 1983.

Memorial of James Fenimore Cooper. New York, 1852.

[Mercier, Henry James]. *Life in a Man-of-War, or Scenes in Old Ironsides During her Cruise in the Pacific,* by a Fore-Top-Man. Philadelphia, 1841.

Mill, Hugh R. *The Siege of the South Pole.* London, 1905.

Mock, Stanley Upton. *The Morgan Episode in American Free Masonry.* East Aurora, N.Y., 1930.

Morison, Samuel Eliot. *"Old Bruin": Commodore Matthew C. Perry, 1794–1858.* Boston, 1967.

A Narrative of the Facts and Circumstances Relating to the Kidnapping and Presumed Murder of William Morgan . . . Batavia, N.Y., 1827.

National Archives. National Archives Microfilm Publications, Microfilm No. 273. Records of General Courts Martial and Courts of Inquiry of the Navy Department, 1799–1867. Roll 49, vol. 46, case 844. Dec. 28, 1842–March 28, 1843. Citations from this source are followed by the number on the film margin where the relevant document begins.

Nevins, Allan, ed. *The Diary of Philip Hone, 1828–1851.* 2 vols. New York, 1927.

New-York Historical Society. In addition to various relevant letters, the society has a lengthy manuscript, attributed to Montfort Mahon, entitled "Slidell Mackenzie's Vengeance: The True Story of an Awful Tragedy." The title reveals the bias of the account, which was written around 1880 and submitted to the *Magazine of American History.* It was not published there or, presumably, anywhere else. Though lively, "Slidell Mackenzie's Vengeance" is for the most part a retelling that leans heavily on Benton's account in *Thirty Years' View,* which in turn was drawn from Cooper's "Review of Proceedings" and from the court-martial proceedings themselves.

New York Newspapers. *New York Commercial Advertiser. Courier and Enquirer. New York Evening Post. New York Herald. New York Tribune.* These are available on microfilm at the annex of the New York Public Library.

New York Public Library. Rare Books and Manuscripts Division. Among materials at the library that pertain to the mutiny and court-martial are some thirty-five pages of letters and five pages of clippings, including Catherine Mackenzie's biographical sketch of her husband, letters from Silas Stilwell and John Lorimer Graham, and a letter from Mackenzie to George L. Duyckinck.

Niles' National Register. Washington. This weekly collection of contemporary documents, editorials, and news items extends through the period of Mackenzie's adulthood; it ceased publication in 1849.

Nordhoff, Charles. *Man-of-War Life.* New York, 1855/1883.

Outland, Ethel R. "The 'Effingham' Libels on Cooper." *University of Wisconsin Studies in Language and Literature,* no. 28 (1929). Madison, Wis.

Parker, William Harwar. *Recollections of a Naval Officer, 1841–1865.* New York, 1885.

Parton, James. *Life of Andrew Jackson.* 3 vols. New York, 1860.

Paullin, Charles Oscar. *The Battle of Lake Erie: A Collection of Documents.* Cleveland, 1918.

_____. *Commodore John Rodgers . . .* Cleveland, 1910.

Philbrick, Thomas. *James Fenimore Cooper and the Development of American Sea Fiction.* Cambridge, Mass., 1961.

Pierce, Edward L. *Memoir and Letters of Charles Sumner.* 4 vols. Boston, 1877–93.

Polk, James Knox. *The Diary of James K. Polk . . .* Edited by Milo Milton Quaife. 4 vols. Chicago, 1910.

Proc CI. Proceedings of the Court of Inquiry Appointed to Inquire into the Intended Mutiny on Board the United States Brig of War Somers, on the High Seas; Held on Board the United States Ship North Carolina Lying at the Navy Yard, New-York; with a Full Account of the Execution of Spencer, Cromwell and Small on Board Said Vessel. Reported for the *New York Tribune.* New York, 1843.

Proc CM. Proceedings of the Naval Court Martial in the Case of Alexander Slidell Mackenzie, a Commander in the Navy of the United States, &c. . . . To Which is Annexed an Elaborate Review, by James Fennimore [sic] Cooper. New York, 1844.

Proctor, L. B. "John C. Spencer." *The Bench and Bar of New-York . . .* New York, 1870, pp. 304–53.

Putnam, George Haven. *George Palmer Putnam: A Memoir,* containing "Recollections of Irving, by His Publisher," New York, 1912, pp. 253–72.

Ramon, the Rover of Cuba, and Other Tales. [John Lauris Blake?] New York, 1843.

R. C. R. [Robert C. Rogers]. "Some Reminiscences of Philip Spencer and the Brig 'Somers.' " *The United Service: New Series* IV, no. 1 (July 1890): 23–36.

Reeves, Jesse S. *American Diplomacy under Tyler and Polk.* Baltimore, 1907.

Ryan, Paul B. "USS *Constellation* Flare-up: Was It Mutiny?" *United States Naval Institute Proceedings,* Jan. 1976, 46–53.

Sears, Louis Martin. *John Slidell.* Durham, N.C., 1925.

Semmes, Raphael. *Service Afloat and Ashore During the Mexican War.* Cincinnati, 1851.

Seward, William H. *William H. Seward: An Autobiography from 1801–1834. With a Memoir of His Life, and Selections from His Letters 1831–1846 by Frederick W. Seward.* New York, 1877.

Shufeldt, R. W. "An Interesting Historical Letter: Commander Alexander Slidell Mackenzie to Honorable Ogden Hoffman, 1843." *Magazine of American History* XVII (Jan.–June, 1887): 128–31.

[Slidell, Alexander]. *The American in England, by the Author of "A Year in Spain."* 2 vols. New York, 1835.

_____. *Spain Revisited . . .* 2 vols. New York, 1836.

_____. *A Year in Spain, by A Young American.* 2 vols. London, 1831.

[Slidell Mackenzie, Alexander]. "Cooper's *Naval History.*" *The North American Review* 49, no. 105 (Oct. 1839): 432–67.

_____. *The Life of Commodore Oliver Hazard Perry*. 2 vols. New York, 1840. Fifth edition, New York, 1844. The latter contains the appendix (II 271–328) answering Cooper's charges in *The Battle of Lake Erie*.

Smith, Justin H. *The War with Mexico*. 2 vols. New York, 1919.

Spencer, John C. "Correspondence Between the Hon. John C. Spencer and a Committee of the Friends of the General Administration." New York, 1842.

_____. "A Portrait of Masonry." In John Quincy Adams. "Letters Addressed to William L. Stow, Esq. . . ." Providence, 1833.

Strong, George Templeton. *The Diary of George Templeton Strong: Young Man in New York, 1835–1849*. Edited by Allan Nevins and Milton Halsey Thomas. New York, 1952. This is the first of four volumes that extend to 1875.

Sturgis, William. *Letters . . . In The Cruise of the "Somers" . . .* 3d ed. New York, [July] 1844.

[Sumner, Charles]. "The Mutiny of the Somers." *The North American Review* LVII (July 1843): 195–241.

Sutton, Charles. *The New York Tombs: Its Secrets and its Mysteries . . .* New York, 1874. The account of the Colt murder, including Colt's confession, is at 64–80.

Thompson, Lawrance. *Young Longfellow*. New York, 1938.

Tuckerman, Bayard. *The Diary of Philip Hone*. 2 vols. New York, 1889.

Tyler, John. "Letters of John Tyler" (two previously unpublished letters to Daniel Webster). *William and Mary College Quarterly Historical Magazine* 18, no. 3. (Jan. 1910): 172–76.

Tyler, Lyon G. *The Letters and Times of the Tylers*. 2 vols. Richmond, Va., 1884–85. Contains "The Dead of the Cabinet," an address delivered by former President John Tyler at Petersburg, April 24, 1856.

Van De Water, Frederic, *The Captain Called It Mutiny*. New York, 1954.

Wallace, Edward S. "Border Warrior [Ranald Mackenzie]." *American Heritage* IX, no. 4 (June 1958): 22 ff.

Waples, Dorothy. *The Whig Myth of James Fenimore Cooper*. New Haven, Conn., 1938.

Warren, Gordon H. *Fountain of Discontent: The* Trent *Affair and Freedom of the Seas*. Boston, 1981.

Weed, Harriet A. *Autobiography of Thurlow Weed*. 2 vols. Boston, 1884.

White, Andrew Dickson. *Autobiography . . .* 2 vols. New York, 1905.

Williams, Stanley T. *The Life of Washington Irving*. 2 vols. New York, 1935.

Wilson, Beckles. *John Slidell and the Confederates in Paris (1862–65)*. New York, 1932/1970.

Zabriskie, Luther K. *The Virgin Islands of the United States of America*. New York, 1918.

ACKNOWLEDGMENTS

OF THE MANY INDIVIDUALS AND INSTITUTIONS THAT have helped me in the various stages of preparing this narrative, I would like to thank in particular Cynthia English and her associates at the Boston Athenaeum; James W. Cheevers, Senior Curator of the Museum of the United States Naval Academy, Annapolis, Maryland; Paul Johnson, Director of the United States Coast Guard Academy Museum, New London, Connecticut; Herbert P. Carroll, Executive Director of Chi Psi Fraternity at Ann Arbor, Michigan; Valerie Ripley of John Murray Publishers, London; and the staffs of the American Antiquarian Society, Worcester, Massachusetts; the Boston Public Library; the Massachusetts Historical Society, Boston; the Houghton Library of Harvard University; the New York Public Library; the New York Historical Society; the Library of Congress; the National Archives and Records Service, Washington, D.C.; the Joint Free Public Library of Morristown and Morris Township, New Jersey; and the Historical Society of Pennsylvania, Philadelphia. The notes acknowledge my indebtedness to scholars past and present.

INDEX